CULTIVATING REVOLUTION

BOOKS BY JAMES F. PETRAS

Politics and Social Forces in Chilean Development
Latin America: Reform or Revolution (co-editor with M. Zeitlin)
Fidel Castro Speaks (co-editor with M. Kenner)

CULTIVATING REVOLUTION

The United States and Agrarian Reform in Latin America

JAMES F. PETRAS and
ROBERT LaPORTE, Jr.

Random House New York

ISBN: 0-394-46789-2
Library of Congress Catalog Card Number: 70-140722

Book designed by Paula Wiener

Maps and charts by Anita Karl & Bruce Kennedy

Manufactured in the United States of America by H. Wolff, N.Y.

9 8 7 6 5 4 3 2

FIRST EDITION

Acknowledgments

Many individuals made contributions to this work. Specifically, we would like to kindly acknowledge the following: Professor Robert J. Mowitz, Director, Institute of Public Administration, The Pennsylvania State University, for his continuous support, criticisms, and suggestions; the faculty and secretarial staff of the Institute of Public Administration for their collective assistance; Professor Marion Brown of the Land Tenure Center and Dr. Arthur Domike of the Inter-American Development Bank for their helpful suggestions and comments on portions of our manuscript; Dr. Helan Jaworski and the DESCO (Lima), Professor Solon Barraclough and the ICIRA (Santiago), Professor Joseph Thome and the Land Tenure Center (Santiago), and the Instituto de Estudios Internacionales (Santiago) for their collective assistance in our research; Michael Konnick whose untiring efforts in data collection greatly facilitated our examination of U.S. AID; Nelson Rimensnyder and Jeffrey C. Rinehart for their assistance; numerous Chilean, Cuban, and Peruvian officials whose time we imposed upon and whose activities we either praised or criticized; our families upon whom this research effort imposed certain hardships; and the generous financial support over the years of the Ford Foundation, the Social Science Research Council, the Rabinowitz Foundation, and the Research and Graduate Study Office of the College of the Liberal Arts, The Pennsylvania State University. Special thanks to John Simon, Alice Mayhew and Nancy Inglis for their help in producing this work. Finally, acknowledgment should go to Sage Publications for their permission to reprint our article, "A Methodological Note on the Comparative Study of Bureaucracy," from *The Journal of Comparative Administration*, I, No. 2 (August, 1969), 234–248.

*To our families and to our friends
in North and South America*

Contents

PART ONE

THE REVOLUTIONARY

CHALLENGE

1

Internal and External Factors Affecting Socio-Political Change in Latin America

An analysis of socio-political change[1] which presents merely an inventory of factors without specifying why certain factors were selected, or which factors have greater significance, is of little value. Meaningful study of socio-political change requires identification of those dimensions and issues that illuminate particular problem areas of specific concern to the researcher and his readers. Since the choice of dimensions to be researched has both theoretical and practical consequences, there must be a clearly stated rationale for the selection of research areas.

We are largely concerned with change processes in a variety of political systems and their subsystems, both with factors which influence the formation of policies aimed at change, and with policy output—the extent to which change has occurred. More specifically, we are concerned with socio-political change policies in the dependent countries of Latin America. Our approach is comprehensive but not exhaustive; there are areas, which could shed additional light, that we do not consider.

Our approach to the change process (1) identifies strategic sectors and critical problem areas of society that have a direct effect on the change process; (2) identifies the issues that emerge from the sectors and problems under consideration; (3) identifies the conflicting strategies that are proposed by the social forces attempting to deal with the problems of socio-political change; (4) identifies and compares contrasting approaches to socio-political change in terms of the formulation and implementation of publicly stated goals; and (5) identifies and measures the impact of external as well as internal factors on decision-making which attempts to respond to demands for change.

In a discussion of change, the term "strategic" is meaningful only in the context in which it is used. We consider a socio-economic sector strategic when sectoral policy decisions or lack of decisions significantly affect (a) a major proportion of the population, (b) the use or ownership of a major economic resource, (c) the distribution of political power and the structure of political authority, (d) the overall functioning of the economy.

Thus, the agricultural sector in Latin America is a strategic sector: it employs a majority of the economically active population, land is an important economic resource, the distribution of economic resources has a profound effect on national as well as sectoral politics, the performance of the agricultural sector has a decisive impact on the capacity and output of other sectors.

"Critical issues" are those which (a) generate conflict between major social forces—issues involving large numbers, force, and significant economic and political resources; (b) affect the interests of important social strata; (c) potentially or actually re-order society. Political action involving critical issues would imply changes in the pattern of authority, the sources of legitimacy, and the bases of political participation in the polity.

Agrarian reform, which involves redistribution of land and social and political power, is such a critical issue. Abolition of privileges and expropriation of land are resisted by the landed elite who frequently resort to violence to prevent change. Conflict between peasants and landlords usually results in the intervention of the state—the social conflict immediately becomes politicized. The role of the state in the process of conflict resolution is especially crucial; depending on its policy, the state can become the ally or enemy of one or both antagonists. While the peasantry is numerically the largest single group in Latin America, the large landowners continue to exercise a more important voice in national policy. Agrarian reform pits numbers against wealth, and thus the issue cuts deeply into the political and social system.

Conflict between different class interests results in conflicting strategies for change. Partisans of the landowners describe change in terms of elite-introduced modernization. These modernization strategies serve the interests of the large landholders who then become associated with policies to transform the agricultural environment. Partisans of the peasantry stress the need for mobilization and change of tenure as preconditions for socio-political change. The different strategies embrace differences in political style and content and have very different political consequences. In the process of transforming a traditional, underdeveloped society several change choices and variants emerge from political and social conflicts—and none of them is predestined to succeed.

Policy decisions emanating from great powers may be linked with domestic policy groups, serve as a constraint on decision-makers, or come into conflict with the policies of indigenous elites. When a great power favors elite modernization and an indigenous elite seeks to promote mobilization from below, there is an obvious conflict. In some situations there are crisscrossing patterns—coalitions between external and internal elites and counter-elites from both areas of the world. Conflicts in the international sphere are frequently transferred into the domestic politics of dependent countries, complicating the problem of policy decisions affecting change. Within the dependent countries cleavages have emerged between "modernizers" and "mobilizers."

Elite modernizers ("gradualists") largely rely on a

legalistic, "insider" approach—the initiation of change is constantly subject to bargaining processes between a variety of established groups negotiating settlements designed to safeguard their vital interests. This bargaining process results in the fragmentation of legislation—each section and paragraph of change-oriented legislation is subject to judicial, executive, and administrative interpretation and reinterpretation. Often, the affected elites have access to the presiding authorities at each stage, and thus are in a position to delay, emasculate, or circumvent the process of change.

Mobilization from below frequently begins as an extralegal phenomenon, and frequently, when established elites perceive an effective mobilization effort, they resort to official violence. Hence, violence becomes an important factor in the resolution of conflict over change policy—the policy outcome being imposed largely by force.

However, there is not always a clear line separating the elite-gradualist approach from the mass mobilization approach. Hostile reaction to gradualist changes may result in an intensification of conflict and political polarization. Not infrequently, the gradualist approach itself is imposed through violence and force, and thus one of its unintentional consequences may be to create the conditions for more comprehensive changes rather than to institutionalize limited change. Likewise, violent mass revolution may result in a new social order with the capacity to routinize change; peaceful, gradual change can occur as a postrevolutionary political phenomenon. Nevertheless, in both the gradualist and mobilization approaches there are constant, hostile pressures from internal counter-elites and external policy-making centers. These pressures may force decision-makers to alter or modify priorities and/or intensify or soften their commitments in directions not originally foreseen. The problematic nature of policy-making in dependent countries results largely from the accumulated disadvantages of past changes and the intricate web of dependency woven by centuries of external penetration. Change choices in dependent countries are always "costly" and the benefits are not always apparent—at least in the short run. The process of policy reversal—the redirection of a society away from underdeveloped dependency toward an independent developing state—is made doubly difficult by external decision-makers who reinforce policies chosen by indigenous elites. Reversing or changing existing change patterns and the societal structures which provide their support has largely become a task for revolutionary elites.

Systemic transformation can be attempted through a variety of revolutionary approaches; for example, revolutionaries may function largely as an "autonomous elite." [2] An autonomous elite may seek to impose change without the use of mass organizations. It may then seek to legitimate change choices by relying largely on a plebiscitory mandate from the people and specific welfare pay-offs directed to the immediate needs of the populace. Revolutions that begin from above may at some point stimulate social forces to act on their own account. Likewise, subsequent to a revolution through mass mobilization, the leadership which emerges may attempt to institutionalize changes and direct the bases of support toward less politicized and more pragmatic goals.

Mass mobilization politics vary in scope and impact. They may turn out to be largely uncoordinated peasant land seizures; or forces throughout the society may coordinate efforts to completely transform their society.

Policies of great powers have a great impact on the internal development policies of most underdeveloped countries. In our approach to this problem, we distinguish between policy statements made on ceremonial occasions and policy statements made in an "operational setting" (appropriation hearings, etc.).

Until recently, most studies have suggested that the policies of the great powers have changed—though not all specified exactly how. Instead, they ritualistically reiterate

8 : CULTIVATING REVOLUTION

"concern" for fundamental democratic goals, although this
liturgy of liberal concern frequently obscures crucial policy
changes.

The notion of *a* policy-making center is useful in fixing
political responsibility, but it is too crude a notion to apply
to the overall study of great power policy-making. Actually,
a variety of political and administrative institutions participate, with varying degrees of importance, in the policy-
making process. In studying U.S. policy-making toward
Latin America it is especially important to focus on the several administrative agencies which are responsible for implementing official policy—to analyze how the outlook and
perception of top administrators lead to alterations and
revisions of policy enunciated on ceremonial occasions.
There tends to be a gap between expressed policy purposes
and the criteria which inform routine decision-making. The
revision or attrition of general goals can eventually result in
a redefinition of the whole problem. The two levels on
which policy-makers function—the ceremonial and the operational—largely reflect a need to maintain publicly acceptable political postures while actually developing (and
covertly practicing) new approaches. Appeals to abstract
ideals are frequently used to obscure the actual linkages between external and internal elites who may be the major
beneficiaries of policy output. The perceptions, decisions
and policies of officials are shaped by socio-economic interests which they perceive to be of critical importance in the
change process.

Utilizing this framework, we concern ourselves with
the role of public administrators (U.S. and Latin American) in the area of agricultural development. We examine
the underlying issues and problems that shape the relationships between legislation, public policy, and socio-political
change. Our focus is on the administrative structures that
are strategically situated between legal documents and society. The specific policy focus throughout is on the issues of
agrarian reform and agricultural development. The study

covers three Latin countries (Chile, Peru, and Cuba) and the great power of the hemisphere, the United States.

Our study is concerned with two interrelated problems in agricultural development: (a) internal efforts to transform Latin America's anachronistic and inefficient agricultural sector and the obstacles encountered by those who have undertaken this task, and (b) the policies and attitudes United States officials have adopted toward those efforts. Through a detailed examination of a series of case studies, largely focusing on the 1960s, we compare and analyze a number of alternative approaches to the problem of agricultural modernization.

In Part One we survey the existing literature on agrarian reform and change. Previous studies, while casting some light on particular problems, lack detailed accounts of a number of areas of crucial importance. For example, little or no attention is paid to the role of great powers in helping or hindering internal change.

In Part Two we turn to the socio-political change policies of the dependent nations. First we consider two cases which have been widely heralded as models of peaceful, gradual change: agrarian reform in Chile under President Frei and agrarian reform in Peru under President Belaunde. Here we attempt to analyze the forces behind the policy decisions or lack of decisions, focusing on the linkage between social forces and administrators.

In Part Three we analyze three cases where revolutionary approaches at the system and subsystem levels have been attempted as means to transform the agrarian setting. We consider peasant politicization in Chile, the Peruvian military junta (since October, 1968), and the Cuban experience since 1959.

The position taken by the United States with regard to agricultural development is considered in Part Four. We note two conflicting approaches: the "reform-from-below" approach enunciated by President Kennedy at Punta del Este in 1961, and the policy subsequently put into practice by a variety of government officials. Through extensive interviewing, we attempt to describe the official perception of past and present agrarian problems and issues.

This volume deals with the problems and obstacles (real and imagined) facing change-oriented decision-makers in dependent countries. By combining detailed case studies with a problem-oriented comparative approach we hope to point out not only the obstacles to change, but to suggest some means by which they can be overcome.

NOTES

1. We are purposively avoiding the term "development" because it implies a sense of progress which we are not convinced has occurred in Latin America. The term "change" is more neutral, allowing for regression as well as progression.

2. Revolutionaries may be from the Marxist Left or from traditional, elite institutions as are the military "revolutionaries" of Peru. See Part Three, "Non-Bargaining Politics and Socio-Political Change."

2

Agrarian Reform and Socio-Political Change in Latin America

This section will critically assess the literature dealing with agrarian reform and its impact on agricultural development and social, political and economic change. By surveying the literature we will determine (1) if a consensus exists among scholars and officials regarding the concepts of agrarian reform and agricultural development, (2) the role assigned to agrarian reform within agricultural development plans, and (3) the role of agrarian reform in social and political development.

The literature in these areas is either largely theoretical or based on limited empirical findings. Frequently it fails to consider agrarian reform or even agriculture. Agricultural studies have largely been concerned with problems of capital accumulation, savings and investment, and increased productivity through technological innovations to the exclusion of problems related to changes in land tenure. This shows an overconcern for a purely economic approach which accepts existing social and political structures as given and which seeks to discover development strategies only within these parameters.

Most studies of agriculture and agrarian reform consider agrarian reform as only one component of a cluster of activities that together induce development. They consider agrarian reform to be a necessary but not a sufficient condition for overall development. The agrarian reform school perceives it as a necessary prerequisite for development. Others conclude that while it is an important component of a modern agricultural policy, it is not generally a requisite for development.

Most writers conceive of agricultural development in terms of increased production and income. This involves seeking means to produce adequate foodstuffs to provide proper caloric intake for current population and increases for future population growth. Where local conditions do not permit growth of all necessary foodstuffs, agricultural specialty exports are to be expanded sufficiently to earn foreign exchange to purchase imported foodstuffs. Agricultural development involves the full and efficient utilization of land and human resources. It includes raising the income of rural laborers and farm owners to levels at least equal to other sectors of the economy. As a consequence, agricultural development is seen as a means for reducing the flow of rural migrants to urban areas, thus stabilizing the agrarian labor source and relieving the pressure on other economic sectors. It is assumed that as capital-intensive agriculture is developed, the earnings from the surplus of agricultural exports will provide capital for industrialization. Industry then is to provide jobs for the rural labor surpluses displaced by agromachinery.[1]

Despite the numerous conceptions of agrarian reform, they can be classified into three groups: (1) "mild" reforms, involving limited government intervention through some public regulation and assistance—laws governing landlord-tenant relations and leasing arrangements, colonization and settlement of unused lands, development programs (infrastructure projects, fertilization, and soil conservation), credit facilities, the creation of cooperatives; (2) "stronger" reforms short of expropriation, such as rent control or rent reduction (the most important) and mandatory consolidation and/or limitations on the extent of parcelization or extent of holdings; (3) "strongest" reforms, including expropriation programs either with or without compensation to landholders, the redistribution of this land to the tillers, or public ownership and collectivization of the expropriated land.[2] Most authors would generally accept the classificatory scheme, although some maintain that development-type programs, credit facilities and the formation of cooperatives are part of an overall development perspective but are not reform per se. Agrarian reform implies a set of public policies designed to (1) readjust land tenure arrangements so as to limit land holdings through expropriation or consolidation or both—actual ownership of the land may rest with individuals or the public sector[3]—and (2) improve or maximize land utilization, facilitating the application of efficient farming methods to increase agricultural production.[4]

Agrarian Reform and Economic Development

We will begin our discussion of agrarian reform and its role in economic development by considering the broader problem of whether industrialization should have priority over agriculture in maximizing overall economic growth. Twenty years ago, in line with the generally held notion that industrialization was the key to development and should be given top priority, P. K. Chang[5] declared that industrialization was necessary for agrarian reform (especially if higher production and greater efficiency are the goals) and not vice versa. In 1951 a conference on agrarian reform at the University of Wisconsin produced a document 700 pages in length which contained 127 papers.[6] Unlike Chang, the consensus of this conference and subsequent works places more emphasis on the interrelationship of economic development and agriculture and the central role of agrarian reform in the development process rather than as a product of it.[7] One contributor noted, "Land tenure adjustments appear essential in many countries to facilitate the development of the economies." [8] He went on to warn that "it must be recognized that land reform is not a cure-all and that it can be productive of social and economic benefits only as part of comprehensive programs of development." [9]

There was some dissent within the conference. For example, Dennis Fitzgerald argued that economic development rests "in the last analysis, on the accumulation of capital," [10] and that economic development "is at once an essential prerequisite to land reform and a partial consequence of it." [11] He then explained that agrarian reform should occur first in those rural areas where there is little population pressure, because when population pressure is great the only lasting solution is the orderly transfer of the excess rural population to nonagricultural pursuits. This would allow redistribution of land to the exact number of farmers who would balance the amount of land resources available, producing reasonable farm size and income.[12]

The great majority of authors followed the central theme set by Barlowe:

> When it is used alone, land reform may bring almost immediate benefits such as lower rents or opportunities for land ownership to large segments of the population. These benefits can be used to stimulate programs of economic development. Past experience, however, suggests that they often have little effect in promoting this goal.[13]

This is true because,

> if land reform is to be used as a tool of economic development, it must be used in conjunction with a number of other programs. Among other things these programs should stimulate local desire for economic development, and promote capital accumulation and investment, higher work productivity and an increase in total production.[14]

Also,

> At this point, one should take care not to overemphasize the importance of land reform. Economic development can

and has taken place without land reform (because) . . . one of the strategic issues in the relationship between land reform and economic development necessarily rests on the emphasis given to economic development as one of the goals in land reform programs.[15]

Continuing the academic debate over agrarian reform, in the 1950s Doreen Warriner[16] viewed the prime economic effects of land reform to be increases in investment and productivity.[17] She saw reform as only a condition for development, which cannot *cause* investment.[18] As to increased production, "we can only say that results will depend on how far the new owners can intensify farming, either by the use of more labor on the land, or by the use of more labor and more capital." [19] She concluded that,

> land reform in the conditions of many underdeveloped countries, is certainly a condition of development. [But] . . . it can only be the first step towards breaking the circle of getting a more balanced development.[20]

Turning to the demographic problems involved (the population pressure mentioned by Fitzgerald), Warriner adds,

> from a demographic standpoint, we can therefore regard the relation of reform to development in a new light. To make reform successful, development—i.e., investment in agriculture and in industry—is needed . . . to provide wider opportunities of employment. . . .[21]

Barlowe, unlike Warriner, viewed land reform as only a marginal factor in the developmental process:

> In conclusion, emphasis might well be placed on the point that land reform by itself provides no guarantee of economic development . . . it must be used carefully or it may only complicate the problem of development. . . . Even under ideal circumstances it must be recognized that land reform cannot do the job alone. Other programs must be used in conjunction with land reform. The process of economic development involves the interplay of numerous

factors, many of which play a more strategic role in the usual process of development than does land reform.[22]

The Warriner-Barlowe views typify most views on the relationship of agrarian reform to economic development. Differences occur in priority ranking. For some writers reform is considered a vital factor while others consider numerous other factors ahead of it in importance.

By the end of the 1950s some variations on these themes became visible. In 1959 Sayigh concluded that there could be no worthwhile development in any sector of the economy without attention to agriculture, especially to modernization of agricultural techniques. He criticized economists for equating industrialization with development and argued that agriculture was the necessary starting point. He saw agrarian reform as the first step in agricultural development, but went on to argue that it must be designed to complement the industrial sectors.[23] In the same year Aziz reached a similar conclusion but specifically criticized "piecemeal land reform." He argued that problems in implementing a reform program were to be found in the lack of planning and organizational skills that allowed reform, rural credit programs, and technical assistance to become disassociated from each other and from the development of nonagricultural sectors.[24]

In 1961 the Eleventh International Conference of Agricultural Economists perceived changes in land tenure merely as a means of gaining time:

> Land policy should be regarded as part of larger policy issues such as population and development policy. Land reform was described as a means of getting breathing space within which to implement other important aspects of development policy.[25]

On the other hand, Alexander saw reform as fundamental to development and stated, "it [the *latifundia* in Latin America] hampers both the further expansion of agriculture and the growth of the industrial sector of the economy.[26] This is because the current agrarian structure:

(1) Prohibits development of a significant market economy;

(2) Does not produce sufficient food for national consumption, causing importation of foodstuffs to the cities and loss of foreign exchange;

(3) Does not create capital for industrialization.

Elsewhere, in the same vein, Alexander connected reform with other programs:

> The mere distribution of land is not, of course, a sufficient reform by itself. An effective program of agrarian reform must make sure that the new proprietors have access to credit to finance their crops and to buy equipment and it must provide technical assistance and help in marketing.[27]

Taking a long-range economic view, Horowitz concluded that "there is little doubt that land redistribution is fundamental to any long-run increase in output in most of the Latin American countries," and that the present *latifundia* structure cannot produce adequately.[28] Likewise Rezsohazy, writing with special reference to Latin America, agreed that the basic cause of underdevelopment is "reluctance to accept indispensable reforms (agrarian most of all) by the ruling class." [29] He further stipulated that land reform must be complemented and coordinated with other programs to improve the process of urbanization, the taxation system, and the promotion of industrial development.[30] In a more limited vein, Balogh called for rural reform but tied it to the joint activities of rural public works and the formation of cooperatives to insure success, ignoring nonagricultural sectors and the socio-political aspects of the problem.[31]

From 1962 to the present—even after the Alliance for Progress—the same basic conception recurs: agrarian reform is viewed as a desirable but not a necessary requisite for development. Galbraith,[32] Alpert,[33] and Hunter[34] argued

that agrarian reform was necessary for agricultural development, but that it must be tied to other programs of technological aid, "modernization," and "social progress."

Other writers continued to reject the notion that agrarian reform was the "vital first step to development" (as
Doreen Warriner has called it, "the end of the beginning").
While believing in the centrality of agriculture in economic
development, Lauchlin Currie[35] argued in terms of increasing farm income. Currie did not favor land redistribution.
Instead, he advocated industrialization to absorb excess
rural population. As a result of increased food demand from
increases in nonagricultural employment and wages, those
remaining in the rural areas would need to expand production and increase their income. Fewer farmers with larger
tracts would thus bypass the need for land redistribution.

Theoretical argument over agrarian reform produced
the same results, i.e., increased production and farm income.

Irving Horowitz summarized the crucial problem:

> Land reform is an issue charged with political emotion,
> and it is often viewed as an economic panacea. It is vital
> that there be some evaluation of what it can and what it
> cannot do.[36]

A number of empirical studies attempted to test the hypothesis already formulated.

Agrarian Reform and Social
and Political Development

On a theoretical level, discussion of the social and political
effects of agrarian reform are very general and limited only
to Barlowe[37] and Warriner.[38] In the main, conclusions are
reached with little evidence to support them, such as Alexander (cited above), concluding that agrarian reform is a
"basic need . . . for the achievement of political democ-

racy." Barlowe concluded that reform may help create a climate in which democratic political institutions may develop[39] and may improve the peasant's social well being,[40] adding:

> But again the process is not an automatic one. For land reform to bring these results it must provide increased production, higher family incomes, and units of economic size. Even when reforms result in increased income and production and in peasant contentment and well-being, a certain amount of promotion may be needed to direct peasant desires and expenditures in the direction of economic development. Without this direction the benefits may easily be hoarded or dissipated with little net gain to the economy.[41]

Going further, Warriner stated that the "most important" results of reform are unmeasurable—the complex and nebulous feelings of more dignity and more freedom gained by the peasants who receive land.[42] Rezsohazy (for Latin America) also saw the vital effects of reform as political and social rather than economic. He contended that only by breaking up the large *fundos* could the political power of the landowners be reduced and redistributed more equally.[43] In this brief statement, Rezsohazy focused on the crux of the situation—to understand the social, political, and economic effects of agrarian reform, one must understand the relationships between economic power, social status, and political influence. Only in this way is it possible to understand both the difficulties of reform and its effects. Meager as it is, the available data show the complex interrelationships involved and raise economic considerations once again.

Of the seventeen works[44] which presented some empirical evidence of the effects of agrarian reform, all generally found the same pattern of results—all reforms had at least some very limited positive effects, but the more closely they were tied to other programs of development (both within agriculture and in other sectors) the more successful agrarian reform appeared. Warriner, a supporter of agrarian reform, found only limited successes in her study of Egypt and Syria. She conceded that in Eastern Europe and in Mexico where peasants received only land without credit, marketing facilities, or technical guidance the results varied, with production rising in some places while declining in others.[45] She concluded that the "wider conception" of land reform as part of a comprehensive development policy is a better approach as long as the policy is not blunted by excessive broadening.[46] Egypt's agrarian reform of 1952 had three goals: expropriation, raising of rural income, and reduction of rents.[47] With regard to the first, the reform was a success.[48] With regard to the second, although some increases had been made, they fell short of expectations.[49] Lastly, although rents dropped initially, nine years later they had returned to, and in some cases, surpassed pre-reform levels.[50] Also, she discovered that most increases in income went to landowners, while wages to laborers remained static largely because the mandated increases were not enforceable. Production increased, but only slightly, while there seemed to be some increase in investment in both industry and agriculture.[51] Warriner suggested that the agrarian reform in Egypt gave more "social equality" to the peasants and produced a more stable society.[52] Several authors studying land tenure measures in Asia found few concrete benefits accruing without additional public efforts.[53] After examining historical evidence, Marburg concluded that only when a political regime took measures that combined investment with innovation did economic development result from changes in land tenure.[54] Hoselitz, writing on Asian experiences, found that the results of land reform did not contribute significantly to immediate economic development. He withheld final judgment pending further industrialization in order to determine if reform is "economically rational." [55] For the Philippines, Cook found that after five years of reform only small increases in production resulted. He also found that income distribution and long-run human resource development have increased.[56] Krishna determined that the cooperative farms of India have had little effect on productivity and capital formation. He concluded that a better tax structure and overall redistribution of all wealth were prerequisites to developing the country.[57] Lastly, in Pakistan, Bredo found that reform attempts were too insignificant to have any effect.[58] In 1962 Coutsoumaris reverted to industrialization and organizational changes in reference to Venezuela:

> I may state in conclusion that the land reform problem under Venezuelan (and other similar Latin American) conditions is one of creating practically a new farm organization adjusted to the prospects of a country having possibilities of rapid industrialization, in contrast to many earlier European and Asian reforms whose basic problem was to modify the existing set-up through a redistribution of land ownership and changes in the conditions of control. This explains why all previous attempts at land reform based on broad social objectives or political expediency have encountered so many difficulties in their realization.[59]

Largely concerned with increasing efficiency, Coutsoumaris argued for modernizing existing farms to serve the rapidly changing needs and preferences of an industrializing society.[60]

Horowitz argues for rapid industrialization and sees agrarian reform as a consequence of this process, eventually resulting in greater social equality:

> In the main, when land reform is undertaken without reference to general industrial change, as in South Korea, the development process is abortive—even in the agricultural sector. When land reform is taken as a general consequence of industrialization, as in Japan, the development process is highly successful—even in the argicultural sector. The reform narrowed the traditional differences between classes in the villages . . . the distribution of land ownership among the multitude of farmers contributed to the foundation of a more satisfying rural life, and to the beginning of local control of the decision-making processes.[61]

A fundamental shift in the locus of power is a prerequisite for development through reform:

> In many countries land reform is thwarted not because there is a lack of technical knowledge, but because the political apparatus is wedded to the economic status quo. It is no accident that in both Japan and South Korea land reform was externally induced.[62]

Duff supports this observation in reference to Colombia, where political opposition surrounding proposals for compensation of expropriated land (cash versus bonds; amount of compensation) and proposals for financing the program resulted in compromise solutions which were inadequate.[63] Feder reached the same conclusions regarding the Colombian experience.[64] Hildebrand, writing on Guatemala, concluded that political opposition from entrenched elites was a roadblock to wider and more effective reform measures.[65]

Cohen, analyzing the Peruvian attempt at land reform under the Prado regime, described many of the political difficulties in reform. A commission appointed by Prado and composed generally of members of the traditional upper class (Prado's supporters) recommended measures that would have left the social, political, and economic structure of Peru unchanged while not significantly increasing agricultural production.[66] Innocuous proposals failed to pass the Peruvian Congress (with the exception of a proposal to colonize remote regions) despite the emphasis on increasing production rather than on social reform.[67] The landed elite possessed the political strength necessary to dominate the commission and circumvent demands for change.[68]

Elias Tuma[69] has taken, perhaps, the most extensive look at the effects of agrarian reform. On the basis of eleven cases (from the Greek reforms of Solon in the sixth century B.C. to the Egyptian reform of 1952), Tuma examined the background, type, and effects (social, personal, economic, and political, over the short and long run) of reform in each instance.[70] With two significant exceptions, he found that neither revolutionary nor nonrevolutionary land reforms achieved sweeping effects, especially in the long run. Only the French reforms following the revolution of 1789, and the Soviet reforms (collectivization) after 1917 have had any long-term effects. Tuma tied the more successful reforms to antecedent dynamic social and political movements, emphasizing that any successful reform was a result of, rather than a cause of, "modernization and developmental forces." He argued that reforms attempted in the absence of this "dynamism" are caught in a set of "static features" in the society and are doomed to failure.[71] He concluded that agrarian reform's direct effect on economic development is a function of its integration in larger development policies.[72] Tuma's study suggests that only short-run political goals were obtained unless reform was applied uniformly to all land and all tenure groups and had the support of a significant urban class.[73]

Tsui Young-Chi's study of Taiwan's reform argues that tenure reform must be integrated with other agricultural programs to insure economic growth.[74] Basic measures of land-to-the-tiller and rent limitations contributed significantly to increased production only when coordinated with programs of water resource development, fertilization, multiple cropping, development of marginal lands, tidal lowland reclamation, highway and housing programs, among others.[75] Successful agricultural development programs resulted from carefully coordinated efforts of reform, colonization, and production-oriented programs. In discussing the same reform (Taiwan), Bandyopadhyay and Ghosh (1967) reach similar conclusions on the importance of technical assistance and integration of reform measures into broader programs of agricultural development.[76]

The same authors, in evaluating the Indian reform, found that only one objective had been achieved—removal of intermediaries between the *ryots* (peasants who farm the land) and the state. Other objectives were not achieved due

to evasion of the law and lax enforcement.[77] In the same
vein, Klein observed few long-range changes resulting from
the Indian reform and ascribed its failures to lack of mass
participation.[78]

Three articles dealing with the Mexican agrarian reform—Saco,[79] Felix,[80] and Bandyopadhyay and Ghosh[81]—
found that a decrease in production occurred between the
pre-reform period of 1900–1909, and 1930–1934. From
then on, however, very rapid increases occurred, with production doubling by the mid-1940s.[82] This was explained by
a lack of technical assistance and credit, poor administration, and a paucity of capital investment until after 1934.
Felix observed the same phenomena. He explained the
changes in terms of the establishment of a "favorable climate" for, and consequently an increase in, public investment in agriculture and a new sense of national unity and
social mobility. The result was an environment in which
ambitious agricultural development programs could gain
public support.[83] Saco's study of Mexico found that the drop
in production after 1900–1909 was attributable to insuffi-
ciencies in technical knowledge, managerial ability, and
capital. He related the subsequent doubling of production to
increases in yield and acreage, reflecting increasing application of technological inputs.[84] He concluded that the production drop was the result of upheavals of the revolution
and that the interrelationship between land reform and general economic development is a two-way process, each
affecting the other (as Tuma maintained).[85] Increased vertical and horizontal mobility to the peasants was the most
important social result.[86] Saco suggests land reform can help
"consolidate democracy" by broadening the ownership of
land—the economic base of political power in agricultural,
underdeveloped countries.[87] Initial production declines resulting from an agrarian revolution and subsequent social
dislocation may be considered part of the overhead costs
prior to an agricultural development take-off.

Summary

Most writers contend that the effects of agrarian reform, their extent and intensity, stem from the forces that create the reform in the first place more than from the reform itself. Broad reform measures spring from dynamic social and political forces which push for "modernization" in general. These forces give rise to a broad scope of programs and projects—land tenure reform, education, peasant organization, enfranchisement and political participation, interest articulation and aggregation. Agrarian reform is as much a result of development as a cause of it. As a result, it is difficult to measure the specific short-term effects of reform. When static or only partially dynamic conditions prevail in a society, tenure reform (as a single program to "get breathing space" or to re-establish the status quo) may result only in a set of compromised, poorly financed programs with little impact on long-range development.

The growing trend among writers is to see agrarian reform as essentially both a cause and an effect of development—a "catalyst" as Barlowe phrases it. It is one of a number of programs that grow out of, and in turn, fertilize dynamic social forces bent on changing a society. It assumes prime importance because agriculture is the largest economic sector in the less-developed nations and because the rural populace is the largest, poorest, most poorly educated, most exploited, and is largely the most completely unorganized (unmobilized politically) stratum of these societies.

Agrarian reform can affect the total structure of rural society with considerable, critical spillover into the urban sector. As yet, we have few empirical studies designed to test theory as it has presently evolved. Instead, we have empirical studies that look at agrarian reform alone, with only generalized reference to its connections with other sociopolitical forces and programs. Only tentative conclusions

26 : CULTIVATING REVOLUTION

can be reached at this point. What is needed now is a series of case studies of national reform movements, which are specifically designed to test reform's role as a result as well as a cause of economic, social and political development.

NOTES

1. For an elaboration of this argument, see Simon Kuznets, "Economic Growth and the Contribution of Agriculture: Notes on the Measurement," *International Journal of Agrarian Affairs,* 3 (April, 1961), pp. 56–75.
2. Raleigh Barlowe, "Land Reform and Economic Development," *Journal of Farm Economics,* 35 (May, 1953), pp. 176–79.
3. The goals of readjustment may be a mixture of economic requirements—to maximize agricultural production and raise farm incomes, and social justice requirements—to eliminate or minimize economic, political, and social inequalities resulting from a grossly unequal distribution of land.
4. Programs designed to achieve this goal include: mechanization or intensification; credit facilities development; water resources development; "infrastructure works"—market-to-farm roads, marketing facilities improvements, price stabilization or guarantees, etc.; technical assistance via improved fertilizers and seeds; in short, those programs which contribute to improved production but have nothing to do with altering the prevailing land tenure arrangements.
5. P. K. Chang, *Agriculture and Industrialization* (Cambridge: Harvard University Press, 1949).
6. K. H. Parsons, R. J. Penn and P. M. Raup, eds., *Land Tenure* (Madison: University of Wisconsin Press, 1956).
7. *Ibid.,* p. 12.
8. *Ibid.,* p. 20.
9. *Ibid.,* p. 20.
10. *Ibid.,* p. 46.
11. *Ibid.,* p. 45.
12. *Ibid.,* pp. 45–46.
13. Barlowe, *op. cit.,* p. 176.
14. *Ibid.*
15. *Ibid.,* pp. 176, 180.
16. Doreen Warriner, *Land Reform and Economic Development* (Cairo: National Bank of Egypt, 1955) and *Land Reform and Development*

in the Middle East, 2nd ed. (London: Oxford University Press, 1962).

17. Warriner, *Land Reform and Economic Development, op. cit.*, pp.17–18.

18. *Ibid.*, p. 18, Warriner's emphasis.

19. *Ibid.*, p. 20.

20. *Ibid.*, p. 21.

21. *Ibid.*, p. 30.

22. Barlowe, *op. cit.*, p. 187.

23. Yusif A. Sayigh, "The Place of Agriculture in Economic Development," *Land Economics*, 35 (November, 1959), pp. 297–305.

24. Ungku A. Aziz, "The Interdependent Development of Agriculture and Other Industries," *Philippine Journal of Public Administration*, 3 (July, 1959), p. 313.

25. Eleventh International Conference of Agricultural Economists (Discussion Group Reports), Cuernavaca, Mexico, August, 1961, in *International Journal of Agrarian Affairs*, 8 (September, 1962), p. 139.

26. Robert Alexander, "Nature and Progress of Agrarian Reform in Latin America," *Journal of Economic History*, 23 (December, 1963), p. 561, and "Agrarian Reform in Latin America," *Foreign Affairs*, 41 (October, 1962), pp. 191–207.

27. Alexander, "Agrarian Reform in Latin America," *op. cit.*, p. 203.

28. Irving Horowitz, *Three Worlds of Development* (New York: Oxford University Press, 1966), p. 207.

29. Rudolph Rezsohazy, "Events and Trends: Economic, Social and Political Problems in Latin America," *World Justice*, 4 (September, 1962), p. 77.

30. *Ibid.*, pp. 79 ff.

31. T. Balogh, "Agriculture and Economic Development," *Oxford Economic Papers*, 13 (February, 1961), pp. 27–42.

32. John Kenneth Galbraith, *Economic Development* (Cambridge: Harvard University Press, 1964).

33. Paul Alpert, *Economic Development* (London: Colber-MacMillan Ltd., 1963).

34. Chester Hunter, *Social Aspects of Development* (New York: McGraw Hill, 1966).

35. Lauchlin Currie, *Accelerating Development: The Necessity and the Means* (New York: McGraw Hill, 1966).

36. Horowitz, *op. cit.*, p. 202.

37. Barlowe, *op. cit.*

38. Warriner, *Land Reform and Economic Development, op. cit.*

39. Barlowe, *op. cit.*, pp. 180–82.

28 : CULTIVATING REVOLUTION

40. *Ibid.,* p. 182.
41. *Ibid.,* pp. 182–83.
42. Warriner, *Land Reform and Economic Development, op. cit.,* p. 31.
43. Rezsohazy, *op. cit.,* pp. 78–79.
44. The seventeen works are: Doreen Warriner, *Land Reform and Development in the Middle East,* 2nd ed. (London: Oxford University Press, 1962); Robert Alexander, "Nature and Progress of Agrarian Reform in Latin America," *Journal of Economic History,* 23 (December, 1963), pp. 559–73, and "Agrarian Reform in Latin America," *Foreign Affairs,* 41 (October, 1962), pp. 191–207; Irving Horowitz, *Three Worlds of Development* (New York: Oxford University Press, 1966), p. 207; Walter Froehlich, ed., *Land Tenure, Industrialization and Social Stability* (Milwaukee: Marquette University Press, 1961); George Coutsoumaris, "Policy Objectives in Latin American Land Reform with Special References to Venezuela," *Inter-American Economic Affairs,* 16 (Autumn, 1962), pp. 25–40; Ernest A. Duff, "Agrarian Reform in Colombia: Problems of Social Reform," *Journal of Inter-American Studies,* 8 (January, 1966), pp. 75–88; Ernest Feder, "When is Land Reform a Land Reform?: The Colombian Case," *The American Journal of Economics and Sociology,* 24 (April, 1965), pp. 113–34; John Hildebrand, "Latin American Economic Development, Land Reform and U.S. Aid, with Special Reference to Guatemala," *Journal of Inter-American Studies,* 4 (July, 1962), pp. 351–61; Alvin Cohen, "Social Structure, Agrarian Reform and Economic Development in Peru," *Inter-American Economic Affairs,* 18 (Summer, 1964), pp. 45–59; Elias Tuma, "Agrarian Reform in Historical Perspective: A Comparative Study," *Comparative Studies in Society and History,* 6 (October, 1963), pp. 47–75. See also Elias Tuma, *Twenty-six Centuries of Agrarian Reform* (Berkeley: University of California Press, 1965); Tsui Young-Chi, "Land Use Improvement: A Key to the Economic Development of Taiwan," *Journal of Farm Economics,* 44 (August, 1962), pp. 363–72; Bandyopadhyay and Ghosh, "Role of Agrarian Reform in Agricultural Development in Mexico, Taiwan and India—A Comparative Study," *Indian Journal of Agricultural Economics,* 22 (January, 1967), pp. 37–48; Sidney Klein, "Land Problems and Economic Growth in India and China," *Malayan Economic Review,* 5 (October, 1960), pp. 66–80; Alfredo Saco, "Land Reform as an Instrument of Change with Special Reference to Latin America," *FAO Monthly Bulletin of Agricultural Economics and Statistics,* 13 (December, 1964), pp. 1–9; D. Felix, "Agrarian Reform and Industrial Growth," *International Development Review,* 2 (October, 1960), pp. 16–22.
45. Warriner, *Land Reform and Development in the Middle East, op. cit.,* p. 3.
46. *Ibid.,* pp. 3–6.
47. *Ibid.,* p. 32.

48. *Ibid.*, pp. 32–36.
49. *Ibid.*, pp. 37–38.
50. *Ibid.*, p. 39.
51. *Ibid.*, p. 40.
52. *Ibid.*, pp. 184–90.
53. Walter Froehlich, ed., *Land Tenure, Industrialization and Social Stability* (Milwaukee: Marquette University Press, 1961).
54. Theodore Marburg, "Land Tenure Institutions and the Development of Western Society," in Froehlich, *ibid.*, p. 75.
55. Bert Hoselitz, "Land Reform, Industrialization and Economic Development in Asia," in Froehlich, *ibid.*, p. 113.
56. Hugh Cook, "Land Reform and Development in the Philippines," in Froehlich, *ibid.*, pp. 168–80.
57. Rau Krishna, "Some Aspects of Land Reform and Economic Development in India," in Froehlich, *ibid.*, pp. 214–56.
58. William Bredo, "Land Reform and Development in Pakistan," in Froehlich, *ibid.*, pp. 260–72.
59. George Coutsoumaris, "Policy Objectives in Latin America Land Reform with Special References to Venezuela," *Inter-American Economic Affairs*, 16 (Autumn, 1962), p. 38.
60. *Ibid.*, pp. 38–40.
61. Horowitz, *op. cit.*, pp. 205 and 203–204.
62. *Ibid.*, pp. 205–206.
63. Ernest A. Duff, "Agrarian Reform in Colombia: Problems of Social Reform," *Journal of Inter-American Studies*, 8 (January, 1966), pp. 75–88.
64. Ernest Feder, "When is Land Reform a Land Reform?: The Colombian Case," *The American Journal of Economics and Sociology*, 24 (April, 1965), pp. 113–34.
65. John Hildebrand, "Latin American Economic Development, Land Reform and U.S. Aid, with Special Reference to Guatemala," *Journal of Inter-American Studies*, 4 (July, 1962), pp. 351–61.
66. Alvin Cohen, "Social Structure, Agrarian Reform and Economic Development in Peru," *Inter-American Economic Affairs*, 18 (Summer, 1964), p. 46.
67. *Ibid.*, pp. 53–59.
68. *Ibid.*, pp. 46–47.
69. Elias Tuma, "Agrarian Reform in Historical Perspective: A Comparative Study," *Comparative Studies in Society and History*, 6 (October, 1963), pp. 47–75. See also Elias Tuma, *Twenty-six Centuries of Agrarian Reform* (Berkeley: University of California Press, 1965).
70. Tuma, "Agrarian Reform in Historical Perspective: A Comparative Study," *op. cit.*, p. 50.

71. *Ibid.*, pp. 72–73.
72. *Ibid.*, p. 73.
73. *Ibid.*
74. Tsui Young-Chi, "Land Use Improvement: A Key to the Economic Development of Taiwan," *Journal of Farm Economics,* 44 (August, 1962), pp. 363–72.
75. *Ibid.*, pp. 365–71.
76. Bandyopadhyay and Ghosh, "Role of Agrarian Reform in Agricultural Development in Mexico, Taiwan and India—A Comparative Study," *Indian Journal of Agricultural Economics,* 22 (January, 1967), pp. 46–47, 48.
77. *Ibid.*, p. 47.
78. Sidney Klein, "Land Problems and Economic Growth in India and China," *Malayan Economic Review,* 5 (October, 1960), p. 77.
79. Alfredo Saco, "Land Reform as an Instrument of Change with Special Reference to Latin America," *FAO Monthly Bulletin of Agricultural Economics and Statistics,* 13 (December, 1964), pp. 1–9.
80. D. Felix, "Agrarian Reform and Industrial Growth," *International Development Review,* 2 (October, 1960), pp. 16–22.
81. Bandyopadhyay and Ghosh, *op. cit.*
82. *Ibid.*, p. 43.
83. Felix, *op. cit.*, p. 19.
84. Saco, *op. cit.*, p. 4.
85. *Ibid.*
86. *Ibid.*, p. 7.
87. *Ibid.*, pp. 8–9. Alexander's "Agrarian Reform in Latin America," *op. cit.*, briefly summarizes the Mexican, Bolivian, Guatemalan, and Cuban reforms and seems to concur wholly with the above.

PART TWO

ELECTORAL BARGAINING

SYSTEMS AND

SOCIO-POLITICAL CHANGE

Perhaps the deepest and most widely held belief among western social scientists has been that electoral bargaining systems are ideal forms through which developing societies should realize changes. Western scholars and journalists have almost obsessively reiterated the claim that ordered social change based on elections, party competition and negotiations between political bodies is in the interests of all the citizens.

This section will examine two political systems (Chile and Peru) which attempted to bring about a major transformation of land tenure (and hence, structural change) through the mechanisms of a bargaining system. The effectiveness of bargaining political systems will be measured in terms of their actual output: the degree to which social, economic and political resources are redistributed among new social strata.

An analysis of the success of bargaining political systems requires a detailed account of legislative and executive behavior as well as administrative structures and practices, which we undertake in the hope of explicating the reasons behind policy outcomes.

3

Gradualism in Belaunde's Peru

Introduction: The CIDA Report

To introduce the problem of agrarian reform in Peru under Belaunde and his *Accion Popular* (AP) government, we will examine the evaluation of a team of OAS specialists.[1] This was the most comprehensive appraisal of the Peruvian situation prior to our study. The following is a condensation and analysis of the OAS findings.

There are approximately one million landless or land-short (less than subsistence) *campesino* families:[2]

> If in Peru 75 percent of those families needing land, which in 1966 was approximately 714,000 families, were to receive lands which are now owned by multi-family *haciendas* or in zones opened up for agricultural exploitation, and if the large *hacienda* lands were to be distributed at suggested rates of 36,000 or 48,000 families per year, present inequalities in land distribution would be eliminated in a period of fifteen or twenty years. This program, however, does not include the 11,000 or more new rural families that would be added to the rural population annually after 1966 as a result of demographic growth.[3]

Under Belaunde's Agrarian Reform Law 15037 (which will be discussed later) it was difficult to find out how much land was subject to expropriation and redistribution to the landless rural poor. Accurate information on the exact amount and quality of land resources in the hands of big landowning families and corporations was lacking. However, some idea of land tenure patterns and the amount of large *hacienda* lands that could be affected by Law 15037 was obtainable from the 1961 agricultural census. Multi-family *haciendas* along the *Costa* (coast) controlled 1.1 million hectares of the 1.3 million in farmland; they controlled 12.2 million hectares out of 15.3 million in the *Sierra* (mountains); and 1.7 million hectares out of 2.1 million in the *Selva* (jungle). Multi-family *hacienda* owners controlled 15.0 million out of a total of 18.2 million hectares of farmland. Irrigated land owned by large landowners accounted for 1.08 million hectares. Only about 50 percent, or 540,000 hectares, of this irrigated land was subject to be expropriated under Law 15037. Accordingly, under Law 15037, only 21.7 percent of the best *Costa* lands, 55.6 percent of the best *Sierra* lands and 82.9 percent of the best *Selva* lands could have been expropriated. In addition, special provisions for exempting various lands, which are evident in Articles 25, 31, 32 and 34 of Law 15037, further constrained expropriation proceedings.[4]

By May, 1966, of the approximately 120,000 *feudatarios* (sharecroppers—those working land under verbal agreement or written contract, but not having title to the land) who had registered with ONRA (the National Office of Agrarian Reform), only around 32,000 had received their *certificados de posesion* (certificates of possession). These certificates establish their rights to occupation and profits from the land but do not concede ownership of the land until the *hacendados* (landowners) receive payment from the government. No such payments had been made. Some preliminary measures had been taken to begin the expropriations of some private and public lands. In January, 1966, for example, a total of 1.2 million hectares were in "the process of affectation" (subject to expropriation). About 1.1 million hectares were located in the three zones of agrarian reform. In six months very few expropriations had been concluded and very little land had been distributed to the proposed beneficiaries of agrarian reform.[5] The biggest failure of ONRA was its inability to expropriate the lands of the U.S.-owned Cerro de Pasco Corporation.[6] Political parties reflecting agricultural and business organizations successfully opposed the Cerro expropriation. ONRA's failure to redistribute Cerro's lands to *campesino* families was a decisive setback for agrarian reform in Peru.

ONRA officials and employees were generally competent and dedicated, according to the CIDA report. The real problems in implementing the reform were, according to the report, lack of funds and personnel and the failure of upper-echelon government decision-makers to give it high priority. Instead, President Belaunde encouraged industrialization and the extractive industries at the expense of agrarian reform.

Law 15037 contains a number of articles which limited the application of the law and prevented it from becoming an effective instrument for large-scale change.[7] The major limitation to extensive agrarian reform appears in Article 25, which expands the amount of unaffected (exempted) lands under the law. For expropriation purposes, one hectare of irrigated land is equivalent to three of "dry" land (unirrigated—vaguely but broadly interpreted) and to 100 hectares of pasturage. As a result of the equivalence tables, of the 890,000 hectares owned by multi-family units in the *Costa* and *Selva,* only about 250,000 hectares are expropriable after all exceptions allowed under the law. These exceptions and others reduce the extent of lands vulnerable to expropriation.

As a consequence of the limitations imposed by Article 25, lands available for expropriation could only provide 6.5 hectares of land per family to a maximum of 95,000 families, which represents only 13 percent of the 714,000 families which should reasonably have benefited from a valid agrarian reform. Other articles, such as 29 and 34, listed numerous reasons for exempting certain types of *hacienda* lands. These reasons were vague and open to considerable subjective interpretation by agrarian reform officials and later in courts of law and before special agrarian reform evaluation committees. At various stages in the bureaucratic and judicial processes, a *hacendado* could have virtually all or at least large sectors of his lands exempted from expropriation. Exemptions were allowed for (1) specific types of *haciendas*, (2) methods of operation or quality of agricultural administration evident (efficient and productive), (3) topography of the property, (4) high income of the *haciendas*, (5) capital investments made by *hacendados*. Article 25 permitted each member of a corporation (*sociedad*) or partnership (*condominio*) to claim individual exemptions. Thus, if 150 hectares of coastal land could be exempted per individual, a corporation owned by fifty persons could exempt a total of 7,500 hectares. This provision allowed for the total exemption of all the coastal and *Sierra* sugar and cotton *haciendas*. Title XV of the law also worked contrary to the goal of a family farm of 6.5 hectares. Title XV, when applied to areas outside of agrarian reform zones, permitted only the distribution of certificates of possession to *feudatarios*. This meant that tenant farmers were given legal possession of their subsistence plots. Title XV did not permit consolidation or expansion of these tiny holdings through expropriation of adjacent *haciendas*. In effect, *minifundismo*[8] was actually perpetuated and strengthened through the application of Title XV. The actual consequence of the law contradicted the stated purpose of ending *minifundismo* as stated in Articles 1, 2, 6 and 95. If the ONRA bureaucrats had chosen to apply Article 52 liberally—it provided for the expropriation of *hacienda* lands outside of officially designated zones of agrarian reform—they could have avoided this pitfall. In another area, Law 15037 did not provide clearly for transfer to peasants of lands owned outright by the government or by government corporations. The law merely said that such government-owned lands were "to be designated in totality to the ends of the agrarian reform." As a result, *hacienda* properties owned by the ministries of Education, War, Aviation, etc. were not to be used for agrarian reform puposes because ONRA's and CORFIRA's (the Agrarian Reform Finance Corporation) rights of acquisition were not specifically stated in the law. Instead, there were reports that government lands were being sold freely and openly to "third parties" (presumably persons outside the government).

Another serious defect of the law was the inadequate specification of water rights. This was of particular importance along the *Costa*. The law did establish clearly the objectives and criteria for the use of water in relation to land tenure (see Articles 81, 84, 109, and 121), but the qualifications and exceptions of Articles 110 and 123 largely annulled the intent of other articles relevant to water rights. On the one hand, land and water were considered indivisible; but on the other hand, the water needs of the larger *haciendas* which had access to rivers and subterranean water sources determined if these waters were to be shared with adjoining smaller farms. Article 114, which specifically stated how to obtain water rights, was limited to agrarian reform zones.

Finally, the law lacked strong sanctions for those who did not comply with it. Articles 65 and 240 did establish sanctions for noncompliance, but they were very benign. In addition, no sanctions were established in the law against large landowners who violated Articles 27 or 55, nor for violations of Titles XIV and XV. The law did establish severe penalties against *campesinos* who invaded adjoining lands. At times these invasions were encouraged or provoked by large landowners in order to create further legal problems for the *campesinos* and to confuse the agrarian situation that much more.

After careful study of the Peruvian law, the CIDA Report noted: "Law 15037 with its 248 articles, attached administrative directives, and a multitude of implementative regulations (*reglamentaciones*), is a law that is too extensive, difficult to interpret and, in addition, difficult to administer in many cases . . . in many aspects the law is almost inoperable."

One of the consequences of the extensiveness and complexity of the law's text involved misinterpretation of certain sections and attendant conflicts with other laws. Conflicts, for example, existed between Articles 41, 42, 72A and E. Article 118, *"Reglamento de Tierras,"* allowed for suspension of land distribution procedures, while the law itself did not allow such suspensions or other delaying tactics. These delays occurred in almost all phases of agrarian reform and, along with the many exemptions and allowances, the lack of resources and other factors converted the law into an unworkable instrument for expeditious redistribution of land. The numerous administrative obstacles that were encountered in the implementation of various agrarian reform projects resulted in administrative costs and procedures absorbing most of the economic resources and energy of the agencies. It was estimated that the minimum period necessary to implement the expropriation of land would be about 392 days (13 months) without counting the time necessary for declaring an area a zone of agrarian reform, nor the time required to effectively survey and subdivide the *haciendas* and settle the *campesinos*. In practice the "normal" period was approximately 490 days (16 months). However, the normal time estimate was often totally dependent on the length of legal litigations. More often than not, litigation exceeded the maximum time allotted for various court actions at different stages of the affectation and expropriation processes. The 16-month estimate was actually the "minimum" time period; the real time period stretched out into the distant future.

The administrative procedures outlined in the law allowed excessive delays. Provisions permitted *feudatarios* to obtain their parcels of land only after the owners had been compensated by ONRA. Before such compensation was paid only certificates of possession could be issued. Ownership documents (*titulos*) could be issued only after the original owners were paid. It was the issuance of these *certificados de posesion* that ex-President Belaunde and ONRA officials often cited as yearly figures for land redistribution. Since they were not actually documents of ownership (deeds) the *feudatarios'* ability to apply for loans and other government assistance was restricted. Furthermore, ONRA did not have the discretionary power to recommend agrarian reform zones based on local social needs. Article 50 made the declaration of agrarian reform zones contingent upon the approval of local legislators. These legislators had virtual veto power over ONRA decisions. In addition, ONRA was required to make extensive, time-consuming studies of local conditions and then produce detailed reports in order to justify declaring an area a zone of agrarian reform. In actuality, studies of Peru's land tenure situation already existed (see section on administrative structure) and such studies by ONRA were unnecessary and only contributed to further delays. Also, the description of the four factors designated in Article 50 was not considered adequate for determining priorities in declaring zones of agrarian reform. The official declaration of a zone of agrarian reform required the President of the Republic to sign a *decreto supremo,* making it so. This increased the opportunities for the landowners to exercise political pressure to undercut ONRA's efforts.

Excessive compensation allowed for expropriated *haciendas* and time-consuming procedures for setting land prices as designated by Articles 75 and 77 created further problems. The high valuations given by large landowners were too often accepted by the *Comision de Tasaciones de la Propiedad Rural de ONRA* (Rural Property Evaluation Commission of ONRA) with little downward adjustment. As a result, scarce economic resources were paid as compensation, limiting the number of expropriations and the amount of funds available for investment in developing the land of the beneficiaries.

In addition, a number of related administrative problems impeded implementation of the agrarian reform law.

The first problem related to organizational recruitment and responsibility. The second dealt with coordination, or lack of same, between agencies responsible for implementation of agrarian reform and other government agencies connected with agriculture. Fragmentation of the administrative structure dealing with agrarian reform provided opponents with numerous points of access to undermine efforts at implementation. ONRA, under Law 15037, could not appoint its own employees nor assign directors of zones of agrarian reform. These administrators were appointed instead by the *Consejo Nacional Agrario* (CNA) and they were subordinate to CNA, although they were employees of ONRA. This situation created a system of indefinite hierarchical relationships and confused lines of responsibility and authority. These appointees responded to CNA pressures and undermined ONRA's ability to carry out reform. Because ONRA could not control recruitment, top officials could not control personnel and therefore could not assure loyalty to the goals of the organization. ONRA, the agency closest to agrarian problems and the rural population through its field offices and zonal headquarters, had the least decision-making power. The real policy-making center of agrarian reform was CNA, which designated projects. However, neither ONRA nor CNA controlled the vital area of financing, which was handled by a separate agency, CORFIRA, under the Ministry of Treasury and Commerce. It was CORFIRA's responsibility to request bonds from the *Banco Central* to finance expropriations (payments to large landowners). Thus, key administrative functions were divided among numerous agencies each responsible to a different set of authorities, who in turn were responsible to conflicting clientele groups.

Lack of *campesino* representation and failures in implementing the law were noted by the CIDA team:

> It is important to indicate that this lack of *campesino* representation at the CNA (decision-making) level affects

campesino representation at all levels of the agrarian reform program. We did not find any *campesino* leaders in central offices of ONRA either as chiefs of important sections or as advisors. Neither were the capacities of these leaders used in field offices. This is a deplorable situation in that many of these *campesino* leaders are well informed, competent, and influential leaders in the rural zones where they work. Their assistance would be invaluable in carrying out the programs of agrarian reform. A truly democratic agrarian reform must put enormous emphasis on the cooperation of the *campesino* from the lowest to the highest levels of the bureaucratic hierarchy. . . .

Although it meets regularly every week in Lima, the CNA has very little direct contact with some of the acute regional problems of an economic, social, and political nature which from time to time flare up in various parts of Peru. As a matter of routine, members of CNA cannot contribute the necessary time to these problems, probably, in part, because of other pressing responsibilities which they must attend.

Dominated by a body (CNA) remote from peasant problems and largely influenced by landowning groups, lacking a chief with sufficient decision-making authority and executive support to overcome particular interests, ONRA's administrative problems (largely a reflection of political realities) doomed it to failure. Whatever the internal weaknesses of ONRA—and they were serious enough—the hostile organizational-political environment in which it functioned played a much more important role in undercutting the efforts of the many dedicated field workers who attempted to administer the law.

Inter-bureaucratic rivalries certainly cut down on the effectiveness of operations. The relationship between ONRA and SIPA (Agrarian Research and Promotion Service), both of which were parts of IRPA (Institute of Agrarian Reform and Promotion), is illustrative. SIPA had two functions: (a) promotion of agricultural development through extension services and research; and (b) activity in "support" of agrarian reform.

The presence of two agencies with overlapping functions and separate lines of authority hampered coordination and cooperation between ONRA and SIPA administrators. When ONRA settled peasants on new lands, more likely than not SIPA did not follow with the needed technical assistance.

A number of decisions and lack of decisions by ONRA policy-makers contributed to the failure of the agrarian reform effort. Title VII of the law acknowledged large landholdings as the "concentration of plots of land" but fragmentation was not recognized as a problem closely associated with the *campesinos'* lack of access to the land. It was thought that over the long run the redistribution of the *haciendas* would bring about a solution to most *minifundio* problems. However, the *Division de Parcelaria* within ONRA only carried out experimental pilot projects which were highly costly in terms of financial and personnel resources in relation to benefits realized, thus further adding to the ineffectiveness of agrarian reform administration. In its pilot settlement experiments, ONRA restricted its activities to *feudatario* lands. It did not include adjacent *hacienda* lands nor did it deal with the problem of the *minifundio,* thus demonstrating the ineffectiveness of the agrarian reform and ONRA's repeated reluctance to change old land tenancy patterns. Preoccupation with resettling tenant farmers on small plots of land became ONRA's substitute for dealing directly with the politically abrasive issue of expropriating the *haciendas*.

Established agencies in the Peruvian government did not promote agrarian reform, and in some cases contributed to its failure. The Ministry of Agriculture, the Agrarian Promotion Bank (*Banco de Fomento Agropecuaria*) and the Ministry of Labor and Indian Affairs failed to cooperate with the *Instituto Nacional de Planificacion,* ONRA, and SIPA in drawing up a plan which should have included specific objectives, such as: (1) the number of *campesino* families to be settled annually; (2) the number of hectares of land to be expropriated annually; (3) the respective administrative agencies to be assigned to various tasks; (4) the financial and technical resources necessary for meeting the established annual objectives. Frequently, older government agencies worked at cross purposes to ONRA and SIPA. This was especially true of the Ministry of Labor in the settlement of labor disputes, the *Direccion de Asuntos Indigenas* in respect to the Indian communities and the *Direccion de Aguas y Irrigacion* in relation to the distribution of irrigation waters. Cases were confirmed where government employees were openly sympathetic to *patron* interests over those of the *campesinos,* making agrarian reform that much more difficult.

In implementing Law 15037 a preponderant emphasis was placed on establishing new individual parcels of land. Administrators failed to create new agricultural enterprises using collective or community property. The law, though not disposed to the establishment and organization of new communities (*comunidades*), permitted the expansion of already established communities. In addition, the law was vague in respect to forms of tenancy arrangements such as agricultural cooperatives. In this respect, the law created policy rigidities by not taking into account diverse patterns such as individual, cooperative, communal, or collective ownership which reflected the wishes of those benefiting from agrarian reform.

Law 15037 united the political forces that opposed agrarian reform. The focus of their political pressure was the administrative agencies responsible for implementing the law. Propaganda campaigns were conducted to discredit the feeble gestures which ONRA undertook. Inside the legislative and executive branches, APRA[9] and other sociopolitical forces hostile to agrarian reform organized a campaign against the effective implementation and financing of the law. ONRA officials reported organized and concerted campaigns by landowners to undercut their efforts. The counter-reform movement had a snowball effect; the more it impeded the progress of agrarian reform, the more time it had for organizing larger and broader bases of support and provoking social conflicts.

The opposition sought to discredit ONRA policies and personnel. Most of the newspapers and magazines owned and operated by reform opponents carried stories of corruption, incompetence, lack of accomplishment, and "subversion." [10] ONRA officials became defensive and devoted a great deal of time and resources to refuting these charges. Bogged down in answering charges, ONRA was unable to take the offensive in the countryside. Continual harassment had a detrimental effect on the morale of ONRA personnel and caused excessive personnel turnover.

In addition, the opposition evaded or openly violated implementation of the law. *Hacendados* organized a systematic campaign of persecution. *Campesinos* who talked to ONRA field officials about their agrarian needs and aspirations were threatened with salary reductions and expulsion. *Hacendados* closed off the irrigation canals that carried waters to the plots of small sugar growers along the coast, causing their crop to fail and causing them to leave the land. Entire irrigation canals were bulldozed by *hacendados* who then had these closed canals watched by armed guards to prevent the desperate *campesinos* from reopening them. Property owners upheld "law and order" as long as it was to their advantage; otherwise they took the law violently into their own hands. *Campesinos* received little or no support from the government in their efforts to oppose the illegal activities of the landowners. Furthermore, the government discouraged the formation of peasant unions which might have enforced the law and upheld peasant rights. The Peruvian government gave little or no financial support to *campesino* organizing efforts. In fact, peasant unions organized by radicals and others were frequently suppressed by the government, and quite often local officials worked with large landowners to discourage peasant unionization. Only when peasants organized independently of the government were they able to negotiate and significantly enlarge their holdings. The program advanced only to the degree to which agrarian reformers in government had strong peasant organizations to counter the landowners.[11]

In specific instances, government officials allocated funds for large irrigation projects on the coast which directly benefited only the large landowners. Thus, scarce funds were diverted from possible use in expropriation and redistribution of land. This policy was in violation of Article 81, which established irrigation priorities in the valleys and zones predominantly farmed by small landowners, Indian communities and/or cooperatives.

The long-run financing of agrarian reform under Law 15037 was to have been paid for ultimately by the *campesinos* and not the middle and upper classes including the large landowners. In the short run, most of the payments for expropriation and land redistribution were based on bonds to be paid over a twenty-year period. The *campesinos* ultimately were to pay these bonds and the interest on them through mortgage payments on the land they received under agrarian reform. No land was *given* to *campesinos* under agrarian reform. They were expected to pay for it in time payments.

The CIDA Report, as a preliminary evaluation of Belaunde's agrarian reform, was an unflattering, objective appraisal. Because of its criticism, it was suppressed by the government and its internal circulation was severely limited. However, it provides a good backdrop for our examination of the Belaunde reform. Therefore, we will proceed by discussing (1) the Peruvian law, including events leading up to agrarian reform legislation, congressional consideration, and the law itself; (2) the administrative structure of the reform program, including organization and administration of reform programs, personnel problems, and financial constraints; (3) the reform effort, measuring land expropriation and redistribution efforts, the number of families affected by all reform efforts, and agricultural production and employment; and finally (4) the FAO (Food and Agriculture Organization) Report as a postscript to the Belaunde period.

The Peruvian Law

Land reform in Peru had not been seriously discussed during a presidential election until 1956. At that time, various catalytic circumstances and personalities, internal and external, precipitated rhetorical, demagogic debate concerning land tenure in Peru. The Bolivian social revolution of 1952, no doubt, aroused the expectations of Peru's southern *Sierra* peasants, many of whom had petty-trade and family contacts with the newly landed peasants of Bolivia's *Altiplano*.[12]

In the election of 1956, the "forty ruling families," the core of Peru's oligarchy, were represented by Manuel Prado, while the emerging "middle sector" of Peru was represented by Fernando Belaunde Terry. Haya de la Torre (of APRA) was excluded from that election, as were hundreds of thousands of illiterate, landless, or marginally landed peasants.

Prado was victorious. Upon assuming office, he created the Commission for Agrarian Reform and Housing. The commission was to study the land tenure patterns and recommend policies and programs to change the maldistribution of land in the agrarian sector. Many have argued with substantiation that Prado only established this commission as a political gesture designed to blunt increasing demands for a comprehensive agrarian reform which would significantly alter the social structure of the country.

The commission strongly represented the economic and political power of the oligarchy—its members came largely from the ruling elite. Its first chairman was Pedro

Beltrán, publisher of the mass circulation Lima daily *La Prensa* and a member of the Peruvian oligarchy. His successor was the chief legal counsel for the vast U.S.-owned Cerro de Pasco Corporation. At various times the commission included officials from Grace and Company (a U.S.-owned firm operating large sugar estates on Peru's northern coast) and the National Agrarian Society (an association of Peru's 7,000 largest landowners who collectively controlled over 80 percent of the commercially viable cultivable or pasture lands).[13] In addition, many commission members were clearly linked to the oligarchy through marriage, commercial attachments, or patronage. As a result, the commission's recommendations were mild and proposed no policies or programs which would threaten existing land tenure or the prevailing political power structure. The proposed agrarian reform law which the commission drafted was not even discussed in the Chamber or the Senate.[14] In short, Prado attempted to sidestep the issue of agrarian reform.

Land reform would not remain dormant as a political issue, however, In the early 1960s, a series of effective peasant invasions of large estates in the southern *Sierra* region of Peru kept the issue alive. Hugo Blanco, a Quechua-speaking Peruvian agrarian technician indigenous to the area, gained national attention through his group's successful harassment of the military. Blanco's ability to mobilize peasants disturbed the Peruvian oligarchy. Increasingly, the central government in Lima reacted to the land invasions with force, often killing dozens of unarmed peasants.[15]

Prado once more reacted administratively in an attempt to mollify the demands of the peasants. In 1959 he appointed Pedro Beltrán premier, and he, in turn, created the Institute of Agrarian Reform and Colonization. The institute had broad paper powers which included expropriation and redistribution of private property, provided that adequate market value compensation was paid. A subsequent decree broadened the scope of the institute's authority. This time the Peruvian Congress made the reform gesture ineffective by appropriating money only for limited *Selva* colonization and conspicuous public works projects in those rural areas where peasant agitation was the greatest.

Concurrent with rising peasant unrest and mounting guerrilla activity, the Peruvian Congress began to debate the necessity for agrarian reform and its feasibility. A committee of eight representatives within Congress was created, but no bill ever emerged. It is, perhaps, no profound mystery since five of the eight members of the committee were members of Peru's largest landowning families. Hence, peasant invasions, guerrilla activity, and two external events —the successful Cuban revolution and the Alliance for Progress—set the stage for the 1962 presidential election.

The 1962 election was unique in two respects. Victor Haya de la Torre of APRA was permitted to run, and agrarian reform was advocated by all candidates as the paramount solution to Peru's increasing rural class conflict. Ex-dictator Odria offered the least radical agrarian reform plan. Belaunde and Haya de la Torre also offered rather mild schemes, perhaps not wanting to become anathema to the military which would ultimately have to pass on the sanctity of the winner. None of the candidates advocated expropriation without "adequate and just" compensation—a euphemism for higher-than-market payments to landowners.

Before the election was held, the military intervened, established a junta, and promised elections within one year.[16] The military, however, did not repress peasant unrest and land invasions in the La Convencion Valley. Instead, the government entered into negotiations with peasant leaders, offering to buy land for distribution if the invasions were halted. The estate of La Convencion was designated for purchase and redistribution, since large sections of this estate were already being held by invading peasant squatters. When peasant leaders refused to agree to the government's proposal they were arrested. Finally, in May, 1963, Hugo Blanco was arrested and imprisoned—a move which further defused peasant resistance. Docile peasant leadership emerged and agreed to the government proposal. In July, 1963, land deeds were given to 260 peasants out of an estimated 16,000 in need of land in the area. The peasants, however, had to buy their land. It was not given but sold to them (to be purchased with yearly payments), as has been the case in all subsequent Peruvian land reform. However, the junta introduced a new strategy in response to increasing stresses on the political system: token land distributions in areas of maximum unrest in order to establish a renewed social equilibrium. To augment this new strategy the junta increased funds for politically prudent and strategically located colonization programs and rural development projects under the auspices of the Institute of Agrarian Reform and Colonization.[17]

Meanwhile, on the electoral front, the junta allowed political campaigning to take place and scheduled presidential and congressional elections for June, 1963. Haya de la Torre, Manuel Odria, and Belaunde were again the candidates. Belaunde, however, seemed best to fit the "moderate reformer" image desired by the military. His rhetoric on agrarian reform, the "development of Peru by Peruvians" theme, and his clever inclusion of the military in his plans to develop the country seemed to make Belaunde the military candidate and assure his victory. Fernando Belaunde Terry was inaugurated President in July, 1963, amid internal demands for immediate and comprehensive agrarian reform and what appeared to be an external imperative for a meaningful agrarian reform law. Continuing peasant unrest remained the dominating internal impetus while Alliance for Progress, with its infrastructure development aid allotments contingent upon the enactment of an agrarian reform law, became the new external factor.

On August 12, 1963, Belaunde introduced his agrarian reform bill to Congress which was controlled by an UNO [18] (Odrista)-APRA coalition, promising Belaunde no support. By November, the Congress had several bills to consider: Belaunde's, the old standing proposal from Prado's administration, APRA's, UNO's (Odrista's), FLN's (National Liberation Front, pro-Moscow Communist), and one submitted by an individual deputy. It was evident that a compromise bill would have to be written by Congress so the Chamber of Deputies appointed an ad hoc committee of thirteen members, six from the AP-DC (Accion Popular-Christian Democrat) government coalition,[19] six from the now established APRA-UNO coalition and one FLN deputy. Debate within the committee soon focused on two points: the methods and forms of compensation and the handling of the highly productive and scientifically managed sugar operations of the northern coast.[20] The committee heard a great deal of testimony from representatives of the oligarchy since this group could best afford articulate and convincing advocates. In January, 1964, the Chamber of Deputies approved and sent to the Senate a bill guaranteeing full compensation in bonds and cash for expropriated land and facilities. The bill also provided loopholes which permitted the exclusion of the northern sugar estates.[21] Subsequently, in May, 1964, the Peruvian Senate approved the bill essentially as proposed by the Chamber. Belaunde promulgated this bill as Agrarian Reform Law 15037.

Belaunde's electoral coalition with the Christian Democrats became a political party coalition in the Chamber of Deputies and the Senate.[22] While APRA and UNO ran individual presidential candidates, these parties soon began working as a coalition in the Congress, which they could effectively control. The following breakdown of representation in the National Congress resulting from the 1963 elections reveals its coalitions:

Senate			*Chamber of Deputies*		
AP-DC	19		AP-DC	52	
APRA	18	} 25	APRA	58	} 82
UNO	7		UNO	24	
			OTHER	6	
Total	44		Total	140	

The first four months of Belaunde's tenure witnessed intensifying peasant mobilization and land seizures in the southern *Sierra* region. During that time, Lima newspapers reported 30 land seizures in the country against a total of 100 for the period 1959–1966.[23] Congressional leaders, however, did not respond to the demand for immediate action. In fact, the first period of congressional debate on agrarian reform centered around compensation. Under the Constitution of 1933, land ownership was guaranteed and land could not involuntarily be expropriated or paid for in anything other than an immediate cash settlement based on market value of the land and facilities. The UNO faction in Congress opposed any land compensation payable in long-term bonds and therefore opposed any such amendment to the Constitution. Ultimately enough APRA defections allowed both the Chamber and Senate to approve a constitutional amendment permitting bond payments. Settlement of this issue permitted Congress to consider other issues of agrarian reform, including (1) estate size and the productive activity of the estate, and (2) alternative methods of compensation. The first point of these debates concerned the coastal commercial sugar plantations which earned Peru around $50 million annually in foreign exchange.

From the beginning, Belaunde was prepared to accept a bill providing for only limited agrarian reform. He wanted a bill that could effectively be applied in the areas of greatest peasant unrest so as to give him time to implement his infrastructure development plans which he saw as the ultimate solution to Peru's land tenure and agricultural production problems. Writing in 1959,[24] Belaunde proposed that redistribution of land should be secondary to an overall agrarian policy that emphasized opening up the eastern highland jungle lands (*Ceja de Montaña*) to colonization, developing animal husbandry in the *Sierra,* and establishing market-oriented cooperatives and large coastal valley irrigation projects.[25]

In 1965, in an edited English-language version of his

book (obviously directed to advocates of the Alliance for Progress), Belaunde reiterated some of his views:

> Peru needs tillable land now to meet pressing problems of malnutrition and population growth and the *Ceja de Montaña* is the only solution.[26]

In the same book, Belaunde stated his conservative fiscal position—a position that maintained traditional spending priorities:

> Before anything else, the national treasury must cover the general expenses of administration and public education, finance the large public works of regional importance, and maintain the efficiency of the Armed Forces. But once these missions have been cared for, there is little left to dedicate to local investment or local needs, which, because Peru is predominantly a rural country, affect the majority of the population.[27]

Despite Belaunde's apparent willingness to accept a watered-down agrarian reform bill, the AP-DC coalition submitted a strong bill which would have paid for all expropriations in long-term bonds and limited the size of the coastal sugar estates, using excess land to provide lands for worker-managed, profit-sharing cooperatives.[28] Vice-President Edgardo Seoane was influential in writing the AP-DC proposed bill, and acted as its chief advocate before Congress. Seoane believed that an agrarian reform must have a strong land redistribution emphasis to gain the enthusiastic support and cooperation of the peasantry. To maximize Seoane's advocacy of a strong agrarian reform, Belaunde created the National Office of Promotion and Agrarian Reform (ONRA), and appointed as its first director general, Dr. Enrique Llosa, a Christian Democrat.

While APRA and UNO maintained a tactical and convenient congressional coalition, the parties represented different constituencies and ideologies. Therefore, they submitted separate and differing agrarian reform bills. It was no surprise that UNO's bill called for cash indemnification prior to expropriation, no limit on the size of holding, priority consideration of "unworked" estates, and a maximum colonization effort. APRA, however, submitted a bill that was far more conservative than Belaunde's. APRA's bill called for exclusion of the large coastal sugar estates. Thus APRA actually became the leading advocate of the traditional landowner's voice in Congress.

Why did APRA, supposedly the peasants' and workers' party, open the way for the approval of a weak agrarian reform law? Informal interviews with APRA leaders in 1967 revealed that jealousy of Belaunde's seizure of agrarian reform as a major issue was at least the privately-stated reason for this position.[29] In addition, the FLN submitted a radical bill that called for the seizure, without compensation, of all lands above a certain size and their immediate redistribution to the peasantry.[30] While their proposal was never seriously considered, the FLN did help maintain pressure for some type of agrarian reform and was really the only persistent national advocate of peasant needs and aspirations.

The law that resulted was never capable of providing even a modest change in Peru's land ownership patterns. Specific provisions assured that the large industrial-commercial sugar complexes of the north would remain intact as well as any large agricultural entity that met high production qualifications. The long legal delays provided in the law gave ample time for large landowning interests to mobilize legal talent, resources, and influence to impede expropriations. In addition, the heavy cash requirements of the law presented budget problems to the reform agencies, exposing the agrarian reform program to a hostile Congress, many of whose members did not consider Peru's landless, unenfranchised peasantry as their clientele. Edgardo Seoane, Belaunde's Vice-President, articulated the major shortcomings of the 1964 law:

The Agrarian Reform Commission in the Chamber of Deputies interjected far reaching changes that negated the ends of the law. In the case of sections granting exceptions to the industrialized estates of the coast, Article 25 constitutes the deepest defect because it makes impossible the affectation of the rural properties that belong to corporations or partnerships and which therefore allow the large landowners to carry out a counter-agrarian reform through stages of affectation along the coast that are not just, while the declaration of the zones of agrarian reform have turned out to be cumbersome and complicated, and have slowed the implementation of the administrative processes and the valuation of land. On the other hand, the selection of adjudicated lands does not correspond to a technical criterion and the dispositions contained in Title V concerning the Water Code which are anachronistic; Title XII which refers to the executing agencies of agrarian reform and which created at the same time a bureaucracy, a National Council of Agrarian Reform easily dominated by the landowning oligarchy; and finally Title XV, frankly demagogic, created serious problems for the small farmer renting land on large estates, a fact confirmed in practice.[31]

Even Belaunde's own party expressed harsh criticism of the law. In December, 1964, Oscar Trelles, then secretary general of *Accion Popular,* stated:

The agrarian reform was born dead because of the Christian Democrats' deletions and the amendments of the APRA-UNO coalition. . . . The conception of the law is good, but it is Article 15 which I have always opposed.[32]

Before discussing the various restrictive provisions of the law, we will define some of the legal terms of the 1964–68 Peruvian agrarian reform procedures such as "affectation," "expropriation," "adjudication" and terms relevant to types of land titles.

"Affectation" means that a piece of property can be considered legally for initiation into the process of agrarian reform. Affectation occurs after a property has been studied and judged affectable under the law. The owner is then informed of the amount of his land that is subject to expropriation, or what is actually to be purchased, in bonds and cash, of property, livestock, equipment, and structural facilities.

"Adjudication" is a very broad legal term which refers to all aspects of the entire process, from affectation through expropriation to the final contractual sale of the land to a *campesino*. In most cases, adjudication refers to the final distribution and sale of the land to a *campesino* while the other preceding legal activities are referred to as the process of adjudication. When reading figures on the amounts of property and *campesinos* involved, one must be careful to observe the subtleties of the terms employed; often these terms can refer to property which is no closer to actual redistribution than a property very recently affected (considered for inclusion in the expropriation and adjudication process).

Often the terms applied to distribution do not reveal the true status of land ownership. Sharecroppers (*feudatarios*), for example, could be given certificates of possession which permitted them to stay on the land they were working, work that land, and sell its produce without rendering compensation to the owner. These certificates were not deed-titles which were given only as the final step in the adjudication process—the signing of a mortgage agreement whereby the *campesino* was committed to make yearly payments with interest at the administratively and judicially established price. Often, however, politicians and reform apologists would refer to figures far in excess of the 11,000 deed-titles of land distributed by ONRA over four years of Belaunde agrarian reform.

Most critics of the 1964 law agree that Article 25 severely restricted the potential for widespread land distribution. This article permitted lands owned by corporations or partnerships to be exempted from consideration as one entity for affectation purposes and to be considered as segmented units based on number of owners. For example, if an estate owned by ten shareholders as one unit could qualify for a 300 hectare exemption from expropriation, each shareholder could take a 300 hectare exemption, yielding a total of 3,000 exempted hectares. This article, therefore, kept virtually intact the collectively owned sugar and cotton estates of the coast and the large sheep and cattle ranches of the *Sierra*.

Title V of the 1964 law was also almost universally denounced by critics of that law. This section permitted landowners to retain water rights and thereby refuse water-use privileges to surrounding small farmers. *Feudatarios* and newly landed *campesinos* were often subjected to intimidation under the provisions of Title V. Provisions should have made the commercial sharing of water a legal requirement for land ownership at the very least, if not guaranteeing reasonable access for landowners needing irrigation water.

Title XV of the 1964 law was to provide almost immediate land ownership status to *feudatarios*—a term broadly applied to *campesinos* working land on a renting, sharecropping, or lease arrangement. Often, these arrangements were verbal. When written, the agreements were held only by the landowner who could destroy them at will, thus ending any legal basis for the *feudatarios'* occupation and use of a parcel of land. In fact, this provision of the law allowed many large landowners to deny any agreements, indirectly forcing the ejection of thousands of *campesinos* from lands they had worked for extended periods of time. The provision that was to give tens of thousands of *campesinos* early land ownership actually became the impetus for their further legal separation from the land.

From hindsight, it is apparent that the reform effort was actually doomed before the law was enacted. Unfortunately, post facto observation does not change what occurred. We will now examine the administration of the reform.

Administrative Structure

In their evaluation of the Peruvian agrarian reform effort, the Inter-American Committee on Agricultural Development (CIDA) listed five obstacles to agrarian reform in Peru: (1) legal limitations imposed by Law 15037, (2) difficulties of execution, (3) institutional and administrative bottlenecks, (4) activities of counter-reform groups, and (5) budgetary cuts and lack of financial resources.[33] Of these five, four (the exception being the law itself) relate to the administration of the reform effort. The Chilean case reveals[34] that reform programs can be achieved partially under laws designed to delay reform efforts if administrators are committed to the larger goals. In Peru, however, this desire to use the law as fully as possible and then circumvent it when it hindered program implementation was absent.

As in the Chilean case, the Peruvian public sector agencies servicing rural clienteles were semiautonomous agencies established apart from functional administrative departments. This practice of establishing new public agencies to perform new public functions rather than having an established ministry assume new responsibilities is characteristic of many industrial as well as underdeveloped countries.[35] Peru's administrative practices are similar to other Latin American countries in terms of formal organizational structure. The Peruvian government, in attempting to stimulate public activity in the area of agricultural modernization, established the *Servicio de Investigacion y Promocion Agraria* (the Agrarian Research and Promotion Service or SIPA). Established by Law No. 13408 of March 10, 1960, SIPA was integrated into the government's agrarian reform program formally by Law No. 15037 of March 21, 1964.[36] Although SIPA and later ONRA were loosely connected to the Ministry of Agriculture, they maintained separate legal identities and independently solicited funds from the President and the Peruvian Congress.

Peruvian attempts to change existing land ownership patterns actually predate the establishment of SIPA in 1960. As did other Latin American countries (Brazil, Chile, Argentina, and Venezuela to mention the larger nations), Peru attempted to encourage land development through foreign immigration and colonization of new lands. Hence, attempts to develop the Peruvian jungle (*Selva*) through government-sponsored colonization date back to legislation in 1909.[37] However, aside from policies designed to open new territories to farming, no attempts were made to deal with established patterns of land tenure. The year 1960 marked the first attempt to examine existing land tenure patterns and agricultural productivity with the specific end of modernizing the agricultural sector. The activities of SIPA marked the beginning of a comprehensive, systematic examination of land resources and their uses in Peru, as one official stated:

> (SIPA's) main objective was to study the entire country. It now has divided the country into 12 zones. . . . SIPA's second objective was to study these zones in order to examine specific, local problems of cultivation. . . . SIPA has an obligation and duty to render technical assistance in all the areas of the country, including those not declared as zones of agrarian reform.[38]

In assigning SIPA the task of canvassing land resources and analyzing productivity, the Peruvian government followed the common Latin American practice of establishing formal institutions and laws to deal with issues and then failing to provide the political muscle to carry through. One author describes the formal commitments that Latin governments embraced:

> The most frequent procedure is the setting up of agrarian reform institutes, whose task is to conduct a census of land, decide which estates must be expropriated because their

yield is too low, and provide for their redistribution and the organization of community services. These services are intended to enable poor, uneducated peasants to make good use of the land they receive. . . .[39]

Where the Peruvian experience (as well as those of most Latin America countries) deviates from Lambert's account is that little expropriation occurred. SIPA conducted a land census and organized and provided technical assistance to a few peasant families, but as officials emphasized, SIPA did not consider itself an agrarian reform institute. Instead, officials construed their administrative responsibilities to include *all* residents of the agrarian sector, which in a period prior to land reform, largely meant the large landowners.

SIPA officials considered themselves "technical evaluators" [40] rather than mobilizers or promoters of change. Their activities convinced agrarian reformers of the need for new government organizations to assume responsibilities for agrarian reform. Belaunde's election in 1964 was secured with considerable support from these reformers, largely found among the Christian Democratic party.[41] As a result, Agrarian Reform Law No. 15037 was passed in March, 1964. This legislation publically recognized the inability of the existing administrative structures to "modernize" Peruvian agriculture. Hence, the law established the Institute of Agrarian Reform and Promotion, created the National Office of Agrarian Reform, and placed SIPA within the institute.[42]

It is important to note that, as in the case of Chile,[43] Peruvian efforts to induce change in the countryside were launched from an experience of public land development through colonization (primarily in the *Selva*) after four years of technical study of land use and productivity. Peruvian politicians and officials justified inaction by citing "insufficient technical capability and experience." This is clearly an indictment of their own policies, which included the *Selva* development experience of some sixty years duration coupled with four years of land use study by SIPA. In other words, the technical basis for agrarian reform could only be established while the ground was being pulled out from under the old political and social elites who dominated the financial resources that could fund the technical training programs.

Party politics and the reform tendencies of Peruvian politicians during the Belaunde period cannot be divorced from an analysis of the organization and administration of agrarian reform. As one leading politician stated:

> The coalition (AP and PDC) was able to initiate the first step toward agrarian reform: to have a law passed, create an organism to carry it out, and create a consciousness among some sectors of the peasantry . . . (however) the PDC resigned (from the Belaunde government) because of lack of support from the President. He didn't want agrarian reform but colonization of the jungle. There was always a lack of resources to finance agrarian reform.[44]

The initial success but eventual failure of Peruvian agrarian reformers, therefore, was related to the same phenomenon —the "pragmatic, adapting position"[45] of AP leadership which refused to respond with the vigor and decisiveness needed to meet the demands for reform when they were articulated. The evasive and indecisive nature of the Belaunde regime was one of the factors triggering the military coup in October, 1968. The pragmatic political behavior of the highest civilian leader was a key factor affecting the performance of agrarian reform organizations and administration.

It is important to examine the formal structural changes introduced by the Agrarian Reform Law of 1964. Chart I reveals the organizational relationships of Peruvian government agencies involved in the agrarian reform process.

As Chart I reveals, the 1964 Agrarian Reform Law sought to provide formal representation on the National Agrarian Council (CNA) to all agrarian interests, including those most hostile to any change in land ownership.[46]

CHART I

PERUVIAN GOVERNMENT AGENCIES INVOLVED IN THE AGRARIAN REFORM PROCESS, 1964-1968

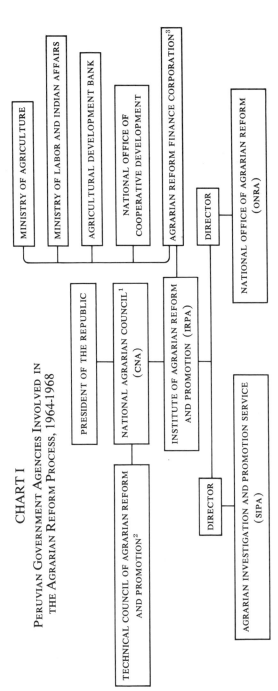

Source: Articles 191 to 223, Agrarian Reform Law No. 15037, Republic of Peru, May 2, 1964; and interviews with ONRA and SIPA officers, 1968.

1. Membership on the council includes the Minister of Agriculture (presiding) and two additional Ministry of Agriculture representatives; one representative each from Labor and Indian Affairs, the Agricultural Development Bank, the National Office of Cooperative Development, the Agrarian Reform Finance Corporation, the agricultural societies, the livestock associations, the Confederation of Peruvian Workers (CTP) and the National Federation of Campesinos (FENCAP).

2. This is an advisory council composed only of university, public, and private representatives. See Article 209.

3. This corporation was established "to finance the administrative budgets and [sic] the formulation and execution of the programs prepared by the Institute of Agrarian Reform and Promotion." (Article 217).

Labels in chart:

MINISTRY OF AGRICULTURE

MINISTRY OF LABOR AND INDIAN AFFAIRS

AGRICULTURAL DEVELOPMENT BANK

NATIONAL OFFICE OF COOPERATIVE DEVELOPMENT

AGRARIAN REFORM FINANCE CORPORATION[3]

PRESIDENT OF THE REPUBLIC

NATIONAL AGRARIAN COUNCIL[1] (CNA)

TECHNICAL COUNCIL OF AGRARIAN REFORM AND PROMOTION[2]

INSTITUTE OF AGRARIAN REFORM AND PROMOTION (IRPA)

DIRECTOR

NATIONAL OFFICE OF AGRARIAN REFORM (ONRA)

DIRECTOR

AGRARIAN INVESTIGATION AND PROMOTION SERVICE (SIPA)

CHART II
ADMINISTRATIVE ORGANIZATION OF ONRA[1]

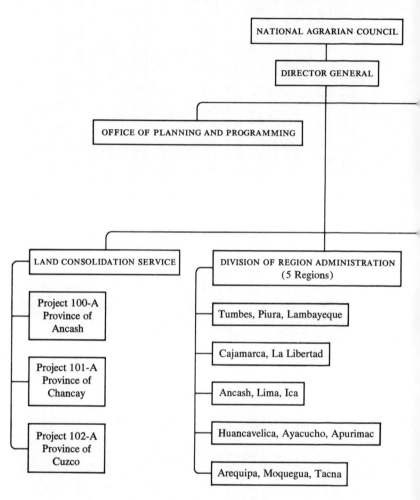

Source: Interviews with ONRA officials, 1968; and ONRA, "Informe de Actividades de la Oficina Nacional de Reforma Agraria al Consejo Nacional Agrario al 30 de Setiembre 1965," mimeographed (Lima: September 30, 1965).

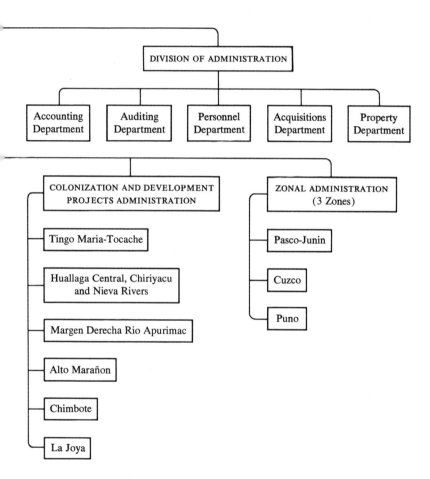

1. This is a translated reproduction/construction of ONRA's formal organization. The authors do not suggest that the hierarchical relationships noted graphically above exist in reality. This chart was
presented to illustrate the kinds of functions or divisions ONRA was
responsible for and was divided into.

CHART III

Organization of the Research and Agrarian Promotion Service (SIPA) [1]

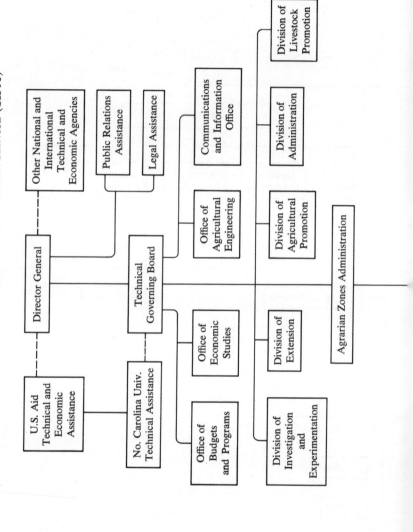

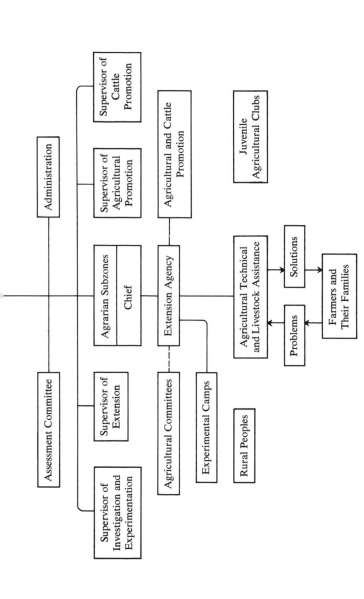

Source: Ministerio de Agricultura, Servicio de Investigacion y Promocion Agraria, "Organizacion, Funciones, Programacion y Metas, Reparticiones y Dependencias" (Lima: September, 1967), p. 63.

1. This is a translated reproduction of SIPA's formal organization. The authors do not suggest that the hierarchical relationships noted graphically above exist in reality. This chart was presented to illustrate the kinds of functions or divisions SIPA was responsible for and was divided into.

One source observed, "the divisions of the council are not by political groups but reflect different socio-economic interests." [47] However, as was the case of the Agrarian Reform Council in Chile, the director general of ONRA was a most influential individual on the National Agrarian Council due to his expertise and proximity to information on the agrarian sector.[48] Nevertheless, the law provided the conservative sectors of the Peruvian countryside considerable representation on the body responsible for formulating and supervising agrarian reform policies and programs.

The conservative position of the CNA on agrarian reform was not only the product of the private agricultural and livestock societies' representatives. The so-called "peasant representatives"—the FENCAP official—had close ties with the APRA and shared APRA's position on agrarian reform:

> one ought not to take all the land from the larger *haciendas*. . . . APRA is for 'social justice' but to expropriate large *haciendas* is stupid, and not even necessary. The large *haciendas* are heavily industrialized and we should protect private industry. We have to replace feudalism but not in the plantations.[49]

Thus, at best, the Peruvian peasant had a formal representative (FENCAP), negatively oriented toward expropriation of plantations. At worst, the FENCAP representative acted in collusion with the representatives of the large landowners to prevent expropriation of land for the benefit of landless or land-poor peasants.

One official commented on the administration of agrarian reform in late 1968:

> Lacking legal-administrative effectiveness, the law will not be complied with. Presently, administrative operations are unsystematic, ad hoc, and there is a jungle of rules; there is a lack of scientific and technical personnel; there is complexity, disorder, and procedures are long and arduous. There is a lack of trained civil servants . . . there is a

lack of financial support to provide an adequate number of lawyers—there are only ten lawyers for the whole country; the local administrators carry out passive resistance (to agrarian reform). . . .[50]

Chart II (Administrative Organization of ONRA) and Chart III (Administrative Organization of SIPA) support Figallo's description of complexity and disorder (functional overlap).

As preceding Charts II and III reveal, an imposing array of divisions, offices, departments, and subdepartments were established to administer the functions associated with agrarian reform in Peru. Many of these offices and personnel staffing them were located in Lima, even though theoret-

TABLE I

COMPARISON OF ONRA's ZONES AND REGIONS
WITH SIPA's ZONES

ONRA		SIPA
REFORM REGIONS (Departments Served)	REFORM ZONES (Departments Served)	AGRARIAN ZONES (Departments Served)
I Piura, Lamba- yeque, Tumbes, and Jaen	I Pasco and Junin	I Piura and Tumbes
II Cajamarca and La Libertad	II Cuzco	II Lambayeque, Ama- zonas, and part of Cajamarca
III Ancash, Lima, and Ica	III Puno	III La Libertad and parts of Cajamarca and Ancash
IV Arequipa, Mo- quegua, and Tacna		IV Lima and part of Ancash
V Ayacucho, Apurimac, and Huancavelica		V Ica and parts of Ayacucho and Are- quipa
		VI Most of Arequipa (see Zone V)

ONRA		SIPA
REFORM REGIONS (Departments Served)	REFORM ZONES (Departments Served)	AGRARIAN ZONES (Departments Served)
		VII Tacna and Moquegua
		VIII Most of Loreto (see Zone IX)
		IX San Martin and parts of Loreto and Huanuco
		X Junin, Pasco, Huancavelica, and parts of Huanuco and Ayacucho
		XI Cuzco, Apurimac, and Madre de Dios
		XII Puno

Source: Interviews with ONRA and SIPA officials, July, 1968; ONRA, "Informe de Actividades de la Oficina Nacional de Reforma Agraria al Consejo Nacional Agrario al 30 de Septiembre 1965," mimeographed (Lima: September 30, 1965); and Ministerio de Agricultura, Servicio de Investigacion y Promocion Agraria, *op. cit.*, pp. 31–58.

ically both agencies were responsible for making changes in the countryside.[51]

Tables I, II, and III and Maps I and II compare the zones and regions of ONRA with the agrarian zones of SIPA and the personnel distribution of both agencies along geographical lines. These tables and the maps reveal how differently ONRA and SIPA divided up the country for the purposes of serving their respective clientele. SIPA did not consider itself as an agrarian reform agency; rather its officers and policy-makers considered the agency as a servicer of all agrarian interests, including those large landowners who had profited for centuries from either government non-involvement in land ownership and management or from government subsidies through the Ministry of Agriculture or other public agencies working in the agrarian sector. The geographical distribution of SIPA and ONRA organizational structures further reveals the extent to which coordination of the activities and services of both agencies would have been almost impossible even if their managements had been in agreement on policy goals and objectives. The geographical overlap of both agencies would have been a real obstacle to any type of coordinated action in serving landless or land-short peasants.[52]

Both agencies shared the organizational feature of centralized decision-making. In theory, ONRA field representatives (in particular regional and zonal directors) possessed considerable latitude in the reform process. In reality, the CNA and other Lima-based ONRA officials could effectively block any expropriation or other reform activity by a number of means, including the replacement of personnel:

> The zonal authority initiated proceedings for expropriation but depended on the National Agrarian Council for approval of such actions. . . . Though expropriation can take place before court proceedings, the CNA undermined many zonal chiefs' decisions on expropriation actions. The law allows for expropriations but political decision-makers undermine attempts to carry it out.
>
> Administrative changes were keys in frustrating agrarian reform. CNA did not rule that a zonal chief's decisions to expropriate were illegal but they could and did change administrative personnel in the zone hence overturning decisions to expropriate. The CNA also limited funds, staff, etc. at the zonal level as a means of control. In the relations between the zonal directors and the CNA, administrative regulations created dependency of the zonal directors on the CNA and the director general thus undermining the autonomy specified in the agrarian reform law.[53]

Administrative organization, as it evolved in ONRA, permitted centralized control over field activities, thus limiting the extent to which administrators could actually initiate reform actions. This pressure from the national level coupled with pressure from landowners, politicians, and other high-

MAP I
GEOGRAPHICAL DISTRIBUTION OF SIPA PERSONNEL
BY AGRARIAN ZONE

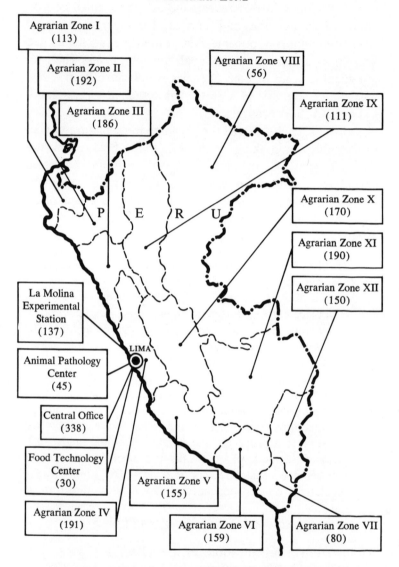

Agrarian Zone I (113)

Agrarian Zone II (192)

Agrarian Zone III (186)

Agrarian Zone VIII (56)

Agrarian Zone IX (111)

Agrarian Zone X (170)

Agrarian Zone XI (190)

Agrarian Zone XII (150)

La Molina Experimental Station (137)

Animal Pathology Center (45)

Central Office (338)

Food Technology Center (30)

Agrarian Zone IV (191)

Agrarian Zone V (155)

Agrarian Zone VI (159)

Agrarian Zone VII (80)

P E R U

LIMA

Source: Ministerio de Agricultura, Servicio de Investigacion y Promocion Agraria, "Organizacion, Funciones, Programacion y Metas, Reparticiones y Dependencias" (Lima: September, 1967), p. 61.

Note: The numbers in the parentheses indicate total personnel in the unit.

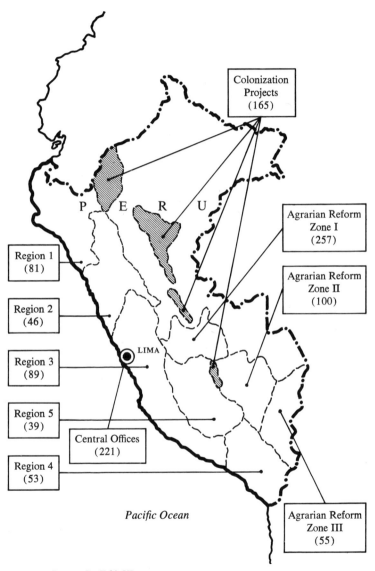

MAP II
GEOGRAPHICAL DISTRIBUTION OF ONRA PERSONNEL
BY AGRARIAN REFORM ZONES AND REGIONS

Colonization
Projects
(165)

P   E   R   U

Agrarian Reform
Zone I
(257)

Region 1
(81)

Agrarian Reform
Zone II
(100)

Region 2
(46)

LIMA

Region 3
(89)

Region 5
(39)

Central Offices
(221)

Region 4
(53)

Pacific Ocean

Agrarian Reform
Zone III
(55)

Source: See Table VI.

Note: The numbers in the parentheses indicate total personnel in the unit.

TABLE II

SIPA PERSONNEL BY GEOGRAPHICAL LOCATION

LOCATION	SUBUNIT OR PROGRAM	NUMBER	PERCENT OF TOTAL
Lima:	Central Office	338	14.7
	La Molina Agricultural Experimental Station	137	5.9
	National Center of Animal Pathology	45	2.0
	National Center of Food Technology	30	1.3
Subtotal		550	23.9
Agrarian Zones:	Coastal Operations	812	35.2
	Sierra Operations	730	31.7
	Selva Operations	211	9.2
Subtotal		1,753	76.1
TOTALS		2,303	100.0

Source: See Table I.

level bureaucrats who perceived reform as a threat was enough to prevent the formulation, let alone the implementation, of a coherent set of objectives aimed at inducing or stimulating structural change in the countryside.

The absence of clear-cut objectives, mutually agreed upon among SIPA and ONRA personnel and supported by high-level politicians and bureaucrats, was one obstacle to reform. A second was the fact that neither agency was committed to reform, regardless of high-level obstacles. This lack of commitment also was prevalent among other Peruvian agencies whose activities touched upon the life of the low-income peasant:

> The salaries of the Water Administration are paid for by the present users of the water—the large landowners—and hence they (water officials) don't support the peasants for fear of losing their posts. Labor officials, because of a lack of resources, do not feel any responsibility to the peasants

or for the new status (of the peasants) assured by law.
Police stations in the countryside depend on the landlords
for light, loans, food, etc.—in all cases, there is a strong tie
between government officials and the large landowners. In
general, the public administrator is not interested in co-
operating in agrarian reform.[54]

Unlike the Chilean case, neither SIPA nor ONRA (nor any
other public agency) existed solely to organize peasants and

TABLE III

ONRA PERSONNEL BY GEOGRAPHICAL LOCATION

LOCATION	SUBUNIT OR PROGRAM	NUMBER	PERCENT OF TOTAL
Lima:	IRPA	11	1.0
	Central Administration	90	8.1
	Operations Administra-tion	94	8.5
	Land Consolidation Serv-ice	26	2.4
Subtotal		221	20.0
Zones and Regions:	Pasco and Junin Zone	257	23.2
	Cuzco Zone	100	9.0
	Puno Zone	55	5.0
	Colonization Projects[a]	165	14.9
	Region No. 1	81	7.3
	Region No. 2	46	4.2
	Region No. 3[b]	89	8.0
	Region No. 4	53	4.8
	Region No. 5	39	3.5
Subtotal		885	79.9
TOTALS		1,106	99.9

Source: See Table VI.
a These projects were started before the ONRA was established. Many agrarian
reform experts question the classification of colonization projects under
the category of agrarian reform. If manpower assigned to the colonization
projects was subtracted, then those assigned to field operations would be
720 or 65.0 percent of ONRA's total manpower.
b Region No. 3 includes Lima, Ancash, and Ica departments. Since many of
those officials working in region No. 3 resided in Lima the total number
of centrally (Lima) located officials increases to around 25 percent.

promote their rights. Little attention and fewer funds were devoted to peasant organization than was the case in Chile.

Organizational structure for reform seems to have been a means for isolating and identifying possible "troublemakers" in the Peruvian bureaucracy—individuals who might seek to change the status quo in the countryside—and make them easier to control by those opposed to reform. Those disinterested in structural change but needing the image of the reformer (including President Belaunde) could, at the same time, point to ONRA and SIPA as examples of agrarian reform.

It is important to point out that ONRA did engage in some land tenure change activities—not by design but by default. Chart IV (pages 76–79) is a flow diagram illustrating the cumbersome process of land transfer.

Most land transfers (from large estates to small peasant farmers) occurred as a result of illegal land seizures and occupations which were later "legalized" by the Belaunde regime.[55] The government and its agrarian reform apparatus played a passive, reactive type of role—moving in to legitimize what the peasants had done under various leaders without government direction, guidance, or counsel. The legal difference between the agrarian reform regions and the more closely scrutinized agrarian reform zones was really a difference in peasant unrest. In this regard, ONRA and SIPA were the Peruvian government's agents in a kind of agrarian reform under duress. A second set of functions, aside from isolation and identification of agrarian reformers in the Peruvian bureaucracy, was to implement the Peruvian government's reaction to land seizures when and where they occurred. Government officials reacted to rather than initiated planned social change. And this was a dominant characteristic throughout the Belaunde period:

> The difference between Chile and Peru is that in the former country there is a political decision to make the agrarian reform. In Peru there is not that decision.[56]

Although this statement is somewhat inaccurate with regard to Chile, it is totally accurate with regard to Peru. The absence of this decision is reflected in the organization and administration of agrarian reform in Peru.

There were several differences between the Peruvian and Chilean attempts at agrarian reform in the 1960s; one important difference concerned the emphasis given to collective forms of social organization and peasant unionization. In Peru, the government parceled out what land it obtained on an individual basis rather than encourage collective cooperatives along the Chilean *asentamiento* line.[57] In Peru, agrarian reform was seen largely as redistribution of land without any serious attempt to create political organizations; the government's program did not include training peasants for political action. In fact, only in Cuzco was there any *campesino* federation similar to the peasant unions organized by INDAP in Chile and these were *not* the products of government-sponsored activity. These differences are reflected in the manpower of SIPA and ONRA agencies. To a great extent, recruitment to the ONRA and SIPA bureaucracies resembled more a "civil service" operation than the Chilean experience:

> (All) applicants are interviewed. Then among those selected we give a general test. Thirdly there is a special test in the specialty to which they are applying. Final selection is made among the top three; some discretion is left to the personnel officer. The potential employee then must present required documents, i.e. medical examination and social security. . . . An employee can join a party but cannot function in a partisan fashion on the job. He cannot wear buttons or display political material in the office. Only the national directors (CNA) and the director general are political appointees.[58]

Thus, the absence of the objective of politicizing the Peruvian peasant to express his demands and interests was reflected in the attempt to recruit political eunuchs to ONRA and SIPA. The absence of overt partisanship was more ob-

CHART IV
FLOW DIAGRAM OF LAND TRANSFER PROCESSES

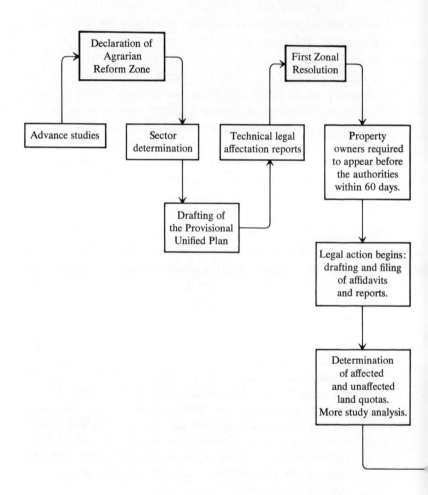

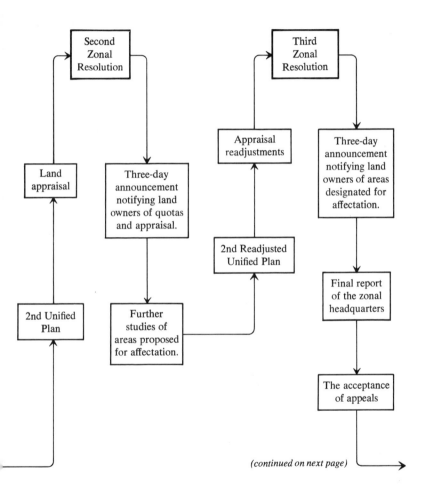

(continued on next page)

CHART IV
FLOW DIAGRAM OF LAND TRANSFER PROCESSES

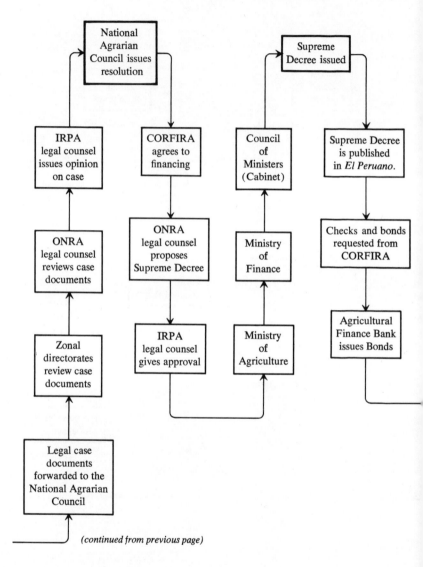

(continued from previous page)

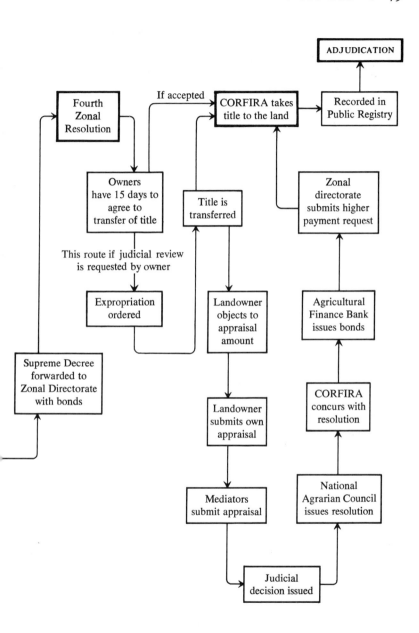

servable in SIPA, even though the director general of SIPA relied on the political judgment of the vice-president of FENCAP (the peasant organization supervised and supported by APRA). Various reasons were offered for ONRA's attempt to maintain an apolitical position which left the peasants in an unorganized state. For one, the claim was made that ONRA and SIPA were merely "technical organizations" serving the state and not any particular political party or ideology. Since Peruvian peasants, a second argument went, were more "explosive" than Chilean peasants they should not be "agitated" or organized into trade unions lest they engage in action that goes beyond the law.[59] A third reason (and perhaps most important) may be found in the counter-reform strategy employed by those opposed to change—they simply kept out any individuals seeking to organize the peasants; when some potential organizers penetrated the agencies, they were dismissed. The extra-official peasant organizers such as Hugo Blanco had their careers prematurely terminated. ONRA-SIPA had no individuals possessing skills in peasant organization and promotion. In their place, one finds an abundance of "paper administrators" and technicians. Tables IV, V, and VI reveal the personnel make-up of both agencies.

In both agencies there is an overabundance of ONRA-

TABLE IV

SIPA PERSONNEL BY OCCUPATION OR PROFESSION

OCCUPATION OR PROFESSION	NUMBER	PERCENT OF TOTAL
Agronomists	442	19.2
Veterinarians	85	3.7
Other Professionals (Civil Engineers, Architects, Lawyers, Chemical Engineers, Doctors, Biologists, Economists, Teachers)	24	1.0
Rural Home Improvement Technicians and Specialists	54	2.3

OCCUPATION OR PROFESSION	NUMBER	PERCENT OF TOTAL
Agrarian Technicians, Farming Demonstrators, and Other Specialists (Grade I)	239	10.4
Agrarian Technicians, Farming Demonstrators, Technical Assistants and Supervisors	719	31.2
Administrators	534	23.2
Secretaries	158	6.9
General Service Employees, Drivers, and Clerks	48	2.1
TOTALS	2,303	100.0

Source: Ministerio de Agricultura, Servicio de Investigacion y Promocion Agraria, "Organizacion, Funciones, Programacion y Metas, Reparticiones y Dependencias" (Lima: September, 1967), pp. 59 and 60.

SIPA bureaucrats engaged in "administering" either "paper" or some small impact programs.[60] For SIPA, the number of nonprofessionals, nontechnicians was 735 or about 32.3

TABLE V

SIPA PERSONNEL BY PROGRAM/FUNCTION

PROGRAM	NUMBER	PERCENT OF TOTAL
Management and Administration		
—General Management	13	0.6
—Management of Staff Services	175	7.6
—Technical Assistance Management	60	2.6
—Agrarian Zone Management	179	7.8
Subtotal	427	18.6
Research and Experimentation	296	12.9
Agricultural Extension	1,030	44.7
Agricultural Development	305	13.2
Livestock Development	245	10.6
TOTALS	2,303	100.0

Source: See Table II.

TABLE VI
ONRA PERSONNEL CLASSIFIED BY PROGRAM OR ADMINISTRATIVE UNIT AND PROFESSION
(as of March, 1968)

	PROFESSIONALS AND NONPROFESSIONALS			TOTALS	
PROGRAM OR ADMINISTRATIVE UNIT	Agronomists	Animal Husbandry Specialists	Civil Engineers	Geologists	Architects
1. Institute of Agrarian Reform and Promotion	—	—	—	—	—
2. Central Management and Administration	3	—	—	—	—
3. Operations Administration	26	—	7	6	—
4. Land Consolidation Service	6	—	1	—	—
5. Zonal Administration: Pasco and Junin	43	2	5	—	1
6. Zonal Administration: Cuzco	14	—	4	2	—
7. Zonal Administration: Puno	13	1	1	3	—
8. Colonization Project: Tingo Maria-Tocache	11	—	2	—	—
9. Colonization Project: Huallaga Central, Chiriyacu, and Nieva Rivers	13	1	3	2	—
10. Colonization Project: Margen Derecha Rio Apurimac	3	—	—	—	—
11. Colonization Project: Alto Marañon	2	—	—	—	—
12. Agrarian Reform Region No. 1	12	—	2	—	—
13. Agrarian Reform Region No. 2	6	—	1	—	—
14. Agrarian Reform Region No. 3	18	—	2	3	—
15. Agrarian Reform Region No. 4	10	—	2	1	—
16. Agrarian Reform Region No. 5	3	—	1	1	—
TOTALS	183	4	31	18	1

Source: Information was supplied by Saudi Palacios Lopez, chief, Department of Personnel, ONRA, July, 1968.

PROFESSIONALS AND NONPROFESSIONALS							TOTALS				
Chemists	Surgeons	Veterinarians	Lawyers	Economists	Accountants	Anthropologists	Sociologists	Social Workers	Home Economists	Journalists	Clerical Supervisors
—	—	—	3	—	—	—	—	—	—	—	2
—	—	—	4	—	3	—	—	—	—	1	52
—	—	—	4	2	—	1	—	—	—	—	8
—	—	—	—	—	—	—	—	—	—	—	1
—	1	12	5	—	1	1	—	3	2	—	67
—	—	—	4	—	1	—	—	3	1	—	16
—	—	1	2	—	—	—	—	2	—	—	6
—	—	—	2	—	—	—	—	1	—	—	20
1	—	—	—	—	—	—	1	—	—	—	5
—	—	—	—	—	—	—	—	—	—	—	3
—	—	—	—	—	1	—	—	—	—	—	2
—	—	—	7	—	2	—	—	—	—	—	9
1	—	—	5	—	2	—	—	—	—	—	6
—	—	1	6	—	1	—	—	—	—	—	14
—	—	—	2	—	2	—	—	—	—	—	10
—	—	—	3	—	—	—	—	—	—	—	10
2	1	14	47	2	13	2	1	9	3	1	231

(continued on next page)

TABLE VI

ONRA PERSONNEL CLASSIFIED BY PROGRAM OR ADMINISTRATIVE UNIT AND PROFESSION
(as of March, 1968)

PROGRAM OR ADMINISTRATIVE UNIT	TECHNICIANS AND SKILLED WORKERS				TOTALS
	Secretarial/Clerical Workers	Photographers	Photo Interpreters	Aerial Photographers	Surveyors
1. Institute of Agrarian Reform and Promotion	6	—	—	—	—
2. Central Management and Administration	19	—	—	—	—
3. Operations Administration	19	—	—	—	2
4. Land Consolidation Service	3	—	—	—	5
5. Zonal Administration: Pasco and Junin	16	1	—	3	14
6. Zonal Administration: Cuzco	11	3	—	—	8
7. Zonal Administration: Puno	8	—	—	1	2
8. Colonization Project: Tingo Maria-Tocache	2	—	—	—	12
9. Colonization Project: Huallaga Central, Chiriyacu, and Nieva Rivers	4	—	2	—	7
10. Colonization Project: Margen Derecha Rio Apurimac	—	—	—	—	4
11. Colonization Project: Alto Marañon	1	—	—	—	4
12. Agrarian Reform Region No. 1	11	—	—	—	16
13. Agrarian Reform Region No. 2	3	—	—	—	11
14. Agrarian Reform Region No. 3	9	—	—	—	13
15. Agrarian Reform Region No. 4	2	—	—	—	9
16. Agrarian Reform Region No. 5	3	—	—	—	6
TOTALS	117	4	2	4	113

(continued from previous page)

| TECHNICIANS AND SKILLED WORKERS | | | | | | | | TOTALS | | |
Cartographers	Draftsmen	Clerks	Land Appraisers	Radio Operators	Agricultural and Meat Technicians	Cooperative Supervisors	Nurses	Maintenance Mechanics	Other Technicians	Totals
—	—	—	—	—	—	—	—	—	—	11
—	—	—	—	3	—	—	—	3	2	90
1	7	5	—	—	3	—	—	—	3	94
—	4	2	—	—	—	—	—	—	4	26
3	8	7	19	1	31	4	—	1	6	257
1	2	6	—	2	16	3	—	1	2	100
1	4	—	—	1	7	—	—	1	1	55
—	5	5	—	1	14	—	2	1	2	80
—	8	1	—	2	5	—	—	—	—	55
1	1	—	—	—	2	—	—	—	2	16
—	1	—	—	—	1	—	—	—	2	14
—	15	2	—	—	4	—	—	—	1	81
—	9	—	—	—	2	—	—	—	—	46
—	12	3	—	—	7	—	—	—	—	89
—	8	1	—	1	1	1	—	—	3	53
—	7	1	—	1	—	1	—	—	2	39
7	91	33	19	12	93	9	2	7	30	1,106

Source: Information was supplied by Saudi Palacios Lopez, chief, Department of Personnel, ONRA, July, 1968.

percent of the total personnel; for ONRA this figure was higher—448 or 40.4 percent of the total personnel cadre. This means that a good portion of resources (manpower and financial) were invested in activities related to internal organizational operations rather than in change in the countryside. This "supercargo" alone cannot be blamed for the failures of the Peruvian reform attempt—though it probably was a contributing factor. Organizational investments in these activities did little to make scarce resources available for activities in the countryside.

There is some similarity between personnel recruitment for ONRA and the reform agencies in Chile. According to one source:

> ONRA originally paid higher salaries than other public institutions but now pays an average wage—and there is a tendency for its pay scale to go below the average. There are two reasons for this decline—because of the restrictions on autonomous state institutions from 1966 to the present and because of the salary freezes from 1966 to the present. Generally the incentive to work for ONRA was originally the higher salary, but some professionals joined for ideological reasons, i.e. to implement the agrarian reform.[61]

As in the case of Chile's reform agencies, ONRA's autonomous status permitted it to offer higher salaries at first. However, autonomous status was a two-edged sword; salaries actually were reduced by the squeeze of a salary freeze and inflation (coupled with a currency devaluation). In effect, this meant that anyone who began working for ONRA in 1964 made less in real terms in 1968. As in Chile, the agencies found it difficult to maintain qualified personnel: material loss tended to overshadow any rewards stemming from the work itself.

Unlike Chile's CORA or INDAP, neither SIPA nor ONRA were able to recruit many individuals who were motivated by the opportunity to bring about change through the public sector. Although the personnel director alludes to the fact that some professionals joined ONRA to implement agrarian reform, the bulk were recruited because of ONRA's economic ability to outbid its competition in the public sector. Furthermore, those who did join for "ideological" reasons did not last the entire Belaunde period. Many resigned by the end of 1967; those who remained were, in many cases, thoroughly discouraged.[62]

A substantial number of high-ranking ONRA officers cited three problems of implementing reform in Peru: lack of a "political decision" (strong presidential leadership) to make the reform, lack of consciousness of need for reform among other administrative agencies, and lack of financial resources—not necessarily in that order. The third problem, finance, was a critical one for Peru. The situation in late 1968 was dramatized by one observer:

> We need 300 million *soles* to complete the currently projected expropriations but we only have 46 million *soles* so far.[63]

As the CIDA report emphasized, budget cuts and general lack of financial support for reform activities severely hampered ONRA for the entire history of its operations.[64] According to Articles 216 and 217 of the 1964 Agrarian Reform Law, 3 percent of the total revenues of the General Budget of the Republic were to be assigned to the Agrarian Reform Finance Corporation for a period of twenty years for the financing of reform activities. This assignment was never fulfilled. In 1965, 3 percent of these revenues was estimated at around 735 million *soles*—only 445 million or 60 percent was ever authorized. In 1966, these revenues were estimated to be around 800 million; only 530 million or 66 percent was authorized. The same pattern held true for 1967 and 1968.[65] Hence, internal financing of the reform effort never reached the legally mandated amount established by the 1964 law—yearly amounts which were, as it turned out, underestimations of what should be spent to effect the kind of reform vaguely promised by Belaunde in 1964.

Coupled with the lack of financial support was the cost of securing land and the other assets connected with individual properties. In part, this was a politically inspired legal handicap; while the land deposit was minimal and the land itself could be paid for over a twenty-year period, all farm installations including barns, machinery and cattle had to be paid for in cash. The price of a farm was determined by taking into account three factors—declared tax value, potential earnings, and market or commercial price.[66] Hence, the price of landed property was higher than what the landowner had declared it to be for tax purposes. In fact, in most cases the price was higher than market value since the landowner could benefit from claims of loss of "potential earnings." Most of the land ONRA purchased was land that was unprofitable to the owner; the owner actually received more money for his land than he probably could have obtained if forced to sell commercially or if he had retained it. In the final analysis, the high prices and the requirement of immediate cash payment insured that few actual expropriations would occur, given the financial resources available to ONRA.

In addition to a lack of internal financial resources for the proposed reform, external aid promised by the U.S. never materialized.[67] No external banking or quasi-banking institution was willing to commit the necessary funds to finance the most expensive aspect of the reform:

> The Inter-American Development Bank, The World Bank, and U.S.A.I.D. have emphasized that they will not provide funds for expropriation of land to achieve agrarian reform.[68]

The financing of the agrarian reform program never reached the legal level authorized by the Agrarian Reform Law of 1964. It is clear that the agrarian reform program was being sacrificed, financially, for other programs and activities of the Belaunde government:

> the government gives agrarian reform last priority. This is a matter of national policy, not techniques. High priority

for road building exists—a mistake in my opinion—but low priority for agrarian reform. I don't know how to get out of the present situation. Every year our budget has been lower and lower. More grave this year because even with devaluation, our total budget was lower in *absolute* figures than last year.[69]

It is evident from the above that the financial constraints placed on the reform program seriously limited the extent to which any reform could be effectively carried out. The primary responsibility rested with the President and the Peruvian Congress to provide the necessary funds from internal sources. At the same time, external sources, especially the U.S., had led many Peruvians to believe that if Peru would provide some funds, external sources would make up the difference—an assumption that never materialized beyond the pledging stage. Finally, Peruvian reform administrators themselves must share some of the blame in that they publicly maintained the illusion that reform activities could be undertaken with considerably less money than legally stipulated or formally estimated by the agrarian reform agencies.

Measuring the Reform Effort: Social, Economic and Political Development

In late 1968, the director general of ONRA summarized the agrarian reform problem in Peru.

> At Punta del Este, we (the United States and Latin America) were committed to agrarian reform, to cooperation, to work. But there was a misunderstanding over the meaning of agrarian reform. Agrarian reform is an integral part of change. In 1966, W. W. Rostow presented a formula —no longer of agrarian reform but of the modernization of agriculture. This is a euphemism and is dangerous. To efficiently run and routinize the operation of agrarian re-

TABLE VII

OFFICIAL ACCOMPLISHMENTS
OF THE PERUVIAN REFORM
(May, 1968)

ACTIVITIES	Hectares
Lands Affected	2,762,657
Lands Expropriated:	
—Pasco and Junin Agrarian Reform Zone	346,344[3]
—Cuzco Agrarian Reform Zone	124,804
—Puno Agrarian Reform Zone	92,307
—Total from the Five Regions and Colonization Schemes	59,573
TOTAL LAND EXPROPRIATED	623,028[4]
Lands Completing Part of Expropriation Process but Funds Insufficient to Complete Takeover (Process Blocked at CNA level)	374,419
Lands Adjudicated (last step in Expropriation Process—see Chart IV)	353,204
Lands Charted Topographically and Aerially Photographed	4,076,525
Credits Granted (1965–67)	
Cooperatives Formed	

Source: ONRA, "Cuatro Años de Reforma Agraria en el Peru, 24 Mayo 1964–24 Mayo 1968" (Lima: ONRA, May, 1968).
[1] In millions.
[2] Refers to percentage of total land expropriated in each zone.
[3] Includes one large expropriation (Algolan) of 309,079 hectares or 89.2 percent of the expropriated land in Pasco-Junin zone. The expropriation pro-

Families Affected	OUTPUT Individuals Affected	Number	*Soles*[1]	Percentage[2]
				28.7
				22.0
				10.5
				N/A
11,163				
			309.7	
	8,868	40		

ceedings against these properties (Algolan) were begun under the military junta which preceded Belaunde. Hence, political and other pressures for expropriation had already massed prior to the Belaunde regime.

[4] The total amount of land expropriated during the Belaunde period was finally estimated at 770,000 hectares. See: "The Land Reform Situation," *Andean Air Mail & Peruvian Times*, 29, No. 1488, June 27, 1969.

form one cannot use euphemisms. Rostow and the U.S. undermined efforts at agrarian reform. We (Peruvians/ Latin Americans) had to defend agrarian reform not only at home but at international conferences against the U.S.[70]

Peruvian agrarian reformers felt that the U.S. was at least a contributing factor if not the main factor leading to the maintenance of the status quo in the Peruvian countryside during the Belaunde period. Peruvian officials exaggerated their own commitments to agrarian reform while accurately assessing the U.S. lack of interest. This section will detail the lack of positive results—the little change that did occur —and the minimal impact that the Belaunde "agrarian reform" had on the condition of peasant life.[71]

Official, published information concerning the amount of land expropriated for redistribution clouds rather than clarifies what actually was accomplished during the Belaunde period. Official information distorts the actual output of reform activities. While we will present the official account of reform accomplishments we will then crosscheck it with reports and information gathered from a number of other nonofficial sources.

Official results are presented in Tables VII and VIII; these charts include the evaluation of the reform effort as well as how these accomplishments measure up to the agrarian reform needs projected at the beginning of the Belaunde period.

An analysis of the two tables reveals:
(1) only 18.9 percent of the land that agrarian experts projected as the minimum total amount needed to execute an effective agrarian reform was made expropriable under the Belaunde Agrarian Reform Law of 1964;
(2) only 45.3 percent of the land made expropriable under the 1964 agrarian reform law was actually acquired by the government;
(3) only 44.4 percent of the land the government ac-

TABLE VIII

PROJECTION OF LAND NEEDS, EXISTING DEFICITS
IN IRRIGATED LAND, AND EFFECTS OF THE
PERUVIAN AGRARIAN REFORM
(land in hectares)

	TOPOGRAPHICAL AREA			NATIONAL TOTAL
	Costa	*Sierra*	*Selva*[1]	
No. of Landless and Land-short Families	69,368	911,079	111,973	1,092,420
Estimated Farm Size Required Per Family	6.5	6.5	30.0	—
Projected Total Land Required	450,892	5,922,014	3,359,190	9,732,096
Existing Land in Subfamily Units	129,000	355,000	272,600	756,600
Total Land Required	321,892	5,567,014	3,086,590	8,975,496
Land Expropriable Under Law 15037	121,000	145,000	1,431,900	1,697,900
Percent of Land Expropriable Under Law 15037	37.6	2.6	46.4	18.9
Land Expropriated or Sold to Government Under Law 15037	4,186	397,963	25,347	427,496
No. of Families Benefited	400	10,094	849	11,343
Percent of Families Requiring Land Who Received Titles	0.6	1.1	0.8	1.0

Source: ONRA, "Cuatro Años . . . ," *op. cit.;* and CIDA, "Peru, Tenencia de la Tierra y Desarrollo Socio-Economico del Sector Agricola," mimeographed (Lima: 1965).
[1] Figures for the *Selva* include all colonization projects.

quired was through actual expropriation—the bulk, 55.5 percent, was sold to the government at prices in excess of market value;

(4) only 0.8 percent of the total land needed to exe-

cute an effective agrarian reform was actually acquired by the government.

If one subtracts the expropriations known to have been initiated prior to Belaunde and land acquired through colonization efforts (colonization projects are not considered to be agrarian reform efforts by many experts), then the total amount of land acquired by the government under the label of agrarian reform is 435,574 hectares or less than one-half of one percent of the total land needed to execute an effective agrarian reform.

If we use as a measure of agrarian reform effectiveness the amount of land acquired for redistribution, the results indicate that the Peruvian agrarian reform effort under Belaunde fell drastically short of even its own goals which in turn were less than what was projected as a minimum for an effective agrarian reform.

On December 16, 1964, in a speech before the graduating class of the National War College in Lima, President Belaunde stated that 1965 would witness the establishment of 56,000 new landowners in Peru and that agrarian reform would be "vigorously pursued" in 1966.[72] On December 11, 1968, former President Belaunde claimed that over 60,000 cultivation certificates had been issued.[73] The difference between temporary cultivation certificates and permanent title to land is significant. Likewise, the difference between a paper designation of being "affected" by agrarian reform and actual benefits derived from agrarian reform is obvious. There was an important difference between government promises and government performance.

The above figures are the official, published statistics and those offered by the individual who was president of the Agrarian Reform Institute during the period of time studied.[74] If one measures the reform effort in terms of the number of peasants who actually received clear title to new land, then the number of reform beneficiaries is indeed small (see Table IX).

TABLE IX

PEASANTS, *Fundos,* AND HECTARES AFFECTED
BY THE PERUVIAN AGRARIAN REFORM
(July, 1968)

STEPS IN THE REFORM PROCESS[1]	*Fundos* AFFECTED	PEASANTS AFFECTED	HECTARES OF LAND
Declaration of Intent to Reform	17,000	126,000	N/A
CNA Approval of Expropriation Proceedings	1,200	25,000	N/A
Expropriation Proceedings Completed	226	3,748	41,000
Cases Adjudicated and Titles to Land Given by Government	89	1,900	6,200

Source: Interview with Otto Schultz, director of agrarian reform regions, ONRA, July 3, 1968.

1 These are the major steps in the reform process. There are a total of 51 (See Chart IV). Unlike the Chilean case, the Peruvian law did not establish special tribunals to handle appeals by landowners against ONRA's expropriations. Hence, the exceedingly lengthy reform process is further complicated by the right of landowners to appeal expropriation decisions through regular judicial channels. This obviously had a dampening effect on: (1) ONRA's declarations of intent, and (2) the CNA's approval of expropriation proceedings.

Hence, in terms of new landowners with clear title to their land, the Peruvian reform effort was a failure. Only 1,900 peasants were given clear title—this figure represents 0.1 percent of landless and land-short peasants in Peru! One must also remember that a large number of new landowners stimulated their own land reform through land seizures. In other words, even the 1,900 figure may not represent government initiative, but rather government recognition of a de facto situation.

By employing a very broad definition of agrarian reform, we find there were other beneficiaries of the Peruvian effort—specifically those peasants who colonized the *Selva* (jungle) with government assistance[75] and those peasants who were organized into cooperatives. The total figure for colonizers was 849; membership in cooperatives was 8,868. In short, even by stretching the definition of agrarian reform, Peru's efforts have been meager, to say the least.

No efforts were made by the government (ONRA-SIPA) to unionize landless peasants to make their own demands for improved conditions in the countryside. As the Chilean chapter will indicate, peasant unionization (a form of politicization) has at least created the potential for structural change in the Chilean countryside. In Peru, no such activities were undertaken by government officials. Furthermore, whenever government officials in ONRA suggested such steps be initiated, they were either ignored or removed from office.[76]

Part of the rationale behind the Peruvian agrarian reform effort was to increase agricultural production. The following table reveals figures on coffee and tea production in La Convencion—an area in which a relatively large amount of land did change hands from large landowners to peasant occupiers of the land:[77]

TABLE X

COFFEE AND TEA PRODUCTION IN LA CONVENCION, 1958–67
(in *arrobas*)[1]

YEAR	COFFEE	PERCENT INCREASE	TEA	PERCENT INCREASE
1958	208,212	—	49,680	—
1959	345,900	+ 66.1	50,560	+ 1.02
1964	210,629	− 39.1	10,894	− 46.8
1965	435,956	+107.2	61,794	+591.2
1966	410,955	− 5.9	66,814	+ 10.9
1967	468,608	+ 11.4	57,798	− 8.6

Source: Interview with Benjamin Samanez, director of zones, ONRA, July 3, 1968. These figures were gathered by the Banco de la Nacion, as of May 24, 1968.
[1] One *arroba* equals 25 pounds.

According to our sources, the Cuzco area, in particular La Convencion, has witnessed the most successful land reform. However, the initial impetus and organization of land distribution took place through violent illegal seizures, not through conventional government channels. The Belaunde administration, after repressing the movement, proceeded to legalize the changes. The peasants have been relieved from working for the large landowners; prior to 1964, they worked up to 180 days each year for the landowners. There are 10,000 families in La Convencion, of which 6,500 are members of cooperatives and now receive credit for fertilizer from the government, to promote the export of coffee. Hence, after a brief period of dislocation due to the extralegal form of land reform, La Convencion area is producing export crops at a much higher level than previously.

Unfortunately for Peru, La Convencion is the exception to the rule. Agricultural production in Peru remains unchanged since 1964. Furthermore, agrarian migration to urban areas has maintained its intensity; Lima's slums and *barriadas* have grown steadily with no indication of a diminution in absolute or relative terms. In other words, the Peruvian agrarian reform effort during the Belaunde period succeeded only in raising hopes:

> The most dangerous stage of reform is now. The peasant is now a protagonist of agrarian reform. The peasants know there is no money for further expropriation. The peasants are thinking that agrarian reform is a deception but are not sure. The peasants may take action in their hands. . . .[78]

Postscript: The FAO Report[79]

One of the first acts under the military junta was to commission an evaluation of the Peruvian agrarian problem. This study by experts of the Food and Agriculture Organization (FAO) was to determine the extent to which land tenure and agricultural production had been affected in any way by the agrarian reform program of the Belaunde regime. What the junta wanted was a description, analysis, and evaluation of the past and a set of recommendations for the future. The intent of the military was to secure the best available advice on the possibilities and costs of agrarian reform in Peru. The following describes and analyzes the work of this FAO team.[80] Since an evaluation of the implementation of the team's recommendations would be premature, we will present their report basically as it was presented to the junta.

The FAO Report supported the government's target of 100,000 peasant family beneficiaries each year for the next five years. However, the team considered it necessary for the government to specify who will be affected and what types of cooperative organizations will be established through the reform. Planning of the reform, therefore, must be improved.

At present, a major weakness exists in planning the reform; there are some general plans at the national level but there is very little integration of these plans with existing zonal and area plans. In addition, there is little participation in planning by the agrarian reform administrators and the peasant leaders who, in the final analysis, will have the responsibility of implementing the plans. Also, planning of the projects of the agrarian reform must be done by area and not by *hacienda*.[81]

There are a number of problems in administration, especially in relation to the absence of adequate training for reform administrators in both techniques and substance. Organizationally, there is duplication of services and agencies responsible for helping and training peasants, which results in confusion in regard to lines of responsibility and authority. One solution suggested by the FAO mission would be to transform the present Ministry of Agriculture into a Ministry of Agrarian Reform and Rural Development. Finance is another problem. If the annual goal of approximately 100,000 families during the next five years is assumed as a given, the problem of financing could be very serious; at least the government should take measures to meet the expected demand by reorienting its credit, implementing a tax reform, and other fiscal measures. However, the mission emphasized that the rhythm of reform must not be slowed down because of possible financial problems.

The mission found the problem of underemployment in rural areas to be very serious. [Apparently, Belaunde's reform did little to alleviate this problem.] The government should make a maximum effort within the agrarian reform to promote rural employment and at the same time adopt measures (i.e., public works projects, investments in physical infrastructure, and the promotion and/or creation of new industries in rural areas) to broaden employment opportunities in rural areas. This implies fundamentally that agrarian reform must not be focused on each expropriated property but cover whole areas.

The mission advised that the policy of private parcelization could seriously limit the agrarian reform. Reform must be implemented along with the formation of cooperatives capable of confronting the other centers of economic power in the country in order to provide support for the agrarian reform. [Cooperatives would become, *ipso facto,* political advocates demanding an accelerated reform.] The mission also considered it very important to change the traditional orientation of technical assistance so that in the future it will serve primarily the *campesino* beneficiaries of the agrarian reform. Currently there are almost 500 professionals and technical experts allocated to technical assistance and extension programs in the countryside. If the government is to meet its objective of 100,000 *campesino* beneficiaries per year, and if there should be one technician for every hundred families benefited, then it will be necessary to train at least 5,000 functionaries in technical assistance skills. Further, it is not possible to give technical assistance in an efficient and immediate manner to a great number of peasants if they are not organized to receive this assistance. In this respect, the government must work through the existing trade unions and cooperative organizations.

The Agrarian Reform Law (15037) was the legal instrument for reform under President Belaunde. This law was put forth to solve the agrarian problem, but it had very serious deficiencies. Firstly, many exceptions to the agrarian reform were established; for example, it did not affect industrial complexes of the coast. Secondly, it dealt with farms and properties unit by unit, excluding large-scale expropriation, basically a piecemeal and fragmented approach to the expropriation. Thirdly, the complexity of the legal/administrative proceedings seriously delayed the process of affectation and made it inoperative. Lastly, the very slowness of the procedures allowed the counter-reform groups many opportunities to influence public opinion against the reform. Expropriations that did take place were not the result of Belaunde's agrarian reform; expropriations may have been completed under Law 15037, but they were initiated prior to the Belaunde period under Law 14444 of March, 1963,[82] and under the special law affecting the *fundo Algolan* in the central *Sierra* which was passed during the first stage of the Belaunde government in August, 1963. On the other hand, some of the achievements associated with the application of Law 15037 were not the effect of expropriation but merely the transfer of public properties to the agrarian reform institutions.[83] Between 1964 and 1968 under Law 15037, 2.7 million hectares of land were "affected." According to official sources, almost a million hectares of land were expropriated of which about 353,000 hectares were adjudicated to the benefit of 11,163 families. (It is important to note, however, that in March, 1969, the Council of Ministers pointed out that between May, 1964, and September, 1968, 698,000 hectares of land had been expropriated of which only 313,000 had been adjudicated and there were only 7,224 beneficiaries.[84] It is not clear why this discrepancy exists.)

Given the ineffectiveness of Law 15037, the present government passed Decree Law 17716 designed to break the power and influence of the oligarchy and correct the defects which weakened the previous law, without reaching the extreme of confiscation. This law has overcome, in many ways, some of the deficiencies pointed out earlier. But the most significant indicator of change of orientation is not in the law but in its application under the military government. The agrarian reform law has been applied immediately and, initially, energetically. Simultaneous with the publication of this law, almost all the great sugar complexes of the coast were affected. The new law is not concerned solely with agrarian reform but aspires to convert itself also into an instrument of industrialization by a policy of bonus payments for the expropriations.

The new actions, however, have not stirred and mobilized the peasantry as expected. In fact, the implementation of the reform process has been delegated to what is the old ONRA and despite its increased personnel, it still does not have sufficient technical and administrative capabilities to assume so great a responsibility. The other state organizations which must participate in the implementation of the agrarian reform are not well integrated. As a result, a very complex organizational structure has emerged which prevents quick solutions.[85] At the same time, there is the risk of creating parallel organizations which would impede the agrarian reform. There is also confusion regarding the new structures and models derived from the new law. Organizational confusion must be resolved.

The government has outlined a number of objectives in regard to agrarian reform. The first is to break up the old *latifundio/minifundio* structure and establish and organize cooperatives for commercialization, credit, and technical assistance. Second, to redistribute income in favor of the least-favored *campesino* and to reorient the provision of such services as irrigation, credit, and technical assistance in favor of reform beneficiaries. Along these lines, a new general law of water rights is contained in Decree Law 17752. Third, to increase agricultural production, promote the application of modern agricultural technology, and to stimulate greater productivity of capital and labor in rural areas. Fourth, to stimulate rapid industrialization based on expansion of internal markets. Finally, to increase and guarantee greater participation of the peasantry in the social, economic, and political life of the nation. [In short, a revitalization of the agrarian sector on the basis of increased benefits to peasants is the goal of the junta.]

The greatest deficiency observed is the absence of operational connections between the policies of the government, as expressed in the law and in the diverse ideological pronouncements of government spokesmen, and what is actually occurring in the countryside. There is, indeed, weakness at the operational level. If the laws are to benefit peasant families directly, actual and immediate distribution of personnel, technical and financial resources, and creation of new institutions is required.

It is now necessary to define what *campesino* groups will be the first beneficiaries, what lands will be affected, what types of cooperative organizations must be created, and what personnel, financial, and technical resources will be assigned to the agrarian reform program. It appears to be extremely difficult for the government to develop a program of this magnitude (100,000 families benefited each year) with the existing planning techniques, administrative structure, personnel, technological resources, and finances. The mission found little evidence of planning in order to implement the agrarian reform at the zonal level, notwithstanding the importance that this has for the development of agrarian reform. The absence of a definition of goals at the national level and the local level restricts the possibilities of effective planning. There are as yet no criteria for officials at the zonal level for planning and programming.

Specific models of the types of cooperatives that must be installed at the regional and national level have not been established. There is a broad range of interpretation of government policies among different official groups, causing a good deal of confusion among the peasants. The lack of general criteria undercuts attempts at the local level to devise and form cooperative organizations. For example, in the agro-industrial complex at Tuman, the chief administrator expressed the belief that it would take many years to form an effective cooperative organization. Until that time, the workers would not play even a minimum role in the reform process. In another unit (the Cayalte agro-industrial complex), the chief administrator was already promoting the active participation of the agricultural field workers as well as the workers in the sugar mill. Thus, there are different interpretations of what should be done, depending on the local administrator.

Another problem in relation to goals or reform guidelines is finding out if the government wants to benefit all the *campesinos* in a particular area or only those who are working within expropriated *haciendas*. Also, some agrarian cooperatives have very few resources while others are very rich. The problem then becomes one of equalizing the benefits within the cooperative program.

Even if the general objectives of the agrarian reform were agreed upon, there is considerable variance in opinion regarding the form this process should take. Some officials have little confidence in the capacity of the peasants to participate in administrative decisions without endangering the level of production. Other officials are unclear as to what form and what level peasant participation should take, even when it is desirable. In this regard, the government should seek the cooperation of peasant leaders for the implementation of the agrarian reform program.

The first problem that was observed was that planning at the national level was not integrated with zonal plans and area plans which are more specific since they deal with specific units of production. In fact, no zonal or area level plans, as presently devised, could be integrated into existing national plans. Related to this is the difficulty in planning for the agro-industrial enterprises since these units already have been designed to achieve maximum productivity. The new law gives the impression that these complexes will be affected, expropriated, and adjudicated while some legal authorities maintain that the industrial enterprises such as the paper mills and alcohol distilleries located on the same property will remain under the control of the old owners. Because these industries are complementary and supplementary to the enterprises of primary production (sugar cane), they are absolutely dependent on the constant production and input of raw materials and, therefore, separation of the industrial plant from the agricultural plant would be arbitrary as well as uneconomic. In Paramonga, the mission was informed that the production of sugar was a losing proposition while the paper, plastics and distillery industries earned large profits. Obviously, this means that expropriation of the unprofitable enterprises would not serve the government purposes very well.

The difficulties inherent in comprehensive planning, however, appear to be the prime obstacles. Zonal directors control the budget and personnel of their zones and must plan accordingly for their use. In some zones the land limitation could be very serious, making it impossible to benefit a great many peasants directly without profound changes in the strategy of adjudicating land. The mission discovered that in the zone of Puno, it is most probable that even with the expropriation of all the land expropriable under the law and its adjudication to *feudatarios* and other workers in minimum economic units, more than 80 percent of the peasants will still be landless. At the national level, sector and subsector plans must be linked up with zonal plans. The means employed to make these national plans effective could include expropriation proceedings, the budget, credit, and prices. On the national level, there must be a reorientation of private bank credits from other sectors to the agrarian reform sectors. Also national policies must be established to control profits with the objective of stopping the flight of capital since, in certain parts of the country, the *haciendas* being expropriated must be paid for in cash (i.e., improvements and cattle on the *haciendas* must be paid in cash).

The organizational structure that the government has created to promote agricultural development and agrarian reform has serious defects, which affect the government's reform goals negatively. In the first place, the process of planning is not linked to administration. Secondly, there is duplication of agencies responsible for performing the same function. The best example of this is in the case of the Agrarian Reform Administration (*Direccion de Reforma Agraria* or DRA)[86] and the Agrarian Cooperative and Promotion Administration (*Direccion de Promocion Agraria y Ondecoop* or DPAO)[87] that are both assigned the task of instructing and assisting peasants without any close and continuous interorganizational coordination. Parallel to these agencies are others providing such services as communal development which are not integrated into the reform process. The creation of the DRA has not meant, in effect, any alteration in the methods, procedures, style, and clientele of the public agencies. They continue operating in traditional ways. The new DRA, even though responsible now for implementing a reform program of great magnitude, continues to be a small organization subject to control by the Ministry of Agriculture (of which it is one subordinate unit), organizationally equal to other agencies in the ministry.[88] The DRA has not been given the status nor the resources that it needs to function effectively. Experiences in other countries demonstrate the need to reorganize and reorient the operations of public agencies to accomplish agrarian reform goals.

There are other problems regarding administration. The lines of responsibility and authority are not clearly defined, giving rise to duplication of command. For example, zonal chiefs theoretically have broad control over the reform process in their territorial areas. However, administrators

of expropriated lands receive their orders directly from central offices; they are not channeled through the zonal chiefs.
At the same time, the mission could not establish what section or which administrators in Lima were responsible for
supervision of the administrators of expropriated *haciendas*.
They had been informed that there were two or three administrators assigned that responsibility.

Administration of the reform is concentrated in Lima
and the departmental [89] capitals. This is another aspect
causing a number of problems. The agrarian reform officials
responsible for assigning personnel to rural areas have their
task complicated by the lack of resources, such as gasoline,
to transport men and materials to the countryside. Existing
organizational procedures (red tape) have contributed to
the confusion. Another problem is the absence of sufficiently motivated and trained personnel. This is, perhaps,
inevitable given the fact that the government is trying to accomplish a revolutionary program which is qualitatively and
quantitatively new with personnel who are oriented to old
norms and structures. A director of projects stated to the
mission that it would be much more efficient to work with
one-fourth of the personnel at his disposal if it were possible
to train them and transfer them directly to the countryside.

One solution offered by the mission is to restructure
the present Ministry of Agriculture, converting it into a
Ministry of Agrarian Reform, Agrarian Development and
Fisheries. The key to effective reform, however, is to have
personnel committed to agrarian reform. No efforts can be
successful without a high degree of leadership on all levels.
The efficient administration of reform implies transformation (retraining) of the old bureaucratic cadre and recruitment of new officials with better training. This assumes
rapid organization of *campesinos*, which reinforces the need
for administrative leadership and the training of personnel
on all levels.

In regard to financing agrarian reform, the new law
facilitates the expropriation of land greatly by reducing the

necessary cash payments which, in turn, makes larger amounts of financial resources available for expenses in the operation of the farm and in productive investments. As was noted earlier, a real constraint on financing Belaunde's reform was the legally-required large cash payment. Nevertheless, the present law still requires cash payments for livestock and improvements, based on commercial value. The initial cost of these is relatively high even though it is lower than prior to the coup. This cash payment could cause the flight of capital out of the country unless the government adopts stringent controls. According to a CIDA study, the totality of agricultural credit presently administered by state and commercial banks would be the amount necessary to finance the agrarian reform. The budget for agrarian reform for the year, estimated at one billion *soles* more or less, has been earmarked for indemnification and administration. The 1970 governmental objectives are 63,320 adjudications of land and the expropriation of 1,470,309 hectares. It is assumed that the affectations in 1970 will involve 100,000 families. The argument that the reform must be made on a small scale owing to its cost lacks validity. The actual problem is not limiting the achievements of the reform, but reducing the cost to a feasible level and mobilizing the necessary financial resources in order to implement it.

The mission observed serious problems of unemployment and underemployment in almost all the places that it visited. In spite of this problem, the majority of the sugar plantations have not hired new workers during the last few years owing to the introduction of modern technology and accelerated mechanization. Within the agricultural sugar communities, very few young, employable men could find work in the local labor market and had to migrate to the city. The problem of underemployment is much more acute in the *Sierra* then it is on the coast. Owing to the limited quantity of land, water, credit, markets, and technology in the *Sierra,* the greater part of the labor force there is unemployed only half the year. A CIDA study calculated that in

Peru, on the average, there is an excess of agricultural labor by practically one-third and there is no possibility of giving each peasant family the amount of land necessary to assure its total employment, even if all the land were expropriated and redistributed. In 1969 CIDA reported that even if there was no increase in the total rate of migration from rural areas to urban, by 1975 there would be an increase of one million persons in the agricultural sector despite the rural exodus and the diminution from 47 to 41 percent in the proportion of the persons actively employed in the rural sector.

Rural unemployment has been caused by many factors. In the first place, landowners have been reducing the size of their permanent labor force in order to reduce the possibility of labor conflict. Secondly, because of government and trade union pressure to raise salaries and living conditions, landowners are reducing to a minimum their dependence on contracted labor and sharecroppers. In the third place, government employees have been encouraging mechanization, and commercial farmers have accepted it even when it was not economically feasible because of the prestige which goes along with this type of modernization. To solve rural unemployment the government needs to promote more intensive use of the land and the elimination of technology that saves labor, at least until it is clearly desirable from all points of view. Also, the government must give priority to the use of excess local agricultural labor through the operation and development of roads and schools for example. Thirdly, it must invest in economically viable rural industries as quickly as possible in order to create alternative employment.

Agrarian reform under the junta is characterized by speed, the massive character of the expropriation, the affectation of the agro-industrial units of the coast, and the formation of worker cooperatives on the expropriated property —a severe break with the past.

Application of agrarian reform by regions or by areas will give greater flexibility to the policy of land settlement. It will improve the conditions of small peasant holdings and peasant communities which operate on the frontiers of the *haciendas,* and it will open the possibility of basically modifying the traditional use of land, water, and forest resources. The project of reorganizing fifty cattle farms with nearly 300,000 hectares into seven units for 2,000 families, a project promoted jointly by the DRA and Rural Settlement Administration in the Department of Puno, exemplifies the policy of applying the agrarian reform by areas. Under Law 15037, ONRA's operations in the zones of agrarian reform were not designed for radical and massive change in the structure of land tenancy in a region (which would facilitate remodeling and planning for new use of resources) but were limited to changing tenure only in certain areas of intense social tension. The policies of the Belaunde government with regard to affectation and adjudication in the zones of Quillabamba and Pasco-Junin had a regional impact but did not fundamentally change the area. There is a tendency to transfer land and installations to cooperatives not only in the coastal valley but in the areas of the *Sierra* (such as the Anta valley in the Department of Cuzco). This could be the basis of a policy of agrarian reform by areas, especially through regional integration of the cooperatives. This area approach would also involve the peasants not currently employed or resident on the large farms. The new law does leave open the possibility that the cooperatives could transform themselves into individual enterprises in order to maintain control over the land. Three types of societies could be established: cooperatives, peasant communities, and agricultural societies of "social interest." Individual ownership, defined in terms of associations of persons, runs the risk of allowing corporations to adopt the façade of personal ownership in order to maintain control over agricultural land and distort the goals of the agrarian reform. The broad exceptions to the affectation of land by the previous agrarian reform law limited its effectiveness as a reform device and constituted a means by which the large landowners impeded the process of redistribution. Within this institutional framework, the old law limited itself to reproducing the traditional scheme of the small family farm (individual plots) and reiteration of purely formal attitudes toward the Indian community.

Prior to October, 1968, the cooperative movement in Peru was a consumer movement of limited extent, found in urban and marginal rural operations with no connections to the productive structure of the economy. Its philosophy was inspired by the most limited and orthodox approaches, mainly oriented toward credit unions and savings and loan associations. The annual rate of growth of the population associated with cooperatives has been only 1.8 percent while the rate of population growth in Peru has risen to 2.9 percent. In the departments (with the least proportion of the urban population) the proportion of co-op members to total population is almost 2.3 percent in Ancash, 1.38 percent in Chicama, 2.88 percent in Pasco, 1.48 percent in Cuzco, and 3.33 percent in Lambayeque. The agricultural cooperative movement has had little socio-economic significance or role in the agrarian reform process or in conventional programs in community development. In 1965, of 102 cooperatives, it was reported that 70 percent had less than 60 members each and capital of less than 20,000 *soles*. This situation reveals the structural inequalities of Peruvian society and explains the extremely weak impact that the cooperatives have on the national economy. Agricultural cooperatives' production represents 1.5 percent of the gross internal product and the capital of the cooperatives amounts to only 2.5 percent of national savings. At the beginning of 1965 there was an attempt to create a cooperative movement to develop and integrate the Indian communities. Its organic and operational weaknesses have been the same as those of the cooperatives not involved in the process of agrarian reform and structural change. The new cooperative program began in 1969 with the initiation of the new agrarian reform. The agro-industrial cooperative of Castavio has 1,676 workers in the sugar mill and fields and 396 supervisors. The Tuman agro-industrial complex has 1,477 workers and 247 supervisors and technicians. These cooperatives are not composed of a small group of individuals lacking financial resources. Under the military government, the big agro-industrial complexes are now the bases of cooperatives. This process of change obviously is related to the larger changes taking place in society.

Nevertheless, there has been a proliferation of agencies that operate at the level of the peasant communities and are involved in the process of change. These organizations operate in isolation from each other, leading to confusion. Lines of command and authority become distorted. The first attempt of the cooperative movement to operate on a regional economic basis occurred in the valley of La Convencion where ten coffee cooperatives are in operation handling 15 percent of the external coffee trade. The ten cooperatives have a membership of 4,300 families in the central region. In 1968 the older form of administration through agrarian reform functionaries was replaced by a system of direct peasant policy-making supported by technical assistance from the government. The trade union tradition of the La Convencion valley could explain the speed of the organizational process. The three cooperatives with 320 members and less than 300,000 *soles* of capital as described in 1964, has become, in 1968, ten cooperatives with 4,144 members and capital of nearly 3,000,000 *soles*. Nevertheless, while the great landowners have been eliminated, the cooperatives have run into the problem of a defective social structure based on the old inequalities with respect to sharecroppers and subsharecroppers, who were employed by the sharecroppers to do some of their work. This pattern of social stratification has not only caused new social tensions but these conflicts have been interjected into the operation of the trade unions and the cooperatives.

The cooperatives now operate the major sugar plantations of the coast and have fundamental responsibility for running the complex agro-industrial enterprises and for developing the agricultural regions of the coast (an activity which involves nearly 26,000 workers on eight of the largest *haciendas* expropriated). Organizing and designing cooperatives to fit the needs of different areas and the peasants of different parts of the country is a major problem. Training on several levels within the cooperatives could be effective only if it is related to the management of specific models and adjusted to the problems of the agro-industrial unit of the coast, the small costly units of La Convencion valley, and the communities of the *Sierra*. There is, at present, no direction from the directors of the national cooperatives program. The special study committee of Tuman (one of the biggest sugar *haciendas* on the Peruvian coast) is composed of eighty-eight persons from fourteen commissions, but they lack specific, concrete objectives. The Tuman plantation's management, inspired by traditional and paternalistic concepts generally found in traditional cooperative organization, depends almost exclusively on the technical staff. The old method under Belaunde was to expropriate and operate each *hacienda* separately. This is a problem which should be overcome by programs of mechanization and by participation on a regional basis. Area co-ops can make up for the inequality between co-ops. This inequality can be seen in terms of the efficiency of output which varies between a 4.8 hectare ton of sugar in one plantation to a 14.2 hectare ton in another.

One of the major administrative problems confronting agrarian reform in Peru is providing technical and credit assistance to the peasant beneficiaries of the reform. The extension services in Latin America have not been oriented toward the landless peasants or toward the small landholders. To substitute the landless and land poor (and reform beneficiaries) for the present large landowner clientele of the extension services, it is necessary to change the objectives and methods of the extension agents. It is paramount, above all, to make them understand the psychology of the peasants. Law 17716 states that peasant beneficiaries of the agrarian law should receive preference in technical and credit assistance from the Ministry of Agriculture or other state agencies. It should be noted that under the old law of 1964, the director generals of SIPA and ONRA were not voting members of the National Agrarian Council. In accordance with the present organization of the Ministry of Agriculture and Fisheries, the responsibility of giving technical assistance to the peasantry falls on the DPAO.[90]

The agricultural extension and education services (administered through DPAO) presently can count on 137 extension teams which include 42 agricultural engineers, 26 veterinarians, 39 social workers, 234 field demonstrators, and 144 general administrators.[91] At the agricultural zone level of the Ministry of Agriculture and Fisheries, there are 12 regional supervisors of extension (one in each zone) plus 10 credit specialists, 3 communication specialists, 4 regional social workers, 6 technical assistance specialists, and 17 administrators. The central office in Lima includes 13 agricultural engineers, 15 technicians, 2 social workers, and 11 administrators. This is very inadequate staffing, if we consider that according to preliminary figures, 60,000 families must be benefited by the sugar expropriations during 1970. The mission had the opportunity of visiting the community of Chicama in the Province of Anta in the Department of Cuzco where it observed that 1 administrator was assigned to provide technical assistance and credit to 168 peasants. It is very obvious that the agrarian reform is drastically understaffed.

Also important is the relationship between the technician and the peasant in the process of technical assistance. Despite the fact that the mission had few contacts with the extension officials in the field, it gathered the impression that a strong element of domination by the technician was present in this relationship. The official often imposed his criteria without involving the peasant. One of the strategic factors in the implementation of the agrarian reform is the mobilization of the peasantry, whether this is through cooperatives or trade unions. Although some trade unions have developed, large-scale peasant mobilization has yet to occur. (Official paternalism will not facilitate peasant participation.)

The government has made clear its interest in training personnel to carry out the agrarian reform. There is now an inter-agency commission for agrarian reform training, established by Decree Law 17269 of September, 1969. The absence of precise objectives in regard to the number of families which will benefit from agrarian reform suggests another serious obstacle. It is very difficult to determine the magnitude of training programs if one does not know how many families in how many areas are going to be serviced. The mission estimates that it will be necessary to train at least 5,000 functionaries in professional and technical fields related to agrarian reform and 50,000 *campesino* leaders to achieve the goal of 500,000 families benefited in the next five years. International assistance (financial aid) for agrarian reform has not been forthcoming. The Peruvian decision to make an authentic agrarian reform, concludes the mission, provides such international organizations as the Inter-American Development Bank and the World Bank the opportunity of demonstrating their interest and willingness to financially support, through relatively large loans, specific programs related to the agrarian reform.

This synopsis of the FAO Report presents the current state of Peruvian agrarian reform; a situation which holds promise if the junta maintains its current level of support for reform and if the ever-current problems of finançe and personnel can be resolved. Comparing the junta period with that of the Belaunde period is revealing. The comparison does not provide encouragement to those Latin American reformers who seek to attempt structural changes within the electoral bargaining system. Rather, it illustrates, perhaps, the bankruptcy of political parties and electoral politics—

two pillars of political democracy—in responding effectively to the economic, political, and social demands of the majority of Peruvian citizens, the peasantry. It is, indeed, an unflattering commentary on the capabilities of supposedly democratic regimes if population demands and needs can be met only when an authoritarian military regime takes control of the system.

NOTES

1. In 1966 a team of OAS experts under CIDA (*Comite Interamericano de Desarrollo Agricola*) auspices was invited by the Peruvian government to come to that country to study agrarian reform in Peru. See: Union Panamericana, Secretaria General de la Organizacion de los Estados Americanos, Comite Interamericano de Desarrollo Agricola, "Una Evaluacion de la Reforma Agraria en el Peru" (Washington, D.C.: Pan American Union, December, 1966). One statement in the introduction of the final CIDA report perhaps best summarizes the purpose of the report: "to determine the principal institutional, technical, financial, and other obstacles which are confronting the execution of agrarian reform" (p. 3).

2. These figures were cited for 1961 when the total population of the country was about ten million. Multiplying the one million figure by five for the average family unit, one can calculate that five million Peruvians were in want of land.

3. CIDA, *op. cit.,* p. 5.

4. CIDA, *op. cit.,* pp. 6–7. Since the amount of land held by multi-family *haciendas* is not sufficient for all those *campesino* families who aspire to land ownership, lands not now open to agriculture in the *Selva* and irrigable areas of the *Costa* must be made suitable for colonization on a massive scale. However, the report adds, this colonization must be carried out as an auxiliary agent and not the only agent of agrarian reform.

5. *Ibid.,* p. 7. "Hardly any action has been taken in areas that would effect a redistribution of land to *campesino* families."

6. *Ibid.,* p. 8. The 320,000-hectare Cerro de Pasco *hacienda* was "a test of fire that could determine the fate of agrarian reform in Peru."

7. ONRA and several political groups had already (by May, 1966) proposed amendments.

8. *Minifundios* are small plots of land not viable economically. The production from a *minifundio* would not be enough to support a peasant family without additional, external income. Another term used to

describe this problem is "subfamily-scale farm." For an excellent treatment of this concept, see: Solon L. Barraclough and Arthur L. Domike, "Agrarian Structure in Seven Latin American Countries," *Land Economics,* Vol. 42, No. 4 (November, 1966), pp. 391–424.

9. *Alianza Popular Revolucionaria Americana.*

10. CIDA, *op. cit.,* pp. 28–29. "There rumors are evidently false, since there are very few Latin American entities that operate as competently, efficiently and as cheaply as ONRA. The threats, open and anonymous, against ONRA personnel or attempts at bribery are also not infrequent. They threaten the professional careers of ONRA technicians and experts by branding them as *'subversivos'* simply because ONRA personnel are carrying out their responsibilities under the law."

11. The CIDA team noted, "In reality, it is easy to show that reform has been successful only in areas of Peru where effective *campesino* organizations existed or were organized."

12. See Cesar Guardia Mayorga, *La Reforma Agraria en el Peru* (Lima: Imprenta Minerva-Miraflores, 1962), pp. 1–10.

13. For a detailed presentation of Peru's land tenure situation circa 1960, see Ernest R. Deprospo, Jr., "The Administration of the Peruvian Land Reform Program" (Ph.D. dissertation, Department of Political Science, The Pennsylvania State University, 1967).

14. For an in-depth critique of the commission's proposed agrarian reform law, see Roberto Mac-Lean y Estenos, "El Proyecto de Reforma Agraria en el Peru," *Estudios Agrarios,* 1, No. 3 (May–August, 1961), pp. 141–158.

15. See *Hispanic American Report,* 14, No. 7 (September, 1961), p. 632 and *ibid.,* 15, No. 3 (May, 1962), p. 251.

16. There is no consensus among scholars as to why the military intervened, but some claim that the fear of an APRA victory strongly motivated older military officers whose distrust of Haya de la Torre and his party dates back to the 1932 APRA-inspired "massacre" of a military garrison at Trujillo.

17. For an expansion of these points see *New York Times,* February 6, 1964, pp. 11–12 and J. V. Fajardo, *Leyes Sobre la Reforma Agraria y Colonizacion en el Peru* (Lima: Editorial Mercurio, S.A., no date).

18. *Union Nacional Odrista.*

19. AP was the President's party; DC was a party supporting the President. Together they provided support for the ruling coalition.

20. *Hispanic American Report,* 16, No. 11 (January, 1964), p. 1082.

21. *Andean Air Mail and Peruvian Times,* 23, No. 1200, December 20, 1963, p. 2.

22. Belaunde assured the continuity of the AP-DC alliance by promising the agriculture and justice ministries to the Christian Democrats.

23. Julio Cotler and Felipe Portocarrero, "Peru: Peasant Organizations," in Henry A. Landsberger, ed., *Latin American Peasant Movements* (Ithaca, New York: Cornell University Press, 1969), p. 311.

24. See Fernando Belaunde Terry, *La Conquista Del Peru Por Los Peruanos* (Lima: Tawantinsuya, 1959).

25. *Ibid.,* pp. 3–9. Belaunde maintained his faith in his road-building solutions to development even after his dismissal from office. See the next section of this chapter.

26. Belaunde, *op. cit.,* p. 177.

27. *Ibid.,* p. 100.

28. For a discussion of the key sections of the various agrarian reform proposals submitted to Congress for consideration, see Deprospo, *op. cit.,* pp. 68–78.

29. Deprospo, *op. cit.,* p. 72.

30. *Ibid.,* p. 73 (especially footnote 39).

31. Edgardo Seoane, *Ni Tiranos Ni Caudillos* (Lima: Partido Accion Popular, 1968), p. 16.

32. *La Prensa,* December 4, 1964.

33. Union Panamericana, Secretaria General de la Organizacion de los Estados Americanos, Comite Interamericano de Desarrollo Agricola, "Una Evaluacion de la Reforma Agraria en el Peru" (Washington, D.C.: Pan American Union, December, 1966). CIDA was created by five organizations, including: Organization of the American States (OEA or OAS), Inter-American Development Bank (BID or IDB), Economic Commission for Latin America (CEPAL or ECLA), the Food and Agriculture Organization (FAO), and the Inter-American Institute of Agriculture Sciences (IICA). This report had been suppressed by the Belaunde government.

34. See Chapter 4.

35. See administrative structure section of Chapter 4. The Latin American designation for this sector between the public and the private is "autonomous subsector."

36. Ministerio de Agricultura, Servicio de Investigacion y Promocion Agraria (SIAP), "Organizacion, Funciones, Programacion y Metas, Reparticiones y Dependencias" (Lima: September, 1967), p. 1. SIPA became part of the Instituto de Reforma y Promocion Agraria (Institute of Agrarian Reform and Promotion or IRPA). ONRA was created by Law No. 15037 of 1964, also as a part of IRPA. See Chart I.

37. The 1909 *Ley de la Selva* was cited by Alberto Gazzo, director, Office of Jungle Colonization Projects, ONRA, as the starting point of organized public sector activities in land management and development. Interview with Sr. Gazzo, July 3, 1968.

38. Interview with Abelardo Baracco, subdirector general, SIPA, July 11, 1968. Sr. Baracco is an agricultural engineer who had worked for

over twenty years in the private sector as the manager of a large *hacienda* before joining SIPA. His hostility toward agrarian reform through expropriation was apparent in this interview.

39. Jacques Lambert, *Latin America: Social Structures and Political Institutions* (Berkeley: University of California Press, 1967), p. 97.

40. This was the term applied to SIPA by Carlos Bohl, technical director, SIPA. As further evidence of its purely technical role, Bohl mentioned several plans that SIPA devised, including *Plan Costa* (technical improvement of coastal lands). *Plan Sierra* (modernization of land resources use in the mountain area of Peru—never fully developed "because the banks refused to provide the necessary loans"), and *Plan Comunidades* (a plan designed to replace *Plan Sierra* which combined several programs in health, technical assistance, but not expropriation and redistribution of land). There is no evidence that any of these plans has been extensively carried out. Interview with Sr. Bohl, July 8, 1968.

41. Support for Belaunde from Peruvian Christian Democrats has been documented elsewhere, including Lambert, *op. cit.*, p. 220. The reform orientation of these CD supporters of Belaunde is evidenced by the fact that the first director general of ONRA was a Christian Democrat, Dr. Enrique Torres Llosa. Llosa's tenure as well as those of other Christian Democrats in the Belaunde government was not long—most Christian Democrats had resigned by 1968.

42. This was not the last time SIPA suffered an administrative reorganization. In August, 1968, this agency was disestablished and its personnel were reassigned within the Ministry of Agriculture.

43. See Chapter 4.

44. Interview with Javier Silva, former minister of agriculture (1965–67), July 2, 1968. Sr. Silva and Cornejo Chavez lead that sector of the PDC (i.e., DC) which supports the industrial entrepreneurs and the electoral system. Silva's sharpest criticism of Belaunde was that he was not interested in agrarian reform and failed to see its importance as a part of the overall economic development picture—the need to create new markets for Peruvian manufactured products:

> An agrarian reform is needed to create markets for goods. The problem is too urgent. Hence, the need to ally with the industrial sector and the middle class. This alliance of urban forces is necessary to carry out the agrarian reform based on the appeal of expanded markets. Peasant organization is too difficult. One needs to train officials, etc. Agrarian reform and industrialization unite urban and rural forces.

45. Interview with Jaime Llosa, former secretary general of the Department of Lima of AP, July 8, 1968. Llosa resigned his post early in the Belaunde regime. He is now active in implementing agrarian reform under the Velasco regime. At the time of the interview, he was on the faculty of La Molina University outside Lima. His situation

(the change from leadership in *Accion Popular* to working with the military) plus the experiences of a number of other intellectuals tends to refute the North American stereotype of Latin American military regimes as conservative, reactionary governments. Actually, as Chapter 6 will reveal, the military under Velasco is far more leftist than Belaunde's regime. Llosa's opinion on the electoral process, "We must denounce elections as not being conducive to change," is shared by many Peruvian and other Latin American scholars.

46. These groups included the various agricultural societies (including the Peruvian National Agricultural Society or SNA) and the livestock associations. Any expropriation of private lands would mean direct losses to the individual members of these societies and associations. A functional equivalent in the United States would be the appointment of railway presidents to the Interstate Commerce Commission.

47. Interview with Guillermo Figallo, legal adviser, National Agrarian Council (CNA), July 4, 1968.

48. *Ibid*. Sr. Figallo's comments on this subject are of interest:

   The most influential person on the council is the director of ONRA because of his technical knowledge and because he represents the executive. The second most important person is the president of the council, the Minister of Agriculture. . . . All executive power is in the CNA. As a legal formality, the Council of Ministers approves the CNA's actions. The initiatives and proposals of the director (of ONRA) are *generally* accepted by the CNA.

49. Interview with Ramiro Priale, senator from Junin Province and third in command in APRA, July 9, 1968. Senator Priale provided us with a letter of introduction to Romulo Jimenez, head of FENCAP. Priale also gave us a lengthy assurance that he and APRA were "very pro-American" and that neither he nor APRA was for expropriation of American property in Peru. In fact, he was against the Belaunde government's feeble attempt to expropriate the properties of Cerro de Pasco (a U.S. firm)—expropriation of which occurred shortly after the military coup in October, 1968.

50. Interview with Sr. Figallo, *op. cit.*

51. Problems of duplication and overlap of services (especially in the areas of agricultural extension work and credit) constantly plagued the ONRA-SIPA operation. The 1964 law stipulated an "integration" of these two organizations; however, this "integration" never occurred and the coordination of efforts desired by the authors of the law was never achieved. See: FAO, "Informe de la Mision de la FAO para Evaluar los Requerimientos de Asistencia Tecnica para la Reforma Agraria Peruana," mimeographed (Santiago de Chile: October 1, 1969), p. 52.

52. Only on one geographical area, Puno, was there agreement between SIPA and ONRA.

53. Interview with Cesar Fuentes, former zonal director, ONRA, July 1, 1968. Sr. Fuentes gave an example of how tightly the CNA and the director general exercised control over field activities:

    In April and May of 1967, a zonal director initiated proceedings to expropriate the land of a corporation, the Ganaderia del Centro. Two days after initiation of expropriation proceedings, the director general accused the zonal director of malfeasance of duties before the CNA. The zonal director (Central Zone—Cuzco) was fired. The entire zonal staff was replaced (some 100 individuals). Since May of 1967, the changes implemented prior to this date have been maintained but no new changes have been initiated. No decision was ever made on the national level to carry out agrarian reform; on the regional and zonal levels in some areas, there were commitments and actions in the direction of change, but they have been severely restricted by Lima.

54. Interview with Pablo Salmon, director of rural development, ONRA, July 4, 1968.

55. Interview with Otto Schultz, director of region administration, ONRA, July 3, 1968. Sr. Schultz admitted that in both the agrarian reform zones and regions, ONRA merely legalized what had occurred. Administratively, "this means we give peasants titles to the property that they are working."

56. Interview with Pablo Salmon, *op. cit.*

57. *Asentamientos* are government-owned collective farms whose workers are the former workers of the landowner's lands. After the government secures land by expropriation or purchase, the peasants are organized into an *asentamiento* to work the land. In the Chilean scheme, the *asentamiento* may or may not be a temporary phase between large landlord exploitation and individual peasant exploitation of land.

58. Interview with Saudi Palacios, director, Department of Personnel, ONRA, July 5, 1968. For some interesting comparisons with CORA in Chile, see the comments of the director of personnel for CORA in Chapter 4.

59. Interview with Benjamin Samanez, director of zones, ONRA, July 3, 1968.

60. Except for the director general of ONRA, all the other high- and and middle-level management personnel of ONRA-SIPA interviewed for this research were professionals—that is, agronomists, civil engineers, anthropologists, etc. No one was classified as an "administrator." The conclusion drawn is that administrators tended to occupy either nonprogram positions or very low-level positions in program implementation.

61. Interview with Saudi Palacios, *op. cit.*

62. This facilitated our research effort. See Appendix.

63. Interview with Benjamin Samanez, *op. cit.* The situation was even more drastic than alluded to by Sr. Samanez. Of the 46 million *soles* appropriated, 16.2 million had to be used to service bonds already issued and 6.5 million for servicing various other debts contracted by CORFIRA. This would leave a net of only 21.3 million for expropriation in 1968–1969. IRPA, Oficina Nacional de Reforma Agraria, "Cuatro Años de Reforma Agraria en el Peru, 24 Mayo 1964–24 Mayo 1968," (Lima: ONRA, May, 1968).

64. CIDA, *op. cit.*, pp. 30–36.

65. CIDA, *op. cit.* Interviews with ONRA-SIPA officials. Former President Belaunde blamed the Peruvian Congress for this lack of financial support:

> I did not have power over fiscal matters. You know I didn't have a majority in Parliament. I must explain that agrarian reform is very expensive. . . . (Interview with former President Belaunde, Ithaca, New York, December 11, 1968.)

Other interviews with ONRA officials contradict Belaunde's "passing the buck" to the Congress. Even ONRA officials who maintained leadership positions in Belaunde's *Accion Popular* admit that the President was more interested in building roads than altering land tenure or other agrarian reform activities. Both the President and the Congress were equally responsible for the failures.

66. Interview with Benjamin Samanez, *op. cit.* Information concerning farm prices and how Peruvian landowners actually profited from the limited expropriation that did occur was supplied by Sr. Samanez.

67. See Part Four for a full discussion of U.S. nonsupport of agrarian reform.

68. Interview with Benjamin Samanez, *op. cit.*

69. Interview with Alberto Gazzo, *op. cit.*, his emphasis.

70. Interview with Lander Pacora, director general, ONRA, and AP leader, July 5, 1968. Sr. Pacora is now residing in the United States.

71. Analysis of policy formation, implementation, and evaluation is a difficult, complex task. A number of constraints on research in the area of agrarian reform in Latin America were operating—of prime importance are data availability and consistency. This constraint should be borne in mind in evaluating our work.

72. *La Prensa* (Lima), December 17, 1964, p. 1. According to Belaunde, most of these new landowners would be in Pasco and Junin departments. In 1966, the emphasis would be shifted to Ancash and Apurimac departments.

73. Interview with former President Belaunde, *op. cit.*

74. Other statistics are available. For example, the Social Trust Fund recorded that some 20,706 peasants were affected by Peruvian reform efforts. Even this figure, according to our sources, was an over-

estimate. The number of individuals and families affected by reform efforts was incredibly small in absolute as well as relative terms. For the Social Trust Fund statistics, see: Inter-American Development Bank, *Socioeconomic Progress in Latin America* (Social Progress Trust Fund, Seventh Annual Report) (Washington, D.C.: 1968), p. 271.

75. It is interesting to compare government assistance to colonists in Peru and Ceylon. In the former, the peasant family clears its own tract; pays for its transportation to the jungle; and pays for all equipment, seed, materials at market usury credit rates. In contrast, the government of Ceylon selects all colonists rather carefully, transports them at government expense to the jungle; clears the family tract, provides credit for equipment, seed, and other materials (sometimes building the house for the peasant); and provides credit for living expenses until the first crop is harvested. The Ceylonese colonist pays for his land, equipment, and house over 20 to 30 years. Ceylon's colonization efforts have been relatively more successful than Peru's. One colonization project in Ceylon has settled over 100,000 peasants on new land.

76. Interview with several ONRA officials.

77. As it was pointed out earlier, agrarian reform has been successful only in areas where peasants have generated sufficient demand and actions in support of this reform. La Convencion is such an area. The government in legally sanctioning land tenure change in this area was responding to rather than initiating actions.

78. Interview with Lander Pacora, *op. cit.*

79. *Informe de la Mision de la FAO para Evaluar los Requerimientos de Asistencia Tecnica para la Reforma Agraria Peruana,* mimeographed (Santiago de Chile: October, 1969).

80. Except for occasional bracketed comments and footnotes, the following is a translation and synopsis of the FAO mission's report. An attempt was made to preserve the wording and emphasis of the original document.

81. What planning that did occur under Belaunde's reform used the *hacienda* as the focal point.

82. The FAO mission cited the initiation of large-size expropriations in La Convencion and Lares in the Department of Cuzco as the example.

83. For example, in the Department of Puno the farms that belonged to the *Beneficencia Publica* (Department of Public Assistance) were transferred to ONRA.

84. For still another figure, see Table X, page 96.

85. Organizational complexity and its resulting confusion is not a new phenomenon for Peruvian agrarian reform. The same situation existed during the Belaunde period. See the section on administrative structure in this chapter.

86. The old ONRA with some additional personnel.

87. A new agency which included part of the old SIPA.

88. Such as those engaged in research and soil control.

89. The Peruvian territorial equivalent of a province (or state in a federal system).

90. It is important to recall that this is really the old SIPA organization whose officers never considered their agency to be part of the agrarian reform process. See the section on administrative structure, page 57.

91. The total figure of DPAO field personnel is less than that employed by SIPA. See section on administrative structure, page 57. However, it is suspected that when SIPA was integrated into the Ministry of Agriculture in July, 1968, personnel of the agency were assigned to different agencies within the ministry.

4

Frei's Gradualistic Approach in Chile

Introduction

In describing the triumph of the Chilean Christian Democratic party (PDC), Jacques Lambert observed:

> Christian Democracy has the President and the majority in Congress on its side, is assured of the neutrality of the armed forces, and therefore is able to carry out its program. If the Christian Democrats prove that the antiquated social structure of Latin America can be changed rapidly by non-violent means and a revolution can be combined with freedom, as President Frei has said, the conditions of Latin American political life might be transformed.[1]

Most Latin Americanists viewed Eduardo Frei Montalva's election as President of Chile in 1964 and his party's congressional successes in March of 1965 as the end of old-style Chilean politics and national life and the beginning of so-called "democratic social restructuring." This prognosis (which appeared more realistic, perhaps, at the beginning of Frei's tenure) and emphasis upon the "reform" nature of the Frei government led many North and South Americans to believe that change was inevitable. The advent of electoral victories by the Chilean Christian Democratic party was welcomed, therefore, as the "answer" to Castro's socialism. Frei's *Revolucion en Libertad* called for revolution, not evolution, but within the framework of electoral bargaining politics.

Now, however, it is quite clear to all except PDC partisans that Frei's "revolution" matured only slightly beyond the rhetoric stage; that some emotions, hopes, and fears were aroused but mobilization of "revolutionary forces" was constrained. This chapter will describe, analyze, and evaluate the extent to which existing Chilean political, economic, and social institutions were changed by the policies adopted by the Frei government. We will analyze the areas of change as well as continuity, evaluating the overall impact of government decisions on the process of social change.

We will focus on agriculture and the agrarian policy which was designed to achieve extensive changes in the economic, political, and social structure of rural Chile. The agrarian reform policy of Frei was presented as a "radical" departure from the policy advocated and implemented during the previous (Alessandri) government. We will examine the implementation of agrarian reform during the Frei administration (1965–70). Agrarian reform has been a much-discussed and debated issue in Latin America as well as in Chile. It has both short- and long-range significance in terms of the crucial development problems the country faces: an underproductive agrarian sector (vis-a-vis domestic food demands), an embryonic stage of industrialization (which increasingly cannot employ Chile's working-age population), an increasingly urbanized population (or, as two scholars have labeled it, "hyper-urbanization").[2] The attempts to bring about agrarian reform and socio-politico-economic change in Chile are closely linked to the fortunes of Chilean Christian Democracy. A discussion of agrarian reform will throw light on public policy formulated and implemented during the last six years and will provide us with a basis for measuring the effectiveness of government policy on the process of "directed change."

To examine continuity and change in Chile, the following propositions will be investigated: (1) that the campaign promises of the Christian Democrats exceeded what

Frei and his advisors planned to accomplish in the area of agrarian reform; (2) that the Frei government presided over the rise and fall of PDC-directed and led attempts at reform which may have led to the electoral resurrection of the Chilean right wing, delaying necessary structural reform, exacerbating tensions, and producing spillover effects in urban areas and in national politics.[3]

We will use: (1) the original public statements articulated during the election campaign, (2) the conditions during the previous Alessandri government. Our approach will be to (a) examine the legal measures advocated by the Frei government (the 1967 Agrarian Reform Law No. 16, 640) and enacted by the PDC-dominated Chilean Congress, and the administrative "strategy" employed by Frei to implement his agrarian policy. It is suggested that administrative strategy negated administration of reform by: dispersion and dilution of administrative powers and responsibilities for agrarian policy implementation among three public corporations; the establishment or continuation of ideological counterbalances between left- and right-wing PDC leaders within the bureaucracy; inability or unwillingness to provide the kind of continuous political and economic resources needed to see through public policy of a radical, structural nature; and the strangulation of functioning, effective programs within the agrarian reform program by withholding finances and/or political support or refusing to commit finances or presidential power at strategic points or junctures in the reform program; (b) enumerate such policy outputs as land expropriated and other land transfer changes, income redistributed, and peasants politically mobilized.

The overall success or failure of the Christian Democratic government's attempt at social revolution in rural areas is an underlying theme. By focusing on that part of the Chilean administrative system responsible for program formation and implementation of agrarian reform and its immediate environment, the factors facilitating or obstructing the realization of program goals, both inside and outside the bureaucracy, are illuminated.

Many development theorists argue that electoral politics can facilitate rapid socio-economic change defined as redistribution of wealth and elimination of gross economic inequalities. The Chilean experience seriously challenges this belief. It is also commonly assumed that administrative systems in countries like Chile impede development by being unresponsive to societal needs and demands.[4]

The Chilean experience with agrarian reform in the past six years raises serious questions about the validity of prevailing theories of "democratic" and administrative development. Finally, the Chilean experience provides us with case material for evaluating the effectiveness of reformers who work within existing electoral systems to secure their objectives. The Chilean case allows us to see constraints on the behavior of political and bureaucratic leaders in positions to effect socio-economic change.

The Chilean Law

The Chilean political system has been characterized by what many observers call bargaining politics—a domination of the national decision-making apparatus by congressional "brokers" constantly securing legislative coalitions for immediate short-range goals. When pointing to examples of electoral, parliamentary-style politics in Latin America, Latin Americanists always place Chile at the forefront. The operation of the Chilean system when confronted with the agrarian reform issue in the early 1960s was not atypical. Congressional debates and maneuvers, activities of various interest groups and representatives, and the resulting law itself merely reinforce the traditional view of Chilean politics. But with agrarian reform, the Chilean political life style may be changing from this historical "bargaining system" to what some have called "mobilization politics" [5]—a political life style which might ultimately undermine existing elites and eventually replace them with new elites whose power is based on their ability to mobilize and maintain popular support of peasants, lower middle-class white-collar workers, and the industrial worker, or some other coalition of groups outside the present reward structure. However, the legislative struggle over agrarian reform must be viewed within a framework of traditional Chilean politics, the initiation of incremental changes through "bargaining"—the covert goal of almost all major participants in legislative struggle.

The legislative struggle over the agrarian reform law had an impact on later attempts to implement it through administratively designed and executed programs. In our discussion of the legislative struggle we will consider inter- and inner-party debate and actions within a broader discussion of the economic and political issues which underlay many of the specific points.[6]

The enactment of a particular law does not guarantee its implementation. The Frei government proceeded on a legal basis provided by the Agrarian Reform Law of 1962[7] for almost two years before the passage of the 1967 law. The delayed passage of the 1967 law, although important, was not a critical obstacle to implementation of the proposed agrarian reform program. The legal mechanism, viewed in this context, has more symbolic than real or functional value. With this in mind, let us examine the background to Chilean agrarian reform.

Since the 1920s, agricultural production has been declining vis-a-vis production in other sectors of the Chilean economy.[8] In 1962 the agricultural product of Chile represented 10.9 percent of the Gross Domestic Product. At the same time, the rural population is steadily declining: 31.8 percent in 1960 and estimated to be around 26 percent in 1970.[9] Even after a net rural-to-urban migration of about 685,000 (or 29.0 percent of the rural population and about 11.9 percent of the total population) from 1950 to 1960, some 305,000 rural families had an average family income of less than E°966 (E° = 1 U.S. dollar in 1960).[10] A greater proportion of these families (about 80 percent) earned less than E°636.[11] There is little doubt that Chile has an underproductive, stagnant agricultural sector whose low productivity requires the importation of about $150 million in foodstuffs annually. For a country which is attempting to industrialize, the expenditure of relatively large sums of foreign exchange for goods that could be produced indigenously is economically unsound. There is also little doubt that prevailing land tenure patterns have adversely affected the agricultural sector:

> studies leave little room for doubt that existing tenure institutions are primarily obstacles to economic and social development. These institutions maintain and legitimize the existing inequalities in the distribution of wealth, power and social status, which in turn impede the efficient use of disposable resources, depress the rates of investment in industry as well as agriculture and prevent the achievement of minimum social and political stability. . . .[12]

Chilean agricultural development has been affected by shifts in investment in the twentieth century as well as by antiquated social and political patterns. Historically, the agrarian sector can trace its organizational development (land tenure arrangements) back to the same kind of colonial institutions which prevailed in other Spanish-held territories of the New World.[13] Except for a smaller Indian population (and the impact of this important variable on present-day land tenure arrangements), Chile's agricultural evolution is similar to its neighbors'. Even today, the effects of the colonial institution of *encomienda* (an arrangement whereby the landlord provides certain benefits to his workers in exchange for their labor) can be seen in that more than 80 percent of farmland in Chile requires a "permanent work force of twelve or more workers." [14] The concentration of land in the hands of a few does not mean that the land is *ipso facto* underproductive or poorly utilized. For example, in the mid-nineteenth century, Chile was a principal source of wheat and flour for California, Australia, and Latin American nations. In fact, Australia was a major purchaser of Chilean wheat from 1850 to 1885.[15]

For a long time landowners have wielded a considerable measure of power within the country. The SNA (National Agricultural Society—an elitist organization of Chilean landowners) was quite successful in extracting government services (funds for agricultural education, irrigation works, and use of government forces against rural unrest) from the middle of the nineteenth century up to and including the 1930s.[16] The importance of land and landowners to national political life has been shown:

> In 1938, with the victory of the Popular Front, the political axis definitely shifted from the traditional land-based right wing to the urban middle class. However, the right-wing parties and traditional elites continued to control the countryside. They strongly influenced Congress, and, through the conservative wing of the Radical party, the Presidency. . . .[17]

The Christian Democratic victory in 1964 was hailed as a *coup de grace* to national right-wing influence. However, Frei's own Christian Democratic party contains influential members of the landowning elite who intervened directly and indirectly in the implementation of the agrarian reform program to impede or cushion the effects of the reform measures on large landowners.

Although Chilean agriculture was expanding in terms of per capita agricultural production and exports as late as the 1930s, there were indications that the large landowners were neither investing the required capital nor showing any interest in improving land productivity significantly.[18] Increases in agricultural production after the mid-thirties were offset by population increases.[19] In short, the political power and influence of Chilean landowners are disproportionate to their productive contribution to the national economy.[20]

The power of the large landowners is also manifested in their relationship with agricultural workers, tenants, or small "competitors" (*minifundistas*). The powerful position of large landowners during the nineteenth century is revealed in Schneider's work.[21] The *Sociedad Nacional de Agricultura* (National Agricultural Society—SNA) was founded in the nineteenth century to promote the interests of large landowners; the total membership of this organization was only 370 in 1890.[22] More important than its restricted membership was its orientation—particularly the values shared by its membership and the kinds of activities it engaged in or sought to promote. Schneider mentions the concern over property rights expressed by the executive officers of the SNA (acting for the membership):

> agriculture is the foundation of all national prosperity and [that] all development is a result of a viable agrarian base. . . . Among the measures whose implementation is dependent upon the government and whose adoption will assure the urgent demands of the nation's agriculture, is that of guaranteeing security in the countryside. As long as the life and property of agriculturalists is not sufficiently guaranteed, industry cannot progress adequately or justly. The state must, therefore, procure it (security) at all costs . . . the attainment of (security of property) must take priority (over everything else). . . .[23]

This concern for security of property in the countryside was underscored by the SNA's attempts to improve the operations of Chilean rural police. For example, in 1872, the *intendente* of Santiago, Benjamin Vicuna MacKenna (a former SNA president), "cooperated" with other SNA members in demonstrating the feasibility of establishing a rural police force in Santiago Province.

Other SNA activities in the late nineteenth and early twentieth centuries led to government subsidies to SNA members for the purchase and distribution of fertilizers, agricultural education, low-interest loans, as well as tariff protection for certain crops and products (Chilean wines among others). They also gained government-subsidized freight rates, and government-financed irrigation works. In short, the SNA was able to secure for its membership the many advantages available from a friendly public sector.

Those who owned smaller plots of land (and did not qualify for SNA membership) did not enjoy the same benefits from government resources. Some spillover did occur when small landowners could tap into irrigation canals built to service the large *fundos* or when farm-to-market access roads (built by the government to service the large landowners) happened to pass by smaller holdings. But smaller plots become even smaller through division upon the death of the holder. In Chile, as of 1950 land was intensely concentrated in the hands of a few large owners while a small amount of land was held by the majority of landowners.

In essence, land concentration and fragmentation have not been lessened from the nineteenth to the late twentieth

TABLE I

DISTRIBUTION OF FARM FAMILIES ACCORDING TO SOCIO-
ECONOMIC STATUS, REPUBLIC OF CHILE* (1950)

Thousands of Families in Agriculture	344.9	
Upper-Total		9.5%
Operators of large-sized farms	3.0%	
Operators of medium-sized farms	6.5%	
Middle-Total		19.8%
Administrators of large and medium-sized farms	2.1%	
Owners of family-sized farms	14.8%	
Tenants with family-sized farms	2.9%	
Lower-Total		70.7%
Communal owners	16.6%	
Subfamily-sized farm operators	6.5%	
Landless farm workers	47.6%	

* Source: Solon Barraclough and Arthur Domike, "Agrarian Structure in Seven Latin American Countries," *Land Economics,* Vol. 42, No. 4 (November, 1966), Table II, p. 397. Data derived from Interamerican Committee for Agricultural Development (ICAD) of the United Nations FAO.

centuries. On the contrary, disparities in land ownership and, hence, the economic gap between the large landowner and the landless or land-poor *campesino* are greater than in the mid-nineteenth century.

The Chilean *campesino* shared about the same class status as his counterpart in the rest of Latin America. However, in some areas of Chile, even in the nineteenth century, the grip of the large landowner was not always absolute. In 1870 Chilean wheat cultivation was "threatened" by an acute labor shortage when some 30,000 Chilean peasants went to Peru to work on railroad construction.[24] The shortage was so acute that the Archbishop of Santiago issued a letter to all parishes condemning the peasants' "desertion" from Chilean wheat fields and issuing instructions to priests to discourage any more peasants from leaving the country.[25] The peasants involved were seasonal agricultural workers, however, and not those (*inquilinos*) who resided permanently on the land of the *patron*. Nor were they the *minifundistas* who owned less than subsistence plots and who worked for the large landowner to supplement family income. But on the whole, in the nineteenth century and on into the twentieth century, the large landowner enjoyed political, economic, and social control over the *inquilinos,* the *minifundistas* and migratory labor. The extent to which this kind of control persists today in Chile depends on the landowner's political skill and his involvement with his land.[26]

The paternalistic relationships which were characteristic of the nineteenth and early twentieth century have not been totally preserved. These relationships were partially altered as early as the 1920s. The Chilean Constitution of 1925 contained a provision which made the "proper distribution of land" a legitimate concern of the Chilean government.[27] This new constitutional power led to the promulgation of Law No. 4496 in 1928 (amended in 1931 and 1933). This law created a Bureau of Agricultural Colonization (*Caja de Colonizacion*)[28] whose funds were to be used to establish agricultural settlements in the Central Valley.

Under the law, land for these settlements (*colonias agricolas*) was to be purchased if possible; if purchase was not possible, the President of the Republic was empowered to expropriate the necessary lands on the grounds of "public need and utility." The expropriation power was severely limited and it is difficult to ascertain any case in which this power was employed. So violent was the opposition of the SNA to the expropriation features of this law that *hacendados* were a major influence in overthrowing the government.[29]

The chief beneficiaries of this "agrarian reform" were foreigners, primarily German immigrants. Few *inquilinos* obtained land in any of these colonies, though on a number of occasions they organized and formally requested land to cultivate. Only a few thousand parcels of land were created from *haciendas* under Law No. 4496.[30]

Forces and events converged in the early 1960s and produced a climate for agrarian reform. Peasant politicization and the success of the Cuban revolution in 1959 influenced Chilean political leadership as well as various sectors of society.

As many writers have pointed out, John F. Kennedy's Alliance for Progress was the U.S. response to the agrarian-based revolution in Cuba. U.S. politicians and technicians as well as their non-Marxist counterparts in Latin America felt that if "something wasn't done" about this "threat" from Cuba, then more American republics would "go Communist." Combining reform rhetoric with grandiose pledges of technical and financial aid and military assistance to arrest insurgency, the Alliance promised to support those Latin American nations who would make efforts at socio-economic change and development. Kennedy's initial statements gave agrarian reform a high priority, although his immediate advisors and the officials charged with implementing the Alliance program had important reservations.[31] The new Pan American development partnership was based in large part on agrarian reform. The attention devoted to agrarian reform in Latin America during the 1960s is suggested by counting the number of agrarian reform laws enacted by the Latin nations—a total of fifteen including two in Chile (1962 and 1967).[32] Chile, with its highly politicized population and its selection as a "showcase" for U.S. Alliance aid,[33] found itself immersed in the rhetoric of agrarian reform. U.S. promises and the experience of Cuba contributed to a climate favorable to enactment of change-oriented legislation in Chile.

The second, internal variable—peasant politicization and radicalization—is not difficult to document.[34] These indicators support the contention that peasant politicization is a factor promoting the popularity of agrarian reform. All major political parties were aware of the *campesinos'* potential as sources of electoral support. The presidential elections of 1958, and especially 1964, were hard-fought in the countryside, and the peasants were heavily propagandized by the leading candidates.

For a variety of reasons, the Chilean *campesino* has not reacted as violently as his counterparts in Bolivia or Peru. For example, Lambert[35] cites rioting and uprisings as the means available to peasants to press demands. He includes Colombia, Brazil, and the social revolutions of Mexico, Bolivia, and Cuba as examples of peasant-based movements. Peruvian peasant uprisings have been, in recent years, sources of encouragement for those Marxist and neo-Marxist leaders such as Hugo Blanco.[36] Chile, however, appears not to have had this kind of historical peasant violence.

Concurrent with the decline in importance of the agrarian sector as a major contributor to the Chilean national economy "the secure if impoverished position of the agricultural laborers" has been undermined by the mechanization of Chilean agriculture.[37] This may have increased peasant politicization. Politicization has taken two forms principally—unionization and interest articulation. Demands for better working conditions and wages are made directly to landowners[38] and through political "brokers" (such as the established political parties)[39] or illegally through such means as direct seizures of land.[40] By the end of the 1960s, however, peasant unionization and interest articulation were common throughout most of the countryside.[41]

Peasant unions tend to organize peasants around a particular *fundo,* confederating with other *fundo*-based peasant unions. Exclusion of nonattached agricultural workers and *minifundistas* from peasant unions could increase the possibilities of more land seizures.[42] Throughout the 1960s, the unstabilizing political impact of the Chilean peasantry contributed to a climate conducive to some governmental efforts toward agrarian change.

By the early 1960s a convergence of forces and events occurred to encourage reform efforts in the agrarian sector. The stagnation in agricultural production, a decrease in the landowners' hold over national political and economic life, an increase in the government's role in economic and social life, the legitimization of agrarian reform by the Alliance for Progress, and the increasing politicization of the peasants all contributed to an awareness of the need for change in the Chilean countryside.

The "pressure" for change forced even the right-wing government of Jorge Alessandri (1959–1964)[43] to enact a weak agrarian reform law (No. 15,020). This law served as the vehicle for Frei's agrarian reform program until passage of Agrarian Reform Law No. 16,640 on July 16, 1967. It is within this setting that the legislative struggle over the Christian Democratic agrarian reform law occurred.

A little more than a year after his election, President Frei introduced his long-awaited agrarian reform bill.[44] The 1962 Agrarian Reform Law No. 15,020 was used as both a model[45] and a "straw man." Frei emphasized the production orientation of his reform as well as the inadequacy and conservatism of the 1962 law.[46] However, observers quickly detected the moderate tone that Frei's "Revolution in Liberty" would maintain regarding private enterprise:

> He and other government spokesmen have said many times that, far from doing away with private property, the new law will merely extend the privilege of ownership to a wider segment of the rural population.[47]

Even before Frei announced the agrarian reform law (November 12, 1965) the lines of congressional support and opposition were developing. The March, 1965 congressional elections[48] witnessed an overwhelming victory for the PDC. Running on a pledge of structural change, the party won 82 of the 147 seats in the lower house (Chamber of Deputies) with 41.06 percent of the popular vote. In the Senate, the PDC increased its strength by 11 seats for a total of 13 or 28.8 percent of the 45-member body. FRAP (composed principally of the Socialist and Communist parties) controlled 15 seats while the Liberals (5 senators), Conservatives (2 senators) and Radicals (10 senators) accounted for the remaining senatorial seats. The congressional results indicated a clear shift from the right to the left. The strong senatorial position of the FRAP ensured the PDC of pressure from the left on all reform measures. At the same time, right-wing forces were found among the Conservatives, Liberals, and some Radicals and included sympathizers among PDC politicians who were to later be known as *Oficialistas* for their "official" support of Frei against the PDC left wing. The right wing was strategically placed within both the government and the Congress.[49] Congressional maneuvering in terms of left and right strategies began even before Frei introduced the agrarian reform bill.

The positions of the conflicting political parties were expressed during congressional debate on the agrarian reform law. The executive branch, including the political and administrative leadership of the three major PDC groupings —*Rebeldes, Terceristas, Oficialistas*[50]—and the important interest groups including the Church, the SNA, and the agrarian reform bureaucracy all became involved in the details of the debate and took sides.

After Frei introduced his agrarian reform bill, it was sent to the respective committees of the Chamber of Deputies and the Senate. In the Chamber of Deputies the Agriculture and Colonization Committee presented its report.[51] The report summarized the proposed legislation by stressing (1) the overriding priority for increasing or augmenting the "physical volume of agricultural products";[52] (2) raising the standard of living of peasant families culturally, socially, economically, and educationally. The report then analyzed the existing structure of agricultural land tenure, emphasizing the inadequacies of the Agrarian Reform Law (No. 15,020) of 1962 in terms of land available for expropriation, financing of expropriated lands (no deferred payments provisions), and the general slowness of expropriation procedures. The committee's report called for an immediate amendment to Article No. 10 of the Constitution which would then permit deferred payment of expropriated land. With the PDC-dominated Chamber of Deputies (and, as a result, a PDC-controlled Agriculture and Colonization Committee), the bill received a favorable reporting. As considered by the committee, Frei's agrarian reform bill contained a total of 170 articles compiled into 10 titles (which were subdivided into many chapters). Few modifications were made by the committee.

Debate in the Chamber began with Julio Silva Solar's[53] presentation of the report and the "popular basis for the agrarian movement." Citing both Frei's and Allende's[54] support for agrarian reform in the 1964 presidential election, the Radical party's approval of policy calling for agrarian reform in 1961, and the Chilean bishops' Pastoral Letter,[55] Silva stressed the universality of support for reform. Even the parties of the Right,[56] argued Silva, claim to favor agrarian reform. His attack was addressed to the Right (Liberals, Conservatives, and some Radicals) for equating reform with the pricing policy of agricultural products, leaving land structure (including tenure) unchanged. Silva set the early tone of debate by stressing that the new agrarian reform bill:

> is based on a concept of social function of land—a concept which is developing in most nations. The classic concept of the unalienable right of ownership is a thing of the past.[57]

The first criticism from the Left centered on the amount of land which the bill exempted from expropriation. Citing the Province of Llanquihue as an example, the Socialist deputy Sepulveda stated that under the PDC-proposed reform, no landholding in the province could be expropriated.

Zepeda (Liberal party—PL) speaking for his party, opposed the procedure by which the Provincial Agrarian Tribunals would handle contested expropriation cases. Initially the Liberals argued against the "excess power" given the President in appointing individuals to these courts and the role of bureaucrats in expropriation proceedings:

> Having a public functionary (official) as a judge is objectionable because the organization to which he belongs might have interests in the reform, the expropriations, and in the fixing of indemnities.[58]

The first Communist party (PCCh) attack came from Montes in connection with proposed Article 151. This article permitted the President to intervene with force to end any work stoppage in agricultural production. Montes, representing the Province of Concepcion which has a large lumber industry, maintained that this article would effectively prohibit workers from striking.

In answering Montes, Silva (PDC) explained that Article 151 was aimed not only at workers who strike but also at the employers. Garces (PDC) attempted to mollify Montes by expressing a similar concern and promising that the article would be more clearly defined.[59] Other conflicts between the Centrist PDC deputies and the Socialist and Communist deputies were not so easily resolved.

While the left-wing deputies were attempting to liberalize the PDC bill in favor of the peasants, the Right led by the Liberal party with support from the Conservative party (PCU) attempted to maintain the prerogatives of the large landowners by resorting to nationalist rhetoric. For example, Zepeda (PL) attacked the bill because it placed a limit on the land owned by Chileans, limiting, in the process, national enterprises. Zepeda carefully pointed out that the bill did nothing about foreign-owned land without, however, mentioning that foreigners owned relatively small amounts:

> It would be better that there should reign a national "oligarchy" rather than a foreign one.[60]

The Radicals (PR), on the other hand, at first took a rather self-serving position, arguing that the PDC did not create the agrarian reform movement, that, in reality, a Radical started the fight for reform in 1923. Depending on the agrarian middle class, the PR argued against the proliferation of *minifundios,* and then accused the PDC of establishing a "biased table of equivalence," insinuating rather strongly that Christian Democrats lived in areas where this table was most lenient. Rioseco (PR) also attacked the expropriation exemption granted to corporations owning vineyards, arguing that "within the perfect philosophy and integral harmony of this proposal there have infiltrated, through some cracks, spurious interests." [61] In this last charge, Rioseco raised the question for the first time of possible landowner influence over the PDC in Congress as well as the government.

The Right in the personages of Phillips (PL) and Ochagavia (PCU) also attacked the bill's provisions concerning expropriation exemptions for vineyards, but from the landowners' instead of the peasants' perspective. Phillips suggested that the PDC should decide whether they were in favor of commercial agricultural enterprises, but not leave exceptions for special sectors (such as vineyards). Ochagavia defended commercial enterprises as the "only adequate wine producers because they outlive individuals." He criticized the fact that only about ten and not more than twenty vineyards in Chile could be maintained intact under the PDC bill, "If the country wants to develop a wine industry, then all concerns in production should be declared safe from expropriation."

Although some observers[62] attribute the slow passage of this bill to the PDC's minority position in the Senate, Aravena of the PS gave a different set of reasons:

> The Socialist party is doubtful as to the outcome of the project (implementation of Frei's agrarian reform program). The conciliatory tone used by Frei and the Minister of Agriculture Trivelli (to wealthy landowners) and the ever greater concessions granted to the wealthy agrarian sector point up the differences between PDC theory and practice. Delays in passage and implementation of the bill will allow for more compromises which are often initiated by militant Christian Democrats who are well-known *latifundistas* or who have close connections with those that are. The Socialists condemn the slow pace at which the PDC is dealing with this issue. Any attempt at changing the critical agricultural situation will prove futile unless it is done within a different social, political, and economic system (with) a government that will struggle (sic) initiated and backed by the working classes.[63]

The charge by the PDC and its intellectual boosters in the U.S. that the delay was due to the opposition of *both* the Left and Right is false. By way of clarifying his party's position vis-a-vis the Frei bill, the Socialist deputy Aravena pointed out the aspects of the proposed bill that the PS supported: (1) the categorical declaration of the social function of land; (2) the expropriation or forced sale of land not serving a social function; (3) the transfer of expropriated

land to the peasant; (4) the recognition of various types of
tenure, including collectivist; and (5) the proposed changes
in water rights and use of water resources. The aspects of
the bill which his party ignored or considered regressive included: (1) the absence of peasant representatives on
agrarian tribunals in a reform which claims to desire direct
participation of peasants; (2) the intent to strengthen the
capitalist regime by establishment of 100,000 new property
owners, turning the "beneficiaries of the reform into guard-
ians of the capitalist system while leaving hundreds of thousands of other peasants without access to land"; (3) the absence of definite targets defined by time limitations, leaving
to the discretion of the government the complete enactment
of the law's provisions; (4) the absence of programs designed to alleviate the problem of the *minifundio*—in fact,
the government program of settlement would tend to aggra-
vate this problem; (5) the large grant of power to the President; (6) the inclusion of proposed Article 151 (see above)
which would annul the organized struggle of the *campesino;*
and (7) the absence of any program to alleviate the plight
of the Chilean Indians.

In one of the few statements made by the National
Democrats (PDN), Tuma supported the PS position in regard to the plight of the Chilean Indians. He pointed out
that since the Indians live on and work their own land and
are, therefore, not tenants or renters, they are not eligible to
receive redistributed land. His second point dealt with the
bonds used to compensate landowners for expropriated
land. He was concerned that such bonds would remain inac-
tive, "under the pillows of the ex-*latifundistas.*" In short, the
PS and PDN positions were constructively critical of the
PDC bill; both deputies sought to strengthen it in ways that
would make it more effective in dealing with a broader con-
stituency of peasants.

The PCCh through Carlos Rosales delineated the
party's position on the PDC bill. After brief reference to

their own goals as a way of making a mild criticism, the Communists gave their support, considering that the bill represented "an important advance," constituting a possible change in the land tenure system. Rosales had specific criticisms for what he considered "grave concessions": (1) the nonexpropriation of vineyards; (2) the inclusion of the landowners' houses in the reserves which can be retained after expropriation—in most cases this is the core of the property with many important installations; (3) the "modifications" in the table of equivalences; (4) the fact that lands partitioned between November, 1963 and November, 1964 remain on the margin of the bill; and (5) the fact that Article 151 (which is mentioned above) denied to agrarian workers the rights enjoyed by industrial workers.

The Radicals' position was summarized by Fuentealba. He criticized the bill for failing to provide a "coordinated plan of development in such areas as education, industrialization, transportation, communication, and commercialization." In agreement with the Socialists, he criticized the fact that no attempt was made to solve the problem of the *minifundio*. The PR promised to vote in favor of this measure, offering amendments to improve it.

In this first session, the Right stressed the "Marxist" nature of the bill, along with its technical shortcomings, its "sacrifice" of individual property rights, and its "foreign," anti-Chilean national origins and tendencies. To illustrate, Phillips (PL) offered a comparison between expropriation of national land and the nationalization of foreign property. Under the proposed agrarian reform law, Chilean landowners are compensated for land over a period of twenty-five years at 3 percent interest. In comparison, the *Compania Chilena de Electricidad* (a U.S. firm) receives cash (in U.S. dollars payable in New York) for its assets, paid for over a period of only seven years, with an annual interest payment of 6.5 percent—plus exemptions from all taxes, charges, or other fees. According to Phillips, the proposed bill, fulfills the designs of North American imperialism: accept agrarian reform in those countries in which U.S. interests own almost all the mines and permit mine reform in those countries where U.S. interests are in land.

Part of the Liberal party argument also rested on abstract philosophical issues involving the supposed conflict between individualism and collectivism. According to Phillips, Frei's election reflected popular rejection of Marxism, and depended largely on the support of the independent and traditional parties. These forces, Phillips argued, joined together to back Frei because they expected democracy and liberty, not "communism" in the agrarian reform bill which eliminated the current agricultural proprietors who, he felt, had a clear right to their lands. Attacking the increasing involvement of the public sector in agricultural change and development, Phillips argued that the law would subject *campesinos* to government functionaries who would operate the land. Phillips concluded that the *campesinos* would not own any land, would be completely dependent upon the state, and would be under the absolute tutelage of government functionaries.

De La Fuente (PL) continued the Right's attack, relying on nationalist and economic arguments. He stated that the proposed agrarian reform would cause production to stagnate and force the country to rely on agricultural imports from the U.S.[64] He argued that the U.S. was promoting agrarian reform to increase Chilean dependence and hence that U.S. economic interests rather than Frei or Chonchol, the head of INDAP, were behind the agrarian reform movement. The only conditions under which his party would accept agrarian reform would have to include (1) "just"[65] compensation for expropriated land, (2) bonds which could be immediately redeemed, (3) division of the land into private holdings, and (4) expropriation proceedings to be heard in regular courts, not special tribunals.

Ochagavia (PCU) concluded the Right's case against the reform by declaring that the proposed agrarian reform bill was not technically, but politically inspired and was largely based on "foreign solutions." The real purpose, he stated, was the attempt by the PDC to gain votes through government patronage, sacrificing the hard-working landowners in the process.

With the close of the first Chamber session on the proposed agrarian reform bill, the battle lines between the Left, the Center, and the Right had been drawn. Broadly, the Left's strategy was to "beef-up" the bill so as to permit even greater, bolder revisions in land structure and tenure. Furthermore, the Left (including the PS and the PCCh) saw many provisions in the proposed bill designed to satisfy the right wing of the PDC (Article 151 which exempted vineyards from expropriation, the equivalence tables, among others). In subsequent sessions, both leftist parties intervened in the legislative process, attempting to change these specific provisions, while giving support to the overall movement toward agrarian reform. The Right's strategy was the same, but the goals were just the opposite—to tone down all "radical" features of the bill by relying generally on anti-U.S. and anti-Communist demagoguery, branding the PDC as both a Marxist and imperialist (U.S.) "tool." The Center (including the PDC and some PR members) attempted to mollify both sides while maintaining the intentions Frei had written into the bill. Adjustments, when they were made, were slightly to the left—but not always. On some issues the PDC was adamant; for instance, the exemption of the vineyards.

During the second session on July 6, 1966, the Chamber continued its debate of the agrarian reform bill.[66] The National party (PN)[67] began a detailed attack, beginning with indemnification of expropriated landowners as outlined in proposed Article 39. Ochagavia (PN) argued that the value set on the land for tax purposes did not reflect the true commercial worth of the land. He alluded to a campaign promise of the PDC in which Frei promised that "the landowner could declare the value of his land and on this figure he would pay taxes. This figure would also be the one paid in case of expropriation."

A Communist deputy, Tejeda, defended the PDC, stressing the immorality of quoting more than that stated for tax purposes. Likewise, Aravena (PS) affirmed that his party would vote in favor of this article. Finally, Valdés (PDC) rebutted the right-wing critics, emphasizing two points: (a) the higher the price paid for land expropriated, the fewer funds would be available for an integral agrarian reform, and (b) land traditionally had not been used for commercial agriculture but for security against inflation. He claimed that the highest priority now would be the incorporation of the *campesino* into the reform process.

The Right (Phillips—PN) responded by raising the nationalist issue claiming that in the case of U.S.-owned *Compania Chilena de Electricidad,* the government compensated the foreign investors above the appraised value while Chileans were to receive only 70 percent of the appraised value of their land. The Communists rose in defense of the PDC indemnification proposal, pointing out the injustices caused from the present land situation and arguing that society should be compensated, not the *latifundista.*

The struggle around the indemnification clause exemplifies the coalition possibilities between the Left and Center parties. Article 39 passed on a vote of forty-nine to six and was incorporated as Article 42 in the law. On the issue of *campesino* property rights raised by the PN, the Left-Center coalition supported Silva's (PDC) declaration that:

> The capitalistic concept of ownership is not compatible with the ideas of this agrarian reform bill . . . the PDC feels that the landowner is subordinated to the community and the state in the name of the community should make the landowners comply with their social duty. . . .

Proposals on the margin of the reform and not detrimental to PDC interests were accepted without hesitation by PDC congressmen.

For example, the PCCh-PS-PR sponsored portion of Article 62 (incorporated as Section C of Article 67), dealing with education, directed CORA to designate land for the construction of schools and living quarters for teachers.

The right wing's attempt to tone down the "collective character" of land ownership as proposed in the bill's land assignment and *asentamiento*[68] system provisions was not successful.

The issue of political representation of new social forces on policy-making bodies forged a new majority coalition right-wing center group which blocked changes aimed at increasing peasant influence. For example, during the third session, held on July 7, 1966, a Left coalition (PCCh-PS) voiced opposition to the absence of a *campesino* representative on the National Agrarian Council (*Consejo Nacional Agrario*)—the agency established to decide appeals by expropriated landowners against CORA.[69] The Center-Right held firm, however, and Article 135 as drafted by the PDC remained unchanged.

There were issues in which the PDC and the Left were in conflict and in which the Center-Right coalition was not operative. For example, during the July 7 session, the Left coalition (PCCh-PS) raised the issue of "foreign intervention" in the area of education—in particular, the activities of the *Instituto de Educacion Rural* (Institute of Rural Education).[70] Both the Communists and the Socialists charged that such foreign groups as the Institute of Rural Education, the U.S. Peace Corps, the German and Belgian peace corps equivalents, various Church-affiliated groups and other religious organizations, CARE, and the U.S. Economic Mission played significant roles in the education of Chilean *campesinos* and youth. The PCCh and PS spokesmen argued that these activities should be performed by INDAP, CORA, and the Ministry of Popular Advancement (*Promocion Popular*). Although this was a side issue in the debate, the PDC supported the activities of foreign-based groups, which suggests that the PDC's influence may have been maintained in part by external assistance.

The final issue of importance raised during this session was proposed Article 150 (which became Article 157 in the law). This article prohibits the formation of private corporations or limited or joint-stock companies whose main or secondary objective is agricultural or livestock development. The intent of this article was not to attack existing agro-commercial firms (since the article does not call for the elimination of existing concerns) but to limit the creation of new corporations. Two issues enter the debate over this provision—the exemption of wine/vineyard operations and the exemption of certain provinces where, it was alleged, certain PDC members owned shares in corporations.[71] The Communists supported the article but opposed the exemption of the wine industry. The Socialists opposed both exemptions. The Left coalition (PCCh-PS) often joined with the PDC in coalition against the Right (PL, PCU, and later the fused PN). Cooperation of the Left and, at times, members of the PR was necessary and/or desirable. One PDC official described Senate action on the Agrarian Reform Act of 1967 as follows:

> A lot of congressional compromise. However, in the long run we gave away practically nothing. The action . . . took place in the Senate Agriculture and Finance Committee. The rightist opposition was stupid—that is, they made bad moves. We had four Christian Democrats and four leftists on the committee so we dominated.[72]

In the end, compromises and revisions expanded the original document from 170 to 333 articles.[73] Compromises when they occurred did little to alter the basic content of Frei's original bill. Given the overwhelming majority in the lower house and a strong minority in the Senate, the PDC was able to exert strong pressure on other political parties to ensure passage of the legislation. The PDC Left (The *Rebeldes*) were still working within the party apparatus, thus permitting PDC to present a united front to opposition parties. Outside of the legislative chambers and inter-party fighting various interest groups were organizing support for and against the agrarian reform law.

Several major "interest groups" [74] were involved or concerned with agrarian reform legislation prior to or during the Frei government—the Catholic Church (or factions within the Church), the executive branch (including the President, the ministries of Agriculture, Interior, and Labor, CORA, INDAP, and the Chilean Development Corporation—CORFO), and the National Agricultural Society (SNA). The peasants at this point in Chilean history were not directly represented since little organization of peasants had taken place.[75] To a great extent, then, what peasant "representation" that did occur was effected indirectly by elite representation.[76]

Several factors explain why certain factions within the Chilean Roman Catholic Church took an activist role in agrarian reform: (1) translation of the social doctrine of the Church in Chile into concrete programs—a historically cumulative process of liberal interpretations of papal encyclicals (notably John XXXIII's Mater et Magistra); (2) concern for, and an attempt to "lure back" Catholics who had deserted the Church in pursuit of more material, earthly rewards (or, more popularly, an attempt to make the Church "more relevant" to the modern demands of depressed strata of Chilean society); (3) absence of sufficient and "effective public-supported institutions of social action operating in the countryside in Chile";[77] and (4) the Marxist "threat"—the argument that unless the Church responds to new environmentally inspired demands (in this case agrarian reform), then peasants will "go communist." [78]

The Church (in particular, the Bishop of Talca and the Archbishop of Santiago) did play a leading role in the early 1960s in privately financed and administered agrarian reform. Some of the Christian Democrats who followed Frei into government positions in 1964 were influenced by or already trained in the Church's Institute of Agrarian Promotion (INPROA) operations. The operations of INPROA are of interest to anyone examining the genesis of agrarian reform in Chile.[79]

There are many similarities between the operations of INPROA and those of CORA and INDAP. Likewise, the INPROA approach to agrarian reform was obviously in the minds of those Christian Democrats who wrote and defended the Frei bill of November, 1965. INPROA's guidelines for the transitional period between Church ownership and peasant (or cooperative) ownership (guidelines which were based on its experiences in Alto Melipilla, Los Silos, and Las Pataguas)[80] are quite similar to the transition from private, large landownership to CORA-assisted *asentamientos* and eventual cooperative ownership or parcelization. Table II compares the INPROA guidelines with the land assignment provisions of the 1967 Agrarian Reform Law:

TABLE II

COMPARISON BETWEEN INPROA[1] AND CORA[2] GUIDELINES

INPROA GUIDELINES	CORA GUIDELINES
1. INPROA receives land from Church; has rights to: (a) sell, cultivate, rent; (b) manage the farms, contract necessary services (assistants, technicians, professionals); (c) contract loans and credits; (d) make necessary investments; (e) perform studies of the land/property;	1. CORA receives land through expropriation (and other means) from private ownership (Article 2 through 57) and has basically the same rights (Article 224); these rights are more finitely described;
2. Colonists (recipients) must pay for land over a twenty-year maximum—price of land determined by INPROA according to its commercial value as measured by productivity;	2. The assignee (recipient) must pay for land over a thirty-year maximum—the "payment will be made partly in cash with the balance in equal annual quotas (Articles 88 and 89)"; CORA determines the price;

INPROA GUIDELINES

CORA GUIDELINES

3. Colonist must pay INPROA 10 percent of the value of the land as a down payment upon parcelization;

3. Cash down payment not cited specifically in law—only phrased as above (Article 88);

4. In first year of operation, land is administered by INPROA and peasants are organized into a cooperative; during this time, the number of families that the farm can support is determined; eventual parcelization is based on production;

4. CORA administers expropriated land for at least three years (Article 67) and maybe five, through presidential/ executive order (Article 67); CORA forms an *asentamiento* (kind of a cooperative); land is divided into family agriculture units (defined by productivity—see Article 1, h);

5. After first year, if cooperative decides, the colonist-community may begin cash-renting its land from INPROA— those who enter community at this time are given an option to buy;

5. After three years, the *asentamiento* decides whether to continue as a cooperative or parcel the land; regardless of decision, land is purchased at this time;

6. Selection of final colonist families is made by the cooperative itself.

6. Selection of final assignees determined by law (Articles 71, 72, and 73) which gives highest priority to those who were peasant *asentados* in the rural property when such land was assigned.

---

[1] Thiesenhusen, *Chile's Experiments in Agrarian Reform, op. cit.*, pp. 69–70.
[2] *Ley de Reforma Agraria* (July 16, 1967).

From the comparison above it is obvious that there are great similarities between the Church-sponsored agrarian reform and the PDC government-sponsored agrarian reform activities. It is no coincidence that the gradualistic approach to agrarian reform advocated by Frei and evidenced in CORA's activities even after the passage of the Agrarian Reform Law of 1967 has the same type of step-by-step, slowly evolving set of operating procedures as first developed and utilized by INPROA.[81]

The Church, then (or more precisely, its liberal wing), by its own example, provided a major impetus for the kind of agrarian reform Frei and the PDC sought in November, 1965 and legislatively achieved in July, 1967. Progressive Catholic laymen did not need to pressure individual congressmen—indeed, they often *were* the congressmen proposing and acting upon agrarian reform. The Church hierarchy did not play an overt, lobbyist role in favor of this type of agrarian reform since it was a PDC-proposed agrarian reform. The Church established the model and many of the major procedures later followed by CORA.[82] The Church's role was much more important than a mere lobbyist—it laid down the general policy guidelines that shaped the direction of social change. Since no Church property was planned for confiscation, conservative churchmen had little to fear from expropriation, and the funds accumulated through compensation could be invested in other lucrative endeavors.

The more active and visible segment of the Chilean Catholic Church supported the PDC agrarian reform. To do otherwise would have meant abandoning a social action position that had been developing within the Church since the end of the nineteenth century. Since the PDC law was even more "gradualistic" than the procedures utilized by INPROA (a simple measure being INPROA's one-year cooperative arrangement versus CORA's three-year *asentamiento* process), even those liberal churchmen who were lukewarm over INPROA could find comfort in the fact that as long as the government was controlled by right-wing Christian Democrats like Frei, radical change could be avoided.

The executive branch of the Chilean government was not a monolithic unit working in harmony towards rapid achievement of agrarian reform.[83] There were several positions within the executive branch in regard to agrarian reform during the Frei administration. Executive branch "actors" who in some manner entered into the policy formation or implementation processes in the area of agrarian reform included: (1) the President and his immediate advisers; (2) the vice-president (executive director) of INDAP and his immediate advisers; (3) the vice-president (executive director) of CORA and his immediate advisers; (4) the Minister of Agriculture and his associates; (5) the Minister of Labor and his subordinates; (6) the vice-president (executive director) of the Chilean Development Corporation; and the Minister of Public Works and Communications and his associates and subordinates. Lesser actors included the Minister of Interior. Table III indicates a rough positioning (left, center, right) of these individuals (and their units) in regard to pushing for an effective, comprehensive agrarian reform. An examination of the positions and actions of these seven units in regard to agrarian reform is needed.

The principal units charged with responsibilities for agrarian reform activities were INDAP and CORA. These two semiautonomous public corporate bodies were on the cutting edge of reform activities. Their respective and relative positions on the reform issue were to the left of the rest of the executive branch including the President. It was CORA legal experts who drafted the agrarian reform bill and advised the President on which sections were most legally feasible. Hence CORA attempted to make the agrarian reform program legally and technically feasible. The political "push" of the reform program came from Chonchol's INDAP. Most observers concede that INDAP rather than CORA was responsible for the attempt to politicize (and even radicalize) peasants. Hence, while CORA was concerned with techniques and pressured for a law which would permit gradual reform (principally, drastically improving the Alessandri law of 1962), INDAP chose to abstain from

TABLE III

RELATIVE POSITIONS OF VARIOUS EXECUTIVE BRANCH UNITS WITH RESPECT TO AGRARIAN REFORM*

POSITION	LEFT		CENTER			RIGHT	
UNIT	INDAP	CORA	Ministry of Agriculture	Office of the President	CORFO	Ministry of Labor	Ministry of Public Works
LEADER	Chonchol	Moreno	Trivelli	Frei		Thayer	Zujovic

Source: A combination of a number of sources, including unstructured interviews with individuals involved directly or indirectly with agrarian reform policy and implementation during the Frei administration, press reports in *El Mercurio, El Siglo, Ercilla, La Nacion,* the *New York Times,* the *Washington Post,* and the *Christian Science Monitor.*

* These relative positions are, of course, only crude guides or measures. In addition, although the unit is categorized along with its principal spokesmen, undoubtedly individual functionaries within the particular unit may or may not agree with or behave in a manner that would suggest conformity with his unit's spokesman. Position, in this case, was crudely determined by the attitudes expressed (either through interviews or press reports) by the unit spokesmen and their immediate associates and subordinates.

directly pressuring for a more liberal law (except through particular leftist PDC congressmen who associated with Chonchol) and worked towards generating radical political pressure for expropriation and a more radical reform through *campesino* organization.

The Ministry of Agriculture under Hugo Trivelli maintained a more moderate position, providing "steady support" for an effective law and quietly encouraging Chonchol's organizing efforts and INDAP's programs.[84] The minister attempted to perform a broker's role halfway between the President and Chonchol. Many bureaucrats within the Ministry of Agriculture were Radical party members (and, hence, center or right-of-center as opposed to the left-of-center bureaucrats in CORA and INDAP), and probably desired a more conservative reform bill than Frei's.

The President's position on agrarian reform reflected a concern with directed change, seeking to alter particular areas of the countryside selectively. In the struggles over enactment, he apparently sought and accepted the advice of the more liberal CORA Legal Division. The bill and the resulting law provided adequate guarantees for the large PDC landowners, especially those whose holdings were in vineyards. In addition, it appears that the opposition charges of distorted equivalence tables favoring certain PDC owners could be substantiated. During the legislative struggle over the agrarian reform bill, the President's position was a centrist one—pushing for the law but accepting some compromises that softened its impact on the landowners.

Historically, CORFO (a public corporation) has been a "boon" to the conservative, economic elite providing credits and opportunities for investment of capital.[85] Its "clientele" was not the *minifundistas* but the *latifundistas*. In addition, even though CORFO's major objective was to stimulate economic development in industrial and agrarian sectors[86] the Frei government sought to bypass this agency by giving CORA and INDAP authority to make investments in land improvement for the purpose of increasing productivity. The creation and strengthening of both CORA and INDAP were made necessary because of CORFO's inability to satisfy agrarian-based needs other than those of the large landlords. Because of CORFO's links with the *latifundistas* (CORFO was the greatest source of easy term credit), it could not be part of any public attempt to curtail large landowning privileges. Within the agrarian sector this corporation played a conservative role.

The Ministry of Labor, responsible for implementing labor laws, played a role in the agrarian reform process through the certification of *campesino* organizations and some mediation of agricultural labor disputes. The right-of-center position of the Ministry of Labor was observable in the statements of a subsecretary of labor, José Ilabaca: "The government's role is to play down peasant demands and play up competition between peasants." [87] Ilabaca cited an example of his ministry's attempt to ban a Marxist *campesino* union[88] for "excessive demands." The ministry's highest officials appeared to oppose the mass mobilization style of politics encouraged by INDAP and the peasant unionists. Even in registering *campesino* unions, the ministry impeded the registration process by a general bureaucratic slowdown. The provision of the law which permits the government to intervene in work stoppages originated with PDC functionaries of a similar persuasion as that of Sr. Ilabaca. The Ministry of Labor made only a negative contribution to agrarian reform in the proposed legislation stage; it provided legal clauses (such as Article 171 referred to above) permitting the government to intervene in agrarian labor disputes on the side of the large landowner.

The most conservative sector of the executive branch in the agrarian reform process was the Ministry of Public Works and Communications. It was not the ministry's work, but rather its head, (Minister) Edmundo Perez Zujovic, who played an overt role in the agrarian reform. Zujovic was responsible primarily for forcing Chonchol's resignation.[89] His own statements vis-a-vis Chonchol and INDAP

tend to support the view that Zujovic did what was necessary to keep INDAP from performing its mandated and legally assigned functions. The ministry, of course, had specific functions in the countryside such as improvement of
physical infrastructure. Chonchol's complaints of lack of
cooperation and even overt hostility on the part of certain
ministers in the Frei government appear to center on Zujovic and a few others. The pressure applied against the reform once it was enacted stemmed partly from this ministry.

In summary, as a set of interest groups the executive
branch often appeared to work against itself in the legislative struggle over agrarian reform. Obviously, the agencies
directly engaged in the reform (INDAP and CORA)
pushed for a strong, feasible reform law. The Ministry of
Agriculture tended to support recommendations of these
two semiautonomous public corporate bodies, at least in
principle, and to some degree, in reality. Pressure in the
other direction (away from a strong reform law) came from
the traditional agency of the large landowner—CORFO.
Both the Ministry of Labor and the Ministry of Public
Works and Communications were in league with CORFO.
All three agencies had substantial if peripheral roles in the
reform process. All three, however, intervened overtly and
covertly during and after the legislative struggle to blunt
the reform effort. Frei started in the center but moved
steadily to the right. As a later section of this chapter
will illustrate, the reform was emasculated when the President had moved so far to the right that he ignored the needs
and demands of the countryside as generated and interpreted by INDAP and, to a lesser extent, CORA.

The last interest group to be discussed and examined in
relation to the legislative struggle is, perhaps, the most obvious one—the National Agricultural Society.[90] The SNA, although not as influential in Chile as similar societies in other
countries, still occupies a most important position vis-a-vis
public decisions in the agricultural sector. The active roles

played by the Liberal and Conservative parties in the Alessandri reform resulted in the SNA's grudging acceptance of this very mild measure. The substantial losses suffered by the PL and the PCU in the March, 1965 elections meant that neither of these two parties nor the SNA itself could directly oppose the PDC agrarian reform bill. Instead, the SNA strategy appeared to be,

> based on a perception and acceptance of limitations that were imposed by the radical reduction in the Right's political strength. This strength must be supplemented by a search for allies within the government itself—Christian Democratic landowners, industrialists, and politicians—that might be inclined to listen sympathetically to SNA proposals that were not incompatible with the basic goals of the reform.[91]

This "insiders" strategy coupled with the SNA's considerable financial resources, technical/professional resources, and access to public media partially compensated for lack of direct political representation in Congress.

The indirect approach of the SNA, it now appears, was essentially the most effective means to prevent a more radical law from being passed. The similarities between this more covert role and the roles played by those executive branch units opposed to agrarian reform are obvious. A successful partnership emerged between the SNA and conservative PDC functionaries whose attitudes towards agrarian reform were less obvious at the outset. Furthermore, this indirect, "infiltration" strategy was most successful because of the nature of the PDC government. In Frei's attempt to satisfy the right wing, he appointed men hostile to reform to jobs that were peripheral to the reform effort but essential to its maintenance. It was these functionaries who colluded with the SNA leadership to the disadvantage of the agrarian reform effort.

In short, the SNA did not have to confront directly those in government responsible for agrarian reform during the legislative debate over the law to succeed in softening the reform.[92] Through his powers to appoint functionaries and his desire to secure right-wing support, Frei did the groundwork for the SNA. Direct confrontation by the Right over the agrarian reform law did occur, but it may be interpreted as merely a symbolic struggle. The real modification of the reform was accomplished indirectly and by "pragmatic" conservatives—individuals skilled in the political bargaining process which characterizes the Chilean political system.

The law finally enacted by the Chilean Congress in July, 1967 was basically the bill introduced by Frei almost two years earlier, though it had been expanded by 163 articles. Congressional debate had not changed the gradual nature of the reform, contrary to FRAP intentions. At the same time, the Right had not been able to emasculate those proposed provisions which strengthened the government's power to expropriate.

To better understand the legal product, it is worthwhile to examine in some detail (1) the major provisions; (2) the differences and similarities between this law and its predecessor, the 1962 law; and (3) the extent to which this law, as a product of Chilean bargaining politics, may be viewed as an instrument designed to facilitate reform.

The law is divided into the following functional categories: (1) lands marked for expropriation and the expropriation process (including indemnification, appeals process, and agrarian reform bonds); (2) reorganization and redistribution of expropriated lands (including transitory and final stages of control over land); (3) water resources; and (4) organization of public sector units involved in the reform process. A content analysis reveals that the major portion of the law deals with organization and reorganization of public sector units assigned agrarian reform responsibilities. Some 104 articles were devoted to organizational aspects of the reform. Other provisions in rank order were: expropriation and expropriation processes (61 articles), water resources (50 articles), reorganization and redistribution of expropriated lands (45 articles), and other provisions (63 articles).[93]

One of the reasons for the length of this law lies in the fact that Chilean law is based on Roman law principles. However, another reason is the fact that this law was an attempt to overhaul the Alessandri statute of 1962.[94] Hence, continuity and differences between both laws.

One interpretation of the history of agrarian reform legislation in Chile emphasizes its cumulative, evolutionary aspect. The 1967 law was one step beyond the 1962 law, which was the next logical step after the Colonization Law of 1928. There is evidence to support this interpretation. For example, in examining the public agencies designated to administer the law, we find some historical continuity between the *Caja de Colonizacion Agricola* (the Agricultural Colonization Bank) and CORA—the present institution was actually founded under the 1962 law,[95] though, as we shall see, its duties and responsibilities have been expanded. The same may be said for the *Consejo de Fomento e Investigaciones Agricolas* (Council for the Promotion of Agricultural Investigations—CONFIN) established in 1928 and its successor—INDAP—which was established in 1962. Both the 1962 and 1967 laws broaden public authority in its legal ability (and capability) to intervene in land tenure and land use matters.

Specifically, the 1967 law was designed to streamline the land reform agencies (INDAP and CORA) and provide them with additional powers to administer, coordinate, and stimulate the reform; enlarge the lands that would be subject to expropriation,[96] and improve and liberalize the financing of the reform. Both CORA and INDAP received more legal authority than they possessed under the 1962 law. The features of the 1967 law in regard to enlarging the expropriatable land made it superior to the 1962 law. "Eighty basic irrigated hectares" [97] was established as the maximum farm size. The earlier law did not provide a maximum size. There was a tightening up of loopholes found in the 1962 law[98] regarding exemptions from expropriation. Nevertheless many observers questioned the objectivity of the tables of equivalence[99] which translated the eighty basic irrigated hectares into their functional equivalents in all Chilean provinces.

The new law attempted to overcome the serious financial bottleneck in the 1962 statute which resulted from a stipulation that "full cash payment must be made for expropriated land." [100] The 1967 law permits a minimum cash payment of as low as one percent (for abandoned property) and a maximum of 10 percent for expropriation based on other criteria (over eighty basic irrigated hectares, and other conditions).[101] The rest of the payment is made in Agrarian Reform Bonds[102] issued by the government at 3 percent interest for five-, twenty-five, and thirty-year amortization terms.

Thus, in terms of organization for reform, land available or subject to expropriation, and financing of the reform, one observes certain differences—differences which tend to strengthen the reform by permitting the government to intervene more directly into land tenure and land productivity through the administrative process. It should be emphasized that although the liberalized landholding and financing provisions of the 1967 law appear to be quite a dramatic break with the earlier law, in reality the law merely legitimized some of the practices of INDAP and CORA. In fact, INDAP and CORA operated for almost two years under the 1962 provision; a comparison of accomplishments (which will be detailed later) between the pre-1967 and post-1967 law reveals very little quantitative differences.

The 1967 law was in many ways an improved, liberalized version of the 1962 statute. At the same time, the goals of the Frei law were not a radical departure from the preceding law which was designed to promote land productivity in Chile. Increased productivity was to be accomplished by limited expropriation, limited redistribution of land, and limited government intervention into land use and ownership. It was considered a reform instrument by those who defined reform as increased productivity.[103] It was also a product of compromise, especially within the PDC.

The Frei reform of 1967 must be considered as a limited attempt to appease both left-wing and right-wing critics. To a degree, the law treats government intervention in such a way as to balance the efforts of the reformers as well as those supporting the status quo. Hence, as the discussion and analysis of the administration of the reform will illustrate, the most radical achievements of government reformers were not facilitated by the law. Key administrative personnel within strategic institutions (INDAP, and to a lesser degree, CORA) achieved results by utilizing government resources that probably would have been provided even if the 1967 law had not been enacted.

Administrative Structure[104]

Beneath the sweeping rhetoric of the congressional debate, we noted that the legislative struggle was concerned largely with specific issues and details and intricate maneuvering of left-center, center, and center-right coalitions. The result was a reform bill which was more "reform-minded" when compared to its predecessor, but quite deficient as an instrument to facilitate structural reform. Initial implementation of agrarian reform by the key public agencies (CORA and INDAP) was more of a radical departure from tradition than the legislative handling of this issue. Innovative administrative action in support of peasant mobilization was a major departure from the patterns of bureaucratic and legislative behavior which were traditionally geared toward demobilizing popular movements.

An examination of administrative organizations, personnel, and financial resources of agrarian reform illustrates both the opportunities for structural change in the countryside and the constraints against it. The opposition correctly appreciated the importance of the administrative process in blocking change. Our discussion of personnel emphasized the problem of recruitment and how the agrarian reform agencies faced it. Whether to recruit individuals who were politically reliable or individuals who might be more competent technically but ideologically hostile was one of the dilemmas. The administrative machinery, nevertheless, held together sufficiently to initiate some major changes in the social organization of rural Chile.

Concurrent with the legislative debates over Frei's agrarian reform bill, the agrarian reform program was being implemented under the authority of the 1962 law. The most striking feature of the organization of public resources for agrarian reform purposes has been that new, semiautonomous agencies have been established. These agencies maintain relations with the older, established agencies but are not necessarily subordinated to them. The proliferation of agencies or organizations parallel to existing ones is not particular to Chile—rather this practice is common to other Latin American countries as well as the nations of Asia and Africa.[105] There are a number of reasons why separate agencies for development or reform-type activities are established, such as the desire to bypass existing agencies. In the case of Chile, the bureaucratic institutions involved in agricultural development activities in the past largely served the interests of the large landowners.

As one astute observer of agrarian institutions noted:

> If further proof is needed of the orientation towards the large farmer clientele of the traditional ministries and agricultural development institutions, it is given by the need to create entirely new administrative institutions to reach low-income clientele (small farmers and farm laborers). . . .[106]

Both CORA and INDAP were established to devote their collective energies and available resources to low-income clientele.

The administrative structure which emerged from establishing INDAP and CORA separate from the Ministry of Agriculture had both advantages and disadvantages for reform. The connection between administrative structure (and other organizational features), policy implementation, and output can be understood by examining the organization of agrarian reform activities (1) prior to 1962, (2) from 1962–1964 (initial development of INDAP and CORA), and (3) from 1964 until the end of the Frei period. Under (3) we will describe and analyze INDAP and CORA with regard to (a) formal organization, (b) informal organization, (c) programs goals and objectives, (d) personnel/manpower resources, and (e) financial resources. A discussion of organizational problems follows.[107]

Only by stretching the definition of agrarian reform to its limits can one maintain that there were agrarian reform activities in Chile prior to 1962. There were, however, government agencies operating in the agricultural sector which had a marginal impact on landholding and productivity of the land. Organization of public resources for agrarian reform goals and objectives after 1962 was based, to some degree, on public activities in agriculture prior to 1962.

The 1925 Constitution was the starting point for government intervention into land use and land policy issues in general.[108] Shortly after the adoption of the Constitution, Law No. 4496 was promulgated on December 10, 1928. It created the *Caja de Colonizacion Agricola* (the Agricultural Colonization Bank or Bureau) and assigned it the responsibility of establishing agricultural settlements (*colonias agricolas*) in the Central Valley.[109] Its initial appropriation was one million *pesos*. Although the President was given the power to expropriate the land necessary for the settlements, there is no record of confiscations. The agricul-

tural settlements (colonies) established by the *Caja* benefited immigrants from Europe almost exclusively—the Chilean *campesino* received little of the land in the colonies. As
an indication of the relatively meager results of this effort,
by 1962, the *Caja* had settled only 4,206 colonists.[110]

Another agency of pre-1962 vintage was the *Consejo
de Fomento e Investigaciones Agricolas* (Council of Agricultural Development and Investigation—CONFIN). This
agency was concerned with research and advice to landowners on scientific farming. Though some interesting research
was carried out, little was applied. This agency became the
Instituto de Desarrollo Agropecuario (INDAP) under the
1962 Agrarian Reform Law.

A third agency which was separate from the Ministry
of Agriculture but played a role in agricultural development
is the *Corporacion de Fomento de la Produccion* (the Chilean Development Corporation—CORFO), established in
1939. This agency has been the major channel through
which state funds have been used to promote industrial, and
to a lesser extent, agricultural expansion and promotion.
However, as one INDAP official stated:

> state support is channeled toward big entrepreneurs—dairy
> enterprises and cattle industry—accentuating the effects of
> maldistribution. . . .[111]

In financial terms, from 1960 to 1967 (with a large increase
in 1966–67), CORFO made 217 loans to 90 cooperatives
(large landowner cooperatives) for a total of E° 50.3
million.[112] Total credits extended to CORA by CORFO during 1966–67 equaled E° 286,108.[113] There is little doubt
that CORFO was and is more interested in serving large
landowning interests than in catering to the low-income agricultural owner or worker.

Public responsibilities and activities in the area of
agrarian reform prior to 1962 were limited to piecemeal
colonization by foreigners. Other government or agricultural activities were limited to granting credits and loans to

TABLE IV
AGRARIAN REFORM ACTIVITIES, 1929–1964*

Irrigated Land Distributed (Hectares)	Unirrigated Land Distributed (Hectares)	Total Land Distributed (Hectares)	Total Families Benefited
61,581.17	1,203,575.31	1,265,162.48	4,801 [a]

Source: Corporacion de la Reforma Agraria, *Cuatro Años de Reforma Agraria* (Santiago, Chile: CORA, 1969). This is the most recent publication of the corporation.

* This includes the combined activities of the *Caja de Colonizacion Agricola* (established in 1928) and CORA (established in 1962).

[a] Assuming that CORA's figures are accurate, this means that CORA under Alessandri settled only 595 families. This averages out to about 300 families per year as opposed to the *Caja's* average of about 126 per year as Thiesenhusen notes in *Chile's Experiments in Agrarian Reform, op. cit.*, p. 36.

those individuals who already possessed a substantial portion of material wealth from agricultural pursuits.

The period from the enactment of the 1962 Agrarian Reform Law until the PDC takeover of the presidency can best be described as one of organizational experimentation but limited reform activity. As was mentioned earlier, the 1962 law was an ineffective mechanism for land tenure change. Severe limitations on expropriation and exceedingly high indemnification requirements (including a cash-and-carry provision) prevented any major changes in land tenure from occurring. In fact, according to official Chilean government figures the amount of activity (measured by land acquired and distributed and families benefiting) is incredibly meager.

While concrete achievements were minor, organizational patterns were being developed which would be adopted, with some changes, by the Frei government. The basic organizational structure placed primary responsibilities for agrarian reform activities on two semiautonomous public corporations (INDAP and CORA). Through the 1962 law Alessandri's government was responsible for the conversion of the old *Caja* to CORA, and CONFIN to INDAP. The establishment of CORA and INDAP as entities separate from the Ministry of Agriculture seems to have been motivated by the desire to give an impresson that something was being done to change land tenure patterns and stimulate productivity. Formal separation of INDAP and CORA from the Ministry of Agriculture was maintained, but it was not until the PDC victory in 1964 that personnel differences occurred. The functionaries assigned to CORA and INDAP during the 1962–64 period were either hangers-on from the *Caja* and CONFIN organizations or were from the Ministry of Agriculture. These individuals tended to be politically indifferent or even hostile to low-income agricultural owners or workers. Commenting on the political complexion of agrarian agencies, a CORA officer said:

> operational needs demanded a new corporation. The technical requirements, the specific functions of the agrarian reform depend on new organization for efficiency. There were political requirements as well—the old Radical party and rightists controlled the Ministry of Agriculture. . . .[114]

And even after the PDC victory, rightist influence continued in CORA:

> Technical advisers to CORA recruited from the University are usually from the Right. CORA and the peasants come in conflict with these technical advisers who are under right-wing pressure. . . .[115]

The Alessandri period made one important contribution to organizational structure for agrarian reform. It established CORA and INDAP as semiautonomous public corporations. Although this move might have been motivated by the desire to isolate and control any reform effort, both agencies under Frei initially became centers for attracting the reform-minded left-wing technicians and administrators of the PDC. INDAP under Chonchol and CORA under Moreno were different organizations from the ones established by Alessandri. Although the organizational structure originated during the 1962–64 period, it was not utilized for the purposes of agrarian reform until the early portion of the Frei regime.

> In 1964, CORA was the "status symbol in the revolutionary process." This was the great opportunity to be involved in a change process. This was the symbolic-ideological appeal of the corporation which made it easy to recruit.[116]

In late 1964 the PDC government began to recruit and train personnel to staff the numerous regular and special government agencies. It is difficult to ascertain the magnitude of the personnel turnover. It is apparent, however, that some agencies (in particular those whose functions were more "political" than others—the reform agencies especially) had wholesale changes in administrative, professional, and, to a lesser extent, technical personnel. This large influx of new talent into the reform organizations changed the character as well as the activities of these agencies during the Frei administration. By examining the formal and informal structures of these agencies in some detail we can best understand decision-making (resource allocations), control and supervision, and operations in the field. Both INDAP and CORA will be discussed and where organizational structures are radically different, the particular agency will be designated.

Both INDAP and CORA continued operations under Frei with basically the same formal organizational structure. The traditional Chilean practice of loosely associating public corporations with functional ministries was followed with regard to INDAP and CORA. As one respondent stated: "The Minister of Agriculture lacks the power and cannot intervene in the affairs of CORA (and INDAP) even though (these agencies) are financed through state funds." [117] Hence, although characterized as agencies dealing with agricultural matters, there are no direct links with the Ministry of Agriculture. There are no means by which the

CHART I
Administrative Organization of INDAP[1]
(Santiago)

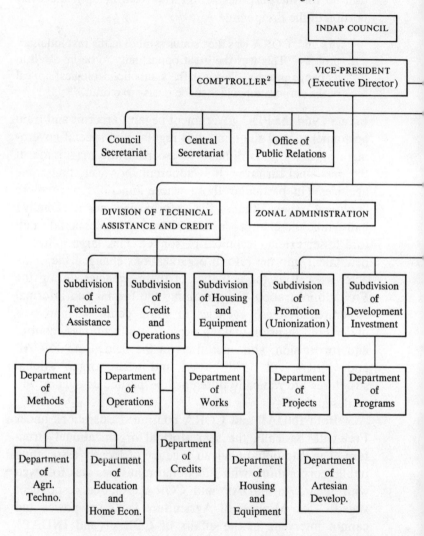

Source: INDAP, "Que es, Como esta organizado, Como actua, Que ha conseguido" (Santiago, Chile: Instituto de Desarrollo Agropecuario, no date), p. 37. Functional equivalents were sought in translating from Spanish to English.

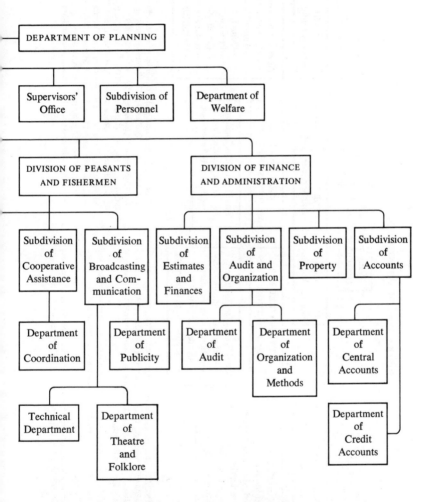

1. Note: This is a translated reproduction of INDAP's formal organization. The authors do not suggest that the hierarchical relationships
   noted graphically above exist in reality. This chart was reproduced
   to illustrate the kinds of functions or divisions INDAP is responsible
   for and is divided into.
2. Includes the Legal Department.

CHART II

ADMINISTRATIVE ORGANIZATION OF INDAP (Field Operations)*

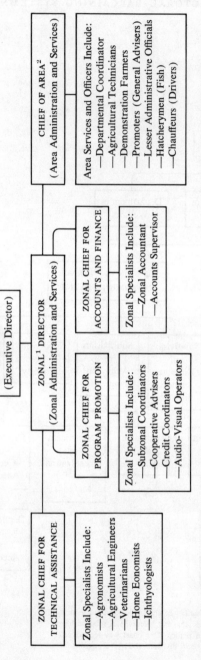

```
                    VICE-PRESIDENT
                    (Executive Director)
                          |
                    ZONAL¹ DIRECTOR
             (Zonal Administration and Services)
```

ZONAL CHIEF FOR TECHNICAL ASSISTANCE

Zonal Specialists Include:
—Agronomists
—Agricultural Engineers
—Veterinarians
—Home Economists
—Ichthyologists

ZONAL CHIEF FOR PROGRAM PROMOTION

Zonal Specialists Include:
—Subzonal Coordinators
—Cooperative Advisers
—Credit Coordinators
—Audio-Visual Operators

ZONAL CHIEF FOR ACCOUNTS AND FINANCE

Zonal Specialists Include:
—Zonal Accountant
—Accounts Supervisor

CHIEF OF AREA²
(Area Administration and Services)

Area Services and Officers Include:
—Departmental Coordinator
—Agricultural Technicians
—Demonstration Farmers
—Promoters (General Advisers)
—Lesser Administrative Officials
—Hatcherymen (Fish)
—Chauffeurs (Drivers)

Source: INDAP, "Que es, Como esta organizado, Como actua, Que ha conseguido" (Santiago, Chile: Instituto de Desarrollo Agropecuario, no date), p. 38. Functional equivalents were sought in translating from Spanish to English.

*See note No. 1 of Chart I. The Chart reveals only one zonal operation and one area. An area generally corresponds to an administrative department.

1. The country is divided into 15 zones. The zones and the provinces they cover and zonal headquarters are: I—Tarapaca and Antofagasta (Arica); II—Atacama and Coquimbo (La Serena); III—Valparaiso and Aconcagua (Quillota); IV—Santiago (Santiago); V—O'Higgins and Colchagua (Rancagua); VI—Curico and Talca (Talca); VII—Maule and Linares (Linares); VIII—Ñuble (Chillan); IX—Concepcion and Arauco (Concepcion); X—Malleco and Bio-Bio (Angol); XI—Cautin (Temuco); XII—Valdivia and Osorno (Valdivia); XIII—Llanquihue and Chiloe (Puerto Montt); XIV—Aysen (Coyhaique); and XV—Magallanes (Punta Arenas).

2. The country is divided into 112 "areas of peasant development."

CHART III

ADMINISTRATIVE ORGANIZATION OF CORA[1] (Santiago)

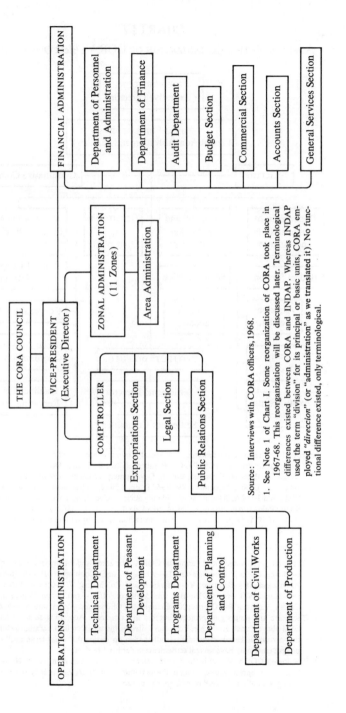

Source: Interviews with CORA officers, 1968.

1. See Note 1 of Chart I. Some reorganization of CORA took place in 1967-68. This reorganization will be discussed later. Terminological differences existed between CORA and INDAP. Whereas INDAP used the term "division" for its principal or basic units, CORA employed *"direccion"* (or "administration" as we translated it). No functional difference existed, only terminological.

CHART IV

Administrative Organization of CORA (Field Operations)*

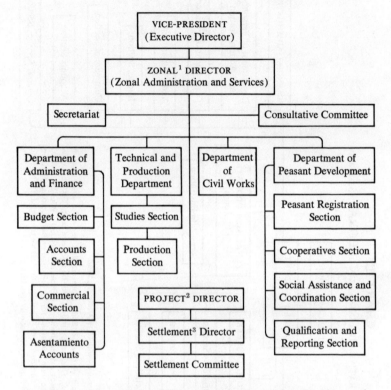

Source: Inter-American Economic and Social Council, Inter-American Committee on the Alliance for Progress (CIAP), CIAP Subcommittee on Chile, "Domestic Efforts and the Needs for External Financing for the Development of Chile" (Washington, D.C.: Pan American Union, September 29, 1967), pp. 124–26; interviews with CORA officers, 1968; and ICIRA, "Organizacion, Planificacion y Coordinacion de las Instituciones del Sector Publico Agricola de Chile, A Nivel de Terreno" (Cuadros Anexos), (Santiago de Chile: ICIRA, Departamento de Administracion en Reforma Agraria, December, 1966), Anexo 17.

*See Note 1 of Chart I.

1. The country is divided into 11 zones by CORA. The zones and the provinces they cover are: I—Tarapaca and Antofagasta; II—Atacama and Coquimbo; III—Valparaiso and Aconacgua; IV—Santiago; V—O'Higgins and Colchaqua; VI—Curico, Talca, Linares, and Maule; VII—Ñuble, Bio-Bio, and Malleco; VIII—Arauco and Concepcion; IX—Cautin, Valdivia, and Osorno; X—Llanquihue, Chiloe, and Aysen; and XI—Magallanes.
2. There are any number of project directors in each zone. According to the CIAP report cited above, "each zone chief (director) divides his territory into agrarian reform areas; this division is based on functional rather than on geographic considerations," p. 125. A project chief may have several settlements under his direction.
3. The lowest CORA official is the *Jefe de Asentamiento* or settlement chief. He is CORA's permanent representative, living in the settlement "and working on daily realization of its plan of operations." CIAP report, *op. cit.*, p. 125.

TABLE V

COMPARISON OF REFORM ZONES OF INDAP AND CORA

REFORM ZONE	INDAP (Provinces Included)	CORA (Provinces Included)	REFORM ZONE
I	Tarapaca and Antofagasta	Tarapaca and Antofagasta	I
II	Atacama and Coquimbo	Atacama and Coquimbo	II
III	Valparaiso and Aconcagua	Valparaiso and Aconcagua	III
IV	Santiago	Santiago	IV
V	O'Higgins and Colchagua	O'Higgins and Colchagua	V
VI	Curico and Talca	Curico, Talca, Linares and Maule	VI
VII	Maule and Linares	Ñuble, Bio-Bio, and Malleco	VII
VIII	Ñuble	Arauco and Concepcion	VIII
IX	Concepcion and Arauco	Cautin, Valdivia, and Osorno	IX
X	Malleco and Bio-Bio	Llanguihue, Chiloe, and Aysen	X
XI	Cautin	Magallanes	XI
XII	Valdivia and Osorno		
XIII	Llanguihue and Chiloe		
XIV	Aysen		
XV	Magallanes		

Source: Composite, see sources for Charts I, II, III, and IV.

policies and operations of either INDAP or CORA are visibly influenced by this ministry or its subsidiary departments.[118]

In addition to this separation from traditional line agencies, both INDAP and CORA were governed by a council (or board of directors) having appointed and *ex officio* members. However, from all the evidence, it appears that the vice-presidents (executive directors) of both

INDAP and CORA had relatively free rein over their agencies, the boards merely legitimizing the actions of the vice-presidents.[119] Unlike other public corporation boards where the board members have functional responsibilities vis-a-vis corporation operations, the vice-president (of both CORA and INDAP) combines the powers of board chairman with those of general manager. Hence, for example, in personnel management, the vice-president exercises the power to appoint everyone down to the fifth or sixth hierarchical level of the corporation—virtually every functionary above the office of section chief must "enjoy the confidence" of the vice-president.[120] Although a formal level (the board) exists between the President of the Republic and the vice-president (of CORA or INDAP), there is virtually no barrier to direct communications between them. Internal structure is reflected in Charts I–IV (pages 170–174).

An obvious conclusion drawn from examining these charts is that both agencies have incredibly complex sets of internal organizational relationships and appear, in many respects, to be engaged in many of the same kinds of activities and services for virtually the same clientele.[121] Both formal organizations (or administrative structures) appear cumbersome. The pivotal position in the hierarchies of both organizations is that of vice-president. The vice-president operates independently from the agency's council in reality if not legally or theoretically. His powers of appointment are large; this was evidenced from information derived from interviews as well as public documents.[122] The extent to which the vice-president of either agency can use or has used his powers to stress one or more aspects of both agencies' operations was in evidence. Hence, the vice-president can selectively use portions of his organization almost at will to effect change if he possesses capable subordinates, or he can choose to use these complex structures to obfuscate operations and activities so as to create the illusion of action. Examples of both kinds of organizational uses were observable in the agencies studied.

The formal administrative structures of both agencies reveal that a considerable administrative "investment" was made in offices and personnel (and also equipment located within the metropolitan limits of Greater Santiago). Even though both agencies' major activities were to take place in the countryside, control and organizational resource allocation (decision-making) tended to remain centralized, although perhaps not to the degree dictated by Chilean or, for that matter, Latin American administrative traditions.[123] According to one source:

> To facilitate planning and control of farming activities in the settlements (*asentamientos* and colonies), CORA has established a decentralized institutional organization that divides the country into . . . zones, each headed by a zone chief who is the maximum local authority of the Corporacion.[124]

Yet, six months after the above statement was made, the Director of the Planning and Control Administration of CORA stated that planning at the lower levels occurs only *"after* the framework of the annual program is received by these (lower) levels," and that the framework is devised by his office in Santiago.[125] He went on to describe the planning process and some of the problems CORA has encountered:

> (after the planning framework has been established by Santiago) plans are then filled in by CORA's zonal people —that is, the technicians, administrators, and *asentamiento* chiefs. Then this (completed) plan is sent for approval (back up the hierarchy) to the chiefs of the zones. Then it is sent to the Planning and Control Administration (Santiago). Then (if approved at all these levels) it is sent to the Vice-President (for his approval) and the process (implementation of plan) is reversed.

This official stated that in 1967, CORA attempted a limited amount of social planning in the countryside in which peasants were involved, prior to the December budgetary submission deadline, but it was not successful. The conclusion, he implied, was that Santiago "could do it better." He noted, however, that "more autonomy" should be permitted at the zonal level to "streamline operations." [126] Although landless and other low-income peasants (*asendados, colonos,* and others being assisted by the government) are the target groups for services, attempts to include their representatives in decisions fundamental to long-range operations (planning and budgeting) have been limited. The CORA official readily admitted these attempts have been unsuccessful from CORA's standpoint. The operations of CORA and INDAP tend to remain in the hands of reform-minded middle-class urban professionals and technicians rather than a coalition of peasant-derived and urban-based leadership or entirely peasant-based, peasant-led leadership. Overcentralization and limited if any participation of clientele (peasants) in decision-making are not the pure products of formal organization structure. Both organizational characteristics have been influenced by informal organization.

In describing, discussing, and analyzing the operations of both CORA and INDAP, one is repeatedly drawn toward the vice-presidents or executive directors of both agencies. In this regard both agencies reveal the particular Chilean (and Latin American) characteristics of executive centralization of decisions (absence of authority delegation) and a stress upon "political reliability." These characteristics are not unique to Chilean or Latin American bureaucracies. Their presence in the agrarian reform agencies, however, tends to diminish the claims of reform promoters that the operations of these agencies are technical or apolitical. This is not surprising as both agencies operate within the constraints of a highly politicized situation. Given the amount of pressure or hostility vested interests and government agents in the field displayed toward INDAP and, to a lesser extent, CORA officials, the vice-presidents' complete support or knowledge of even limited operations was often vital for their success.[127] Political reliability is a rather obvious qualification because of the highly charged political atmosphere and the history of past reform efforts. However, absence of discretionary power has limited speed with which field officials could act.

Control and strict supervision emanating from the executive director's office has meant that both agencies have stressed certain policies and goals above others which were mandated by the 1962 and 1967 laws. The broad range of vice-presidential powers permitted Chonchol to use his director of operations (Nicoli Gligo) as a sort of general manager for INDAP internal operations, while he himself handled the coordination of INDAP's external relations with CORA and other executive branch agencies.[128] The Chonchol-Gligo emphasis was one of peasant mobilization first—other program goals received secondary emphasis. According to Gligo:

> Peasant promotion is our basic work. It involves us in economic as well as social activity. We organize trade unions to promote social development. Our activity in the area of creating infrastructure is marginal compared to peasant promotion. . . . The success of the agrarian reform depends on broad political and economic changes. . . .[129]

Hence, because of executive decisions taken by Chonchol and his immediate advisers INDAP concentrated on unionizing peasants. INDAP's objectives officially covered such "infrastructure" activities as credit extension, technical advice and assistance (agricultural, administrative, and other) housing, and craft development. However, political mobilization and political organization were primary goals of INDAP's efforts. INDAP was organizing peasants in all zones of agrarian reform, partly in competition with other Christian Democrats and Marxists engaged in the same activity. Policy and goal formation in INDAP was a centralized activity; implementation of goals through the attempt to meet certain targets may have had a decentralized character.[130] CORA's policies and goals were not less "political" than INDAP's—although CORA's operations were more cautious. By 1968 CORA's expropriation and family resettlement achievements were meager compared to the original goals. Despite the slow start, some CORA officials were under the impression that rapid changes had been achieved. One CORA official stated that:

> In the beginning CORA needed imagination, speed of operations, creativity, innovation, etc. Now, the process of routinization is most important. Some order to organization chaos is needed.[131]

CORA essentially followed a policy of attempting to reform without directly confronting the existing power holders. CORA moved into areas only where owners showed their incapacity to manage the social and economic problems of their farms, or where social conflict became intense. Legal expropriation was permitted for poorly exploited land but little actual expropriation occurred. CORA's stress on productivity inhibited it from large-scale expropriation proceedings. CORA feared the social dislocation that initially results from large-scale tenure change. According to several sources, CORA's concentration on productivity of land led to the abandonment of structural reform (land tenure reform) long before the final PDC-leftist split in late 1968.[132]

This more cautious, "pragmatic" approach to agrarian reform implementation which characterized CORA's operations can be seen in almost all levels and areas of the corporation's activities. To illustrate this cautious pragmatism, an example from the Legal Division is useful. CORA's lawyers played an important role in drafting the 1967 Agrarian Reform Law and advising the President on the constitutional issues associated with government intervention into land use. Likewise, in terms of implementation of the provisions of this law or its predecessor, the Legal Division of CORA was in the forefront. CORA's lawyers brought suits against landowners and fought cases to expedite the slow process of expropriation. However, at the same time that court suits brought by CORA gave the illusion that change was occurring rapidly, CORA lawyers maintained that the corporation "must be careful" in "this business of expropriation." Agricultural efficiency was cited as the criterion for agrarian reform. Economic criteria were given priority over social justice. According to CORA's highest legal officer:

> From the legal aspect, you cannot have a law with priorities —but CORA can establish priorities in expropriation (through implementation of the law). The most important priority is the worst worked *fundos* (bad owners) not the worst land. Furthermore, the corporation should have a mix of priorities. The aim is for greater agricultural efficiency. Therefore, we need to be very selective in expropriating. We must realize that we lose in terms of economies of scale but must not penalize efficient and good *fundo* owners. . . . We must be selective and careful in choosing expropriation priorities.[133]

CORA's operations, much more so than INDAP's, tend to coincide with Frei's centrist position. The formation of general policy guidelines and the operationalization of these policies were influenced by external and internal politics. Comparing the two agencies, CORA was much more in tune with the "political realities" as interpreted by Frei and other right-of-center PDC officials. INDAP, however, deviated from the Frei position by confronting the PDC right-of-center officials in the field (organizing peasants on all farms including PDC-owned *fundos*). The reorganization of CORA illustrates the difference between this agency and INDAP. The following charts reveal the reorganization of CORA Santiago and CORA Field Operations.

Basically, CORA's reorganization involved both Santiago and field operations. In Santiago, the original two *direcciones* (divisions or, as we have translated the term, administration), Finances and Operations, and part of the *Fiscalia* (Comptroller) were expanded into five *direcciones* (excluding Zonal Administration) which include Planning and Control, Organization and Finance, Technical, Legal, and

Production.[134] One reason offered for this proliferation or expansion of "supercargo" at this level was that the old structure was impossible to coordinate.[135] Reorganizing field oper ations did not increase services but rather formally recentralized services away from the lowest administrative unit in the structure (settlement director's office) to the zonal director's office and staff—two levels higher. Specifically, all technical services (including extension), infrastructural development, finance (budget, audits, and accounting), and many services to peasants (credit extension, etc.) except education and some "social welfare" type activities were reassigned from the settlement level to the zonal level. Even though the settlement director is CORA's link with the peasants, these responsibilities (according to one informant) made for an "impossible job even for better educated, trained, and paid official(s)." [136] The considered opinion of CORA higher authorities was that after three years of operations (1964–1967), the *jefe del asentamiento* (settlement director)[137]—the "critical link" between CORA and the peasant—could not accomplish CORA's assignments. In reality, CORA's collective assessment of the settlement directors' performance was probably accurate; however, the pretense of a "decentralized administrative structure" should not be maintained to describe CORA's organization. Even with the so-called "zonal autonomy move" which was the official description of the reorganization, CORA technicians and other program personnel receive their instructions, at least in part, from the *direcciones* in Santiago as well as the particular zonal directors assigned to direct the area. Hence, in effect, CORA's "decentralized administrative structure" remained highly centralized and even more complex (in regard to lines of authority and areas of responsibilities) after reorganization. Actually, CORA had recentralized formally many powers, responsibilities, and functions it had assigned previously to field personnel.

One further note is needed on the significance of ad-

CHART V

ADMINISTRATIVE REORGANIZATION OF CORA
(Santiago)

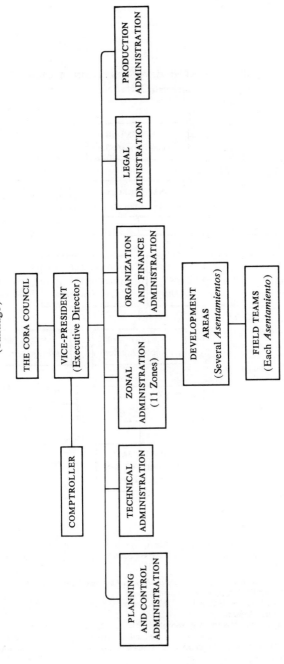

Source: Combined sources included: CORA, *Cuatro Años de Reforma Agraria* (Santiago de Chile: Corporacion de la Reforma Agraria, 1968); and interviews with various CORA officers.

CHART VI
ADMINISTRATIVE REORGANIZATION OF CORA
(Field Operations)

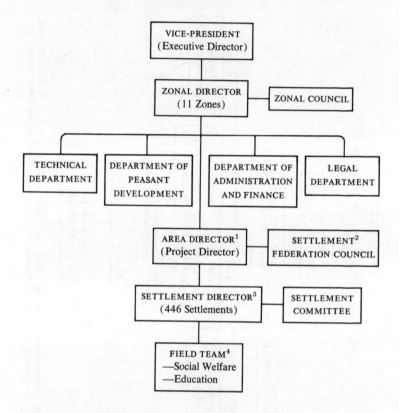

Source: Combined sources included: CORA, *Cuatro Años de Reforma Agraria* (Santiago de Chile: Corporacion de la Reforma Agraria, 1968); and interviews with various CORA officers.

1. Number of areas is not known. One estimate would be slightly more than 100.
2. Settlement is English equivalent of *asentamiento*.
3. CORA's estimate as of June, 1968. This is 180 more than earlier 1968 figures. See last section of this chapter.
4. According to the director of Personnel, CORA, "...organizational reshuffle has eliminated all (of the settlement director's) responsibilities except social welfare and rural education. Other services/functions were handled at higher levels." Interview with Hernan Vera, *op. cit.*

ministrative reorganization of CORA in the context of problems the two agrarian reform agencies faced in the late 1960s. The ICIRA document[138] stressed administrative reform (through reorganization) of both INDAP and CORA (as well as SEAM, SAG, CORFO, ECA, and the *Banco del Estado*) as a solution to agrarian sector problems. The idea was that such reorganization would facilitate and streamline government operations and, hence, achieve government goals. The inability of CORA and INDAP to move quickly in the areas designated for reform was viewed more or less in mechanical, technical, and apolitical terms. The idea was that by improving the administrative structure through rational reorganization and operations reform would be accelerated. Reorganization of CORA did occur, perhaps not exactly along the lines suggested by the ICIRA report, without speeding up the reform effort. If anything, *less* expropriation occurred *after* reorganization (although cause and effect is not suggested here). INDAP, on the other hand, continued to move in the area of unionization—efforts that decreased only after Chonchol's departure. One conclusion that may be drawn from these experiences is that in the late 1960s, if CORA was to increase the pace of reform, the reorganization required was not necessarily in the realm of administrative structure, but in the policy and program development areas. Increased emphasis should have been placed on making a greater impact on existing peasant conditions. By 1967–68, the cautious, "pragmatic" policy and consequent program development and implementation of CORA was not achieving structural reform.

Our examination of administrative structure so far has revealed that the manner in which services to the agrarian sector were organized permitted the President and high right-of-center supporters to indirectly hamper structural reform by pitting competing government agencies against each other. There were at least seven agencies[139] directly involved in providing services to the three distinct categories of agrarian clientele (large landowners, middle-sized landowners, and low-income rural inhabitants) and competing unequally for their share of the *escudos* to be expended in the agrarian sector. This fact underscores how organization or administrative structure could be used to subvert rather than support structural reform. This proliferation of agencies serving different agrarian clienteles coupled with policy and program differences which existed between the two main servicers of the low-income rural inhabitant (INDAP and CORA) meant that no coordinated government efforts could be exerted. This was true even if funds and personnel were earmarked for the low-income rural inhabitant. The decision to divide agrarian reform services between one agency to implement expropriation and farm administration, and another agency to implement other services related to some notion of reform (training, socio-economic organization and mobilization, etc.) [140] may be seen as partial acceptance of the previous regime's ideological hostility toward rapid structural change. A government interested in major rural reform would have merged CORA and INDAP into one agency with funds specifically earmarked for expropriation, farm administration, technical assistance, peasant promotion (socio-economic as well as political mobilization), and credit (as well as other services). Instead, the administrative strategy of the Frei government called for a continuation of an administrative structure which dispersed and diluted authority and responsibility in the area of agrarian reform. Hence, when INDAP's reform-oriented programs or activities began to "outpace" the desires of the more conservative but important backers of the PDC, control was re-asserted over these programs through the bureaucratic apparatus itself. This uncoordinated agrarian reform program which depended upon several bureaucratic agencies (but especially INDAP and CORA) dispersed administrative structure, diluted responsibilities for servicing the agrarian sector, and permitted the conservative elements of the PDC to intervene directly in the implementation process.

Personnel or the human resources committed to public endeavors have often been cited as a factor crucial to the success of such operations. Although exact figures were not available, a reasonable estimate of the total personnel available to both CORA and INDAP operations was around 3,000 or about 1.0 percent of the Chilean bureaucracy.[141] The exact size of CORA-INDAP manpower resources is unknown; for example, the personnel director of CORA estimated CORA's personnel cadre at between 1,500 and 1,600 while CORA documents of the same period placed total personnel at 1,464.[142] Regardless, CORA-INDAP manpower represents the total contribution of the Frei government to its campaign for uplifting the peasant.

Manpower sources for the CORA-INDAP complex differed from other bureaucratic agencies in terms of ideology and age but not in social background. Recruitment was mostly from the universities and not from existing government agencies. In fact, few individuals were recruited for CORA from the established ministries (such as Agriculture) since such individuals tended to be hostile to the goals of agrarian reform.[143] A striking characteristic of the CORA personnel cadre (a characteristic seemingly shared by INDAP's cadre as well) was the youthful nature of these reformers. About 50 percent of CORA's total employment were between twenty-five and thirty years of age. Even upper-level staff (those above the 5 to 6 level) were younger than their counterparts in other government agencies.[144] Unlike the technicians and administrators found in the older public agrarian sector organizations (the Ministry of Agriculture, SAG, that part of CORFO dealing with agriculture, and others), CORA-INDAP personnel were, on the whole, the sons and daughters of middle-class urban dwellers instead of the sons and daughters of the large landowners.[145] Youth, university-to-government service recruitment, and urban origins characterized the personnel attracted to CORA and INDAP during the early years of the Frei administration.

According to some sources, the urban nature of the reform agencies' personnel had certain advantages, including: (1) educational preparedness (at the lower bureaucratic levels primarily); and (2) no "vested interest" in the agrarian status quo and status hierarchy. The CORA-INDAP functionaries were "new" people, not known in the agrarian reform zones, and hence, in theory, not suspect by the peasants. Admittedly, there were several disadvantages, including: (1) urban CORA-INDAP functionaries had different values from rural dwellers; (2) communication was difficult as a result of cultural differences; (3) lack of roots in rural areas accentuated the physical, cultural, and social hardships of rural life for these functionaries.[146] Despite the difficulties surrounding employment in rural areas for the average university graduate, it was not until 1968–69 that recruitment in CORA-INDAP began to wane. There were two primary reasons offered by applicants for wanting to join CORA: (1) symbolic political appeal of being involved in the process of change—Frei's "Revolution in Liberty"; and (2) early salaries were higher than those in other government agencies. From 1964 until 1966, salaries for all functionaries in CORA and INDAP were quite good. In 1966 due largely to budget cuts and inflation, a great leveling off occurred. According to salary surveys in late 1968, CORA's technical salary levels had remained unchanged. By 1968 salaries of technicians and general administrators were rated only "fair," salaries for lawyers were rated "low" and "fair" respectively.[147] As a result there was considerable fear that CORA and INDAP were in a very precarious recruiting position vis-a-vis other public agencies. In other words, although material rewards were secondary criteria for recruitment in 1964, by 1968 they were replacing the "symbolic-political" reason; reform, it was feared, could not be implemented by functionaries symbolically rich but materially destitute.

Recruitment procedures employed by both agencies conformed to those which prevailed for other Chilean agencies. Standardized examinations were given for initial selection and for promotion from one level to another. The first major job of the Department of Personnel in 1964 was recruitment since CORA's turnover rate in 1964–65 approached 75 percent.[148] Some 400 functionaries who retained their positions after Frei's ascent to power were, for the most part, technicians—individuals who possessed skills in great demand but in limited supply. The major source of conservative pressure within the CORA organization was from leftover technical personnel. Many technical advisers to CORA throughout the Frei period tended to identify ideologically and politically with the Chilean Right (PR, PL, PCU, as well as the right wing of the PDC).[149] Thus from the point of view of successful implementation, the need to recruit functionaries with the "proper" political credentials was an absolute necessity. It was evident, however, that because of the reform agencies' technical manpower needs, they had to retain and recruit individuals whose political affiliations were not completely in tune with the reform character of the agencies. This requisite for technical competence may have been a critical factor in the policy formation and program development phases of both agencies' operations. However, technical feasibility or "practicability" is often a convenient argument used by the technician to reject policies or programs that he does not find acceptable politically or ideologically.[150]

Before leaving the subject of reform personnel, Tables VI and VII will be presented and discussed.

The predominance of professional and technical personnel reveals the complex nature of the attempted reform. A total of 1,464 officials (less if one subtracts the manual labor component) is supposed to serve a clientele of over 300,000 peasant families. This indicates the inadequate manpower resources devoted to the reform. Even if one used the Frei target figure of 100,000 peasant families, the functionary-family ratio would be about 70 to 1. Given the manpower resources devoted to CORA's operations it is ob-

TABLE VI

CORA Personnel as of June, 1968

Occupational Speciality or Position		Number	Percentage of Total
I PROFESSIONALS AND TECHNICIANS		897	61.2
—Agronomists	108		
—Foresters	6		
—Veterinarians	5		
—Agricultural Technicians	37		
—Forest Technicians	4		
—Forestrymen	10		
—Farmers	233		
—Civil Engineers	29		
—Architects	14		
—Contractors (Builders)	34		
—Topographers and Map Makers	34		
—Draftsmen	12		
—Lawyers	60		
—Auditors	9		
—Accountants	60		
—Sociologists	6		
—Educators	12		
—Social Workers	18		
—Home Economists	6		
—Cooperative Advisers	14		
—Other Professionals	18		
—Other Technicians	48		
—Personnel with Technical Experience	89		
—Others	31		
II ADMINISTRATORS		414	28.2
III SERVANTS (Manual Labor)		153	10.6
TOTALS		1,464	100.0

Source: CORA, *Cuatro Años de Reforma Agraria, op. cit.,* p. 13.

vious that it could not begin to perform its assigned responsibilities effectively. Even the combined resources of CORA and INDAP could not meet the early targets of the PDC government in agrarian reform. In addition to the insufficient supply of manpower for CORA-INDAP, the lack of financial support was another major obstacle to reform.

Finance was viewed as the critical element for reform implementation from the beginning of CORA-INDAP operations in 1965. According to one report:

> The sizable financial resources required to meet the goals of the agrarian reform program represented the major factor of limitation. . . . The agrarian reform program begun by the government in 1965 . . . has experienced a decline in progress because of financial problems. . . . The financial limitations have brought about the reformulation of goals.[151]

The financial needs of both INDAP and CORA were related to the number of peasant families to be serviced. For CORA, the number of families to be serviced was especially important because of its direct involvement in expropriation and settlement of peasants on the land. Let us examine these costs and estimates of cost as a prelude to a discussion of financial administration.

In 1964, Frei promised to settle 100,000 *campesino*

TABLE VII

FOREIGN TRAINING RECEIVED BY CORA PERSONNEL

SUBJECTS	NO. OF PERSONS TRAINED
Rural Development	15
Agricultural Planning	9
Cooperative Development	8
Rural Administration	5
Agricultural Commercialization	5
Peasant Education	4
Agricultural Techniques	4
Financial Administration	4
Rural Engineering Project Design	4
TOTALS	58

Source: CORA, *Cuatro Años de Reforma Agraria, op. cit.,* p. 14.

families on expropriated land during the period 1965–70. This figure was roughly a little less than one-third of the total landless or land-poor peasantry. Almost immediately, CORA encountered several difficulties.[152] Program revision including the formulation of new goals occurred toward the end of 1966. In October, 1966, the Minister of the Interior stated that the government had reduced its earlier goal from 100,000 to between 40,000 and 60,000 families.[153] Accompanying this goal revision was the estimation of total costs. CORA estimated that it cost about U.S. $18,000 to settle one family—55,000 families would amount to almost E° 2.12 billion (or U.S. $353.3 million) at 1967 prices.[154] Based on the 55,000 family target, CORA provided the cost estimates to the CIAP subcommittee (see Table VIII).

Table VIII reveals the sources of public financing for land tenure change. Of the $353.3 million cost, Chilean internal sources would provide $112.6 million or only about 31.6 percent. The balance ($240.6 million or about 68.1 percent) which was over two-thirds of the total had to be financed from non-Chilean sources. CORA's estimates of its ability to self-finance its operations were premised on an 80 percent recovery on loans provided as working capital to new owners. The CIAP report, however, pointed out that "historical figures on recovery of loans to settlements (under the 1962 law) show(ed) a level of 25 percent." [155] There is no evidence that the recovery rate improved substantially after 1967.

Tables IX, X and XI show CORA's sources of income expenditures and appropriations in relation to other agency appropriations.

Table IX reveals the extent to which CORA has failed to become "self-financing." [156] In terms of administrative goals for the agency many CORA officers that we interviewed gave self-financing a high priority. They felt that as long as the corporation was heavily dependent upon the good will of congressional sources, its autonomy of action was threatened.[157] Regardless of the agency's desires to be-

TABLE VIII

ESTIMATED* COSTS OF AGRARIAN REFORM ACTIVITIES, 1967–1970

(in millions of E° of 1967)

Year	Number of Families (in thousands)	Payment for Land Expropriations	Infrastructure Works	Working Capital	Other Capital Expenses	Total [a] Capital Expenses	Total Current Expenses	Grand Total	Amortizations	Loan Recoveries	Banco del Estado Credit and Others	Total [b] Self-Financing	Financing [c] Requirements
1967	10	33.0	50.7	124.3	37.4	245.4	49.4	294.9	—	21.3	31.1	52.4	242.5
1968	12	34.0	56.2	210.9	44.9	346.8	79.5	426.3	6.0	63.9	45.3	115.3	311.0
1969	15	49.5	89.8	319.1	56.1	514.5	100.0	614.5	11.2	118.1	67.9	197.3	417.2
1970	18	66.3	110.0	418.7	67.3	662.3	122.0	784.3	35.7	184.5	90.6	310.7	473.3
TOTAL FOR PERIOD	55	183.6	306.7	1,073.0	205.7	1,769.0	350.9	2,120.0	52.9	387.8	234.9	675.7	1,444.0

Source: CIAP, op. cit., p. 131. These figures were supplied by CORA. The Escudo-Dollar ratio was about 6:1.

* Some totals may be more than the simple sum. This is due to CORA's rounding-off of figures.

a Total Capital Expenses equals Payment for Land Expropriations (E°183.6) plus Infrastructure Works (E°306.7) plus Working Capital (E°1,073.0) plus Other Capital Expenses (E°205.7); approximately U.S. $284.7 million.

b Total Self-Financing equals Amortizations (E°52.9) plus Loan Recoveries (E°184.5) plus Banco del Estado Credit and Others (E°234.9); approximately U.S. $112.6 million.

c Financing Requirements equals Grand Total (E°2,120.0) minus Total Self-Financing (E°675.7); approximately U.S. $240.6 million.

TABLE IX

CORA's Financial Sources, 1965–1968
(in millions of Escudos)

SOURCES OF INCOME	1965 AMOUNT	%	1966 AMOUNT	%	1967 AMOUNT	%	1968 AMOUNT	%	FOUR-YEAR TOTALS AMOUNT	%
Appropriations	69.1	86.0	131.0	84.0	178.7	70.2	189.5	45.5	568.3	62.6
Properties	6.5	8.1	18.4	11.8	40.7	16.0	92.6	22.2	158.2	17.3
Foreign Credits	4.8	5.9	6.4	4.1	7.3	2.9	36.6	8.8	55.1	6.0
National Credits	—	—	0.1	0.1	27.7	10.9	98.0	23.5	125.8	14.1
TOTALS	80.3	100.0	155.9	100.0	254.4	100.0	416.7	100.0	907.4	100.0

Source: CORA, *Cuatro Años de Reforma Agraria, op. cit.,* p. 18. Four-year totals were added to original table.

TABLE X

CORA's Investments and Expenditures, 1965–1968

(in millions of Escudos)

CATEGORY	1965 AMOUNT	1965 %	1966 AMOUNT	1966 %	1967 AMOUNT	1967 %	1968 AMOUNT	1968 %	FOUR-YEAR TOTALS AMOUNT	%
A. PRODUCTION OF GOODS & SERVICES										
Technical & Credit Assistance to Settlements	24.9	31.0	73.0	46.8	126.7	49.8	268.0	64.3	492.6	54.2
Infrastructure & Constructions	13.7	17.1	26.2	16.8	37.1	14.6	49.8	11.9	126.8	13.9
Credit Assistance to Cooperatives	7.0	8.7	7.5	4.8	12.7	5.0	6.5	1.6	33.7	3.7
Peasant Development	1.8	2.2	7.6	4.9	12.8	5.0	19.5	4.7	41.7	4.6
Other Investments	5.3	6.6	6.9	4.4	12.1	4.7	1.8	0.5	26.1	2.9
SUBTOTALS	52.7	65.6	121.2	77.7	201.4	79.1	345.6	82.9	720.9	79.4
B. LAND PURCHASES	10.3	12.8	15.5	10.0	29.7	11.7	46.5	11.2	102.0	11.2
C. ADMINISTRATIVE COSTS	17.3	21.6	19.2	12.3	23.3	9.2	24.5	5.9	84.3	9.2
TOTALS	80.3	100.0	155.9	100.0	254.4	100.0	416.6	100.0	907.2	100.0

Source: CORA, *Cuatro Años de Reforma Agraria, op. cit.,* p. 21. Four-year totals were added to original table.

TABLE XI

SELECTED PUBLIC SECTOR APPROPRIATIONS BY FUNCTION, 1967

(in millions of Escudos)

SECTOR OR AGENCY	APPROPRIATION	PERCENT OF TOTAL
Education	1,174.2	25.4
Health, Social Security and Social Assistance	608.1	13.1
Housing and Urban Affairs	512.0	11.0
Defense	681.1	14.7
Transportation and Communications	1,056.4	22.8
Agriculture	446.6	9.6
Agrarian Reform Corporation (CORA)	141.8	3.0
TOTALS[a]	4,620.2	99.6

Source: CORA, *Cuatro Años de Reforma Agraria, op. cit.,* p. 21.

[a] These are not all the parliamentary appropriations for 1967; they do, however, illustrate the relative position of the agrarian reform program vis-a-vis government appropriations. Even with INDAP's appropriation included in the reform appropriation, agrarian reform would still remain the lowest funded set of activities in comparison with this select list.

come self-financing, as of 1968, the major source of income remained government appropriations.[158] Furthermore, although income from properties was slowly increasing at a rate of about 5 to 7 percent per year, income from internal credit extension (private banks primarily) was growing at a faster rate than the property resource income. CORA's investment income, such as it was, was not increasing at a rate which would assure self-financing. Financial aid was largely dependent on the good faith of the private investor.

In addition, the hopes for external financing never materialized. In the first four years of the reform, external credit extension or investment never achieved a level of 10 percent, nowhere near the level hoped or asked for.

Finally, considerable doubt still remains with regard to loan recoveries from the settlers, cooperative members, and small farmers. CORA's reporting does not separate these recoveries from the total properties income item so that one cannot ascertain the extent to which CORA is being paid back for credit and other loan extensions. ICIRA[159] personnel connected with the credit extension operation expressed serious doubts about the advisability of CORA's or INDAP's depending very extensively upon this source of income.

In short, it appears that CORA (and INDAP) will not be self-financing by 1970 although reliance upon government appropriation may be reduced. In conjunction with this reduction, however, there has been a service reduction in the reform goals.

As Table X indicates, CORA funds have gone increasingly over the four-year period toward the "production of goods and services" category. This includes everything from technical and credit extensions and assistance for settlements to the vague subcategory of "other investments" (percentage-wise), 65.6 percent to 82.9 percent from 1965 through 1968. On the other hand, CORA's expenditures for land have actually *decreased* in relative terms so that the four-year average as a percentage of total expenditures is *less* than what was spent during the first year. The CIAP report stated that to attain the goal of settling between 40,000 to 60,000 peasant families in the 1965 to 1970 period, CORA would have to secure an area of between 400,000 to 600,000 hectares of irrigated land (more if un-irrigated) which would represent between 15 and 24 percent of all arable land in Chile.[160] CORA has no hope of reaching the minimum figure by 1970 yet it continued to *reduce* its expenditures for land and, hence, its acquisition of land for new settlements.

The reduction of general administration costs was heralded as a major savings by the corporation. This may be true to a certain extent; however, part of the reduced costs are attributable to a policy of nonreplacement of personnel necessary for settlements. Although figures for INDAP were not available, the hiring "freeze" involved almost 10 percent of its manpower.[161]

Although INDAP's appropriation for the same year

was not known, a good guess would place it somewhat below CORA's. Therefore, if one combined both agencies' appropriations, one would discover that together they would not equal the agriculture appropriation—a government financial allocation almost entirely spent on upper- and middle-class landowners. In fact, the agriculture appropriation listed in Table XI may not reflect the entire allocation for large landowners since CORFO's appropriation (and certainly not its total expenditures) may or may not be reported here. In short, Table XI reinforces the hypothesis formulated earlier—that government support in terms of finance has been less than generous, and in fact, less than the support given the already financially secure large landowners.

Before leaving the subject of reform financing, it is important to compare what CORA and its foreign advisers felt should be an effective financial program designed to attain the modest goal of between 40,000 and 60,000 new settlers and what, in fact, was made available from all sources for reform activities. Although complete time series data were not available, we do have four years of expenditure figures and four years of estimated financial needs. Overlap of these two time periods (1965–1968 for actual expenditure and 1967–1970 for estimated need) does occur so that at least trends in terms of the difference between estimated need and actual expenditure may be discerned.[162] The comparison between the estimates and the actual expenditures can be seen in Table XII.

The only category in which CORA spent more than it estimated earlier was in land purchases—but this is not an indicator of sound finance since it largely represented overpayment for land (some E° 9.2 million for both years combined) and did not secure more land for redistribution but really *less;* more funds had to be expended to purchase less land.[163] In all other categories, CORA had fewer funds available than were estimated for the proper servicing of the settlers. In short, lack of funds crippled CORA's modest effort

TABLE XII

A Comparison of CORA's Estimated Financial Needs with Actual Expenditures, 1967–68*

(in millions of Escudos)

CATEGORY	ESTIMATED (1967)	ACTUAL	DIFFERENCE[a]	ESTIMATED (1968)	ACTUAL	DIFFERENCE[a]
Land Purchases[b]	33.0	29.7	− 3.3	34.0	46.5	+12.5
Goods and Services						
—Infrastructure	50.7	37.1	−13.6	56.2	49.8	− 6.4
—Other	211.1	187.6	−23.5	335.3	320.3	−15.0
TOTALS	294.8	254.4	−40.4	425.5	416.6	− 8.9

Source: Raw data for Tables VIII and X.
* What Table XII reveals is the basic financial problems of CORA in aggregate terms. The two years are good indicators of financial problems since they represent neither the beginning nor the end of the Frei period. Rather, reform efforts had been under way since 1965 and would continue (largely in name only) until 1970.
[a] Difference between estimated and actual expenditure.
[b] Based on goal of settling 55,000 families during Frei administration (1965–70). By the middle of 1968, CORA officers privately admitted that at best only 27,000 to 30,000 families could be settled by 1970. Interview with Fernando Yrarrazaval, finance director, CORA, June 18, 1968. However, as the next section will reveal, even this modest target will not be attained.

at resettlement. Rather than attaining a target of settling one-third of the poor peasants on expropriated land, CORA could only settle less than one-tenth!

Measuring the Reform Effort: Social, Economic, and Political Development

Measuring the efforts of Chilean agrarian reformers over the past six years is difficult because of data constraints and the inability to foresee the future. What we can do is point to the deficiencies and advances made by those individuals interested in structural change in the countryside who have used Chile as their laboratory for change efforts.

Many failings in the Chilean effort were not due to incompetence or stupidity on the part of the reformers. Various factors have affected policy formation, interpretation, and implementation, including the bargaining nature of the Chilean political system, the influence of conservative interests on the administrative and political system, and the unwillingness of Chilean political leaders to push structural changes that would alienate the economic elite from the political system.

Our measurement of the effectiveness of reforms uses the same indicators as the reform agencies and the Frei administration. We also include peasant political mobilization (politicization) through unionization as an indicator of change. The indicators of structural change include: (1) land expropriated and distributed; (2) settlements (*asentamientos*) formed and families settled; (3) mobilization of peasants (unionization); and (4) stimulation of production in the agricultural sector (productivity of CORA's *asentamientos* versus land unaffected by CORA or INDAP services).[164]

We have already mentioned the land expropriation targets established first in 1964 (Frei's promise of settling 100,000 *campesino* families), the home minister's 1966 revision (a 40,000 minimum and 60,000 maximum) which was suggested by CORA, and we hinted at further, informal revisions made by CORA and INDAP officials in late 1968. The most optimistic estimate is that of CORA's finance director who gave a maximum-minimum family settlement figure of 27,000 to 30,000 by 1970. These estimates, of course, have been made with reference to families settled on new lands (acquired by the government through expropriation or other means) and not in terms of the actual amount of land needed to settle these individuals. Let us examine the size of land that would have to be acquired to meet these estimates.[165]

Frei's first "promise" made during the campaign would have meant that some 1,000,000 hectares of irrigated land [166] or 4,000,000 hectares of nonirrigated land would have to be acquired, paid for over time, organized, and distributed to qualified recipients. The 1966 revision, as stated earlier, would have entailed the acquisition of between 400,000 to 600,000 irrigated hectares. The 1968 estimate referred to above would have required between 270,000 to 300,000 irrigated hectares of land. However, according to CORA's own figures[167] land acquired by all means including expropriation totaled only 171,623.0 irrigated hectares. The number of *fundos* actually expropriated number only 709. The amount of land acquired testifies to the shortcomings of land tenure change during the Frei period.

Table XIII shows the reasons used by CORA to justify expropriation and Map I (page 203) reveals the geographical location of expropriations.

With regard to distribution of titles to new peasant owners, again the record is bleak. Title distribution depends upon government-acquired land and the whole transitory process of settlement, operation of the settlement (as a collective) for a period of three years, and a decision by each settlement after the three-year period as to whether or not a majority of settlers wish to divide the land or operate it collectively. Therefore, few titles had been distributed until the

TABLE XIII

REASONS FOR LAND EXPROPRIATION, 1964–1968

CAUSE	LAND EXPROPRIATED	
	Number	Percentage
1. Abandoned or Poorly Exploited Land	458	64.6
2. Lands Offered to CORA by the Owners	115	16.2
3. Lands Whose Size Exceeded the 80 Basic Hectares Limit	79	11.1
4. Public and Private Corporate Lands Assigned to CORA	33	4.7
5. Other Causes	24	3.4
TOTALS	709	100.0

Source: CORA, *Cuatro Años de Reforma Agraria, op. cit.,* p. 26.

last three years of the Frei period. One source states that by the beginning of 1969, only 225 *campesinos* from the settlements of Panguesillo, Quelen, Llimpo-Jorquera, and Corron had "received a total of 56,224 hectares under both cooperative and individual titles," and that CORA had programmed title distributions for an additional 900 settlers on 13 more *asentamientos*.[168] Actual and planned title distributions, therefore, as of the middle of 1969 would affect less than 1,500 *campesinos*.

Again, using CORA data, Table XIV illustrates progress in *asentamiento* development and peasant settlement on land. Table XIV reveals the slow pace of family settlement during the first four years of the Frei regime. Only by doubling 1968's estimate of families to be settled could CORA meet the 27,000-family target informally set in late 1968. To attain the minimum goal of 40,000 families, CORA would have to triple its four-year total. Regarding family settlement, Table XV compares CORA's accomplishments with its plans formulated in 1966.

Even if CORA could settle an additional 15,000 fami-

MAP I
CORA's EXPROPRIATIONS BY ZONES, 1965-1968

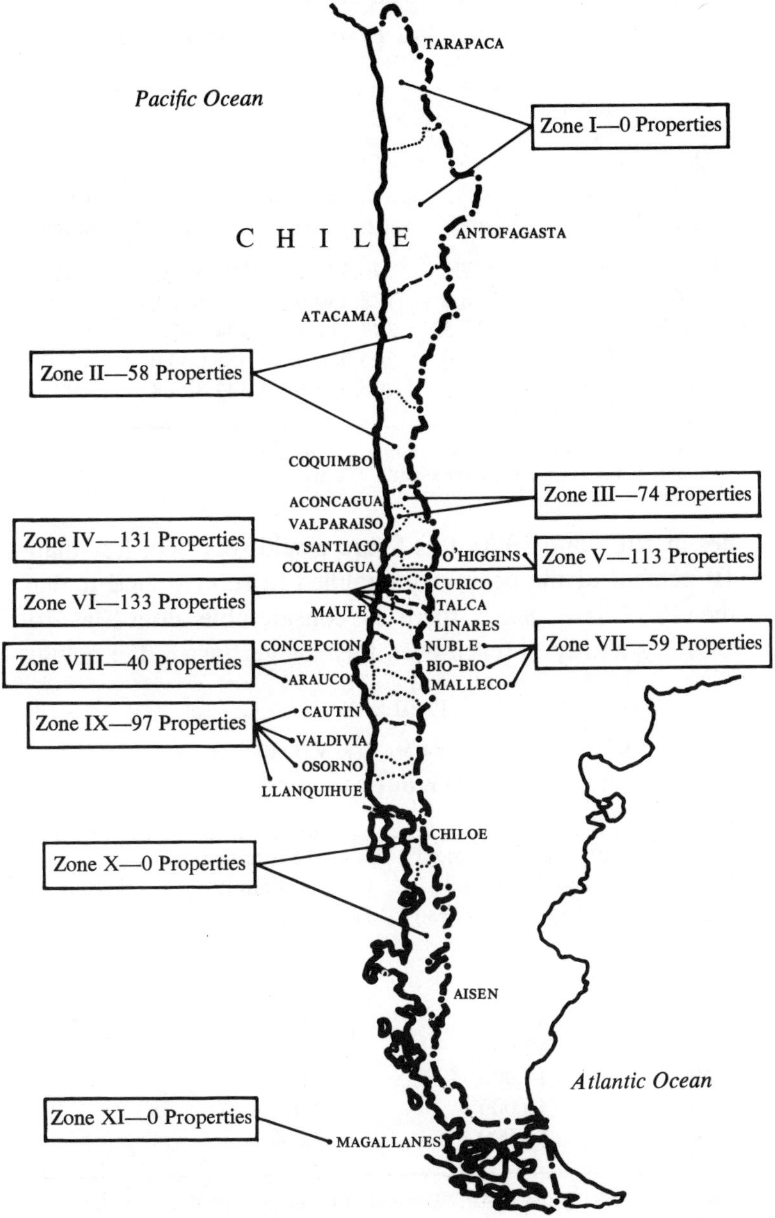

Pacific Ocean

TARAPACA

Zone I—0 Properties

C H I L E

ANTOFAGASTA

ATACAMA

Zone II—58 Properties

COQUIMBO

ACONCAGUA
VALPARAISO

Zone III—74 Properties

Zone IV—131 Properties

SANTIAGO
COLCHAGUA

O'HIGGINS

Zone V—113 Properties

Zone VI—133 Properties

MAULE

CURICO
TALCA
LINARES

CONCEPCION

Zone VIII—40 Properties

NUBLE
BIO-BIO

Zone VII—59 Properties

ARAUCO

MALLECO

Zone IX—97 Properties

CAUTIN
VALDIVIA
OSORNO
LLANQUIHUE

CHILOE

Zone X—0 Properties

AISEN

Atlantic Ocean

Zone XI—0 Properties

MAGALLANES

Source: **CORA**, *Cuatro Anos de Reforma Agraria, op. cit.*, p. 24.

TABLE XIV

ASENTAMIENTOS FORMED AND FAMILIES SETTLED, 1965–1968[a]

Year	Number of Asentamientos Formed	Area in Hectares Irrigated	Area in Hectares Not Irrigated	Total	Families Settled
1965	33	16,247.1	270,592.2	286,839.3	2,061
1966	62	17,286.8	128,330.0	145,616.8	2,109
1967	151	47,736.3	307,111.4	354,847.7	4,218
1968[b]	200	55,000.0	500,000.0	555,000.0	5,500
TOTALS	466	136,270.2	1,206,033.6	1,342,303.8	13,888

Source: CORA, *Cuatro Años de Reforma Agraria, op. cit.,* p. 30.
[a] Thome's figures (*op. cit.*) differ slightly. His may be more accurate.
[b] Estimates.

lies in 1969 and 1970, this figure would represent less than 10 percent of the peasantry qualified to receive land under the 1967 law. Since there is considerable doubt as to CORA's ability to reach even this meager target, the actual

TABLE XV

CORA's ACCOMPLISHMENTS VERSUS ITS PLANS:
FAMILY SETTLEMENTS

Year	Planned Settlement (60,000 Family Target by 1970)	Planned Settlement (40,000 Family Target by 1970)	Actual Settlement[a]
1965	2,500	2,500	2,061
1966	2,500	2,500	2,109
1967	10,000	6,000	4,218
1968	12,000	8,000	5,500
1969	15,000	9,000	—
1970	18,000	12,000	—
TOTALS	60,000	40,000	—

Source: Table XIII and CIAP, "Domestic Efforts and the Needs for External Financing for the Development of Chile" (1967 Report), *op. cit.,* p. 127.
[a] Figure for 1968 was an estimate. As of May 31, 1968, only 451 families had been settled. See Thome, *op. cit.,* p. 5.

final figure might be only slightly more than 5 percent of this potential clientele.

Considerable change has occurred in INDAP's efforts to mobilize the peasantry through unionization efforts. The strategy of peasant mobilization through unionization was apparently conceived early in the reform effort as a low-cost means of activating and stimulating an increasingly political, radical, and exploited social stratum.[169] Most writers on Chilean politics have observed that Chilean peasants played almost no role in politics up to recent years. The potential for change, however, appeared very real as a result of the activities of INDAP during the first four years of the Frei government. Table XVI reveals the progress made by INDAP (under Chonchol) in organizing the peasants and the relative strength of those INDAP-organized peasants in comparison with PDC- and FRAP-organized peasants.

It is important to note that federated *campesino* unions do not account for all peasants organized in some form. The total number of peasants organized to some degree may be as high as 210,000.[170] This means that an additional 160,000 peasants are not listed by the Ministry of Labor as belonging to some organization. Table XVII reveals some relationships between government (INDAP) efforts, populations affected, and actual unionization.

Of course, peasant unionization in terms of its political and social impact is of a potential nature.[171] Widespread land seizures in the Province of Ñuble illustrate what might occur in the future. However, in terms of change, the approach of peasant settlement on land has obvious advantage in personal as well as social, political, and economic terms. The ultimate products of peasant mobilization through unionization might become the basis for a new radicalism— exactly the opposite of what Frei and other leading PDC politicians had hoped would be the result.

TABLE XVI

FEDERATED CAMPESINO SINDICATOS AS OF JUNE 10, 1968

Province	N.C.L.* (PDC)	N.E.T.C.C. † (INDAP)	N.C.I.R. ‡ (PCC-PS)	Others §	Totals
Atacana	—	—	276	—	276
Coquimbo	—	1,985	189	—	2,174
Aconcagua	1,519	1,928	778	—	4,225
Valparaiso	1,448	—	—	—	1,448
Santiago	2,295	3,779	970	1,219	8,263
O'Higgins	718	4,434	1,156	—	6,308
Colchacua	1,070	1,094	1,646	—	3,810
Curio	—	1,498	952	—	2,450
Talca	4,762	1,995	1,958	—	8,715
Linares	972	1,707	—	—	2,679
Ñuble	1,119	2,053	529	—	3,701
Concepcion	685	—	1,039	—	1,724
Bio-Bio	—	—	581	—	581
Cautin	—	1,648	—	—	1,648
Valdivia	1,025	2,638	937	—	4,600
Osorno	—	2,068	—	—	2,068
TOTALS	15,613	26,827	11,011	1,219	54,670
PERCENT-AGE	28.5%	49.1%	20.1%	2.2%	100.0%

Source: *Direccion del Trabajo, Organizaciones Sindicales, "Nomina de Federaciones Provinciales de Sindicatos Agricolas de Trabajadores, con indicacion del numero de Sindicatos que las Componen y Socios Afiliados* (June 10, 1968).

* *Confederacion Nacional Campesino Libertad* (Christian Democratic Party sponsored—International Development Fund supported).
† *Confederacion Nacional El Triunfo Campesino de Chile* (INDAP sponsored —left Christian Democrats).
‡ *Confederacion Nacional Campesino e Indigina Ranguil* (Communist-Socialist Party sponsored).
§ Not affiliated with the other three confederations.

Agricultural Production and Employment

This last area in which substantial advance was promised by the Frei government through its agrarian reform activities has had a mixed history. Several studies of CORA *asentamientos* seem to indicate quite clearly that production and land productivity of these settlements have substantially improved. In other words, when *asentamientos* replaced the traditional *patron*-dominated system of production or cultivation, actual yields per acre have increased.[172] However, *asentamientos* account for only a very small portion of Chile's cultivatable land. In other words, agrarian reform (revisions in land tenure) was not given enough of a test over the entire countryside. Limited trials seem to support the conclusion that productivity can increase.

Measured over the entire countryside for the 1965–1969 period, productivity in the agricultural sector has declined in relative terms. In part this was due to the drought of 1967–68:

> In 1968, the foreign trade balance of the agrarian sector was negative in the amount of U.S. $155.9 million, while there was no significant change in the composition of agricultural imports and exports as compared with 1967. An increase in this deficit is expected for 1969 (estimated at approximately U.S. $170 million), primarily as a result of increased imports of grain to alleviate the effects of the drought.[173]

The drought does not account for this depressing agricultural forecast, however. Some observers felt that the large landowners used the drought argument as a weapon *against* reform efforts:

> Both the opponents and supporters of agrarian reform see in the drought a crucial moment for the program, which is already far behind schedule because of conservative resistance and ineffectual administration.
>
> The landlords, invoking the need to maintain rural social order and sustain food production, have called on the government to suspend land expropriations and invest in relief projects, such as small public works. . . .
>
> Jacques Chonchol . . . said the only solution was to "accelerate the agrarian reform. Give the peasants the land and they will pull in their belts and work. . . ." He said that he believed the landlords were following a political

TABLE XVII

Organized Agricultural Labor, 1968

INDAP ZONES	PROVINCES	TOTAL AGRICULTURAL LABOR FORCE (1967 Projection)	TOTAL ORGANIZED AGRICULTURAL LABOR FORCE	PERCENTAGE OF AGRICULTURAL LABOR FORCE ORGANIZED By Province TOTAL	By Confederation INDAP	FRAP	PDC	OTHER[a]
I	Tarapaca	6,807	N/A	N/A	N/A	N/A	N/A	N/A
	Antofagasta	2,501	N/A	N/A	N/A	N/A	N/A	N/A
II	Atacama	5,394	276	5.0	—	100.0	—	—
	Coquimbo	37,075	2,174	6.0	91.3	8.6	—	—
III	Valparaiso	29,036	1,448	5.0	—	—	100.0	—
	Aconcagua	23,545	4,225	17.0	45.6	18.4	35.9	—
IV	Santiago	81,146	8,263	10.0	45.7	11.7	27.7	14.8
V	O'Higgins	44,508	6,308	14.0	70.3	18.3	11.4	—
	Colchagua	35,201	3,810	10.8	28.7	43.2	28.1	—
VI	Curico	22,291	2,450	10.8	61.1	38.9	—	—
	Talca	38,948	8,715	9.8	22.9	22.4	54.6	—
VII	Maule	17,200	N/A	N/A	N/A	N/A	N/A	N/A
	Linares	36,934	2,679	8.8	63.7	—	36.3	—
VIII	Ñuble	59,565	3,701	6.2	55.5	14.3	30.2	—

INDAP ZONES	PROVINCES	TOTAL AGRICULTURAL LABOR FORCE (1967 Projection)	TOTAL ORGANIZED AGRICULTURAL LABOR FORCE	PERCENTAGE OF AGRICULTURAL LABOR FORCE ORGANIZED				
				By Province	By Confederation			
				TOTAL	INDAP	FRAP	PDC	OTHER[a]
IX	Concepcion	32,060	1,724	5.3	—	60.3	39.7	—
	Arauco	14,462	N/A	N/A	N/A	N/A	N/A	N/A
X	Malleco	32,387	N/A	N/A	N/A	N/A	N/A	N/A
	Bio-Bio	34,563	581	1.7	—	100.0	—	—
XI	Cautin	78,382	1,648	2.0	100.0	—	—	—
XII	Valdivia	43,472	4,600	10.6	57.3	20.4	22.3	—
	Osorno	26,350	2,068	8.0	100.0	—	—	—
XIII	Llanguihue	29,509	N/A	N/A	N/A	N/A	N/A	N/A
	Chiloe	23,793	N/A	N/A	N/A	N/A	N/A	N/A
XIV	Aysen	6,330	N/A	N/A	N/A	N/A	N/A	N/A
XV	Magallanes	6,102	N/A	N/A	N/A	N/A	N/A	N/A
	TOTALS	767,561	54,670	7.1	49.1	20.1	28.5	2.2

Source: Composite; see sources for Charts I, II, III, and IV. See also, source for Table XV.
[a] Includes those unions not affiliated with the other three confederations.

plan of forcing peasant invasions through evictions. "They want the government to send in the police and turn the peasants against the government." [174]

Undoubtedly poor weather can account for low productivity in recent years but the structural changes which technicians and foreign experts concurred were necessary to modernize Chilean agriculture have not been made so that Chilean agricultural production has remained basically unchanged.

Finally, related to the productivity of the agricultural sector is its ability to provide employment. In this regard, Chile has not been able to reverse the urbanization trend of the last few decades. In the year 1967–68 Chile witnessed a decrease of 0.2 percent (some 1,200) in employment in the agricultural sector—the only sector to record a decrease.[175] A conclusion that may be inferred from this statistic is that the "push" off the land and into the city is still occurring in Chile—a situation which most urban specialists deplore as an indication of an unhealthy economic situation.

In the final analysis, direct changes resulting from Frei's agrarian reform program have been meager. Few *campesinos* have directly and immediately benefited from the services of CORA. With regard to INDAP's operations, only the long run will reveal the extent to which organizing peasants into unions will sufficiently mobilize them for collective demands for land and not merely marginal changes. The tactics of the PDC leadership in playing the leftist reformers off against the rightist landed interests proved disastrous to the peasants and the nation's long-term political, social, and economic growth.

NOTES

1. Jacques Lambert, *Latin America: Social Structures and Political Institutions* (Berkeley: University of California Press, 1967, p. 221.
2. John Friedman and Tomas Lackington, "Hyper-urbanization and National Development in Chile: Some Hypotheses," mimeographed

(Santiago: University of Chile, Urban Development Program [CIDU], November, 1966). Another version of this paper appeared in *Urban Affairs Quarterly*, 2 (June, 1967), pp. 3–29.

3. Chile is one of the few Latin American political systems with civilian, electoral politics. It is not unrealistic to envision a change toward the politicization of the military as a response to "civilian unrest" in the urban or agrarian areas. With respect to agrarian reform, Chile's military-governed neighbor, Peru, now appears to be in the position of implementing a strong agrarian reform which was not achieved under a civilian, liberal-reform-type government. It is difficult to assess the extent to which Chilean military leaders might be influenced by the Peruvian situation.

4. In this regard, some argue that U.S. bureaucrats are somehow more attuned to the demands and needs of a democratic polity. The Chilean experience will suggest the opposite; the agrarian reform section of the public bureaucracy appeared more responsive to the needs and demands of Chilean peasants than were political leaders. The Chilean experience with public-sponsored and directed socio-politico-economic development programs compares at least favorably (in terms of implementation) with those of the United States in recent years. Both the U.S. federal bureaucracy and the Chilean national bureaucracy have experimented with social-economic programs as well as those programs which promote political mobilization of disaffected populations. The cross-national conclusions which may be drawn from the Chilean experience with agrarian reform programs and the U.S. experience with economic opportunity programs would include the experimental nature of these types of programs, development of technology for problem solving as well as the importance of political support for experimentation, refinement, and eventual application of these new technologies for public social-economic problem solving. In this regard, Chile is no more administratively "underdeveloped" than the United States. In neither situation does it appear that the "critical mass" needed to initiate, sustain, and eventually accomplish the objectives of programs designed to make significant impacts on socio-economic problems was present. Chilean agrarian reform efforts (administratively speaking) are indicative of the world-wide intervention of the public sector in social, economic, and political restructuring.

5. For example, see James F. Petras, *Politics and Social Forces in Chilean Development* (Berkeley: University of California Press, 1969), p. 5.

6. Too often political analysis is content with describing and analyzing the actions of legislators without examining the context within which their actions take place or the events which occur outside legislative chambers which contribute directly or indirectly to the legal results.

7. Although an understanding of the 1962 law enacted during the Alessandri government is necessary for understanding the 1967 law, the

former has been described and analyzed in great detail elsewhere. For example, see: "The Chilean Land Reform: A Laboratory for Alliance-For-Progress Techniques," *Yale Law Journal,* Vol. 73 (December, 1963), pp. 310–33; and William C. Thiesenhusen, *Chile's Experiments in Agrarian Reform* (Madison: University of Wisconsin Press, Land Economics Monograph No. 1), pp. 36–45. Therefore, provisions of this law will be included only when required for an understanding of the 1967 law.

8. UNECLA, *Estudio Economico de America Latina,* Vol. 2 (July, 1964).

9. S. L. Barraclough and A. L. Domike, *op. cit.,* p. 408.

10. *Ibid.,* p. 407. Rural-to-urban migration has not significantly improved the material position of those peasants who remained behind.

11. *Ibid.*

12. *Ibid.,* p. 409.

13. There have been a number of studies of Chilean agriculture in the eighteenth and nineteenth centuries—in particular, George M. McBride, *Chile: Land and Society* (New York: American Geographic Society, 1936) and Teodoro Schneider, *La Agricultura en Chile en Los Ultimos Cincuenta Años* (Santiago de Chile: Sociedad Nacional de Agricultura, 1904). In addition, William C. Thiesenhusen's section on the historical development of Chilean agriculture, although brief, attempts to relate colonial practices to present-day agricultural patterns. See *Chile's Experiments in Agrarian Reform, op. cit.,* pp. 10–28.

14. S. L. Barraclough and A. L. Domike, *op. cit.,* p. 396.

15. T. Schneider, *op. cit.,* p. 14.

16. *Ibid.,* pp. 139–46 and 205–13.

17. James F. Petras, *op. cit.,* p. 99. Robert J. Alexander in *Labor Relations in Argentina, Brasil, and Chile* (New York: McGraw-Hill, 1962) cites the earlier 1920 election as the watershed whereby "political power in the nation as a whole passed from the rural landlords to the city" (p. 238). This may have been the first step in limiting the traditional (land-based) elite's political hold on Chile but a rearguard action has been successfully fought now for over fifty years.

18. The extent to which incentives à la "economic man" theory of increasing production even affected most large landowners in Chile or Latin America as a whole is effectively discussed by Solon Barraclough in "Agricultural Policy and Strategies of Land Reform," *Studies in Comparative International Development,* 4, No. 8 (Beverly Hills: Sage Publications, 1969), pp. 178–79.

19. W. C. Thiesenhusen, *op. cit.,* p. 14.

20. Chilean landowners in combination with Chilean industrialists and business/commercial elites exercise considerable political and economic power and influence. Furthermore, there are familial as well

as sociocultural ties between the large landowners and new members of the economic elite. For an elaboration on this theme, see: J. F. Petras, *op. cit.*, pp. 51–62.

21. Schneider, *op. cit.*

22. *Ibid.*, p. 181.

23. *Ibid.* This is a translation from the original Spanish. This was Schneider's first recommendation for government action in the agrarian sector. Since his book was published by the SNA in 1904, one may assume that at least there was no large-scale organizational opposition to his findings. The rest of the discussion of SNA activities is drawn from the Schneider work, pp. 166–90.

24. *Ibid.*, p. 11.

25. *Ibid.*

26. There appears to be a high correlation between peasant seizures of land and disinterested or absentee ownership. In one recent case study, while peasants on one farm (*Culipran*) were battling local authorities after seizing the land they worked from a disinterested landlord, peasants on a nearby farm (*San Manuel*) were content to remain as bystanders under a paternalistic but generous *patron*. See: James Petras and Hugo Zemelman, "Peasant Politics in Chile: A Case Study," *LTC*, No. 65 (Madison: The Land Tenure Center, University of Wisconsin, July, 1969).

27. McBride, *op. cit.*, p. 268. The following discussion of early "agrarian reform" stems principally from this source.

28. The *Caja de Colonizacion* was reorganized as the *Corporacion de la Reforma Agraria* (CORA). This reorganization was part of the Alessandri agrarian reform law (No. 15,020) of 1962.

29. McBride, *op. cit.*, p. 271. General Ibanez was ruling Chile at the time that Law No. 4496 was passed.

30. William C. Thiesenhusen points out: "While planned colonization on purchased *fundos* as a means to redistribute land has a long history as a policy of (the Chilean) government . . . relatively little land was given out. What land has been distributed went largely to people who could not have been classified landless laborers by any stretch of the imagination," *op. cit.*, p. 32.

31. For a discussion of the "watering down" of Kennedy's original commitment to agrarian reform, see Part Four.

32. Three had laws prior to 1960—Mexico (1915), Bolivia (1953), and Cuba (1959). Three did not enact legislation in this area—Argentina, Uruguay, and Guatemala.

33. According to former Senator Gruening: "Chile seemed to be one of (the) most hopeful prospects in Latin America for an effective assistance program: stable, homogeneous, literate, with a democratic tradition and a promising resource base, Chile is particularly endowed with the requisites for attaining Alliance for Progress objectives. . . ."

See: U.S. Congress, Senate, Committee on Government Operations, *United States Foreign Aid in Action: A Case Study, op. cit.,* p. VIII.

34. For example, see: James Petras and Maurice Zeitlin, "Agrarian Radicalism in Chile," *The British Journal of Sociology,* 19, No. 3 (September, 1968), pp. 254–70.

35. Lambert, *op. cit.,* pp. 188–90.

36. Furthermore, land seizure in the *Sierra* was the only method of expropriation used in Peru until the 1968 coup. See chapter on Peru.

37. Marvin J. Sternberg, "Chilean Land Tenure and Land Reform" (Ph.D. dissertation, Department of Economics, University of California at Berkeley, 1962), p. 133.

38. See Landsberger's case in Henry A. Landsberger (ed.), *Latin American Peasant Movements* (Ithaca, New York: Cornell University Press, 1969).

39. See James F. Petras, *Politics and Social Forces in Chilean Development, op. cit.,* pp. 256–87.

40. It is difficult to ascertain the frequency and occurrence of land seizures in Chile. Petras in *Politics and Social Forces in Chilean Development* states: "The number of peasants involved in strikes tripled from 1964 to 1965. A number of *fundos* have been taken over by the peasants, sometimes by force, and some *asentamientos* have been established on expropriated lands," (p. 258). Landsberger in *Latin American Peasant Movements* provides no examples of peasant land seizures and presents an eighteen-year-old case study of a Chilean peasant strike. Thiesenhusen, in "Grassroots Economic Pressures in Chile: An Enigma for Development Planners," *Economic Development and Cultural Change,* 16 (April, 1968), mentions eighty land invasions but these were made by Chile's relatively small Araucanian Indian population (p. 416). Finally, only two rather thoroughly documented land seizures have been examined by the authors and both occurred in 1965. These include: Petras and Zemelman, *op. cit.,* and Terry L. McCoy, "The Seizure of *'Los Cristales':* A Case Study of the Marxist Left in Chile," (Santiago, Chile: Land Tenure Center, University of Wisconsin, No. 67/1, April, 1967), mimeographed.

41. This does not imply, of course, that Chilean peasants could not develop into a revolutionary force employing illegal means if their immediate demands are not met.

42. The "land hunger" of those peasants who are already organized and, hence, better off economically is already a problem in Chile. A state of emergency was imposed in Ñuble Province in response to a farm workers' revolt in which 7,000 agricultural workers struck 200 farms and seized 9 of the farms. The workers' demand was immediate distribution of land rather than waiting for the government to expropriate. According to government sources (CORA) 3 of the 9 farms could not be expropriated under the 1967 law. See: the *Washington Post,* February 1, 1970.

43. For a discussion of the agrarian reform politics of this period, see: Constantine Menges, "The Politics of Agrarian Reform in Chile, 1958–1964: The Role of Parties and Interest Groups" (Ph.D. dissertation, Department of Public Law and Government, Columbia University, 1966).

44. For an early precise analysis of Frei's agrarian reform bill, see: Marion R. Brown, "Frei Unveils New Agrarian Reform Bill," *LTC*, No. 11 (Madison: University of Wisconsin, The Land Tenure Center, December, 1965).

45. The administrative organizations of the Agrarian Reform Corporation —CORA—and the Institute of Agricultural Development—INDAP —were maintained unchanged structurally, while strengthened functionally.

46. A critique of the Alessandri law by CORA is contained in a "White Paper" issued jointly with Frei's introduction of his bill. See Brown, *op. cit.*

47. *Ibid.*, p. 1.

48. For a basic discussion of this election, and other election details, see: Frederico G. Gil, *The Political System of Chile* (Boston: Houghton-Mifflin, 1966), pp. 206–43.

49. It is interesting and somewhat ironic that the Chilean right wing was characterized as "mummies" at this time because many North Americans and Chileans considered them politically "dead." The "resurrection" of these "mummies" and the splintering of the PDC in 1969 came as a surprise only to those observers who were ignorant of or discounted the right wing of the PDC—the wing of the party that Frei apparently chose to mollify during his tenure.

50. This configuration was evident in Congress as well as the party apparatus. The three groups roughly corresponded to left, center and right positions.

51. Chilean Congress, Chamber of Deputies, Debates, 90th Session (Thursday, May 19, 1966). The balance of this discussion of the committee's report and the debate of this report is derived from this session (a session equals one meeting of the Congress—see Gil, *op. cit.*, pp. 110–12, for other Chilean congressional procedures).

52. This concern for productivity more than social justice is in keeping with priorities of those supporting agrarian reform—urban politicians backed by an urban population unhappy with food shortages and high food prices. See S. Barraclough, "Agricultural Policy and Strategies of Land Reform," *op. cit.*, pp. 167 and 181. Although others have stressed the urban base of agrarian reformism, Barraclough develops this argument by citing the results of a public opinion poll taken in Santiago in 1966 in which 80 percent believed agrarian reform to be necessary for the nation and 75 percent cited low food production as the reason for supporting reform.

53. Silva was the informant of the committee. Other deputies who presented significant or different comments or positions of their parties included: for the PDC besides Silva, Carlos Garcés Fernández, Luis Maria Aguirre, Manuel Valdés Solar, César Raúl Fuentes Venegas, Narciso Irureta Aburto, Pedro Urra Veloso, and Pedro Alvarado Paez; for the Communists, Carlos Rosales Gutierrez, Luis Tejeda Oliva, Jorge Montes Moraga, and Cipriano Pontigo Urrutia; for the Socialists, José Andres Aravena Cabezas, Francisco Sepúlveda Gutierrez, Eduardo Osorio Pardo, Ernesto Guajardo Gomez, and Carmen Lazo Carrera; Radicals included Manuel Rioseco Vasquez, Clemente Fuentealba Caamano, Jorge Cabello Pizarro, Renato Laemmermann Moresalves, and Samuel Fuentes Andradres; Liberals included Patricio Phillips Pariafiel, Hugo Zepeda Coll, Gabriel De la Fuente Cortés, and Gustavo Lorca Rojas; for the Conservatives, Fernando Ochagavia Valdes; and for the National Democrats, Juan Tuma Masso and Victor González Maertens. This information is derived from an examination of the Chamber debates, from the committee's report on May 19, 1966, through the passage of the bill.

54. Senator Salvador Allende, leader of the Socialist party and the FRAP presidential candidate in 1964; and now president of the Republic.

55. *El Deber Social y Politico* of September, 1962, which attacked, among other problems, the disproportionate distribution of land.

56. It was during 1966 that a merger of the principal parties of the Right into the *Partido Nacional* (National party or PN) occurred. However, for this first session on the agrarian reform bill, separate party identity was maintained.

57. Chilean Congress, Chamber of Deputies, *Debates,* 90th Session (Thursday, May 19, 1966).

58. *Ibid.*

59. Article 151 (proposed) was incorporated into the law as Article 171 with little if any modification. It maintains presidential prerogative of intervention as follows: "In case of an employer's lock-out or an illegal work stoppage that for any reason suspends the agricultural activities on a rural property, the President of the Republic may order that such activities be resumed, with the intervention of the civil authorities. . . . The interventor appointed will have the authority necessary to continue the exploitation of the land." This article also includes compulsory arbitration. See: *Ley de Reforma Agraria,* No. 16,640 (July 16, 1967), pp. 84–5. It is suspected that this article was used to justify the use of government forces to dislodge striking agricultural workers from nine farms they had seized recently in the Province of Ñuble.

60. *Debates, op. cit.*

61. *Ibid.*

62. For example, see Brown, *op. cit.,* pp. 1–2.

63. *Debates, op. cit.*

64. Chile was already importing about $150 million worth of foodstuffs annually.

65. Price to be determined by the landowners.

66. Chilean Congress, Chamber of Deputies, *Debates,* 15th Session (July 6, 1966). The following discussion is derived from the record of this session.

67. Merger of Liberal and Conservative parties plus small fascist groups.

68. The *asentamiento* system will be discussed under the section on "Measuring the Reform Effort."

69. The National Agrarian Council is composed of the Minister of Agriculture, the Minister of Land and Colonies, the executive vice-president of CORA, and "two persons freely selected by the President of the Republic . . ." It appears from a reading of this Article (135) establishing the council that it can overrule CORA decisions regarding expropriation and can exclude lands from expropriation. Chilean Congress, Chamber of Deputies, *Debates,* 17th Session (July 7, 1966).

70. This is a Church-supported "social action" agency. See: Thiesenhusen, *Chile's Experiments in Agrarian Reform, op. cit.,* p. 59, footnote 14.

71. This article (157) reads as follows: "Since the national interest requires it, it is hereby forbidden to form corporations and joint-stock companies that have as their primary or accessory objective agricultural or livestock exploitation. This prohibition will not affect corporations whose primary objective is the preparation of new land for cultivation and its subsequent exploitation in the provinces of Tarapaca, Antofagasta, Atacama, Coquimbo, Chiloe, Aysen, or Magallanes." The last sentence was the one which raised the charge that the PDC bill was a device to protect PDC landowners and/or large businessmen with investments in such corporations.

72. Interview with R. Santa Cruz, chief, Legal Section, CORA, June 24, 1968. Santa Cruz and his staff drafted the 1967 law and advised the CORA and the executive branch on the law's constitutionality. (Most Senate committees have thirteen members—a majority would be seven.)

73. Differences between the bill and the law have already been discussed. Some additional analysis of the compromise process and results will be discussed later. Also, comparisons between the 1967 and the 1962 laws will be made later in this section.

74. We are using the term "interest group" in a very broad sense. Since only congressmen could actually vote on the proposed agrarian reform legislation, those others who represent groups of sorts and who expressed positions for their groups directly to congressmen or indirectly for or against the uplifting of peasants can legitimately be considered as "interest representatives."

75. See Petras, *Politics and Social Forces . . . , op. cit.,* his chapter on the peasantry.

76. For a discussion of this type of representation and access process for articulation of interests, see: Gabriel A. Almond and G. Bingham Power, Jr., *Comparative Politics: A Developmental Approach* (Boston: Little, Brown, 1966), pp. 83–4.

77. Thiesenhusen argues that the parish-diocese arrangement of the Church makes for a more effective administrative set-up than the traditional provincial government administrative apparatus.

78. Thiesenhusen, *Chile's Experiments in Agrarian Reform, op. cit.*, pp. 64–5. For an excellent discussion of the role of the Church in reform efforts prior to 1967, see Thiesenhusen's work, especially Chapter 2, pp. 55–81; see also, his article entitled "Chilean Agrarian Reform: The Possibility of Gradualistic Turnover of Land," *Inter-American Economic Affairs*, 20 (Summer, 1966), pp. 3–22.

79. The source of information for this discussion is Thiesenhusen, *op. cit.*, pp. 65–77.

80. *Ibid.*, p. 70.

81. Thiesenhusen in his *Inter-American Economic Affairs* article uses the INPROA program as an example of successful "gradualistic turnover of land" in Chile. As he himself notes: "Using several private-sector case studies (INPROA operations), this article will argue that the land tenure structure in Chile might be better changed by somewhat slower but nonetheless steady steps toward individual proprietorship," (p. 4). He goes on to imply that the Chilean government might be well advised to follow the procedures and processes developed and employed by INPROA. See: Thiesenhusen, "Chilean Agrarian Reform: The Possibility of Gradualistic Turnover of Land," *op. cit.*

82. The liberal wing of the Church also had the experience of having some of its lands "reformed" and finding out that it would not lose anything. As Thiesenhusen states: "The INPROA program is not set up to lose money for the Church . . . the Church did not give the land absolutely without strings. The general case is that land was sold to colonists over a twenty-year period with 5 percent interest." See: *Chile's Experiments in Agrarian Reform, op. cit.*, p. 67.

83. Alan Angell in "Christian Democracy in Chile," *Current History*, 58 (March, 1970), makes a similar point—see p. 84.

84. Chonchol resigned as head of INDAP in November, 1968. His resignation condemned the PDC right wing but he did not have ill words for Trivelli. Chonchol's exact words (as translated) were: "I would like to emphasize . . . that I received the steady support of the Minister of Agriculture, Sr. Hugo Trivelli." *Ercilla*, November 26, 1968.

85. See Petras, *Politics and Social Forces . . . , op. cit.*, p. 100. For an earlier but excellent treatment of this important financial/investment agency, see: Kalman Silvert, "The Chilean Development Corpora-

tion" (Ph.D. dissertation, Department of Political Science, University of Pennsylvania, Philadelphia, 1948).

86. Agricultural development outside CORA *asentamientos* is the official responsibility of CORFO. See: Corporacion de Fomento de la Produccion (CORFO), Gerencia Agricola, Officina Programacion y Estudios, "Memoria Gerencia Agricola, 1967," (Santiago, Chile: CORFO, 1967), mimeographed. These and similar reports reveal the extent to which CORFO's clientele are the *latifundistas*—almost all investments (credits and loans) in the agricultural sector made by CORFO went to large landlords.

87. Interview with José Ilabaca, subsecretary, Ministry of Labor, June 20, 1968. During the course of the interview, Sr. Ilabaca received a telephone call from a large landowner who was a "friend of the family." The landowner wanted to discuss his "labor problem" with the subsecretary and a luncheon date was arranged. Ilabaca stressed repeatedly that "excessive (labor) demands are driving the landowner to the brink." He emphasized his role in intervening against protest marches of agricultural workers to demonstrate for higher wages and better working conditions. See: Petras and Zemelman, *op. cit.,* for additional information regarding agricultural worker demands.

88. Ilabaca's designation of "Marxist" would seem to indicate that it was a union of the *Confederacion Nacional de Campesinos e Indigenos Ranquil.* See the section on policy outputs in this chapter for a discussion of the relative numerical strength of this confederation.

89. See *Ercilla, op. cit.,* November 26, 1968.

90. There are other large agricultural groups in Chile such as the Consortium of Agricultural Societies of the South (CAS) and the Agricultural Associations of the North. In addition, there are producers' associations whose product would be sugar beets or rice. However, the single most important large landowner group is the SNA. For a discussion of the Right's opposition to agrarian reform up to 1967, see: Robert R. Kaufman, *The Chilean Political Right and Agrarian Reform: Resistance and Moderation* (Washington, D.C.: Institute for the Comparative Study of Political Systems, 1967). Kaufman suggests a very strong tie between SNA membership and the leaders of the parties of the Right.

91. Kaufman, *op. cit.,* p. 42.

92. Nor did the landowners have to resort to extra-legal measures to preserve their privileges, since they were never really in jeopardy.

93. A number of important provisions of the law are found in this category. For example, Article 171 (discussed above) may be found here along with the provincial equivalence tables (Article 172), tax exemption status for CORA and its cooperatives (Articles 168 and 169), among others.

94. Material and comments on the 1962 law were primarily drawn from Thiesenhusen, *Chile's Experiments in Agrarian Reform, op. cit.,*

pp. 36–44; and "The Chilean Land Reform: A Laboratory for Alliance-for-Progress Techniques," *op. cit.,* pp. 310–33. It is interesting to note that the 1962 law contained 104 articles, which the *Yale Law Journal* labeled "elaborate" (p. 315). This law was 205 articles shorter than the 1967 law, which the Inter-American Economic and Social Council labeled "complex."

95. With the creation of CORA from the *Caja,* continuity was preserved through personnel. That is, the functionaries of the *Caja* stayed on in CORA. A greater break occurred in 1964, but even with the PDC victory, some 400 functionaries remained, under PDC supervision. See the section on personnel in this chapter.

96. The *Yale Law Journal* noted, "Outright expropriation as a method for acquisition is severely restricted," and concludes "the provisions of the Chilean land reform (of 1962) dealing with conditions of *minifundia* would appear to be the most promising," since expropriation "obviously does not reach the bulk of the *latifundios* within the country." See: "The Chilean Land Reform . . . ," *op. cit.,* pp. 315, 316 and 318.

97. Article 3, Agrarian Reform Law (July 16, 1967).

98. For example, the "poorly exploited" category as a criterion for expropriation was rendered useless shortly after the law was enacted. The 1967 law included this criterion. However, the 1967 law provided its own set of expropriation loopholes. See Articles 20 through 27 (includes vineyard protection, among others).

99. Article 172, Agrarian Reform Law (July 16, 1967).

100. "The Chilean Land Reform . . . ," *op. cit.,* p. 316. Article 31 of the 1962 Agrarian Reform Law was cited.

101. Article 45. Expropriation based on the "poorly exploited" criterion entitles the owner to a down payment of only 5 percent.

102. See Articles 131–34 for details concerning these bonds. For more detail concerning indemnification, see Articles 45 through 55.

103. This was true for many PDC leaders including Frei. It is, perhaps, related to the fact that Frei's urban middle-class supporters viewed agrarian reform principally as a device to secure greater productivity and, hence, lower food costs.

104. The two agencies examined in depth—CORA and INDAP—were the ones most directly involved with the agrarian reform program during the Frei period. They were not, however, the only public agencies active in the agricultural sector nor were they the best funded or staffed. We have mentioned CORFO whose clientele was primarily the large *fundo* owners. Others that deserve to be mentioned include: the Agricultural and Livestock Service (*Servicio Agricola y Ganadero* or SAG) which works with Chilean middle-class farmers (those farmers who own more than a subsistence-size farm and are, therefore, producers for the commercial market); the

Agricultural Machinery Service (*Servicios de Equipos Agricoles Mercanizados*—SEAM); the State Bank (*Banco del Estado*); and the Commercial Agricultural Enterprise (*Empresa de Comercio Agricola* or ECA). Neither of the latter two provide any substantial services to the 350,000 *campesino* families who are not large- or medium-size agriculturalists.

105. For a discussion of the use of these kinds of organizations for development work, see: Robert LaPorte, Jr., "An Analysis of a Development Strategy: Public Corporations and Resource Development in South Asia," *International Review of Administrative Sciences,* 33, No. 4 (1967), pp. 319–28. At present, Chile has close to 60 semi-autonomous public agencies. This figure included educational institutions such as the University of Chile. These agencies are grouped under the various ministries. The ministerial breakdown is as follows: (1) Foreign Affairs Ministry—1; (2) Ministry of Economic Development and Reconstruction—8; (3) Ministry of Interior—7; (4) Ministry of Public Education—4; (5) Ministry of Defense—6; (6) Ministry of Public Works—3; (7) Ministry of Land and Colonization—9; (8) Ministry of Public Health—4; (9) Ministry of Mining—4; (10) Ministry of Housing and Urban Affairs—5; (11) Ministry of Agriculture—5; and not categorized—1. Data compiled from a number of sources, including: Ministerio de Hacienda, Direccion de Presupuestos, Oficina Central de Organizacion y Metodos, "Organizacion de Gobierno Central," (Santiago, Chile: Ministerio de Hacienda, November, 1964).

106. Barraclough, "Agricultural Policy and Strategies of Land Reform," *op. cit.,* p. 169.

107. Before beginning our discussion, it is interesting to note that, according to our survey, no legislator publicly raised the question of administrative feasibility with regard to Frei's promise to settle 100,000 landless *campesino* families on land secured by the government. Yet, as the following will reveal, only a small part of that relatively modest goal was achieved. Implementation of public programs is not an automatic process. The explicit development of new agencies to administer programs like agrarian reform implies that existing bureaucratic manpower resources as presently organized are insufficient or inadequate in qualitative as well as quantitative terms to implement public policy. The ability or capability of a particular agency to organize; develop a feasible set of program goals and objectives; recruit, train and deploy its human resources; and garner sufficient financial resources to pay for its operations is not a small matter. The following section will be concerned with the concept of administrative feasibility as it applies to the reform agencies' abilities to achieve their stated objectives effectively.

108. McBride, *op. cit.,* p. 268. Thiesenhusen, *Chile's Experiments in Agrarian Reform, op. cit.,* also cites McBride in this respect.

109. *Ibid.*

110. Thiesenhusen, *Chile's Experiments in Agrarian Reform, op. cit.*, p. 36. He does not state the amount of land that changed hands under the *Caja*. McBride, in his 1936 work, states that up until that time, only a few thousand parcels had been created (p. 276). It is safe to say that less than one million hectares changed hands from 1928 to 1962.

111. Interview with Nicoli Gligo, director of operations, INDAP, June 25, 1968.

112. Corporacion de Fomento de la Produccion, Gerencia Agricola, Officina Programacion y Estudios, "Memoria Gerencia Agricola, 1967" (Santiago, Chile: CORFO, 1967), mimeographed, pp. 6–7.

113. *Ibid.*, p. 7.

114. Interview with Oscar Gonzales, director, Public Relations, CORA, June 22, 1968.

115. *Ibid.*

116. Interview with Hernan Vera, director of personnel, CORA, June 24, 1968.

117. Interview with Oscar Gonzales, *op. cit.*

118. This is true for internal operations for the most part. However, as was revealed in an earlier section and which will be discussed in greater detail in a later section, certain PDC ministers were able to circumscribe and hamper the operations of both agencies, especially INDAP. Hence, the operations which relied upon at least minimal cooperation from other agencies were most exposed to negative influences from these agencies.

119. A number of respondents agreed with this description. For example, one official interviewed stated: "All decisions are made theoretically by CORA's council—in reality, by CORA's vice-president." Interview with Ramon Downey, director, Planning and Control, CORA, June 26, 1968.

120. According to one source, the President of the Republic generally appoints the officers in the first two levels of CORA's hierarchy. In reality the President relies upon the advice of the vice-president of CORA with regard to corporation appointments. Interview with Hernan Vera, *op. cit.*

121. This conclusion was reached formally as early as 1966. See: Plinio Sampaio (ed.), "Organizacion, Planificacion y Coordinacion de las Instituciones del Sector Publico Agricola de Chile, A Nivel de Terreno" (Santiago de Chile: ICIRA, Departamento de Administracion en Reforma Agraria, December, 1966), pp. 14–5. This report calls for the "integration of clientele" among SAG, INDAP, CORA, Banco del Estado, Gerencia Agricola de CORFO, ECA, SEAM, and Comites Regionales y ODEPLAN. Some of this report's recommendations were adopted; the particular one mentioned above has not been as yet.

122. For example, in discussing the distribution or allotment of resources of INDAP among its various units, the "allocation or appointment of functionaries is the exclusive responsibility of the vice-president." See: INDAP, "Que es, Como esta organizado, Como actua, Que ha conseguido," *op. cit.*, pp. 26–7.

123. Overcentralization in decision making has been cited as a characteristic of Latin American bureaucracies by a number of individuals, including: Roberto de Oliveira Campos, "Public Administration in Latin America," in Nimrod Raphaeli, ed., *Readings in Comparative Public Administration* (Boston: Allyn and Bacon, 1967), pp. 283–94; and John C. Honey, ed., *Toward Strategies for Public Administration Development in Latin America* (Syracuse: Syracuse University Press, 1968).

124. CIAP, "Domestic Efforts and the Needs for External Financing for the Development of Chile," *op. cit.*, p. 125.

125. Interview with Ramon Downey, *op. cit.* The following discussion of planning stems from this source.

126. This is only one example of one administrative operation—planning. Others exist in goal and objective formation, program development, and program implementation from supplying funds and other resources (human and material) to the accountability processes. This example from planning illustrates not only the centralization issue and the extent to which the Santiago organization tends to dominate in the control and supervision of field operations, but it also reveals some clues as to the decision-making process within the reform agencies.

127. *El Mercurio, El Siglo, Ercilla,* and other Chilean public news sources periodically carried stories of conflicts between INDAP or CORA officials and those connected with other public agencies. For example, Zujovic alluded to such an incident in his defense of his actions in the Chonchol resignation. See: *Ercilla,* November 26, 1968.

128. Interview with Salvador Cox, chief, *Campesino Sindicates,* INDAP, June 27, 1968. The director of operations, according to Cox, "deals with directors of divisions and zonal chiefs" while Chonchol "is in charge of coordination of external relations with CORA, etc."

129. Interview with Nicoli Gligo, *op. cit.*

130. For example, Cox, although admitting that "zonal advisers implement . . . (but) do not make policies" could still describe INDAP as a "decentralized organization" of fifteen "action zones divided into work areas which correspond to an administrative department—that is, slightly larger than a municipality. They are ecological zones rather than political or administrative units." Salvador Cox, *op. cit.*

131. Interview with Ramon Downey, *op. cit.* Downey was, previous to CORA's reorganization, Director of Operations—the position comparable to INDAP's Gligo.

132. Interview with ICIRA officials, June 14, 1968. These same officials stated that CORA's expropriation process was highly political, pointing out that none of the Edwards' lands has been expropriated.

133. Interview with R. Santa Cruz, director, Legal Division, CORA, June 24, 1968. It is interesting to note the double or two-way use of economics to justify limited expropriation. On the one hand, Sr. Santa Cruz argued that agricultural efficiency is the paramount aim. On the other hand, he argued for the non-expropriation of "good *fundo* owners" even though "we realize that we lose in terms of economics of scale." Who determines the "good" *fundo* owners not to be penalized by expropriation? The Agrarian Reform Corporation. An example of obvious nonenforcement of the law's expropriation is the fact that none of the holdings of the Edwards Company has been subjected to expropriation proceedings.

134. Interview with Ramon Downey, *op. cit.*

135. *Ibid.* It is interesting to note that Sr. Downey had been director of operations under the pre-reorganized CORA and is now director of planning and control. However, he considered that his new, reduced *direccion* (Planning and Control) was the hub of the CORA administrative universe since it was the principal gatherer, processer, and redistributer of information for the agency.

136. Interview with Hernan Vera, *op. cit.*

137. The lowest CORA official in rank and pay.

138. ICIRA, "Organizacion, Planificacion y Coordinacion," *op. cit.*

139. This figure does not include ODEPLAN's Regional Committees responsible for planning or the Ministry of Agriculture.

140. A decision made by a rightist government (Alessandri's regime) whose major goal was to impede if not actually prevent structural reform of the countryside.

141. Estimates of the combined CORA-INDAP personnel come from various interviews with officers of both agencies and various documents, including: CORA, *Cuatro Años de Reforma Agraria, op. cit.,* and INDAP, "Que es, Como esta organizado, Como actua, Que ha conseguido," *op. cit.* Total Chilean public bureaucracy is approximately 300,000.

142. Interview with Hernan Vera, director of personnel, CORA, June 24, 1968. The 1,464 figure was found in CORA, *Cuatro Años de Reforma Agraria, op. cit.,* p. 13. This report is a second edition, published on May 26, 1969. The original edition first appeared in 1968.

143. Interview with Hernan Vera, *op. cit.* A large portion of the information on CORA's personnel was derived from this interview and the materials supplied by Sr. Vera.

144. For example, Chonchol's chief assistant and adviser, Nicoli Gligo (director of operations, INDAP), was in his late 20's. Many other division heads, directors, and program and zonal chiefs were in their

20's and 30's. This was true for CORA as well. Youth appeared to be the rule rather than the exception.

145. Interviews with several INDAP and CORA officers. In addition, functionaries from these other agencies openly admit their hostility to agrarian reform and their ties with the traditional landowning elite. Older agencies attempted to maintain the status quo as their clientele orientation might lead one to suspect. CORA-INDAP, on the other hand, was "trying to accomplish rural change with urban personnel" (Vera interview).

146. Interview with Hernan Vera, *op. cit.* Seventy-five percent were from Greater Santiago.

147. This survey was conducted by the Department of Personnel and Administration, CORA, in the spring of 1968.

148. Interview with Hernan Vera, *op. cit.*

149. Interview with Oscar Gonzales, *op. cit.*

150. The use of "experts" to justify, in technical terms, opposing policies or programs is not, of course, unique to Chile. Debate over the ABM or "Safeguard" weapons system in the United States is a prime example of conflicting expert opinion marshalled on both sides of the question.

151. CIAP, "Domestic Efforts and the Needs for External Financing for the Development of Chile," *op. cit.,* pp. 6, 7, and 128. This report went on to state: "An analysis of the figures given (estimates of reform costs) prompts the suggestion that the international financing agencies consider the possibility of extending long-term credits to finance specific programs . . . mak(ing) it possible to alleviate such bottlenecks in the implementation of agricultural development programs" (p. 138). The estimated population of communal owners, subfamily-sized farm operators, and landless farm workers (all lowest income rural dwellers) ranged from about 317,000 (Barraclough and Domike, *op. cit.,* p. 397) to 320,000 families (INDAP, "Que es, Como esta organizado, Como actua, Que ha conseguido," *op. cit.,* p. 4). Using the more conservative estimate of 317,000 resulted in the 17 percent calculation.

152. We will discuss these in the next section. Needless to say, one problem was finance.

153. CIAP, *op. cit.,* p. 127.

154. *Ibid.,* p. 130.

155. CIAP, *op. cit.,* p. 130.

156. An effort to wean itself from total dependency upon government or parliamentary appropriations.

157. As a later part of this study will reveal, an additional push toward self-financing and limitations upon the number of *campesinos* to be affected by CORA-INDAP activities was the unwillingness of the

U.S. to back its earlier Alliance for Progress promises of support for structural change with financial assistance, credits, and grants. See Chapter 8.

158. Perhaps more than a desire to become "weaned" from Congressional appropriations was the main stimulus for self-financing—that is, CORA and INDAP officials realized that presidential support for structural reform was not real and that one effective means of scaling down reform efforts was by withholding or severely reducing government appropriations to INDAP-CORA. This is more than a suspicion since almost all officials in INDAP and many in CORA complained of lack of financial support for reform activities.

159. This is the Institute of Training and Research in Agrarian Reform. This is a cooperative venture between the United Nation's Food and Agriculture organization and the Chilean government. It was established during the early part of the Frei regime.

160. CIAP, "Domestic Efforts and the Needs for External Financing for the Development of Chile," op. cit., p. 127.

161. Interviews with INDAP officials.

162. Observations derived from comparing data in Table VIII with data in Table X. The problem of inflated escudos is controlled since both data were generated at almost the same time (1967–1968).

163. This was not due to poor estimates by CORA. Court rulings required CORA to provide more cash for down payments on expropriated *fundos*. Interview with R. Santa Cruz, op. cit.

164. One note before discussing reform results—some observations made by the Inter-American Committee on the Alliance for Progress (CIAP) on Chile's development are pertinent:

> With regard to the development policy, the subcommittee (on Chile) agreed with the general guidelines of the government's strategy, which gives high priority to increased exports and to investment in the primary and secondary sectors. . . . Progress achieved in the main sectors was recognized and there was agreement with the government as to the need to speed up the agrarian reform process. . . .

[Inter-American Economic and Social Council, Inter-American Committee on the Alliance for Progress (CIAP), CIAP Subcommittee on Chile, "Domestic Efforts and the Needs for External Financing for the Development of Chile" (Washington, D.C.: Pan American Union, December 15, 1969), p. 1. Discussion occurred in January, 1970.] This Chilean government strategy when compared to what was presented a few years earlier clearly demonstrates the fact that in late 1969 the Chilean government had given up almost all pretense of structural change. A content analysis of the CIAP report of 1967 with its counterpart in 1970 underscores the absence of any significant breakthrough in structurally changing the agrarian sector.

Whereas the 1967 report devoted some nineteen pages to Chile's agrarian reform program, the 1970 report vaguely endorsed the government's recognition of the "need to speed up the agrarian reform process"—a polite method of avoiding an obviously unpleasant subject. While politely admitting little progress, the report indirectly pointed to agrarian reform's priority in 1970: "This report does not intend to cover exhaustively the behavior of the Chilean economy over the last two years, and therefore, *only very important aspects of that behavior are analyzed.*" This last statement is qualified by: "it does not take into consideration the significant progress achieved in the fields of education and agrarian reform. . . ." Reading between the lines one can discern the CIAP's opinion of Chilean agrarian reform. "CIAP Report of 1970," *op. cit.,* pp. 1–2.

165. Land size will be given in "basic irrigated hectares." CIAP estimated that available family farm size would be, on the average, ten hectares of irrigated land or forty hectares of nonirrigated but arable land. See: CIAP, "Domestic Efforts and the Needs for External Financing for the Development of Chile" (Report dated September 29, 1967), *op. cit.,* p. 127 and note 1 on same page.

166. This would be about 40 percent of all arable land in Chile.

167. CORA, *Cuatro Años de Reforma Agraria, op. cit.,* p. 24. CORA's figures for part of 1968 were estimates.

168. Joseph R. Thome, "A Brief Survey of the Chilean Agrarian Reform Program," *LTC* No. 23 (Madison: University of Wisconsin, The Land Tenure Center, February, 1969), p. 5. Thome also states that title distributions were planned for nine other settlements sometime in late 1969.

169. Petras and Zeitlin, *op. cit.*

170. This estimate was given by Jacques Chonchol. His breakdown was as follows: 80,000 peasants organized in unions (some 26,000 more than the labor ministry has recorded and, hence, certified); 90,000 peasants belonging to committees of small farmers; and an additional 30,000 peasants belonging to small farmer cooperatives. This is a substantial change in traditional patterns in the countryside. The total set represents a large political potential. Interview with Jacques Chonchol, vice-president (executive director), INDAP, June 20, 1968. He resigned in protest over Frei's policy toward agrarian reform five months after this interview.

171. Gerrit Huizer reached a similar conclusion working from a slightly different perspective. See his study, "Report on the Study of the Role of Peasant Organizations in the Process of Agrarian Reform in Latin America," mimeographed preliminary draft (Geneva: International Labour Office, June, 1969), p. 609. This study was jointly sponsored by the ILO and CIDA.

172. Interviews with ICIRA and CORA officials.

228 : CULTIVATING REVOLUTION

173. CIAP, 1970 Report, *op. cit.*, p. 28.
174. "Chile's Drought Worsens Strife Over Reforms," *New York Times*, September 18, 1968, p. 2.
175. CIAP, 1970 Report, *op. cit.*, p. 28.

PART THREE

NON-BARGAINING

POLITICS AND

SOCIO-POLITICAL CHANGE

Most accounts of social change stress the positive features of a legal and peaceful or "evolutionary" approach. Implicit or explicit is the assumption that such change is feasible and, moreover, that it is the only approach compatible with the democratization of society. Not infrequently when comparisons are made between an evolutionary and a revolutionary approach, the latter is usually described as irrational and antidemocratic mass behavior. In ideological terms the alternative approaches to social change are often posed as either democratic (evolutionary) or totalitarian (revolutionary).

The hostility of most U.S. political scientists toward social revolution is largely a function of their predisposition to idealize the evolutionary alternative. The context in which gradualism occurs, the differential costs that it imposes on various social classes, and the specific outcomes are not seriously examined. On the other hand, when it comes to studying revolutionary change most social scientists tend to focus almost exclusively on the costs and to give only slight attention to the benefits resulting from radical action.

The elaboration of more complex counting techniques (quantification) and the simplification of political action through the manipulation of abstract symbols (mathematical model building) rest primarily on empirically untested assumptions largely derived from the repetitive and pervasive rhetoric of official policy-makers.

During the last twenty years repeated attempts were made, throughout the Third World, to apply the evolutionary approach to social change and development with little or no success. To the "true believers," however, no amount of evidence was sufficient. Variants of the evolutionary approach were elaborated which lengthened the time period during which changes were supposed to occur, rationalized political violence accompanying the "evolutionary" approach as "reactive" or "defensive" action against those who presented alternatives, and apologized for illegally constituted regimes as "temporary" or "necessary" occurrences in unfortunate circumstances. Thus a good deal of the writing on social change has been biased in a conservative direction, an admixture of romantic idealization of abstract processes remote from contemporary realities and hardnose authoritarian realism.

The need for revolutionary change has become a dominant theme throughout Latin America and has already been embodied in at least one ongoing political system. Despite the warnings of U.S. social scientists and policy-makers concerning the "inherent" dangers of totalitarianism, intellectuals and the politically conscious exploited strata are increasingly turning toward revolutionary politics as the only effective way to democratize society.

The politics of existing societies (pluralistic, hierarchical and exploitative) are largely managed by bargaining elites who have little or no interest in redistributing economic resources, especially land. Changes where they occur are marginal, halting and directed from above. Legally sanctioned change usually results in endless procedural and administrative obstacles, reducing the number of beneficiaries and exhausting financial resources allocated for reform. Atomization or organizational subordination of the populace to administrative agencies permeated by traditional values, characterizes societies which have experienced "peaceful" change. The absence of an assertive popular movement which takes the initiative in seeking change on its own behalf is described as "ordered change," while marginal improvements directed from above for a demobilized populace are described as peaceful democratic change. This mythology may have its political uses but it has little value as social science. In our study of peasant politics we have found that illegal and violent land seizures can have a salutary effect on democratic politics. As evolutionary approaches have failed to provide meaningful reforms, peasants, perceiving opportunities for effecting changes, have taken violent actions which have substantially improved their economic and social conditions and encouraged them to participate in civic affairs. In a word, revolutionary action has brought about changes which were sought but unattained by practitioners of evolutionary politics.

5

Subsystem Change—
Peasant Politicization in Chile

Throughout the 1950s and early 1960s an insignificant fraction of the rural labor force was unionized. In 1953 only 1,042 agricultural workers were unionized in 15 unions; in 1963 there were only 1,500 members in 22 unions.[1]

In the 1964 election, the Marxist Left and the Christian Democrats, both strong advocates of agrarian reform, gathered over 95 percent of the vote. When the Christian Democrat Frei took over the Presidency in November, 1964, there were only 1,658 unionized rural workers in the whole of Chile. Spurred on by the election campaign and continuing with increasing militancy afterwards, rural workers began to take direct action. Strikes and work stoppages were occasionally followed by land seizure.[2] The left wing of the Christian Democrats led by Jacques Chonchol was in charge of the agrarian reform. Under its direction government policy began to change significantly.[3] Government officials in many cases began to take a more positive or at least neutral attitude toward peasant demands; the police were less frequently employed to defend the interests of the landlords; and, more important, Chonchol's Institute of Agricultural Development (INDAP) began to actively encourage peasant organization.[4]

The politicization by the Left and PDC during the 1964 elections encouraged peasants to make demands; the expression of collective demands and the success in carrying out struggles encouraged the organization of peasant unions. The growth of an active, socially conscious peasantry and the competition of different political organizations led to the formation of rival peasant trade union confederations.[5] The vast expansion of peasant unions resulted in increased pressure to accelerate the agrarian reform. The agrarian reform officials, especially Chonchol, began to articulate these demands in government policy-making circles. However, the broad scope of the movement and its increasing militancy conflicted with the policies of the executive. The intentions of the latter were to encourage the gradual unionization of peasants who would present moderate demands, compatible with the time schedule and economic activities of the landowners (not at seeding or harvest) so as not to affect productivity.[6] The process of land expropriation was to be selected and tightly controlled by government functionaries who were to exercise their prerogatives in a manner which did not undermine the "confidence" of the agricultural entrepreneurs.[7]

In the first year of the Frei government (1965) very little overt organization took place though rural unrest was increasing; in 1966, the unrest and strikes began to coalesce in an organizational way. The number of trade unions increased fivefold: from 2,118 in 1965 to 10,647 in 1966.[8] In 1967, membership in agrarian trade unions increased four and a half times—from 10,647 to 47,473.[9] The major impetus for organizing peasant unions came from INDAP and secondarily from the Marxist-led federations. While INDAP lacked experienced peasant leaders, it did have access to government officials in resolving peasant demands and it was able to neutralize the effects of adverse decisions by local officials of the Ministry of Labor. While the Christian Democratic agrarian reformers saw peasant agitation and organization as the first step toward a broad transformation of land tenure, President Frei perceived the process as going too fast and threatening the "balance" that he wanted to maintain between big landed entrepreneurs and peasants.[10]

The unionization of the peasants which the agrarian reformers took to be the *first* step toward a social transformation, Frei perceived as the *end* product of a prolonged process of rural education and gradual organization under government tutelage. The executive pressures to slow down government-sponsored peasant mobilization began to be applied in 1967, but the agrarian reformers refused to accede; and between 1967 and 1968 peasant unionization increased by over 50 percent, from 47,473 to 76,356.[11]

By mid-1968, the situation in rural areas appeared to Frei to be getting out of control; Chonchol and his supporters were told to slow down. Despite this pressure, as of September, 1968, the INDAP-supported trade unions had an absolute majority of the unionized peasantry (52.4 percent), followed by the Marxist-led unions (24.4 percent) and the U.S.-backed, pro-Frei *Confederacion Libertad* with 23.2 percent.[12]

By the end of 1968, President Frei decided that the unionization process had gone too far; that the peasant unions were engendering too much conflict; that the growth of a militant peasant movement was a threat to the entrepreneurial farmers. On the other hand, Chonchol and the agrarian reform wing of the PDC became increasingly aware of the difficulties in carrying out an agrarian reform in isolation from other sectors of the economy. As a result, they formulated a strategy which they referred to as the "noncapitalist road to development," which included the nationalization of banks and credits and increased the government's control over the commercialization of farm products.[13] In the meantime, the urban economic elites— construction industry, banking, and commerce—were becoming increasingly preoccupied with the militancy in the countryside. They increasingly gave their support to the large landowners' association. The Christian Democratic coalition, made up of agrarian reformers and urban capital, which Frei had held together, collapsed. Frei was presented with the choice of allying with the economic elites or the agrarian reformers. The choice was never in doubt; Chonchol and a significant part of the left wing departed and formed a new party—MAPU (the United Popular Action Movement).

In 1968, the political Right, directed by the National Party, began to coalesce into a coalition of urban and rural economic elites.[14] Encouraged by Frei's rejection of the agrarian reformers, they began to mobilize their supporters in open defiance of the law. This culminated in the shooting of an Agrarian Reform Corporation (CORA) official involved in expropriating a farm.

Frei's adaptation to the urban elites, the increasing audacity of the landowners, and the departure of part of the left wing of the PDC created the public impression that the program of agrarian reform was ready to be buried. To counteract the conservative image provoked by the sudden aggressive behavior of the "new Right," and under considerable pressure from the remaining reform elements in the Party, the PDC continued to tolerate unionization and expropriation of *fundos*.

Peasant unionism continued to expand. By the end of 1969, 103,043 peasants were organized, 35 percent above the 1968 level.[15]

By June, 1970, CORA estimated that the number of unionized peasants reached 127,688—a jump of almost 25 percent in six months—a figure which is hardly to be trusted.[16] The increased pressure of the election campaign and the competition between the candidates for peasant support undoubtedly have opened up further opportunities for peasant union organizers to enter the field. If we accept CORA's figures, by the middle of 1970 almost 38 percent of the salaried rural labor force of 335,000 was unionized in 488 unions. However, informed sources claim that most likely the unionized peasants do not exceed 105,000. The growing militancy of the peasants, the increasing activity of the trade-unionists, and the promotional activity of agrarian reform officials have increasingly polarized the countryside.

The rural labor force has become cognizant of its exploited position in the "traditional" socio-economic system and has redefined its relationship to the landowners and to the dominant social classes. The rural laboring classes, conscious of their position, have increasingly opted for organizations that can, in the short run, *improve* their class position and, in the long run, *change* their class.

In absolute terms, INDAP—the organized *campesino* confederation (*Triunfo Campesino*)—continued to be the most important (47,609 members).[17] However, in terms of the proportion of trade union members, it declined from 52.4 percent in 1968 to 46.7 percent in 1969. The more conservative confederation (*Libertad*) decreased slightly from 23.2 to 22.6 percent.[18] The Marxist-led confederation (*Ranquil*) increased from 24.4 to 30.3 percent of the organized peasantry.[19] The large landowner-sponsored "United Agrarian Provinces" contained less than one percent. Almost one-half (47 percent) of the increase in peasant union membership between 1968 and 1969 was accounted for by the Marxist peasant unions—a significant change from the preceding years: *Ranquil,* the radical peasant union independent of the Frei government and led by unionists who opposed his policies, showed the greatest gain in 1969. At the same time, the peasant confederation which was most influenced by the former left wing of the PDC (*Triunfo*) was the one which showed a relative decline (in absolute terms it increased its membership by eight thousand). The growth of the Left was also strongly aided by the incorporation of the left Christian Democrats (MAPU) in the left-wing coalition (*Unidad Popular*).

The split in the PDC, however, did not result in a formal split in the peasant unions. To maintain the loyalty of the peasant leaders of *Triunfo,* the Frei government began to increase its social and economic pressures. The government began to tie credit and technical assistance to conformity to the party's political position. Being pragmatists, most of the leaders of *Triunfo* at least outwardly shifted their loyalty from Chonchol to Frei and Tomic. Many of the rank and file of *Triunfo,* however, continue to support Chonchol and MAPU while accepting government economic aid. In the near future, a division may take place within *Triunfo*—one section going over to *Ranquil* and the rest fusing with *Libertad*.

The change of personnel in INDAP is indicative of the changing orientation of the Frei government. The agrarian reformer, Chonchol, was replaced by Luis Marambio at the end of 1968 and he stayed on till the middle of 1969, apparently caught up in the momentum of the organization and thus maintaining to some extent the dynamism of his predecessor. However, in mid-1969, Marambio was replaced by Roberto Infante Rengifo, a large landowner and a member in good standing of the landowners' association (SNA) and vice-president of the *Banco del Estado*. INDAP seriously curtailed its union organizing activities under its new chief. Nevertheless, some of the trade unions developed their own leadership and financial support apart from the government and continued to promote unionization. Thus, despite the departure of Chonchol and his supporters, the peasant organizational effort continued to operate. This accounts for the increase in peasant union membership. Nevertheless, there is some doubt if many of the peasant unions promoted by INDAP could have survived the onslaught of a right-wing government without strong support from urban political and social organizations.

Many of the peasant leaders, especially from the *Triunfo* and *Libertad* confederations, were able to maintain their leadership positions largely due to their ability to resolve problems through contacts within the Christian Democratic government. Their dependent role vis-a-vis the government and the increasing tendency, on the part of the peasant trade union leadership, to lend themselves to clientele politics (that is, exchange of favors for political support) suggests that at least part of the peasant union movement could become a bureaucratic appendage of the government: less concerned with pushing the redistribution of land than with obtaining concessions and consolidating their existing basis of support. The leadership of *Libertad,* partly financed by the International Development Foundation (a CIA conduit), is amenable to maintaining "order" in the countryside in exchange for vehicles, financial support, and government backing.[20] The situation in *Triunfo* is changing; immediately following the exodus of Chonchol and his followers, the pro-PDC and pro-MAPU forces were about equal. However, as the 1970 election campaign developed, the leadership shifted toward Tomic because of their closer ideological affinity and because the government offered services and material incentives. Christian Democratic peasant union leaders are an upwardly mobile group; in a very short time they have catapulted from the lowest status in society to playing an important role as conflict managers for the national government.

The competing confederations concentrated their organizing efforts initially near urban centers, areas of sociopolitical strength, and areas where there existed concentrations of salaried workers. In recent years, however, the peasant unions have spread to the more distant parts of the countryside, especially rural areas of the south which were previously unaffected. The greatest number of organized peasants in decending order, is first, the Province of Santiago (13,443), the proximity of the capital and its political-economic resources is an obvious determinant;[21] second, the Province of Talca (9,344), long a Christian Democratic and Marxist center of socio-political peasant organization;[22] third, O'Higgins (8,588), with its mining centers and their radical traditions which have served to influence and support peasant struggles;[23] fourth, Ñuble, one of the most impoverished and exploited regions, which was swept up in the initial organizing effort of rural areas and in the process accelerated it—in 1969 Ñuble experienced a wave of land seizures.

The confederation of the conservative Christian Democrats, *Libertad,* is a dominant trade union force in Valparaiso (81 percent of the unionized peasants), Curico (39.5 percent), Talca (46.9 percent).[24] The more militant *Triunfo* confederation is dominant or shows equal influence in Atacama (100 percent), Coquimbo (50 percent), Aconcagua (43 percent), Santiago (38.2 percent), O'Higgins (62.8 percent), Colchagua (41 percent), Linares (45.6 percent), Maule (68.5 percent), Ñuble (53.3 percent), Malleco (95.8 percent), Cautin (84 percent), Valdivia (49.9 percent), Osorno (78.7 percent), Llanquihue (56 percent), Aysen (100 percent).[25] The Communist/Socialist-led *Ranquil* confederation is dominant or shares equal influence in Coquimbo (49.9 percent), Colchagua (40.4 percent), Concepcion (52.2 percent), Arauco (87.2 percent), Bio-Bio (37.9 percent), Magallanes (65.1 percent).[26] The forces of *Libertad* tend to be more concentrated on a regional basis (Central Valley) than the other confederations which tend to have more balanced bases of support.

The provinces which show the highest increase between 1968 and 1969 (over 10 percent) were generally those areas where previously peasant unionism was weakest (where less than 23 percent of the salaried rural workers were organized). Two of the three provinces which contained over 35 percent of the unionized salaried workers had increases of less than 3 percent. It appears that the phase of relatively easy expansion of unionism may be coming to an end in some areas. Further expansion will probably occur in less organized areas (such as Maule, O'Higgins, Valparaiso, Linares, Bio-Bio, Osorno, and Aysen).

INDAP's organizational breakthrough which occurred between 1966 and 1968 extended rural unionism beyond the areas adjacent to socio-political centers to strictly rural areas with little prior history of social struggle. In some areas the establishment of Christian Democratic unions facilitated the entrance of the more radical Socialist-Communist unions; in other cases the initial organizers, once having established their predominance, were able to maintain it. It appears that the Christian Democrats, especially in areas of extreme conservatism, legitimized peasant unionism through their initial efforts. However, they have had problems in maintaining their influence once peasant demands began to grow and leftist organizations began to compete for the allegiances of the peasantry.

Summary

The major change in Chile during the Frei presidency was not in the area of land tenure change but rather in the unionization of the rural wage labor force. The rapid growth of unionism was initially supported by all Christian Democrats. As the movement grew in size and militancy, a division developed over the goals of the movement. Frei and his supporters perceived the trade union as a pressure group within the traditional structure. The organization of the peasants was perceived as an instrument to "integrate" them into existing capitalist society, giving them a limited role in determining their terms of employment by the rural entrepreneurs.[27] To Chonchol and his supporters, the union was an instrument to transform rural society and a substitute for the landowner. Consistent with Frei's past support of a "pluralist" capitalist society (including landowners, bankers, and industrialists), Frei never envisioned the approach which INDAP proposed. It is incorrect to state, as do some left Christian Democrats, that Frei "betrayed" his program: he sought to "integrate" new strata of peasant proprietors in the existing capitalist society. What did change was the young Christian Democrats; under the impact of peasant organization and struggle they sought to implement the agrarian reform put forth by Frei; and they became increasingly frustrated as they continued to encounter political obstacles erected by the Frei government. The rebel Christian Democrats were increasingly committed to a general transformation, while Frei became increasingly concerned with limiting the structural consequences of mass social organization. The result of these contradictory approaches was the successful promotion of a mass peasant union movement and very limited redistribution of land.

Land Distribution 1965–1970

During the period 1965–1970, the Frei government expropriated 279 thousand hectares of irrigated land.[28] By June, 1970, the government had expropriated only 17.5 percent of the irrigated land; the large landholder still maintained the great bulk of the best land in the country. During the same period, the government expropriated only 12 percent of the nonirrigated land (3.1 million hectares).[29] Government reporting does not allow us to state the amount of this nonirrigated land that is usable for cultivation. The expropriation program has varied considerably from province to province. In Aconcagua, 34.8 percent of the irrigated land has been expropriated while in O'Higgins only 9.6 percent has been taken over.[30]

Family Settlements in the Agrarian Reform

The Frei government's major failure was in the area of settlement of families on land expropriated through the agrarian reform. In 1964, he promised 100,000 proprietors by 1970. By 1967, the figure was reduced to between 40,000 and 60,000. In the end, only 21,105 families received land (as of July, 1970).[31] In terms of the total peasant population in need of land, about 8 percent were benefited by the "agrarian reform"—almost 92 percent were excluded. CORA's figures on the agrarian reform were frequently manipulated and inflated to give the impression that rapid

TABLE I

FORMATION OF LAND SETTLEMENT COLONIES BETWEEN 1965 AND JULY 14, 1970

	1965	1966	1967	1968	1969	1970*	Totals for 1965–1970
Number of Land Settlement Colonies	33	62	151	158	229	277	910
Amount of Land in Hectares	286,839.3	145,616.8	354,847.7	725,171.9	1,078,210.8	461,328.5	3,052,015
Irrigated Land	16,241	17,286.8	47,736.3	53,661.1	68,432.5	53,344.2	256,708
Nonirrigated Land	270,592.2	128,330	307,111.4	671,510.8	1,009,778.3	407,984.3	2,795,307
Families Benefited	2,061	2,109	4,218	5,644	6,404	8,703	29,139

Source: CORA, "Reforma Agraria Chilena 1965–1970," Santiago, Chile, July, 1970, p. 45.
* The 1970 figures were those projected; as the subsequent table shows, the projection is quite distant from the reality.

changes were occurring—especially from 1968 to 1970. For example, if we compare the tabulations of CORA (Table I) to those presented by a former director of CORA and collected by CORA's Department of Statistics (Table II) we will see marked differences after 1967.

As can be seen in comparing Table I with Table II, CORA manipulated the data for 1968 and 1969 to give the impression that there was a *constant* increase in reform activities, when in fact there was a decline in 1968 followed by an increase in 1969. More important, the data published for 1970 were greatly exaggerated probably to serve the presidential campaign needs of the Christian Democrats.

The agrarian reform program was experiencing stiffer resistance from the landowners: CORA officials were assaulted; landowners armed themselves and prepared to fight against expropriation. In comparison, the first years of the agrarian reform were relatively easy. From the beginning of 1965 to July, 1967, land was expropriated under the 1962 agrarian reform law. Most of the expropriations that took place occurred on abandoned farms or farms that were inefficiently operated. Almost one-half (47 percent) of the irrigated land expropriated occurred under the old law.[32] Under the new law passed in July, 1967 the government continued to expropriate land that was not being cultivated efficiently (20 percent of the total holdings expropriated since July, 1967) but began to move toward expropriation of other lands. In many cases of expropriation (37 percent), the owners offered to sell their holdings to the government because of the high price which the government was willing to pay.[33] However, this option was quickly exhausted and fewer and fewer landowners remained who wanted to sell their *fundos*. Hence the land reform and land settlement process slowed down considerably during 1970. On the other hand, the pressure of the *campesinos* and the peasant unions increased: land seizures multiplied during 1968 and 1969. In May of 1970, a historic nationwide general strike of peasant unions took place, demanding the ac-

TABLE II

LAND SETTLEMENT COLONIES 1968–1970 (JULY 14, 1970)

	1968	1969	1970	Totals 1968–70
Number of Land Settlement Colonies	113	209	99	667
Amount of Land in Hectares	443,061	1,103,125	328,110	2,661,599.8
Irrigated Land	30,136	79,682	22,740	213,828
Nonirrigated Land	412,925	1,013,444	305,370	2,437,772
Families Benefited	2,915	7,315	2,487	21,105

Sources: Jorge Echenique, *Las expropiaciones y la organizacion de asenta-mientos en el periodo 1965–1970,* Universidad de Chile, Santiago, Chile, 1970, p. 21.
Department of Statistics, CORA. Raw data covering the period January–June, 1970, was provided by personnel in CORA's Department of Statistics.

celeration of the agrarian reform and an end to the illegal armed resistance of the big landowners.

The peasants and peasant unions increasingly turned toward direct action, radicalizing their demands, and looking toward support from the Marxist Left. Under Frei, the promised reforms served merely to raise peasant expectations and to provoke right-wing resistance. One former high CORA official who served during the first three years of the Frei government noted:

> In general terms one could conclude that the peasants, through various forms of behavior, have participated in bringing about the expropriations but with the exception of some leaders of land settlement colonies in certain zones, the most representative organizations of the agricultural workers have not had any participation in the programming or formulation of the criteria and agreements concerning expropriations.[34]

The Frei government's policy was to create a new middle-class entrepreneurial farmer group alongside the large efficient farm. The trade unions were to serve as tools to improve the living standards of the rest of the *campesinos*. The few thousand *campesinos* who have received land have experienced a substantial increase in their standard of living. The cost of reform—in terms of payments to the landowners and financing of post-reform development—strained the limits of the government's resources. The agrarian reform program of the Frei government has created a new stratum of relatively better off, middle-class peasants, who now employ labor, mimic the old landowners, and follow their political lead in many cases. On the other hand, Frei allowed a vast number of landless peasants to be unionized without meeting their basic demands. Frei's policies polarized the countryside and in the process undercut the basis of support for the "centrist" Christian Democrats. The vote of the economically active *campesinos*—largely males —shifted to the left (see Table III); the right-wing picked up support precisely in the areas where unionism was weak and among small farmers little affected by the new rural organizations.

Allende gained a plurality of the male votes in ten of fourteen rural provinces—Alessandri captured the remaining four. The Christian Democrat Tomic was the lowest vote-getter in twelve of the fourteen provinces. The countryside polarized with a significant plurality swinging to the left. It is well to remember that the Tomic campaign itself was decidedly more radical than Frei's (he promised to accelerate the agrarian reform). In other words, the total antireform vote (in rural Chile) amounted to only 36 percent (Alessandri's proportion).

It is clear that by 1970 the Chilean countryside was greatly politicized and ready for a rapid and thorough transformation of land tenure, a task which the new Socialist President Salvador Allende will have to face. Allende and the rural laborers who backed his candidacy are intent on realizing the transformation which Frei promised but never achieved. What is equally obvious, however, is that the land-

TABLE III

MALE VOTE FOR PRESIDENTIAL CANDIDATES IN RURAL
PROVINCES DURING 1970 ELECTION[35]

	ALLENDE (Left)	ALESSANDRI (Right)	TOMIC (Center)
Coquimbo	24,859	13,406	11,600
Aconcagua	11,767	8,967	8,879
O'Higgins	24,719	14,350	13,969
Colchagua	9,361	9,345	7,428
Curico	7,487	5,758	4,510
Talca	15,249	8,476	8,828
Linares	9,758	10,061	7,896
Maule	4,837	4,828	3,337
Ñuble	16,794	15,972	12,987
Bio-Bio	10,998	9,401	6,815
Malleco	8,892	9,910	8,056
Cautin	16,209	26,305	21,295
Valdivia	16,369	14,847	11,851
Osorno	9,074	10,291	8,039
TOTALS	186,373	161,917	135,490

owners are now backed by the urban economic elites who stand to lose through government-sponsored nationalizations. Relying on their control over economic institutions (banks and factories), they have begun to apply economic pressures, withdrawing capital, and closing enterprises in hope of provoking a crisis and military intervention.[36] A right-wing coup, however, would be resisted by the great majority of the people (leftists and Christian Democrats) who voted against the Right. In a country where the bourgeoisie has long preached obedience to the law and constitution (as it suited their convenience), a right-wing coup could set off a series of conflicts which could lead to a civil war. The military appears to be divided between those favoring a coup and those who are "constitutionalists." [37]

For the right wing and the big landowners, time is running out; panic has set in. The agrarian revolution is on the door step of the *Casa Grande*. The last best hope for the economic elite is to be found among Christian Democrats who are prepared to create a host of problems in the post-elections period, not excluding certain maneuvers which could undermine the Allende victory.[38]

The election of Dr. Allende, and his subsequent assumption of executive power, does not mean that the politically vitalized peasants and industrial workers and miners who supported him will be satisfied with symbolic rewards. The gulf between the rhetoric of reform and economic redistribution *and* the actual accomplishments during the Frei period was great; in fact, the promises Frei made have encouraged Chilean peasants to demand their fulfillment. President Allende's major task will be to satisfy both rural and urban demands while at least neutralizing powerful counter-interests. An accelerated agrarian reform program which would include major redistribution of land tenure and further unionization, coupled with complete nationalization of major industries and a realignment and redistribution of the products of these industries, are the basic requisites for Allende's objective of laying "the foundations for socialism."

Postscript

An assessment of the first few months of the Allende government is revealing in both early accomplishments and genuine promises for the future as well as symbolic and real impact. Allende appears to be carrying out his program with all due speed. The record of socio-economic change, planned and accomplished, includes: a bill to nationalize the copper mines; the acceleration of agrarian reform to the point that in the first three months several thousand acres (mostly in the south) have been expropriated—in conjunction with this, a national peasant council has been established to participate in the planning and direction of the agrarian reform and agricultural development in general;[39] the nationalization of several banks for their violation of government financial operations regulations; the nationalization of a number of industrial enterprises as a result of their violation of the Chilean labor code; and the implementation of certain basic public-health–social-services programs such as the free distribution of a liter of milk per day to every school child.

The immediate result of these actions (and those which will have longer range effects, such as Allende's proposed judicial reform)[40] has been a sharp increase in the popularity of the Allende government and a subsequent growing hostility to the government among the economic elite. Groups of right-wing extremists, supported by certain members of the economic elite, have turned to violent, terrorist tactics. Party dissension and fragmentation has also resulted. For example, the Christian Democrats have become the major oppositionist group but they have split into two groups—the Tomic section, about 40 percent of the party, seeks to collaborate with the government, giving support on certain measures while using their influence to impede the rapid socialization of the economy; the majoritarian or Frei section, while verbally favoring a "constructive opposition" (theoretically, the supporting and opposing of specific government measures), in practice seeks only to effectively brake and impede the process of change. To accomplish this, the Frei section has developed informal linkages and contacts with the rightist National Party although publically denying these relations.

The events of the past few months appear to have been politically favorable to Allende. It is quite likely that the Popular Unity coalition will increase its electoral base in the municipal elections (scheduled for April, 1971) from the 36 percent of the popular vote obtained in 1970 to an estimated 45 percent. The steady decline in popular support coupled with the acceleration of the rural and urban reforms is leading to increased opposition from the political right. The right-wing's electoral defeat along with their identification with the abortive kidnap attempt and tragic assassination of General Schneider led to general demoralization; however, after a few months, they were active again. Right-wing coup attempts are not to be excluded from the realm of possibility in the coming months—the consequences of which would be a violent civil war.

It is indicative that the Chilean workers and peasants are enjoying, for the first time, a government which is giving primary consideration to their basic social and economic needs and demands. It is hoped that the immoderate, intemperate, and generally misinformed attacks by the U.S. press on the Chilean government will not be translated into official U.S. policy—a step which would once again align the U.S. government with those Chilean elite members and economic forces intent upon maintaining outdated and grossly unjust political, social, and economic privileges in opposition to the popular, majoritarian demands of the Chilean peasantry.

NOTES

1. *Ministerio de Trabajo, Direccion de Estadistica.* Information compiled from raw data presented in a table "Organizacion sindical desde 1953 hasta 1968."

2. Almino Affonso, Sergio Gomez, Emilio Klein, Pablo Ramirez, *Movimiento Campesino Chileno* (ICIRA: Santiago, Chile, 1970), Vol. 2, pp. 7–140.

3. Jacques Chonchol, "Poder y Reforma Agrarian en la experiencia Chilena," *Cuadernos de la Realidad Nacional*, No. 4, June, 1970, pp. 50–87.

4. *Ibid.*

5. Almino Affonso, *et al., op. cit.,* Vol. I, pp. 65–261.

6. "It is an indisputable fact that the most critical point for our economic development resides fundamentally in the backwardness of the agricultural sector. There is no possibility of escaping from stagnation, overcoming inflation and achieving a favorable balance of payments, if we are not capable of carrying out an agrarian policy that substantially increases our agricultural and livestock production." *Mensaje Presidencial al Congreso,* 21 May, 1965.

7. *Mensaje Presidencial,* 1 May, 1968.

8. Organizacion sindical desde 1953 hasta 1968," *op. cit.*

9. *Ibid.*

10. "Neither the small, medium or even the large proprietor that is highly productive and maintains good working conditions is threatened (by the agrarian reform)." *Mensaje Presidencial al Congreso*, 1 May, 1965.

11. "Organizacion sindical desde 1953 hasta 1968," *op. cit.*

12. *Ministerio del Trabajo, Direccion de Estadisticas.* Raw data, "Confederaciones nacionales de trabajadores agricolas."

13. Jacques Chonchol, *op. cit.*, interview with Chonchol, August 31, 1970.

14. Interview with Senator Pedro Ibañez, Partido Nacional, August, 1968.

15. *Fundo de Educacion y Extension Sindical, Unidad de Estudios,* "Afiliacion sindical por confederaciones 1969" (Santiago, Chile, 1970).

16. *Corporacion de la Reforma Agraria,* "Reforma Agraria Chilena 1965–1970" (Santiago, Chile, 1970).

17. "Afiliacion sindical por confederaciones 1969," *op. cit.*

18. *Ibid.*

19. *Ibid.*

20. Almino Affonso, *et al., op. cit.*, Vol. I, p. 186. The peasant unions which were associated with *Libertad* are discussed in some detail.

21. "Afiliacion sindical por confederaciones 1969," *op. cit.*

22. *Ibid.*

23. The impact of mining communities on the peasantry has been discussed in James Petras and Maurice Zeitlin, "Miners and Agrarian Radicalism," in Petras and Zeitlin, eds., *Latin America: Reform or Revolution* (N.Y.: Fawcett, 1968).

24. "Afiliacion sindical por confederaciones 1969," *op. cit.*

25. *Ibid.*

26. *Ibid.*

27. "The Agrarian Reform is a process which respects and guarantees the right of property to those landholders who do not merely accumulate land, but fulfill a social function, who have observed the existing social legislation, and have given over to the peasants the rewards which are theirs as a result of their cultivation of the land, thus creating stability, justice, and welfare." *Mensaje Presidencial al Congreso*, 22 November, 1965. It will be interesting to observe what Chonchol will do as President Allende's Minister of Agriculture. As Frei's INDAP director, Chonchol was a pivotal figure in the agrarian reform program but did not have the power of a cabinet minister.

28. Jorge Echenique, *Las expropiaciones y la organizacion de asentamientos en el periodo 1965–1970,* Universidad de Chile, 1970. Data for 1970 supplied by the Dept. of Statistics of CORA.

29. Echenique, *op cit.*, and Dept. of Statistics, CORA.

30. Echenique, *op. cit.*, p. 8.

31. This data provided by Dept. of Statistics of CORA.

32. Echenique, *op. cit.*, p. 4.

33. *Ibid.*, pp. 4–6.

34. *Ibid.*, pp. 11–12.

35. *El Siglo,* September 6, 1970.

36. *Nacion,* September 8, 1970, p. 1. The situation seems to have eased somewhat since the inauguration of Allende on November 4, 1970.

37. The assassination of General René Schneider, Commander-in-Chief of the Chilean Army on October 22, 1970 (two days before the Chilean Congress was to meet in special session to confirm Allende's election), was part of a right-wing plot to create the incident for a military coup. The fact that the coup did not take place supports the idea that at least for the time being the "constitutionalists" continue to dominate within the military.

38. Some examples of post-election maneuvers illustrate this point. First, the PDC demanded certain constitutional "guarantees" in exchange for supporting Allende's popular victory, in the special session of the Chilean Congress on October 24, 1970. This "Statute of Guarantees" took the form of an amendment to the Constitution attempting to assure legally political rights, including the right to work, to form labor unions, to reside anywhere in the country, and the privacy of mail and telephone conversations. Dr. Allende agreed to this amendment, it was incorporated into the Constitution, and the PDC voted for his candidacy. One objective of this maneuver was to attempt to cast doubts on the democratic nature of the new regime even before it assumed power. A second example may be revealed in outgoing President Frei's "concern" for the preservation of the "opportunity for political alternatives" and his call for the "moral energy and courage" of Chileans to "defend democracy." Again, an attempt to indirectly link the Allende regime with "anti-democratic" forces. See: "President Frei, in Farewell Address, Urges Chileans to Defend Democracy," *New York Times,* November 1, 1970.

39. Peasant participation in the agrarian reform during the Frei period was never accomplished due to the opposition of certain PDC officials even though it was part of the 1967 Agrarian Reform Law. See Chapter 4.

40. See: "Leftist Authorities in Chile Denounce Judicial System," *New York Times,* January 27, 1971.

6

The Peruvian Military as a Revolutionary Modernizer

For the first time in Peruvian history a serious effort to develop a modern industrial capitalist society is being undertaken. A military government closely linked to nationalist professional groups has promulgated a broad-ranging program that includes substantive changes in the system of land tenure and target areas in which public and private investments should be channeled.

The military government has set itself a number of strategic economic goals:

(a) Establishment of a dynamic capitalist industrial society in which public and private Peruvian entrepreneurs will play a dominant role.

(b) Incorporation of the peasantry into the market economy through expropriation of the large traditional *haciendas* of the *Sierras* and the distribution of land to the peasantry.

(c) Exclusion of those foreign firms whose behavior violates the political rules and economic guidelines which have been established to foster national industrial development.

(d) Transfer of private capital from agriculture to nonagriculture pursuits especially in the secondary sector.

The military government is clearly *developmental* in its orientation. The earnest effort at redistributive policies such as agrarian reform are subordinated to the overall effort to create inducements for future industrial growth. Likewise *nationalist* policies such as the expropriation of the International Petroleum Company largely served to provide the junta with great popular support. Subsequent policies regarding concessions to foreign investors in the exploitation of minerals and in manufacturing suggest that the junta is largely concerned with integrating foreign-owned resources and enterprises into a broader national development perspective. The *populist* policies of the junta are mainly concerned with socio-economic improvement of the peasantry without permitting effective peasant mobilization. Land reform will be carried out and administered largely by government-appointed agrarian officials (*tecnicos*).[1] Independent activities which the peasants might take on their own behalf will not meet with the approval of the junta. Activities of the industrial working class which revolve around traditional class organizations and issues are treated as threats to the industrial development orientation of the junta.[2] Paternalistic projects involving profit-sharing and co-participation in management are counterposed to the politics of class struggle. The junta has moved to depoliticize the universities and create a professional, technically-oriented university.

In sum, the horses of populism and nationalism are tied to the carriage of developmentalism. The politics of capitalist modernization from above[3] in a colonial economy require the junta to place restrictions and controls on the economic activities of the traditional Peruvian elite as well as the established foreign investors rooted in their mineral-based economic enclaves. At the same time, it requires the junta to limit the opportunities of the Left in order to maintain and direct the process of social change, especially the transfer of property, and in order to limit the extent to which change occurs. While resisting pressures from the advanced capitalist countries that would distort their development priorities, the junta must also provide incentives and a

favorable investment climate in the urban industrial areas—
hence the need to maintain a docile and "managed" labor
force. Paradoxically, in carrying out policies designed to
produce a modern capitalist industrial society, the military
must overcome the opposition of the center of world capitalism and the reservations of its own entrepreneurial elite. Internationally, it is the communist countries—the Soviet
Union and Cuba—and the Peruvian Communist party who
have shown the greatest enthusiasm for the policies of capitalist modernization from above.[4] The policies of the military junta can best be understood by examining the interplay between recent Peruvian political history and the
process of political socialization of the officer corps—the
strategic policy-making elite in Peru today.

Background

The first indications that Peru's military men differed from
the traditional Latin American military *caudillo* appeared
during the military government of 1962–63. Most com-
mentators assumed that the assumption of power was precipitated by fear of an imminent Aprista (APRA) victory
in the 1962 presidential elections.[5] The military was portrayed as defending the old order against the "populist"
APRA. This account fails to deal with the fact that APRA
had for several years come to terms with the traditional
ruling class, and as we shall see, the military had changed
both in its ideas and in its social composition.

Reasons much deeper and more complex than that of
the old military-Aprista hatreds account for the military
coup. The younger military men in Peru's armed forces
were becoming impatient with the transactions and negotiations of the ruling civilian elites. Development-oriented, socially cognizant of Peru's extreme inequality in the distribution of wealth, they were increasingly apprehensive over
the possibility of a violent revolution emanating from the

country's economically depressed and politically excluded rural and urban poor.

The primary intent of Peru's military government of 1962–63 was to assure the election of a civilian who would develop unused resources, alleviate some of the inequities of Peru's socio-economic structure, and restrain the growing revolutionary movement in rural areas.[6] Radical structural changes affecting the prerogatives and privileges of the elites were not objectives of the military men who ruled in that brief (ten-month) government. The men who ran the military junta of 1962–63 were headed for retirement and were acting to some degree under the influence of younger junior staff officers (majors, lieutenant colonels, and colonels). Largely the products of different social and educational experiences than many of the older generals, many of these junior staff officers later surfaced as the generals who are influential in the present junta.

The military coup of July 18, 1962, occurred during large-scale rural insurgency and while traditional conservative and Aprista politicians were busy putting together a complicated political maneuver to obtain political office. Both the politicking and the insurgency seemed to provoke the hostility of the army. In 1962 the conservative Prado administration, which was elected to power with Aprista backing in return for legal recognition in 1956, returned the favor by supporting Aprista leader Haya de la Torre for the presidency. The other two major candidates were ex-dictator Manuel Odria and Fernando Belaunde Terry. No candidate received a majority in the balloting and Congress was constitutionally charged with selecting the candidate. Subsequent maneuvers in Congress led to the alliance of APRA and the right-wing former military dictator Odria in order to exclude Belaunde from the new government. The political maneuvers in Congress included a deal under which Odria was to become president while APRA dominated the congress. The military intervened and prevented the deal from being consummated. Ten months after the coup, in June, 1963, the military held new elections and Belaunde was elected President.

Politics and social policy during the Belaunde years served to reinforce the feeling among the socially mobile officer corps that Peru needed structural changes capable of generating dynamic development if the capitalist order was to prevent a massive and uncontrollable revolution from below.

The failure of Belaunde's internal development policies were instrumental in provoking the military intervention. During his five years in office, Belaunde failed to implement basic changes in the prevailing socio-economic structure of Peru. The Agrarian Reform Law of 1964 was weak and full of loopholes: it was certainly incapable of giving impetus to substantial change in the life of the *campesino*. Belaunde chose to give agrarian reform low priority, largely confining his policies to encouraging the traditional elites to be more productive. In a word, he attempted to develop Peru within the existing socio-economic structure.

The Inter-American Committee for Agricultural Development (CIDA) estimated that approximately one million *campesino* families in Peru do not have access to or own sufficient land to maintain an above-subsistence living.[7] Taking a conservative average of five members per family, this means that approximately five million persons (or 40 percent of Peru's population) do not have sufficient land to subsist on. These landless families are highly concentrated in the *Sierra* where per capita income averages around fifteen to twenty dollars a year.

According to the National Office of Agrarian Reform, under the Belaunde-sponsored Agrarian Reform Law 11,760 rural families received 380,000 hectares (about 30 hectares per family).[8] This distribution took place over a four and one-half year period. CIDA census estimates reveal that Peru adds 11,000 landless or near landless rural families to the population yearly.[9] Thus under Belaunde

40,000 more families needing land were added to Peru's economically depressed rural poor. His agrarian reform law failed even to keep pace with population growth.

Belaunde favored measures to attract foreign private investment in Peru's extractive industries without limiting their profits or specifying their relationship to Peruvian development needs. He contracted large external loans under unfavorable terms (short-term repayment and high interest rates) to develop a highway and to open the eastern jungle areas to settlement and exploitation. The highway program that Belaunde thought was absolutely necessary was not linked to specific industrial projects designed to develop the interior, or agrarian reform. Social development on the local level was to be provided through Belaunde's *Cooperacion Popular*—the mobilization of volunteer labor to participate in the construction of locally needed services and facilities. After an initial spurt of activity *Cooperacion Popular* turned into a government patronage machine hardly related to social development.

While Belaunde was proving to be impotent to carry out promised reforms, the military was busily engaged in suppressing what might have been the beginning of the revolution from below. Between 1960 and 1965 mass peasant radicalism, especially in the South, was becoming a major concern of many military personnel. It is interesting to note that while the military killed and jailed hundreds of peasants during the repression of 1962–64 it also accepted the de facto seizure of land that had occurred—the first indication of a new attitude.[10] In addition to Belaunde's inability to realize the reforms he promised, his financial policies caused rampant inflation and forced a devaluation of the currency. Massive corruption and speculation were routinized among high-ranking government officials.[11] Manipulation of an agreement in the IPC negotiations in late September, 1969, touched off a nationwide outcry. The accumulation of numerous short-term and long-term grievances contributed to the overthrow of Belaunde on October 3, 1968. The assumption of total executive and legislative power by the present military junta signalled a shift from an impotent middle-class government to a military one rooted in the middle class but committed to overcoming the stalemates in the political system which hindered the emergence of a new and dynamic approach to economic development.

The educational and social backgrounds of the officials in the Revolutionary Military Government, as it is officially called, are important in understanding the policy orientation of the government. Socially mobile, with close links to higher education, the Peruvian military resemble armed intellectuals rather than the stereotype image of the Latin American *guerrilla*. The President of the military government, General Juan Velasco Alvarado comes from a middle-class family of modest means.[12] He enlisted in the army in 1929 as a private, as did at least one other member of the government, and was selected the following year, on the basis of competitive examinations, to attend the Chorrillos Military School near Lima. He graduated first in his class in 1934. All of the government's fourteen cabinet ministers graduated from one of the three military academies in Peru during the late 1930s or early 1940s. Several of the army members of the government were contemporaries at the Chorillos Military School and two of them were roommates for a time, suggesting that we are dealing with a homogeneous close-knit "generational group." Instruction at Chorillos included courses that dealt with Peru's social and economic ills. Many returned to Chorillos as administrators or instructors sometime during their military careers. Only two members of the government came from upper-class families and few married outside of their social background, which is almost exclusively middle-class.

More important from the point of view of intellectual influences was the common experience that more than half of the fifteen members of the government share in having attended special courses in the 1950s at the Center for Higher Military Studies (CAEM).[13] Both the intellectual subject matter and the instructors had a profound effect on the evolution of their political consciousnesses. From their course work came their commitment to developing and changing Peruvian society. Given their middle-class status, they were moved in the direction of a bourgeois revolution from above. For it was at CAEM that the future rulers of Peru were exposed to detailed courses on Peru's socio-economic structure, the dependent nature of its economy, and the vulnerability of internal development to external fluctuations. For the most part these courses were taught by left-wing nationalist academics who were well informed about the problems of Peruvian economic and social development. Many members of the current military government maintain their links with some of their former professors. More recent graduates of CAEM, including many of the younger military officers, continue to receive the same education and to keep the pressure on for change. President Velasco has often sought legal advice from left-wing nationalist elements of whom the best known is the President of the Bar Association, Alberto Ruiz Eldredge.[14]

Politics and Development Strategy

Possessing an awareness of the historical processes which produced the present social structure and the attendant impediments to industrial development, the military has come to view the traditional political institutions as incapable of carrying out the necessary changes. The military will not entrust the leadership of this revolution from above to the Peruvian civilian politicians, legislature, or elected government. In early August, 1969, the military government announced that it would remain in power "until at least 1975" in order to guarantee that Peru will be well on the way to accomplishing the goals of the twenty-year development plan which the military government unveiled in November, 1968, one month after assuming power.[15]

The twenty-year plan is known as "The Strategy for Peru's Long-Range National Development" [16] and reflects the military government's major preoccupation: rapid industrial development and the prerequisite social reforms necessary to assure such development. The plan enumerates five basic reforms: (1) expropriation of all large landed estates; (2) a new mining policy to include more public participation, regulation, and control in integrating Peru's mineral resources into the national economy—Peruvian resources are to be used for internal industrial development and not merely extracted for export; (3) an industrialization policy designed to reduce Peru's imports and increase exports, especially in the growing regional market; (4) reorganization of public administration, recruiting personnel on the basis of technical competence to create a more efficient instrument for implementing development policies; (5) fiscal reform. The national plan is subdivided into five zonal development plans. Zonal plans are based on an expansion of present economic activities and potential additions in each zone. The plan does not envision wholesale nationalization but rather additions and inducements to existing entrepreneurs to expand their activities. Over a twenty-year period the junta hopes to achieve: a greatly enlarged and expanding internal market, a more balanced geographical distribution of population, structural changes that will eliminate present institutional obstacles to development, expanded infrastructure, a more equitable distribution of national income and a doubling of per capita income, subordination of external investment to national development policies, and less economic dependence on and vulnerability to external forces.

The language of the development plan suggests that the military government is not going to reside over a development strategy prescribed by rigid guidelines or accomplished in the space of a few years. In fact, an examination of the government's rhetoric, goals, and accomplishments over the past year provides us with some basis for determining the implications current behavior might have for radical social change and significant economic development.

One week after coming to power, the military government expropriated the International Petroleum Company, IPC, a subsidiary of Standard Oil of New Jersey.[17] The government immediately announced that no compensation would be granted, charging IPC with extracting oil from Peru since 1924 under illegal agreements. The expropriation had two immediate results. It created instant popular support for the military government and it incurred the hostility of the U.S. A U.S.-Peruvian confrontation developed over the threatened implementation of the Hickenlooper Amendment.[18] Under the terms of the amendment, all U.S. government economic aid to Peru under the Alliance for Progress, AID, and similar programs would be cut off if IPC was not compensated. Additional pressure existed in the threat to cut off Peru's sugar quota, a move which would have serious repercussions on the country's economy.

The popular support generated by the nationalist action gave the military government an opportunity to consolidate its power, purge itself of conservative dissidents, and begin its program of development from above within a tranquil and favorable internal environment. The Nixon administration, seeking to avoid a confrontation that might radicalize the junta, has decided not to apply the economic sanctions; instead it has chosen to negotiate, hoping to utilize indirect pressures to obtain a settlement of the IPC compensation demands. Since April, 1969, when negotiations began, the Peruvian military has remained adamant—no compensation. Nor have there been any overt indications that Peru would consider compensation in exchange for increased U.S. economic aid or private investment pledges. Apparently the military government is confident that the Hickenlooper threat is past. In early August, 1969, the Peruvian press reported that the whole affair has been a "meaningless bluff and a most unhappy example of political blackmail." [19] The IPC expropriation is a good indication of the military government's stated intent to make foreign capital subordinate to Peruvian law and to Peruvian economic development needs. In his Independence Day speech on July 28, 1969, President Velasco said that his government considered the case closed and that in the future, decrees affecting the conduct of foreign capital in Peru could be expected.[20] He went on to point to the negative role which unrestrained foreign capital has played in Latin American development. Velasco pointed out that Peru and the rest of Latin America are exporters of capital and that income earned in Latin America finances the development of the highly industrialized nations. Velasco then went on to define his government's attitude.

> This unacceptable situation must be overcome. Latin American development needs foreign capital. But this capital does not come for philanthropic reasons. It is worthwhile for it to come here. There is, therefore, a mutual convenience which must be clearly and justly normalized for benefit of both parties. So foreign capital must act within the legal bounds of our countries under rules which guarantee the just participation of our countries in the wealth which they and their men produce.[21]

The Petroleum Decree—Law 17440, issued in February, 1969—gives some indication of what the military government is intent on achieving concerning the extractive industries. New concessions will no longer be permitted under old laws. All new contracts are to be negotiated on "fixed profit" terms. All concessions are to include provisions for state participation and profit-sharing.[22] In addition, all existing foreign and domestic concessions can be subjected to renegotiation for terms more favorable to the government.

The one act of the government to date, however, that could, if fully implemented, have the most profound effect on Peru's social structure and economic development is the Agrarian Reform Law 17716. Since this law was decreed on June 24, 1969, 66,000 hectares (hectare = 2.47 acres) of the coastal sugar lands[23] were placed under government administration pending the completion of expropriation procedures and the formation of cooperatives. The cooperatives will be under government supervision and function as state enterprises. The large sugar estates along the coast and in the *Sierra* affected by the law included those owned by wealthy Peruvian families and private foreign interests such as W. R. Grace and Co. of the United States.[24] All associated sugar-processing facilities and installations on the plantations are marked for expropriation. The agrarian reform is being carried out "without prejudice or favor," at least along the coast, as promised by President Velasco, in order to "end once and for all the unfair social order that has kept peasants in poverty and inequity." [25] If the military government fully implements the agrarian reform, the large cotton plantations and *Sierra* cattle and sheep operations will also be affected.

The one major nonsugar-growing *Sierra* estate expropriated by the military government was the 247,000-hectare cattle and sheep ranch operated by the U.S.-owned Cerro de Pasco mining company.[26] The Cerro Corporation received $490,000 in cash compensation for the installations on the land. One million, eight hundred thousand U.S. dollars has been paid for 90,000 head of livestock. Twenty-year bonds were issued as payment for the land. This expropriation, however, was officially carried out in January, 1969, prior to the present law, under the authority and provisions of the Agrarian Reform Law of 1964. The property is to be divided among the peasants working on the land and they are to operate the farms under cooperative arrangements. This was the first expropriation activity in the agrarian sector undertaken by the military government and it had wide national support. This may have been a pilot project designed to test the response of antagonists and protagonists in the public at large toward a radical agrarian reform.

Subsequently the government decided to expropriate the large, efficient, modern sugar plantations on the coast, an economically powerful and politically influential sector of the economic power structure.[27] The Agrarian Reform Law was applied immediately along the coast, but application was slower in the *Sierra*. So far little or no defiant opposition has materialized from the large sugar growers of the coast. One possible explanation might be found in the fact that for some time sugar interests have been transferring their investments to other sectors of the economy. The application of the agrarian reform to the coast allows for a smooth and rapid movement of compensation bond payments into the more modern private sectors of the economy. Records show that forty-four major *latifundistas* of the coast now have substantial investments in Peruvian mutual stock funds, the construction industry, insurance and saving companies, mining, public utilities, transportation, and in the mass media of communication.[28] The government is counting on the demonstration effect of the successful and peaceful coastal expropriations to make things easier when the *Sierra* is hit with expropriations.

In any case this strategy will effectively isolate the landed elite and inhibit a united opposition from acting in concert. The clear intention of the junta's agrarian reform law is to encourage capital investment in nonagricultural Peruvian industry and mining. Under arrangements for compensation payment, most bonds can be readily converted to cash if they are immediately invested in Peruvian enterprises designated by the government. This device simultaneously prevents capital outflow and encourages industrialization. The exact manner in which this important provision of the law will be carried out remains to be seen. Nevertheless, the government's intention clearly demonstrates its commitment to harnessing social change to economic objectives. The junta perceives agrarian reform as an aid in the formation of a large internal consumer market, and a provider of capital funds for the industrialization of the country.

Along with the signing of the agrarian reform, changes occurred in ministerial personnel. On June 13, 1969, President Velasco demanded the resignation of the conservative Minister of Agriculture, General José Benavides. The initial appointment of Benavides was viewed by many in Peru, including high officials in the Office of Agrarian Reform (ONRA), as an indication that the military government was not seriously concerned with agrarian change.[29] Benavides was closely associated with members of the National Agrarian Society, the association of large landowners, and expressed strong opposition to large-scale expropriation of land. He was the cause of continued irritation to other members of the government including General Jorge Fernandez Maldonado who was Minister of Energy and Mining. Soon after his appointment Fernandez became the spokesman of the "radical" sector within the government. Benavides was replaced by one of the "radicals," General Jorge Barandiaran Pagador after the former had been quoted in an interview as opposing expropriation.[30] He argued that it was not feasible because of the costliness. He went on to argue that the land tenure system was not a major cause of Peru's agrarian problems. Benavides favored incentives to the current landowners to encourage increases in production, arguing that this would lead to a reduction of the country's high level of imported food.

Apart from the opposition of the traditional economic elite, other vested interests have voiced their opposition to the agrarian reform. The sugarworker unions of the coast have questioned some aspects of the law. These unions were given legal recognition and permitted to organize by the military government of 1962–63. Through organization and pressure the sugarworkers have gained pay raises and many fringe benefits as well. The principal question raised by the sugarworkers is whether in becoming employees of state enterprises they will lose their right to strike and bargain collectively.[31] Workers and labor leaders who have been interviewed expressed their confusion over what their new status would be and indicated concern over losing benefits. Several of those interviewed alluded to political motivations on the part of the military government—that possibly the application of the law was intended to destroy the Aprista-controlled unions that dominate the sugar unions and further undermine APRA power and influence among the working class.[32]

The political strategy of the military government is to reduce the effectiveness of the old electoral party machines and begin to build a new power base of their own among the peasantry and agrarian workers. Government leaders at various times have hinted that a new constitution might give the vote for the first time to all those over twenty-one without regard to literacy or property ownership qualifications. To further debilitate the patronage-based electoral parties, the military government has stated that it will remain in power for at least six years.

Other measures instituted to implement the economic and social goals include reform of the banking system, water rights, and public administration.[33] Banks incorporated in Peru must now be controlled by Peruvian citizens. The Water Code Decree Law 17752 of July, 1969 makes all water state property, no matter what its source. The law establishes a water control authority to coordinate water resource utilization with the agrarian reform program and general economic development policies. The administrative changes were most noticeable at the ministry level. In early April, 1969, the Ministry of Development which had become a catchall for a myriad of functions was eliminated and its responsibilities divided among four new ministries: Industry and Commerce, Energy and Mines, Transport and Communications, and Housing. The ministries of War, Navy, and Aviation are to be consolidated under a new Ministry of Defense. In June, 1969, the Ministry of Finance was reorganized and is now responsible for coordinating national economic activity with the general development policies of the government. In addition the National Planning Institute is now to be under the Finance Ministry and its plans are to be forwarded to the specified ministries and agencies for implementation. Formerly the institute functioned apart from the government and its plans were usually ignored or not given serious consideration. The Planning Institute has become a central agency in designating government priorities and in allocating government funds and hence will play a much more direct and important role in shaping the direction of economic development.

A number of other changes geared toward modernizing Peruvian society are projected. In his Independence Day speech of July 28, 1969, Velasco said that business, fishery, credit, and tax reforms were also being planned.[34] Business reform will reportedly involve profit-sharing by employees in accordance with productivity and cooperative ventures, with labor participating to some degree in management. Tax reform would include control of evasion, reduction of indirect taxes and an effective progressive income tax. Reform of the fishing industry would involve protection of small operators and heavier taxation of larger enterprises.

All of these decrees reflect the military government's dual policy of initiating modernization yet remaining firmly in control of the political situation. The latter can best be seen in the new University Law. Issued in early March, during the annual university summer break, its purpose is twofold: to make higher education relevant to the development needs of the country and to eliminate political activity on the campuses. Professors have been divided on the law, some supporting it and others publicly and privately denouncing it. Student leaders have been highly critical of the law, yet efforts to organize effective protest have been quickly snuffed out by government police activity and university administrative action.

Under the University Law, according to the government, all universities are to maintain their autonomy in administrative, financial, and adademic matters, but a university will no longer have the right of "extra-territoriality" in matters concerning "threats to public order." [35] This provision means that police and military personnel can now freely enter university grounds and buildings, make arrests, and intervene in "riotous and mutinous situations." The law in effect destroys all semblance of university autonomy. In addition, university administration has the authority to expel students who have organized or engaged in political activities. Prior to this law the university administration had to request and receive permission from the University Council, composed of administration, faculty, and students, before a student could be expelled for nonacademic reasons. The clear intention of the junta is to "de-politicize" the university and thereby remove a possible source of left-wing opposition to continued military-directed modernization programs.

External Obstacles to Development

In implementing its plan to modernize and industrialize Peru within a capitalist economic system under domestic and not foreign control, the military government has been confronted by numerous external obstacles. The government has been expending considerable time and effort to overcome or remove these impediments to the execution of its development policies. One of the most crippling obstacles with which the military government is faced concerns repayment of Peru's massive foreign debt.

Under Belaunde, Peru's foreign debt climbed to $847 million, 70 percent of which must be payed off over a four-year period beginning in 1970. The principal creditors are the United States ($200,000,000), West Germany ($157,-000,000), Italy ($87,000,000), France ($52,000,000), followed by Great Britain, Spain, and Japan.[36]

Peru's Treasury Minister, General Morales Bermudez, has made two trips to United States and European capitals in an attempt to obtain agreements extending Peru's payment period. During his July and August trip, Morales Bermudez visited various European capitals trying to win support for his plan for refinancing Peru's payment schedule over a ten-year period. The principal motivation for seeking an extension of the time period for debt payment appears to be the long-range development plans of the military government rather than the country's short-range financial situation. As of August, the reserves of the *Banco Central* exceeded $110 million and the balance of payments has jumped from a deficit of $17 million in the year ending June 30, 1968, to a surplus of $30 million in the period ending June 30, 1969.[37]

The attempt to refinance the foreign debt is reflective of the military government's immediate interest in channeling funds into developmental projects and consolidating reforms already introduced. Instead of allocating funds for the payment of the foreign debt, financial resources would be directed to the target areas in the industrial sector. Opposition to the nationalization program is evidenced, however, by the financial pressures. The Treasury Minister has failed so far to acquire agreements allowing for the refinancing of the debt. The fears of the international financial community have heretofore blocked the development and refinancing plans of the government. Despite some offers from foreign investors primarily interested in obtaining concessions in the mining sector, little positive aid has been forthcoming from the capitalist world. U.S., German, French, and Italian financial and investor groups have refused to consider refinancing current debts or making further investments in existing companies until agreements are reached guaranteeing the security of present and future investments.[38]

The capitalist modernization effort of the military government has been further delayed by the reluctance of U.S. mining companies to sign agreements to expand production and to develop facilities for refining ore in Peru. The military's dependence on foreign investment is based on the assumption that tax revenue from profits, wages, and export duties would alleviate the country's foreign debt payment problems and thereby free more capital for industrialization and government social welfare programs.[39]

Negotiations with U.S. companies over expansion began during the Belaunde period. Recommencing after the overthrow of the Belaunde government, negotiations to achieve the desired agreements committing the companies to massive expansion investments over the next five years have continued without tangible results. The Minister of Economy and Finance, General Jorge Fernandez Maldonado, who is considered by the international business community to have "Nasserist political tendencies," has been the chief negotiator for the junta. He assured General Velasco that a $345 million expansion agreement with the U.S.-owned Southern Peru Copper Corporation would be completed in time for his Independence Day Speech on July 28, 1969. A detailed account of the agreement was to be discussed in Velasco's speech to demonstrate that the military government sought and welcomed foreign capital but wanted to integrate it into the development of Peru's entire economy. The agreement, it was thought, would help to allay some of the fears in the international financial community concerning the military government's motives and attitudes toward foreign capital. The agreement with Southern Peru Copper Corporation, it was hoped, would serve to prompt other major U.S. mining companies operating in Peru to expand their investments.

Besides Southern, the military government has been negotiating with the Homestake Mining Company for a $10 million expansion of its operations near Arequipa, with Anaconda for a $70 million expansion of its Cerro Verde operations in the same general area, with Cerro de Pasco Corporation for a $115 million expansion of its Junin-Ancash operations, with American Smelting and Refining for $250 million and with Kaiser for $91 million. The military modernizers argued that if all investment expansions were begun this year, Peru could double its copper exports to $400 million by 1973 and to $650 million by 1975. Recent history suggests that the military's hope of modernizing through massive foreign investment is overly optimistic. U.S. copper mining companies in Peru have invested very little in new capital or equipment for expansion since 1955.[40] The government is anxious to grant lucrative exploration, exploitation, and domestic marketing concessions to major petroleum companies in an effort to develop what are considered to be rich petroleum reserves of the northern continental shelf and the northeastern jungle areas of Peru. It is also anticipated by the military government that petroleum agreements having similar terms will eventually be reached, following a pattern established by the mining agreements.

To the disappointment of the military government, none of the major U.S. mining companies in Peru has agreed to sign contracts to expand production of Peru's mining industry, especially copper. To a substantial degree the military's program of modernization from above has been dependent on the completion of these agreements.

The only agreement which has been reached concerns a contract with the *Compania Minera de Madrigal* for the development of copper, lead, and zinc. *Compania Madrigal*, a wholly owned subsidiary of Homestake Mining Company, agreed to invest $10 million over the next year and a half. However, only $760,000 of the financing is coming from the U.S. subsidiary, the balance are loans from Japanese firms. In order to extract this agreement the junta granted substantial tax benefits and a favorable exchange rate: income taxes during the first five years will be 25 percent lower and the exchange rate will be 13 percent higher than the free rate. The fact that 92 percent of the new investment funds are coming from Japanese sources suggests U.S. pressure is still on, but that outside capital may take financial and economical advantage of the political stalemate.[41]

Peru is currently seventh in world production of copper, fourth in zinc and lead, and third in silver. The military government views these resources as crucial sources for the revenue needed to modernize the agrarian sector, and to provide the social and economic infrastructure required for industrialization. The choice facing the military modernizers is whether they will sacrifice their plans for national development by making further concessions to the U.S. companies or whether they will turn to public enterprises as the instrument for developing the mineral resources, in which case the modernization-from-above strategy would tend to shift toward a revolutionary collectivist approach. There is a possibility that the military government might not allow itself to be intimidated indefinitely by the refusal of the large U.S. mining companies to accept Peruvian terms.

There is evidence, however, that the military is seeking to "internationalize" the sources of new capital for exploiting minerals, thus breaking their total dependence on the U.S. In September, 1969, Southern Peru Copper Corporation was warned that if it was not disposed to sign an expansion contract, the military government would "act to protect Peruvian economic interests." [42] The Minister of Economy and Finance has said on various occasions that the government would offer Southern's concession at Cuajone for sale on the international market if the company did not sign the expansion agreements. Belgian and Japanese mining concerns have expressed interest in this and other copper concessions.

It is clear that U.S. policy-makers in association with U.S. business interests are applying pressure to weaken the "nationalist" aspects of the Peruvian development program. The U.S.-controlled Export-Import Bank has been reluctant to approve loans, thus providing Southern Peru Copper with a convenient pretext for delay in initiating its expansion program.[43] The bank, largely under U.S. control, is under orders not to approve any new loans involving Peru. In the meantime, Nixon continues to keep the application of the Hickenlooper Amendment in suspension while his representative continues to negotiate over the IPC compensation, attempting to resolve the problem in a manner favorable to U.S. business interests.

The chief objections of U.S. investors go to the very heart of the development program of the junta. One of the conditions that is demanded is a guarantee that profits be allowed remission to foreign accounts over a "tolerable" period of time.[44] U.S. business is resentful of exchange controls that could effectively keep profits in Peru. The military government considers these objections to national controls by Southern and the other companies as serious obstacles to their overall development plans.

The military government is attempting to overcome the opposition of U.S. policy-makers and established interests by appealing, over their heads, directly to the U.S. investment community as a whole. A full-page advertisement entitled "Peru Today: Highlights of Achievements in the Last 12 Months, Financial Summary and Investment Opportunities," appeared in the *New York Times*.[45] The ad emphasized the potential for profitable exploitation of minerals and revealed the opportunities for investors in the development plan, especially in copper and phosphate. It went on to specify the advantageous features of a recent decree guaranteeing new investors reduced tax rates, accelerated depreciation allowances, availability of foreign exchange for profits and services, ability to deduct any losses incurred over a previous five-year period from future profits, and a dispensation which permits up to 50 percent of the profits to be reinvested tax free in refineries and/or plants for treating metallurgic products, five years after a mining contract expires. Investment incentives were offered to potential investors in the petrochemical, carbochemical and fertilizer industry. Tax holidays and other incentives lasting up to 1983 were offered to attract investors in industries producing for the export and domestic market. The military government offers to provide the infrastructure for outside capital if it comes into the growth areas designated by the government for development.

The brand of "nationalism" advocated by the military government is not incompatible with strong doses of foreign capital. The strategy appears to be to diversify the source of capital within the capitalist world. The nationalist component in the ideology of the junta is subordinated to its developmentalist perspective.

Further evidence of its commitment to economic development over ideological considerations can be seen in the new commercial, economic, and diplomatic relations established with the Soviet Union and other Eastern European countries.[46] This policy has also allowed the junta to counter the threat of economic sanctions from the U.S. with the possibility of closer economic and political relations with the Communist world. Once again, however, by creating new options in the Communist bloc the junta might be weakening their appeal for new foreign investment. Up to now, however, trade and aid have been somewhat limited since current Peruvian exports are not in great demand in the Soviet Union and Eastern European countries.[47] The Soviet Union has offered $100 million in trade credits for heavy machinery. Czechoslovakia has offered $6 million in credits for capital goods as well as technical assistance for the development of zinc, copper, and petroleum facilities. Poland has offered $25 million in credits for machinery, food, medicine, and toys. Hungary has offered $5 million, and Rumania an undisclosed amount. Up till now, however, the junta has been unable to persuade the Soviet Union to finance the Olmos Irrigation Project in Northern Peru's Lambayeque Department. The project when completed would bring 247,000 acres of land under cultivation for the first time. The project plans include hydroelectric plants to generate 350,000 kilowatts of power for the industrialization of Piura, Lambayeque, and La Libertad Departments. A U.N. study estimated the cost of the project at $325 million.

As further proof of the junta's lack of concern over ideology in its search for economic aid for development, the military government is seeking financial support from South Africa's General Mining and Finance Corporation.[48] The purpose is the construction of a $22-million tunnel under the Andes in association with the Majes-Siguas Irrigation Project in the desert foothills fifty miles west of Arequipa. This project would bring 140,000 acres of previously uncultivable land under production. On December 16, 1968, Velasco declared that Peru would seek economic support from "any country in the world," meaning Communist, capitalist, and fascist governments.[49]

One of the most widely publicized obstacles confronting the military government's development plans has been its conflict with the U.S. government over the nationalization of the International Petroleum Company (IPC), a Standard Oil subsidiary, on October 9, 1968. The military government gave corruption in high places as one reason why it deposed the Belaunde government. The military charged that top government officials were paid off to allow IPC to obtain a very favorable settlement, resulting in enormous tax evasion and further concessions to operate in Peru.

The military government nullified the agreement immediately after taking power and expropriated all IPC fields and facilities seven days later. From the beginning the military government has refused to pay financial compensation. It claims that the company has been illegally extracting petroleum from Peru since 1924 under agreements with dictator Leguia which never had the approval of a Peruvian Congress. The military government claims that IPC actually owes Peru $690 million, ten times the value of IPC former holdings and cannot expect a cent in compensation. The date of the Act of Talara, as the IPC expropriation is called in Peru, is now known as the "National Day of Dignity" and the military government has been using the popular reception to the IPC expropriation as an effective issue to rally mass support behind the government's development plans.

The problems with the U.S. government center on the

Hickenlooper Amendment which requires the executive branch to suspend all aid to any nation expropriating U.S. property without offering prompt compensation in cash (U.S. dollars assumed). The aid cutoff was to occur six months after the expropriation if compensation payment guarantees have not been made by that time. So far the Nixon administration has sought to avoid a direct confrontation and possible conflict escalation which would result from the application of the Hickenlooper Amendment. Instead Nixon appointed John Irwin of New York, a Wall Street lawyer and financier with the Rockefeller Brothers Association, to negotiate the dispute. There has been continuous pressure from the U.S. to influence the negotiations. Negotiations began in Lima in April, 1969, but nothing has developed to change the military government's decision concerning IPC compensation. Two deadlines for application of the Hickenlooper Amendment have been postponed.

In addition to the Hickenlooper threat, some policymakers have considered cutting the Peruvian sugar quota. Under the Sugar Quota Act the United States buys half (450,000 tons) of Peru's annual sugar production and pays seven cents a pound against the two or three cents per pound which generally prevails in the world market. The remainder of sugar production is marketed domestically. The price differential amounts to about $50 million yearly. A suspension of Peru's sugar quota might create economic problems and social unrest if alternative markets could not be located quickly. The suspension might jeopardize the financing of the government's infant agrarian reform programs, including the funding of the cooperativization of the large sugar estates. On the other hand, it might serve to radicalize the junta, leading to confiscatory measures and nationalization of other U.S. enterprises.[50]

An additional problem which has complicated matters has been U.S. rejection of Peru's claims of a 200-mile coastal fishing limit. Section 3(b) of the Foreign Military Sales Act (Pelly Amendment) dated October 22, 1968, provides for suspension of arms sales to a country if a U.S. fishing vessel is captured more than 12 miles off its coastline and fined. In addition, the amount of the fines paid are to be deducted from foreign aid commitments to that country.[51] After several vessels were seized, on April 3, 1969, Washington began to apply the pressure: the Peruvian ambassador in Washington was informed that military aid was suspended. The Peruvians responded by seizing another ship. More important, the U.S. MAAG (Military Advisory and Assistance Group) mission of about fifty officers was ordered out of the country by the military government.[52] The arms sale ban was lifted on July 3, 1969, but its imposition increased tension between the two countries.

The tension generated by the IPC compensation issue, the Hickenlooper and sugar quota sanction threats, and the fishing vessel arms sale controversy have been viewed by the U.S. investment community in Peru as part of an unfriendly climate. Businessmen have responded by holding back on investment capital. This has all been intently noted by the military government.

The dilemma facing the junta is whether they want to sacrifice their National Development Plan to meet the demands of foreign investors or whether they can locate alternative sources through internal savings, public enterprises, and assistance through closer ties with the Communist countries.

In the fall of 1969, the Velasco government took a series of measures that indicate that the pressures for change may be radicalizing the more militant wing of the junta.[53]

Foreign investors in the mining industry were told to put into operation unexploited mining concessions within seven months or the Peruvian government would repossess them. The "suburban reform law" provides for the rapid expropriation of suburban plots of land in order to eradicate the "barriadas" and to construct private homes. This program, if it is seriously applied, could signify a hard blow to banking and real estate circles. In addition, Vice-Admiral

Enrique Carbonell, who is considered a radical, recently joined the junta. He was responsible for exposing IPC's illegal remission of $18 million shortly after the junta expropriated it, leading to the fall of two of the "moderate" members of the junta.

In the middle of September, the government severely restricted imports, practically prohibiting all luxury items and goods which compete with nationally produced items. The government established a state monopoly in charge of the importation of meat and dairy products in order to end speculation on the food market.

At the same time it was announced that an important Soviet mission headed by a vice-minister would be arriving in Lima to study the possibility of a vast program of irrigation in the northern desert plains.

The government appears to be loosening its authoritarian posture regarding popular demands. The government decreed that striking workers of Cerro de Pasco be awarded a raise 23 percent higher than that offered by the company. The measure was strongly denounced by the business community as "demagogic."

By the middle of September the agrarian reform had been extended to all the coastal sugar plantations and was beginning to be applied in the cattle ranches of Cuzco for the first time.

Though the ideology of the military continues to reflect a developmentalist perspective, the dynamic unleashed in the process of initiating social change may be building up momentum.

Cumulative social changes resulting from piecemeal legislation to achieve specific economic goals may begin to develop their own dynamic. The tension between Peru and the U.S. and the opening of new commercial relationships with Communist and non-Communist nations may lead to closer relations and possibly allow the junta to increase the state's role in organizing and directing economic institutions. Already the original developmentalist perspective has been modified to take account of the intransigent opposition of foreign and domestic investors, and the receptivity of the populace to socio-economic changes and nationalist policies. Whether the military chooses to continue operating on a pragmatic basis, adjusting its measures in response to specific pressures or whether they will formulate a radically new political strategy will depend on whether they will be able to work out a *modus vivendi* with U.S. corporate capitalism.

Peru as a New Model for Latin America

In the course of two years, the Peruvian military government has established a stable political system, initiated a sweeping agrarian reform, and has decreed an industrial development program that far surpasses any previous efforts. Little or nothing is heard among the public concerning the absence of elections, congress, or political party activity. Furthermore, hardly anyone outside of the old, professional politicians is concerned with a restoration of "representative" political institutions. All attention is focused on the social welfare and economic development policies which the government is pursuing, and the political instruments which it is shaping to implement its programs.

The Peruvian experience is being watched carefully in a number of Latin American countries, especially those at a similar stage of underdevelopment. The Peruvian political experience serves as a reference point for other Latin countries. Insofar as the programs of the Peruvian military succeed, the Peruvian experience could become a model for development.

Frequently writers have referred to the Peruvian military junta as "developmentalist," "nationalist," and/or as "leftist"—labels which have little or no analytical value in terms of specific policies adopted by the junta. In a very general way, the junta is "developmentalist"—if by that we mean that it has given a higher priority to investments in productive activity over and against redistributive policies.[54] The key aspects of the junta's policies however are found in the vastly enlarged role which it has given to the state in the development of the economy and in the reorganization of social life.[55]

Statism, or the active intervention of the state in the financial and economic activity of the country, is the key characteristic of the Peruvian military government—and what most clearly distinguishes it from previous regimes. The government has increasingly taken over the commercialization of two major exports (copper and fish-meal),[56] expanded its involvement in finance and banking, nationalized a part of the petroleum and telephone industry, gained a predominant influence in the agro-industrial cooperatives which emerged from the expropriation of the coastal sugar plantations, exercised control over exchange and, most important, reserved the development of "basic industry" to the state. The expansion of state control in commerce and banking and its growing influence in the areas of industrial development suggest that Peru is experiencing a profound transformation: from a laissez-faire capitalist society to a state-capitalist society in which the state has become a major factor influencing investment decisions and growth areas.[57]

The second major feature of the Peruvian model is the strong tendency toward *authoritarian paternalism*. In the area of social policy, the mass of the population—especially in the rural areas—are the *beneficiaries* of socio-economic gains and not the actors who bring about change.[58] The immobilized populace receives socio-economic benefits, largely at the behest of the military leaders; but there is no attempt to encourage popular mobilization to bring about social change. When mobilization did occur independently of the junta—as it did in Ayacucho in 1969—it was vigorously suppressed.

The third feature is *sectoral nationalism*, largely in the

form of national industrialization. The nationalist policies of the junta—apart from symbolic gestures such as the expropriation of the IPC petroleum holding—are largely in the area of industrial development.[59] The industrial law generally confines the development of industry to national entrepreneurs—both public and private.[60] However, in the area of mining, the government has signed a number of agreements with U.S. and European firms.[61] Since the fish-meal industry has reached its ecological limits, copper will increasingly predominate in the composition of exports (copper will be largely in the hands of U.S. investors). In fact, the government *pressured* the foreign firms to expand their operations. As a result, in five years the Peruvian economy, especially its export sector, even more than today will be dependent on a single export, copper, owned by a U.S. firm.[62] If the price should sharply decline it could seriously jeopardize the whole economic development program or force the government to look elsewhere for sources of income.

The growth of the economy—to the extent that it will depend on capital imports—will become increasingly dependent on the performance of the U.S.-controlled mining sector. The government's commercialization and refining of copper will give it some leverage but will not affect the basic dependent relationship. Sectoral nationalism—largely confined to industry—is the most substantive and innovative feature of this particular ideology. Nationalization of existing industrial enterprises has taken place on a very *selective,* legal basis with adequate compensation (telephone, IPC, *Banco Popular,* and the sugar mills). The selective nature of the nationalization process can be seen with regard to the sugar operations on the coast; only the least profitable operations, the sugar plantations and pulp and alcohol enterprises which process sugar cane by-products, were left in private (U.S.) hands.[63] Nationalist industrialization combines incentives to dynamic entrepreneurs and the threat of workers taking over the operation through the formation of an "industrial community." Though foreign capital tends to be relegated to the mining sector there are conditions under the Industrial Law in which mixed national-foreign enterprises can be formed.

The fourth characteristic feature of the Peruvian model is *technocratic planning;* the junta stresses directed and planned development. The execution of policy is largely an executive matter relying little or not at all on "demands" from below or outside of the executive-military, COAP Planning Institute complex. There is little or no evidence of any feedback from the masses.[64]

The fifth characteristic of the Peruvian model is the combination of large-scale social change and tight executive control exercised over the process of change. Controlled social change embodies the dual features of the displacement of the old *patron* and his replacement by a new technocratic executive. This is clearly illustrated in the agro-industrial complexes which have been taken over by the government. The new structure of authority, despite the façade of an elected cooperative, is largely controlled by government-appointed *tecnicos* and administrators.[65] In the agriculture of the coast, the forms of property have changed but the structure of authority persists; the hierarchy of power, status, and life style.[66] In fact, many of the old managerial personnel have stayed on in responsible posts. Executive-centered authority is largely concerned with maintaining social control, increasing production, and dispensing socio-economic benefits according to one's position in the social scale.

The sixth feature of the Peruvian model is the *neutralization of the political opposition.* There is no political competition for office; there are no political institutions where competition can take place. The absence of competitive institutions, combined with the military's control over the process of broad social change and its monopoly over the means of coercion, i.e., the loyalty of a unified armed force, has concentrated power in the military-executive. Political opposition is *tolerated* on the margins of political life; and being on the margin, political criticism is muted and impotent.[67] Symbolic but highly charged nationalist measures (IPC), agrarian reform which cuts into the privileges and prerogatives of the traditional oligarchy, national industrialization which offers pay-offs to dynamic industrialists and industrial workers—these measures undermine the ability of existing parties and pressure groups to rally popular support. The symbols of nationalism, agrarian reform, and industrialism, and the measures taken to implement policies in each of these areas, have neutralized the political opposition of both the Left and the Right and have provided the government with ample popular support. The inability of parties and interest groups to confront the government is largely based on the fact that the policies so far adopted or carried out have been directed at the most mobilizable sectors of the population: the peasants and the rural and urban industrial workers. The large mass of urban poor (the 35 percent of Lima's economically active population which is underemployed)[68] has not received any substantial pay-offs from the government but neither is it available to the existing opposition which has its social base elsewhere.

The *developmental mission* of the current military government defines the last major feature of the Peruvian model. In their totality, the measures adopted by the government regarding the indemnification payments to the old landowners, the tax incentives to the industrialists, the agreements with the U.S. mine owners have one common end: the maximization of industrial investment. The role that the military has chosen for itself is to *concientizar* the holders of wealth.[69] The military is trying to convince, rather forcefully in some instances, potential investors to plow their capital into national industrial development. The devices which the military is depending on include bonds to landowners which can be redeemed through investment in industry, tax concessions, and threats of expropriations.

Through a variety of measures, the military is attempting to create the Schumpeterian entrepreneur: the risk-taking industrial capitalist whose mission is to build industrial empires. The negative reaction of the industrialists is largely a function of their past; protected and subsidized industrial growth encouraged by tax exemptions and import privileges, has little in common with the image of the industrial entrepreneur which the military is trying to cultivate. The military is banking its development plans on its ability to transform a laissez-faire bourgeoisie into an active entrepreneurial collaborator of the state, willing and able to follow the industrial plans outlined by the junta. One of the functions of the state is to create the conditions which make the bourgeoisie aware of its historic role as a developmental force.[70]

The Neo-Bismarckian Model

There are a great many similarities between the Peruvian model of development and the German experience in the latter half of the nineteenth century, especially during the Bismarckian period. The confluence of similar factors in the two cases suggests the appropriateness of referring to the Peruvian experience as a Neo-Bismarckian approach. In both societies there is a strong sense of nationalism. The structure of public authority is strongly influenced by military personnel or values. There is a strong drive toward industrialization linked to the overwhelming sense of building a strong nation. There is the same understanding that paternalistic social legislation administered by the state is necessary to head off a socialist revolution and create bonds of loyalty to the government while undercutting class and populist appeals.[71] There is the same drive for an efficient and orderly society unencumbered by regional rivalries and inequalities—the unification of the coast and the *Sierra* is similar to the attempts of Bismarck to unify the German nation.[72] There is the same concern in both cases to produce a "moral bureaucracy" along Weberian lines: a neutral, efficient, and rational administrative instrument of national policy. There exists the same authoritarian politics where a strong executive rules, drawing on the expertise of professionals and selected advisers. Rulership is exercised through a bureaucratic structure and a vertical line of authority.[73] In external relations in both countries there is an attempt to develop an independent foreign policy, using foreign policy as a lever to permit internal development and to overcome external dependence or influence.[74] There is a strong tendency toward autarchy and reliance on national resources. There is the same dislike of conflict and "foreign" ideologies and a decided preference for technical education geared to nationalist industrial development.[75]

While there are a number of cultural and other factors which are decidedly dissimilar, the striking fact is the similarity between the Bismarckian style and the Peruvian model of development: the nationalist military leadership forcefully pushing for national integration and industrial development subsequent to the failure of liberal experiments and in the face of repeated attempts to mobilize mass support for socialist revolution. In the case of Bismarck's Germany, the industrialization policies achieved a modicum of success because the bourgeoisie responded to the incentives and opportunities which grew out of the state's development policy. The landed aristocracy, the junkers, became increasingly involved in commercial agriculture; the bourgeoisification of the rural elite and its incorporation into the development plans of the state together with the rapid expansion of industrial activity contributed to forging Germany into a powerful nation-state.

In Peru the expansion of the activities of the state in industry is an attempt to take the existing bourgeoisie—a product of the industrialization effort beginning in 1950—and to make it an instrument of state development policy. The substantial group of middle-class farmers which will remain and the more enterprising of the new land reform beneficiaries (Peru's "kulaks") will form the political and social basis of Peruvian development. The military-industrialist–middle-class-farmer alliance, in turn, is dependent on and linked with the foreign-owned, multi-national corporations which are heavily involved in the exploration of the mines and the largest enterprises. It is not altogether certain that the developmental and welfare policies of the authoritarian Peruvian military will have the same type of success in winning middle-class support and creating a powerful nation-state that Bismarck was able to achieve. A key element will be its ability to limit social conflict and control popular demands during the period of industrialization and economic expansion.

Corporatism: Institutions for Political Containment

In the first two years of rule, the Peruvian military ruled directly through the administrative structure. Congress and elections were suspended and replaced by rule through executive decree and executive-selected public officials. Power was concentrated in the executive office. The new decision-making structure was legitimated through nationalist-populist measures—the government acted as if it had a popular mandate to accomplish certain historic tasks.[76] The previous political system was attacked as acting on behalf of the oligarchy and foreign interests. In fact if not in law, political parties, pressure groups, parliament, and elections were deprestigized—and illegitimized in the eyes of the public. Political parties continued to exist on the margins of political life, but since most of their existence revolved around holding office and competing in elections, they slowly withered away or were abandoned by their members and leaders who joined the government. In reality, the experience with electoral politics did not create much public support, hence there is no popular base for the restoration of electoral party politics. The opposition of the landowners and industrialists is based on *selective* criticism of particular decrees and regulations—they have not been an intransigent opposition insistent on the restoration of the previous political institutions. The only other oppositional force, the revolutionary socialist intellectuals, are on the margins of political struggle and their main activity consists in critical analysis of the activities and policies of the junta.

The main arena of political conflict and bargaining is the bureaucracy.[77] Within the public administration most of the conflicting socio-political forces of Peruvian society can be found: from national-populist and collectivist to laissez-faire capitalist, with the bulk made up of proponents of mixed enterprise, social welfare neo-capitalism.[78] The bureaucracy is the functional equivalent of the Congress; different ministries tend to represent different viewpoints and social forces. The present government, through the presence of diverse social and political forces within its administrative orbit, is far more representative of the plurality of social groups in Peruvian society than any other previous regime.[79]

The notion of a "representative bureaucracy" is not incompatible with the authoritarian political structure. The bureaucracy contains agencies which articulate the interests of social forces but are not necessarily subject to their control. The agrarian reform agencies represent the interest of the peasants but are appointed by and responsible to the central government. The Ministry of Labor continues to be influenced by the economic elites but is not selected by any of the interest associations. Though not directly controlled by their constituents, these representative agencies develop ties and linkages with their constituents and are susceptible to pressures. The conflicts and tensions within the Cabinet and COAP are reflected on the lower levels of the administrative structure and to a certain degree reflect the conflicting social interests in Peruvian society.[80] The notion of a representative bureaucracy does not imply that all social classes are equally represented within the bureaucracy or that in fact the balance of forces within the bureaucracy favors the "popular classes." Some classes are better represented than others within the bureaucracy—though not always in the way in which these social classes would like to have their interests represented.[81]

There are three major social forces represented by the bureaucracy: the industrial capitalists, the public entrepreneur-technocratic sectors of the embryonic state enterprises, and the middle-class farmers emerging as the beneficiaries of the agrarian reform. The absence of political parties and professional politicians together with the refusal of the military to deal directly with organized interest groups has created a substantial gap between the bureaucratic representatives of social classes and the organizations of these classes.[82] Thus, it appears at times that the political representatives are acting autonomously of the class structure since formal linkages are not readily visible. Nevertheless a careful examination of the overall frame of reference of policy-makers suggests that policy-measures favor certain classes over others. The agrarian reform clearly represents a transfer of property away from the large landowners toward the promotion of a substantial rural middle class. On the coastal plantations the agrarian reform is creating a new domestic technico-administrative elite which is replacing the former foreign plantation owners.[83] The industrial law will benefit the more dynamic and enterprising sectors of the Peruvian bourgeoisie and the state entrepreneurs, technocrats, and planners who will manage the state sector of industry.[84]

The organizations which will include the lower classes —the cooperatives in rural areas and the "industrial community" in industrial enterprises—are institutions largely designed to co-opt the leaders in management functions, to limit the degree of class conflict, and to increase the productivity of labor and the collaboration between labor and capital within the framework of a capitalist economy. These new social organizations will replace the trade unions and serve to identify the interests of the workers with greater productivity. Membership in the social organizations will include management as well as workers and is designed to undercut class organizations and class struggle by emphasizing "common" interest of the industrial "community." [85] Corporatist politics envision a form of functional representation which will be underwritten by paternalistic social legislation and which is designed to facilitate social integration but not workers' control. In reality the prerogatives of management will hardly be affected and in the long run could be strengthened.

The corporatist political institutions which the government is promoting have their roots in Catholic social doctrines which were popularized to an extent by the Christian Democrats in the notion of communitarianism—an ill-defined idea which was meant to encourage industrial cooperation between employers and employees.

Catholic social thought has from the nineteenth century perceived the destabilizing effects of liberal capitalism, the dangers provoked by the division of society into hostile classes, and the emergence of class conflict. The corporatist notions of Catholic social doctrine are meant to provide social bonds that cushion the harsh effects of capitalist development through worker co-participation in common organization with employers and through paternalistic social legislation. The corporatist structure is inserted in the hierarchical structure and links the bottom to the top through various mutual aid or profit-sharing schemes. The social solidarity of social classes is undermined by cross-class linkages created through formal organizational membership, even though the organizations tend to support the prerogatives of management.

The collectivist or communitarian aspects of the corporatist ideology is strongly influenced by Catholic ideology which imposes obligations and duties on the members of a hierarchical society. The term *trabajador* is sufficiently general to include executives, management, professionals, employees as well as workers; hence an "industrial community" made up of "trabajadores" is not incompatible with the maintenance of a hierarchical society; on the contrary, the presence and active participation of high functionaries in the association of *trabajadores* can result in the easy conquest of policy-making positions. Hence the corporatist industrial institutions which embody the "cooperative" principles that the government is propounding will largely serve as a mechanism of social control, inhibiting the solidarity of the workers and maintaining the social peace necessary to encourage private entrepreneurial activity.[86]

The government's *imposition* of corporate institutions on society was generally *not* favorably received by the business community. The obligations imposed by the government, while securing long-term social peace, are perceived by Peruvian businessmen as infringements on their "freedom." [87] Accustomed as they are to invest and dispose as they please, lacking the minimal restraints or regulations of European capital, enjoying from time immemorial government subsidies and tax exemptions, it was not surprising to find the Peruvian business community citing the Scriptures in defense of their mundane property interests.

The social integration which is envisioned in the corporatist notion conflicts with the liberal past to which the Peruvian business community is accustomed; the loss of some options in the areas of investment and the government's assumption of the role of director of the development process has caused a substantial segment of the business community to invoke nineteenth-century fundamentalist doctrine, including the notion that private property is a God-given right. Corporatist socio-political organization rather than being a threat to private property tends to "encase" the activities of workers and employers in the industrial plans which the government is trying to attain. The business community generally tends to feel that the costs of social peace are too high in terms of the restrictions on their activities.

Accustomed to running their operations exclusively along market considerations, the businessmen view the social proposals for an industrial community as intrusions into a domain which they have perceived, by tradition and custom, as an area exclusively reserved for the *patron*. It is in the area of *methods of operation* not over principles of property that the government and the business community are in conflict.

The "Autonomy" of the Military Government

The means by which the government decides policy tends to exacerbate the differences with the business community. The government refuses to recognize interest groups as legitimate participants in the policy-making process.[88] Only members of the business community in their capacity as individuals are authorized to present their point of view to executive meetings. The closed nature of government discussions, the limited number of individuals who are selectively invited to participate, the cohesive corporate identity which characterizes the military policy-makers, make it quite difficult for the business community to communicate directly, let alone influence the military decision-makers. There is no doubt that individual entrepreneurs have close relationships with key military decision-makers—but these are largely based on personal or family ties: the linkage is only secondarily business, though no doubt this has important repercussions on the socio-economic policies of the government.

More than any previous government the present military one enjoys a great deal of autonomy which allows it to develop broad social and economic policies, informed by the political economy of corporatist-capitalism and unencumbered by the demands of particularistic interests. While the military government has yet to face any serious opposition from labor (on the contrary it appears to enjoy the support of labor despite occasional criticism from APRA),[89] business may play an obstructionist role. In the final analysis, however, it is the military itself which is the final arbiter and which will choose the means to cajole or to coerce.

Agrarian Reform: Social Change and Continuity

The most important redistributive policy pursued by the government is the Agrarian Reform Law. Under the present law, 11,000,000 hectares of land, involving 13,500 land holdings, are susceptible to expropriation.* This includes 500,000 hectares of irrigated land, 570,000 unirrigated land, and 7,000,000 pasture land. The government proposes to settle 260,000 families on this land.[90]

The present military government has accomplished more in one year than the previous Belaunde regime accomplished in five. The number of beneficiaries under the previous government amounts to 14,631 families who received approximately 375,000 hectares. Under the present military government, 28,246 families have received more than 860,000 hectares.[91]

In the six years prior to the present agrarian reform, the previous government allocated the meager sum of 929 million *soles* (43 *soles* = 1 dollar) for agrarian reform, thus undermining the little that was attempted. In the year and a half since the junta took power, it has assigned 1.6 billion *soles* for agrarian reform. The government has already paid in cash a billion *soles* (for land, installations, machinery, and cattle) to the ex-landowners who also are holding bonds worth 2.2 billion *soles* which they can recoup

* This does not include regions which have not yet been declared agrarian reform zones. These include the Department of Ica, Arequipa, Moquegua, Tacna, Cajamarca, Huanuco, Apurimac, and Tumbes.

by investing in industry. Government agricultural credits have also increased substantially—most of them for agricultural reform projects, especially in Chiclayo.[92]

An indication of how smoothly the process is taking place can be seen by the fact that agricultural production is increasing: rice production jumped from 250,000 metric tons in 1968 to 604,000 metric tons in 1970 while sugar production increased by 137,000 metric tons over the previous year.[93]

If the current rate of land settlement continues, it will take a decade to settle 280,000 families (it was earlier stated that the government would attempt to settle 500,000 families in five years—obviously an unrealistic target). In addition, the government allows up to 150 hectares of land to each owner who is affected by the agrarian reform while the average landholding of a land-reform beneficiary will be between 5 and 7 hectares, thus perpetuating substantial inequalities.[94]

The government's policy of redistribution of land is a substantial advance over that of any previous government, though in terms of current peasant needs it is still proceeding slowly, especially in some regions which have yet to be declared agrarian reform zones (for example, in the department of Cajamarca as of August, 1970 only three *fundos* were affected by the agrarian reform).

More important, however, was the tendency for government technocrats to replace the *patron* as the major decision-maker within the farm. The technocrats play an important role in organizing the peasants and are capable of manipulating them to serve government policy ends. Rather than proposing alternative policies so that the peasants can choose, there is a tendency for the technocrat to impose the course of action which he feels is best suited.

To a certain degree it is inevitable that the *tecnicos* will play a leading role in the cooperatives; they have the knowledge, skill, and contacts with the government, and this reinforces their authority. The Agrarian Reform General Headquarters (*Direccion General de la Reforma Agraria*—D.G.R.A.) has made a concerted propaganda effort to orient its personnel toward dealing with the peasants in a nonpaternalistic way.[95] The peasants who have been politicized and organized are less willing to accept a new technocratic *patron;* the pressures for change in the structure of authority both within rural areas and those emanating from urban centers are making it difficult to re-create a paternalistic structure.[96] On the other hand, where the government feels that it has an important stake in the outcome—as in some of the recently expropriated coastal plantations—it has forcefully intervened and established a rigid top-down structure which resembles a military operation more than a workers' co-operative.[97]

The new Agrarian Reform Law No. 17716 and the subsequent decree laws modifying it have substantial advantages over the previous Agrarian Reform Law No. 15037.[98] The amount of land exempted from expropriation has been decreased, the areas subject to expropriation have been expanded, the procedures of valuation and compensation are less complicated, and the terms of payment are less costly to the government. The period between the government's declaration of intent to expropriate a farm and when it actually gives the farm to the peasants has been substantially shortened.

The principal causes for expropriation in the first year of agrarian reform which have been cited by agrarian reform officials include: (a) the need to provide tenant farmers and *feudatarios* extensions of land to complement their inadequate subsistence lots—Articles 17 and 19 of the Agrarian Reform Law; (b) land which is jointly owned (*condominio*)—Article 21; (c) land which belongs to the agro-industrial complexes—Articles 37 and 40; (d) land holdings on which the landowner did not comply with the labor laws—Article 45.[99]

Outside of the coastal areas Article 45 was most frequently applied since almost all landowners were guilty of some violation. However when the article began to be applied in the Department of Lima, the landowners, largely influential residents in Lima, began to put pressure on their contacts in the bureaucracy.[100] As a result, the Labor Ministry intervened and established a commission to review each expropriation based on Article 45. As a result of this, the agrarian reform officials virtually ceased expropriating farms via Article 45 and began to search for other articles which could be used easily to legitimate the transfer of property.[101]

Despite the strong pressure emanating from the economic elites, the agrarian reform continues to move ahead, even in the Department of Lima. In the first six months of 1970 (January 1 to June 24), the agrarian reform agencies had "affected" (indicated to be intended for expropriation) 73,246 hectares of land.[102] The majority of *affectaciones* were occurring in the Province of Canete where peasant pressure and discontent were most intense. The positive attitude of the military government to agrarian reform in comparison with the previous Belaunde government, can be seen in the valley of Canete.

Under the Belaunde law (15037) from May 24, 1964 to June 24, 1969, 29 *fundos* were affected covering 956 hectares; under the new law 25 *fundos* involving 4,000 hectares were affected in the period between March 3, 1970 and June 24, 1970.[103] Four times as much land was affected by the previous government in five years. The zonal leadership for the Department of Lima has indicated that over one-third of the land affected will be expropriated during the year 1970. It appears fairly probable that in the next several years most of the large landholders will have been displaced. The crucial question that immediately arises is who will replace them as directors of the new cooperative enterprises?

Despite the expropriation of land, most of the old administrative and technical personnel remain on the farm, largely maintaining their authority and status despite the formal changes in ownership. Elections in the agro-industrial complexes have been so manipulated that the old administrators continue to dominate the decision-making apparatus along with the government-appointed technical advisers. The police and military control "political activities," eliminating possible sources of opposition, tending to inhibit the development of grass roots involvement.

Apart from the problems presented by the maintenance of the old administrators, the agrarian reform officials themselves have not always been capable of promoting peasant participation and control.[104]

The present officials involved in agrarian reform and development are in most cases the same agrarian bureaucrats who worked under the previous government.[105] As a result, many of their attitudes reflect their previous experiences: they still maintain class-racial prejudices and a paternalistic view toward peasants. The agrarian reformers in large part lack the political commitment which would allow them to involve the peasants in the sweeping changes envisioned in the law.[106] Whenever political divisions occur in the cooperatives there is a tendency for the *tecnicos* to smother the discussion and to impose their views in the name of keeping the cooperatives "apolitical." [107]

Agrarian reform officials claim that many of the problems stem from the fact that much of their personnel are inadequately trained, a problem they hope to rectify through an adequate training school.[108] It is hoped that a new training institute will make the agrarian bureaucrats more sensitive to peasant attitudes. While a new institute may indeed make the *tecnicos* more sensitive and the government's bureaucratic agrarian structure more flexible, it will not change the authoritarian decision-making structure, though it may increase the efficiency of the operations of the cooperatives. Nevertheless, as the peasants become organized and increasingly involved in the cooperatives, it is not excluded that they may displace the *tecnicos* and in the course of time transform the cooperatives into more democratic organizations.

The attitudes of the large landowners toward the agrarian reform have varied considerably. Though the landowners generally opposed the law, they felt that it would be impracticable to attempt to oppose the military's firm commitment and stand a chance of losing their compensation. Active opposition took the form of evasions rather than open confrontations. In some cases, where farms were abandoned, the government merely took over and distributed the land. In other cases, landowners anticipating the reform began to divide the land among members of their family, ejecting peasants and workers in the process, thus generating considerable tension. The strategy of the large landowners was to subdivide the farm to such a degree that they could pass themselves off as middle-class family farmers. They then utilized the ideology of the middle-class family farmer as the basis for their attack on the expropriation procedures initiated by agrarian reform functionaries. While initially surprised somewhat by the landowners' subterfuge, the government later took several measures including the application of Article 45 to expropriate the subdivided farms, and the initiation of a 50 percent profit-sharing scheme to undercut this evasion of the agrarian reform. Not willing to attack directly the agrarian reform law or the military executive, the big landowners association (*Sociedad Nacional de Agricultores*) focused its attack on the agrarian reform functionaries and supposed "abuses" of their authority and misapplication of the law. As a result, the landowners may have been able to slow down somewhat the expropriation procedures but they have not been able to stop it. It appears that the old landholding class is fighting a rearguard action hoping to salvage a reduced part of their property. Two big U.S. firms which owned land, Grace and Company, and Cerro de Pasco, did not resist the expropriations. Lacking political support, the U.S. landowners focused largely on the terms of compensation. More importantly, they hoped to save their more profitable nonagricultural enterprises. Hence, the U.S. companies put little effort into opposition to land reform. In the case of Grace, their primary concern was the industries that work the by-products of sugar cane, which Grace succeeded in having exempted from the agrarian reform process. Cerro de Pasco lost its largely undeveloped landholdings but continues to exploit its mines under profitable terms.

The new peasant leaders of the cooperatives and the agrarian *tecnicos* are emerging as the dominant social forces in the post-reform areas. The privileged status of the agro-technical administrative elite is already becoming obvious in some cases.[109] The implementation of the government's agricultural development policy will be based largely on these new emerging social classes, though the socio-economic position of the small farmers may improve substantially over the past.

In the case of Peru, we find substantial redistribution of land *without* social mobilization; tensions increase as peasants await the land reform but subsequent to receiving the land they tend to become relatively conservative. Land distribution from above tends to reduce class consciousness and to weaken autonomous organization. As a result, in the post-reform period organizations are generally formed through the initiative of government officials. The bureaucratic development state appears to be "de-politicizing" the issue of agrarian reform. The implementation of social-economic innovation through authoritarian political instruments has resulted in a new policy which embodies previously excluded strata largely encapsulated within a hierarchical mold.

The New Industrial Policy

The three key groups involved in the formation and implementation of the new industrial polity include: the generals, the technocratic planners, and the private investors—according to their order of influence. The generals make policy, selectively accepting the advice of the planners; the investors are expected to follow the new directives and invest in the areas assigned to them.

With the passing of the new Industrial Law, Decree Law No. 18350, in July, 1970, the military government's approach to industrial development has become much clearer, though some important areas still need to be clarified further. The Industrial Law is divided into five parts. Part One is a brief declaration of basic principles which states that the government goal of "permanent and self-sustained development" will be based on industrial expansion. Part Two deals with executive norms largely concerned with specifying the priorities within the industrialization program. Steel, metallurgical, and chemical industries, basic industries which provide the inputs for productive activities, and other specific industries such as the capital goods industries are top priority. Second priority is given to industries that produce "essential" goods oriented toward individual needs and those that produce for agricultural development. Third priority is given to the production of "inessential" goods of consumption. Luxury goods have no priority.

The law subsequently proceeds to divide industry into three sectors: the public, the private, and the cooperative sector. Basic industries are reserved to the state (Article 8) but all other industries will be open to private investors. However, the government leaves open the possibility that the private sector could participate in basic industries in partnership with the state or if the state decides not to enter into a particular activity. In either case, the private sector is obliged to sign a contract which includes the rate of profit and the duration of the investment; in the end, the enterprise is supposed to revert to the state in exchange for compensation. To promote industrial investment, the law establishes a series of extremely generous tax, credit, administrative, and technological incentives which, in effect, are government subsidies to the industrial sector (Titles IV and V).

Part Two of the Industrial Law refers to the criteria for rating industries on a point system (nationalist, social, economic, and technological) and the creation of a fund for technological development. Title VI, Part Two, deals with foreign capital. In industrial enterprises which are dominated by foreign capital (within a time span and depending on the nature of the enterprise and its technology), a contract must be signed with the state reducing the share of foreign ownership to no greater than one-third of the capital, allowing for recovery of initial investment and a "reasonable profit." In enterprises when foreign capital is less than 75 percent (but more than 50 percent), contracts are signed in which national capital will eventually amount to 50 percent. Article 18, however, leaves the whole question of the participation of foreign capital in the hands of the executive, for it states that "in each case [the executive] could decide the percentage of foreign capital in the industrial enterprises when it is suitable to the national interest" or when it is necessary for "permanent and self-sustained industrial growth."

Title VII and VIII refer to the participation of the workers and the change in the organization of the firm. Article 21 refers to profit-sharing in which 5 percent of the profits will be distributed equally among all the *trabajadores* (management and workers); and 5 percent will be distributed proportionately according to pay scale. Title VIII refers to the industrial community—a new juridical entity which will include all the personnel (management, salaried employees, and hourly workers) and which is to receive 15 percent of the net profits which are to be reinvested until it progressively accumulates 50 percent ownership. In the case of public enterprises, the workers receive bonds instead of shares (Article 26). Upon leaving the firm, the workers lose all the benefits accumulated by the industrial community.

The executive board of industrial firms are obliged to include at least one representative of the industrial community. The subsequent sections and parts refer to sanctions, complementary and transitory regulations, operative definitions, and a list of industries of primary priority.

An analysis of the Industrial Law reveals several features which allow us to focus on the future direction of government policy.

First of all the Industrial Law makes it clear that the governmental powers over the economy will be vastly expanded,[110] that rapid industrialization is seen as the key to economic development, that the law is open-ended and allows the government to control the options. The government is reserving to itself the final say on what the law will mean, which depends on the responses from the private sectors, both private and foreign, to the incentives which are being offered to induce new investments. If private investors decide to cooperate then the government's activity will be largely one of providing the basic inputs and infrastructure; if the private sector withdraws, the government may substitute state enterprises. In any case the most salient feature of the law is the attempt to concentrate industrial decision-making power in the executive's hands without abolishing private property.

Secondly, the law is clearly a political compromise which in the final analysis attempts to satisfy a variety of political viewpoints. Those forces like General Montagne and General Bermudez who tend to favor a neo-liberal political line were largely influential in having the sections providing incentives for private capital included in the law; General Fernandez Maldonado and his supporters were able to secure a clause reserving "basic industries for the state"; the socially concerned technocratic planners were able to include sections calling for popular participation and profit-sharing for workers.

What is more important was apparently the general agreement to limit the role of foreign enterprise and there was no mention of workers' control (auto-gestion)—the two portions which define the traditional Right and the new Left.

The major problem, however, facing the military government is the high proportion of big entrepreneurs who are linked to foreign capital. It has been estimated that eleven entrepreneurs control or influence 135 enterprises. Of the eleven, nine are linked to foreign capital, mostly U.S. Thus, the attempt by the government to promote *nationalist* industrialization based on the most dynamic sectors of the national bourgeoisie comes into conflict with the linkages and dependence which these sectors have on nonnational capital.[111]

Thirdly, the Industrial Law accepts the existing socioeconomic inequalities—indeed, they are built into the new system of profit-sharing.[112] Because the industrial community includes management, the share of the profits which will go to the workers is reduced to the point where they might even receive smaller raises than they have been accustomed to receive.

Fourthly, it is clear that if the industrialists maintain a moderate re-investment rate equivalent to that of the industrial community, the latter will never achieve fifty percent ownership.[113]

Fifthly, as originally presented, the law ties the workers to the firm (they lose their accumulated shares if they leave), hence lessening their mobility and their militancy.[114]

Sixthly, it appears that the creation of the industrial community is aimed at replacing trade unions; the instruments of socio-economic improvement are meant to induce greater efficiency and productivity, not strikes or class struggle. At the same time, the board of directors of a firm is required to have only one representative of the industrial community (who could be a manager or salaried employee as well as a worker)—the majority will still be made up of the same executives. It seems doubtful that the representative of the industrial community will not be co-opted by the elite.

Finally, the industrial law seems almost exclusively concerned with the goals of modernization—higher productivity, high rates of investment, technification—and little concerned with the problem of developing industries capable of absorbing the underemployed and unemployed. At best, the industrialization effort appears to be aimed largely at benefiting those segments of the working class employed in industry—approximately 7 percent presently, compared to the 35 percent who are underemployed. Despite President Velasco's repeated denials, Peru's effort is largely directed at modernization of existing society; it is not a social revolution basically concerned with the most exploited sectors of urban Peruvian society.[115]

The Entrepreneurial State

The major issues in debate do not concern socialism vs. capitalism especially if by socialism we mean workers' control over industrial enterprises; the military government is firmly committed to the maintenance of private property. What is under discussion is the degree of state involvement in the economy.

Prior to 1968, private enterprise was supremely dominant. National and foreign capital were linked together and economic decision-making was concentrated in a small group of capitalists. The state was largely a spectator, hardly even a guardian of state interests.[116]

Today at least among one sector of the government,

the state's role is described as decisive: under the new government the direct intervention of the state in the planning of economic development, organization of new enterprises, and in the control of trade, commerce, and refining is seen as an integral aspect of the new "entrepreneurial state." [117] The state is perceived as an instrument of creation, not as a pliable tool of private interests.

The activities of private investors are supposed to conform to the demands of the national planners; the proponents of the entrepreneurial state are relying on a "change of attitude" on the part of the private sector; a willingness of the middle class to risk capital and sacrifice for long-term development. It is hoped that the middle class and, more specifically, the private sector will accept the rationality of the process and incorporate itself to the "revolution," that is, the developmental process.

The notion that the problem of development is one of reasoning, of changing attitudes, is somewhat naive; the perception of interests and the problem of power over decisions are what influence the decisions of the private investors. The differences between the advocates of the entrepreneurial state and private investors are considerable though they can be resolved. In any case, the government will press the private sector to cooperate or, failing that, threaten to impose its own solutions.

The key problem facing the military is how to promote an "entrepreneurial state" without entrepreneurs. In the existing bureaucracy it is difficult to find the kind of dynamic organizers capable of directing the new enterprises. The hope is to recruit new personnel, mainly new university graduates and to create new state organizations independent of and parallel to existing bureaucratic structures in the hope of avoiding the conservative and ineffective operations of the past.

The government's control over commercialization, especially in the export of fish-meal, was largely an attempt to eliminate the speculative aspects of capitalist operations.[118]

The "moralization" of capitalist operations is not meant to infringe on the interest of private enterprise but to make sure that they play the game according to the strict rules of the game.

The Technocrats: The Power to Influence

The technocrats have replaced in part the traditional pressure groups as a major influence on government policy. The present government has declared, on numerous occasions, that planning is of capital importance in reaching the goals set forth in its program. Previous governments also spoke of the importance of planning but most of the proposals remained on paper. Presently there is a one-year plan which is supposed to guide government investment policy. However, an evaluation of the plan following the first six months of 1970 showed that the investment goals set up by the plan were not followed largely due to a lack of personnel capable of taking them down to the micro-level and the failure of the private sector to respond. Administrative inefficiency led to development bottlenecks, while the ministries had not prepared concrete programs to invest public funds.[119]

The Institute of Planning participates in COAP through its coordinators and thus directly participates in the deliberations that shape government policy. COAP, together with the cabinet, sets general policy. The institute is called upon to give advice and to implement plans. The Institute of Planning takes the policy framework and proposes a budget for each ministry. The final outcome is largely a result of bargaining between the ministry and the Institute of Planning. Beginning in 1971, the powers of the Planning Institute will increase, they will set the budget and orient the ministries to specific kinds of economic activity.

There is no mechanism that links the planner to the public. As a result, the feedback from the public to the planner is weak. In addition, the planners lack the power to make the private sector comply with their plans. Indirectly, through their ability to influence legislation, the planners can substantially affect the private sector. During the first six months of 1970, the decline of private investment in some lines of industry[120] (mainly cement and textiles) was the result partly of political uncertainty—a political fact which was uncontrollable. The response of the planners to a withdrawal of private capital is to increase the state's role.

Lacking a popular basis, the policy of the Planning Institute largely reflects the technocratic bias of the military; in the industrialization process the emphasis is on increasing production and efficiency and improving technology; little or no thought has been given to developing industry capable of absorbing the underemployed labor force. The assumption, apparently, is that industrial growth will generate a whole series of side effects which will stimulate new employment opportunities. Likewise, the planners and the military have rejected urban reform which would deal with the pressing housing problem.[121] The focus is on productive not social investment.[122] The government will continue to rely on "self-help" and private sector construction for housing—solutions which have had very meager results in the past. Furthermore, the military's unwillingness to alienate the urban middle class has been an important factor forestalling the initiation of progressive taxation. As a result, little income redistribution appears to have occurred so far in urban areas. Even in terms of financing their current programs involving agrarian reform and industrial development (based on tax exemptions for industrialists) the current tax structure may prove to be inadequate and create serious bottlenecks.

The planners are "nationalist" in the sense that they are highly preoccupied with the problem of Peru's "dependence" on the U.S. Yet there has yet to appear a strategy that links copper production to industrial development; the U.S. will continue to absorb the greater part of the copper in its own industries.

The Ministry of Industries has been functioning only since 1969. In the first year there was a constant changeover of personnel in the search for individuals capable of implementing the state's part in the new industrialization effort. As of 1970, few if any studies of projects to develop industries have been carried out. Planners estimate that it may take four to five years to develop industrial projects. The long view which the planners are taking may be justified in terms of what is technically feasible but the popular expectations which have been raised by the government may begin to create difficulties.

The growing influence of the planners can be seen in the fact that in 1971 the Institute of Planning will become the Ministry of Planning. In addition, economic development currently treated by the Ministry of Economy and Finances will be transferred to the Planning Ministry. Furthermore, through budget control and programming the planners will increase their influence. The planners as government advisers will orient policy toward increased involvement of the state in the economy.

The close ties and interaction between the military government and the planners have increased the authority of the planners. This can be seen by the easy access which the planners have to top decision-makers, in comparison to businessmen. The government is more likely to take account of the recommendations of the planners than those of the trade unions or industrial associations.[123]

The planners have focused their attention on increasing the government's involvement in banking and finance, as the new industrialization program depends on financial policies which are congruent with its needs. While banking still rests in the hands of the traditional elites, it is hardly likely that the industrialization goals will be realized.

The growing intervention of the state in agriculture, mining, fishing, industry, and banking is creating an important institutional power base for the technico-intelligentsia. There exists a tension between the new upwardly mobile state-based *tecnicos* and the private investors who feel that the gains of this new stratum are made at their expense.

Private Investors

The initial response of the business community to the military government was favorable; it was perceived as a government of law and order, and little else. The expropriation of IPC was viewed as an exceptional and symbolic measure necessary to legitimize the coup. Since it was largely aimed at a foreign firm, the Peruvian bourgeoisie supported it. The conservative fiscal and monetary policies of the government were along the lines advocated by the International Monetary Fund.[124] Credits and salaries were restricted, imports were reduced, and government spending was restricted. As a result, the economy was stabilized and the balance of payments problem was solved. The Peruvian government's agreement to sign the copper contract expanding U.S. exploitation of copper, together with the decision not to expropriate Grace's holdings in industry, facilitated the refinancing of the foreign debt.

On the Agrarian Reform Law and later, the Industrial Law, the private investors were divided: a small minority of entrepreneurs supported these measures;[125] another group maintained selective opposition; and a third group, which appears to be in the majority, voiced a more general opposition.

Most of the businessmen are disturbed by the relationship which they have with the military government. COAP's refusal to recognize the National Industrialists Association (SNI); the infrequent consultations with businessmen; and the absolute control that the military has over decisions—the closed "caste" of decision-makers—all this appears to the businessmen as an unsympathetic political environment.[126]

For a very small minority of entrepreneurs—who ap-

pear to be among the few dynamic businessmen of
Peru—the agrarian reform was welcomed as an expansion
of the internal market; the industrial law is perceived as
creating a solid basis for development. The profit-sharing
part of the law is welcomed since it will undercut the trade
unions by creating a parallel structure, that is, the industrial
community. With generous tax exemptions and state-
promoted basic industries, a favorable environment for
manufacturing would be created. Given an adequate investment rate, there would be no possibility that the industrial
community would ever obtain 50 percent ownership. For all
these economic reasons and because of the political stability
which is engendered, the pragmatic entrepreneurs are in
favor of the junta's policies if not always in favor of the
methods by which policy is made.

The second group of entrepreneurs feel that in the long
run the law may be to their advantage but feel that in the
short run there are a number of specific problems. These
grievances include: too much *dirigismo* or control by the
government over the rate of profit, membership in director-
ship of enterprise, investment choices, etc.; they are fearful
that the workers will not wait 15 or 20 years—the length of
time it will take for the workers to become partners, according to government promises. The businessmen fear that the
Industrial Law, rather than becoming a palliative, will stimulate the workers to demand that the industrial community
take their share now. The businessmen fear that the government's promise of co-participation in the future could become the demand of the workers for auto-gestion now. Finally, these businessmen are fearful that the government
controls may have an adverse psychological effect on the
majority of businessmen, resulting in a decline of investment that would have a depressing effect on the economy in
general.

The third group of businessmen have opposed the law
as "a radical modification of the right of private
property." [127] Replete with references to the Bible, Christi-

anity, the Pope, Western civilization, and human nature, the Chamber of Commerce of Lima, the National Association of Industrialists, the National Association of Mining and Petroleum, the National Association of Fishing, and the Peruvian Chamber of Construction have condemned the law. This fundamentalist approach is largely a reflection of Peru's past, the complete and absolute freedom to exploit which Peruvian businessmen enjoyed. These attacks on the law are more interesting for what they tell us about the attitude of Peruvian business than what they tell us about the law.

The businessmen are unable to understand the chronic debilities of the Peruvian economy and the weak basis on which recent industrialization took place; the lack of basic industry, the narrow market, and their dependence on government protection.[128] Incapable of understanding their incapacity to develop the basic infrastructure and industries on which economic development could take place, incapable of reacting positively to the government's challenge, they react in a negative, defensive manner reverting to fundamentalist dogma. If we leave aside the religious embellishments the main criticism of the businessmen toward the Industrial Law is not the profit-sharing, or even the partial ownership by workers, but the new juridical entity, the industrial community, which will own half the enterprise and be represented on the board of directors. Not a small factor is the intense dislike by some of the "European" Peruvian businessmen for the *"cholos"* with whom they will have to sit on the board.

The objections of the businessmen are more fantasy than real; they perceive the seeds of a new form of property which could become the basis for a change in property. It is this irrational attitude on the part of the majority that frightens those industrialists who know that this part of the law is not likely to come about; the pragmatic entrepreneurs fear the irrational response to the law may hurt the economy. Thus some pragmatic industrialists object to the law not for what it is but because of its psychological effects.[129] The pragmatists argue that "ideologies frighten businessmen." The pragmatists hope to convince their fundamentalist colleagues to shift their attack to specific features of the law; to focus on its "technical" inadequacy and to show why it is inoperative and then to arrange the suitable regulations.

The opposition of the businessmen has been singularly ineffective and has hardly impressed the Peruvian military. The Peruvian businessmen exhibit very little class consciousness of collective activity. What else explains the little or no interest that SNI exhibited regarding the education of the military in CAEM? Because of their close association with landholding groups and foreign investors, the Peruvian bourgeoisie find it difficult to separate themselves from the "traditional" oligarchy and U.S. interests. In fact, the attitudes of the businessmen are not clearly differentiated. The number of class-conscious, national capitalists is very small. The government has devised a policy to promote the interests of the "national bourgeoisie" but does not call on them for advice, apparently because there is a strong undercurrent within the government that feels that they are not "progressive."

To some businessmen the government's advisers are largely "frustrated intellectuals" who are better educated than most businessmen but who couldn't make it like the successful businessmen.

Businessmen perceive the nationalization of enterprises and statification of the economy as policies which government advisers adopt to enrich themselves.[130] According to some businessmen, the *tecnicos* will utilize the state enterprises to promote themselves at the expense of the private entrepreneurs.

There is a half truth in this view: the backwardness, underdevelopment and dependence of the Peruvian economy has "frustrated" Peruvian intellectuals—as it has many other social strata; the concentration of ownership and the penetration of external capital have limited the options available to university graduates. The military government's industrialization program and agrarian reform are opening opportunities especially for technicians and university graduates. The basis of the government's economic and social program is not rooted in psychological maladjustment; rather the psychological malaise is rooted in socio-economic conditions which have generated sufficient pressure to produce a new political elite which is, in turn, attempting to create from its policies a homogeneous social basis of political support for its economic development policies.

Military Government and Political Forces

The pre-1968 parties are in difficult shape. The only party which maintains a base of support is the APRA. General Odria has dissolved the *Union Nacional Odrista*. Many of the supporters of *Accion Popular* are now working for the government or have returned to private practices. The Christian Democrats are working in the government with the exception of a right-wing splinter, the Popular Christian party, which is in opposition.

APRA presented mild opposition to the government during the first year but has since offered its support to the government which has refused to accept it.[131] Aprista trade union functionaries have tried to separate themselves somewhat from the party and there may be some contact between them and some government functionaries who are ex-Apristas. The conservative politics of APRA, its bureaucratic organization, its aging leadership, and its absorption in electoral-parliamentary politics for fifteen years have made it incapable of seriously challenging the military's political hegemony.

On the left, the Communist party has adopted a position of total, uncritical support of the military government.[132] Describing it as a revolutionary national-democratic government, the Communists have attempted to mobilize support for the government which has, in turn, accepted their support while rejecting any proposal by the Communists to build an organized mass base for the revolution.[133]

The Revolutionary Left is badly fragmented and reduced in size. The three most important groups are the *Vanguardia Revolucionaria* (VR), the Movement of the Revolutionary Left (MIR) and the pro-Chinese Communists (who are subdivided into three or four groups). The Revolutionary Left is still largely confined to the universities, though some effort has been made by the VR to recruit trade unionists and the MIR appears to have influence among some peasant groups in the north. At the present time, the Right appears to be better prepared than the Left for a crisis within the military government, but it is highly unlikely that a crisis will occur.

Most of the non-revolutionary, non-communist Left appears to be within the government, attempting to commit the government to particular reforms within their areas of competence.

At present the military does have the problem of activating its passive supporters.[134] The lack of popular participation in urban and rural areas is admitted even by the generals themselves. The military has given little indication that it is interested in the active mass support needed to overcome the problems of underdevelopment; it has rejected the formal trappings of democracy but it has substituted a corporatist structure which hardly will serve to articulate the needs of the workers; the nationalist ideology and the symbolic expropriation of IPC may have created a sense of solidarity but Peru's increased dependence and vulnerability on a single foreign-owned export (copper) may soon dissolve this bond. Industrialization based on the importation of sophisticated technology will exacerbate existing problems of unemployment and underemployment and will not serve to absorb the landless peasants who will not receive land.

Renaming barriadas "Pueblos Jovenes," self-help, and

penny-capitalism are poor substitutes for an urban reform which provides the services and materials that makes "human investment" a meaningful method of social change. The present political stability and social change could generate new confrontations and more radical social changes in the not too distant future.

In the meantime, the government must confront two points of conflict with its nationalist-state development program: (1) the strong linkage and dependence of the Peruvian entrepreneurs on foreign capital; (2) the high concentration of economic power within a small group of investors who are influential in a number of economic sectors.

The government must face the option of permitting foreign capital and its national dependencies to continue to dominate the industries on which its industrialization is based or have the state take them over and operate them. With few exceptions it is difficult to separate the "dynamic" national industrial bourgeoisie from foreign capital. The nationalist industrial effort conflicts with the foreign dependence and linkage of national entrepreneurs. In addition the sectoral nationalist policies which envision the development of industry are highly vulnerable because the private banking and credit sources are linked to the economic elite. The fifty-eight largest entrepreneurs have links with more than a single sector of the economy. Because of the interdependence of industry and finance the government must either extend its domain into the area of finance or make concessions to the industrial elite. Sectoral changes leave the industrial development program vulnerable to the pressures and policies of the financial elite.

The military government faces a better-than-even chance of gaining and maintaining substantial support, initiating a number of new development programs, consolidating social changes, and bringing about political stability. In the long run the new expectations of the workers for participation will come into conflict with the authoritarian vertical lines of government, which now predominate. The problems

TABLE I
Junta Biographical Data

Name	Position	Rank, Date of Rank	Age	Birth Place	Family Social Origin	Year Graduated From Military Academy	CAEM† Association	U.S. Training or Assignment
Juan Velasco Alvarado	President	Division General, 1965 (Army)	60	Piura	Middle Class	1934*	X	X
Edgardo Mercado Jarrin	Minister of Foreign Affairs	Brig. General, 1966 (Air Force)	54	Lima	Middle Class	1941	X	X
Alfredo Avunseno Cornejo	Minister of Education	Brig. General, 1967 (Army)	54	Arequipa	Middle Class	1939*	X	X
Jorge Barandiaran Pagador	Minister of Agriculture	Brig. General, NA (Army)	50	Chiclayo	NA	1941*	X	X
Armando Artola Azarate	Minister of Interior	Brig. General, 1967 (Army)	50	Moquequa	Upper Class	1940*	X	X
Ernesto Montagne Sanchez	Minister of Defense	Division General, 1968 (Army)	53	Lima	Middle Class	1938*	X	X
Jorge Chamot Biggs	Minister of Labor	Major General, NA (Air Force)	50	Lima	NA	1942	NA	X
Francisco Morales Bermudez	Minister of Economy and Finance	Brig. General, NA (Army)	48	Lima	Grandson of Former President	1943	X	X

Name	Rank, Date of Rank	Position	Age	Birth Place	Family Social Origin	Year Graduated From Military Academy	CAEM† Association	U.S. Training or Assignment
Jorge Maldonado Solari	Brig. General, NA (Army)	Minister of Development	47	Ilo	Middle Class	1941*	X	NA
Eduardo Montero Rojas	Major General, 1963 (Air Force)	Minister of Public Health	51	Yurimaguas	Middle Class	1941	NA	X
Jorge Camino	Rear Admiral, NA (Navy)	Minister of Industry and Commerce	56	Iquitos	NA	1936	NA	X
Alfonso Navarro ‡	Vice Admiral, 1968 (Navy)	Minister of Navy	58	Lima	Middle Class	1934	NA	X
Anibal Meza Cuadra Cardenas	Brig. General, NA (Army)	Minister of Transportation and Communications	49	Bolivar	NA	1942*	NA	X
Rolando Gilardi Rodriguez	Lt. General, NA (Air Force)	Minister of Aeronautics	49	Arequipa	Middle Class	1941	NA	X
Jose Graham Hurtado	Brig. General, 1968 (Army)	Chief, Presidential Advisory Committee	51	Arequipa	Middle Class	1941*	X	NA

* Chorrillos Military Academy.
† Center for Military Studies. Many junta members attended and graduated and later returned as administrators or instructors.
‡ Considered moderate-conservative and often differed openly with more radical elements in junta. Was replaced in September, 1969, by Vice Admiral Enrique Carbonell, a radical.
NA Information not available.

of dependence and the expanded foreign presence which the government has yet to face will provoke new issues for debate and conflict.

Conclusion

The policies of the military aimed at carrying out a nationalist bourgeois revolution are products of their class background, the position of the military in Peruvian society, and their position within the middle class. With few exceptions the military officials are from provincial middle-class families—they were not members of the urban industrial bourgeoisie which is largely linked to and dependent on foreign investors and which tends to subordinate its policy preferences to accommodate those of their foreign partners. Likewise the officers did not originate from commercial families with strong linkages to the large landowning families. From the economic and geographic angle the members of the military junta have their roots in the marginal middle class of the province. Recruited from the marginal middle class they do not identify with the large domestic propertied interests and hence are not as subject to the same direct pressures and influences emanating from these classes. Not faced with these class and family constraints their marginality allowed them to develop nationalist and agrarian reform policies which other middle-class political elites have shunned because of their integration in the international-agricultural-banking economic power structure.

At the same time the middle-class origins and the political education of the officials in the military produced a strong antipathy toward working-class or revolutionary socialist politics. Some of the officials have visited the U.S. as many as six times. Most of the military officials have received instruction and political indoctrination in the U.S. The political courses are partially geared to indoctrinating the military against communism and to the virtues of western-style private enterprise. Apparently the Peruvian military has been selective in what it chooses to learn. Their animosity to communist revolution has been matched by their attempts to modify Peru's current dependence on the U.S., suggesting that the overseas students are not the docile, loyal, and obedient products that the educational program is supposed to turn out. The position of the military is supportive of the middle class but not identical with it. The fact that military officers originate from and lead middle-class styles of life should not obscure the fact that they have to a certain degree an independent base of power outside of the existing property structure which allows them political autonomy. Not linked to the existing "mutual support societies" characteristic of the other middle-class propertied groups they are less susceptible to the log-rolling politics which undermine the formulation of a systematic development strategy. In the final analysis the military shares the same long-term ideals as many of the propertied groups who are opposing its reform measures today. However, what is crucial to the immediate situation is the fact that the military lacks the support of precisely those propertied groups which it needs in order to modernize society and which would be the final beneficiaries of the current policies.[135]

NOTES

1. On the appointment of government officials to supervise the administration of expropriated estates, see interviews in *Caretas* (Lima) Vol. 19, No. 400 (August 14, 1969), pp. 16–19 and 48–50. In addition, imprisoned peasant leader, Hugo Blanco, said at the time that "government bureaucrats and soldiers will bungle successful implementation of the new Agrarian Reform Law." Blanco felt that men like himself who have exceptional ability to organize the *Sierra* peasantry should have major roles in the agrarian reform. See interview in *International Press* (New York), Vol. 7, No. 31 (September 29, 1969), pp. 848–9. Since this statement, Blanco along with Hector Bejar, Ricardo Gadea, and some 100 other political prisoners were granted amnesty on December 21, 1970, and released from prison, an action which may indicate that the junta is confident that it can control the peasantry without jailing its popular leaders.

2. The junta has demonstrated that it intends to keep unions under effective government control. See "Un an de pouvoir militaire," *Front* (Paris), Vol. 1, No. 3 (September, 1969), pp. 38–41.

3. For an excellent discussion of capitalist modernization from above see Barrington Moore, *Social Origins of Democracy and Dictatorship* (Boston: Beacon Press, 1966).

4. On Cuba's favorable response, see Fidel Castro's speech of July 26, 1969, in *Granma,* July 27, 1969.

5. For background information concerning this period in Peruvian politics, see Frederick B. Pike, *The Modern History of Peru* (New York: Praeger, 1967), pp. 282–320, and Lewis Hanke, *Contemporary Latin America* (Princeton: D. Van Nostrand, 1968), pp. 128–32.

6. For an account of the motives surrounding the military coup of 1962, see Peter Nehemkis, *Latin America: Myth and Reality* (New York: The New American Library, 1966), pp. 93–104.

7. See CIDA report, *Una Evaluacion de la Reforma Agraria en El Peru* (Washington, D.C.: Pan American Union, 1966), p. 1.

8. *Boletin Informativo* (Lima: ONRA, September, 1968), and for additional information, see *Peruvian Times,* June 27, 1969, pp. 1–2.

9. CIDA report, *op. cit.,* p. 5.

10. See James Petras, "Revolution and Guerrillas in Latin America: Venezuela, Guatemala, Colombia, and Peru," in *Latin America— Reform or Revolution,* James Petras and Maurice Zeitlin, eds. (N.Y.: Fawcett Publications, 1968).

11. Foreknowledge of the 1967 currency devaluation enabled many high government officials to make substantial sums in the money markets. For IPC-related corruption see, *The Economist para America Latina* (London), Vol. 3, No. 6 (March 19, 1968), pp. 11–12.

12. Biographical data on the junta members was kindly provided by the Peruvian embassy, Washington, D.C. We would also like to thank U.S. Congressman Dante Fascell and Senator Frank Church for their aid in attaining supporting data.

13. See Table I. For a brief background sketch on CAEM and its activities see Frederick B. Pike, *op. cit.,* p. 315.

14. *Vision* (Mexico City), Vol. 37, No. 5 (August 29, 1969), pp. 12–16. (This issue of *Vision* was not permitted to circulate freely in Peru because of its critical observation regarding the junta's lack of wide national support.)

15. *Peruvian Times,* August 8, 1969, p. 1.

16. Institute of National Planning, Lima, November, 1968. (The institute was established by the military government which ruled in 1962–63 and was one of the developmental institutions inaugurated at the time.)

17. For a discussion of the history of petroleum politics in Peru see *Marcha* (Montevideo), No. 26 (June, 1969), pp. 7–29.

18. On the Hickenlooper Amendment see *Congressional Record, Senate,* Vol. 108 (October 2, 1962), pp. 21615–20. For a historical perspective on this highly controversial topic, with excellent documentation, see Marvin D. Bernstein, ed., *Foreign Investment in Latin America, Cases and Attitudes* (New York: Knopf, 1966). General Valdivia, a member of the Peruvian military junta, declared that the Peruvian government had been threatened by the International Monetary Fund with cancellation of credits amounting to $75 million if Peru did not restore the property of IPC. Other agencies alleged to be applying financial pressure include AID, BID and the World Bank. See the *New York Times,* December 8, 1968.

19. *Peruvian Times,* August 1, 1969, p. 1.

20. For summary of Velasco's Independence Day speech see *Peruvian Times,* August 1, 1969, p. 1.

21. *Peruvian Times,* August 1, 1969, p. 1.

22. *Peruvian Times,* February 28, 1969, pp. 1–2.

23. The coastal plantations, including the sugar plantations, were exempt from expropriation under Belaunde's Agrarian Reform Law of 1964. Article 25 of that law allowed individual members of agricultural corporations to declare single expropriation exemptions. The collective declaration of these exemptions would effectively exclude the large estates from judicial or administrative action under the Belaunde law. On expropriations under the junta Agrarian Reform Law of June 24, 1969, see *Peruvian Times,* July 4, 1969, p. 2.

24. W. R. Grace and Co. of the United States lost 12,000 hectares. See *Peruvian Times,* July 4, 1969, p. 2.

25. *New York Times,* June 26, 1969, p. 4.

26. On the expropriation of the Cerro de Pasco lands owned by Cerro Corp. of New York, see *Peruvian Times,* January 3, 17 and May 9, 1969.

27. "La Reforma Agraria y los Empresarios," *Caretas* (Lima), Vol. 19, No. 399 (July 24, 1969), p. 25.

28. *Ibid.,* p. 25.

29. Former director of ONRA, Lander Pecora resigned six months after the military took power and expressed surprise when the new agrarian reform law was decreed. In a private interview in Washington, D.C. on June 25, 1969, he openly admitted that he did not think the military government would decree such an effective, thorough, and radical law.

30. *Correo* (Lima), May 10, 1969, p. 4.

31. Labor leaders and sugar workers expressed their fears in a series of interviews conducted in early 1969 on the *Hacienda Pomalca,* a large Peruvian-owned sugar-growing and processing operation on the north coast. See *Caretas,* Vol. 19, No. 400 (August 14, 1969), pp. 16–19 and 48–50.

32. *Ibid.*

33. *Peruvian Times,* August 1, 1969, p. 1.

34. *Ibid.*

35. For a copy of the University Law see *Marcha* (Montevideo), June 26, 1969, pp. 85–96. For additional information and commentary on the Law see *Vision,* Vol. 36, No. 7 (March 28, 1969), p. 14.

36. *The Economist para America Latina,* Vol. 3, No. 16 (August 6, 1969), p. 14.

37. *Ibid.*

38. *The Economist para America Latina,* Vol. 3, No. 17 (August 20, 1969), p. 32.

39. *Ibid.*

40. *Peruvian Times,* February 28, 1969, p. 1.

41. *Peruvian Times,* August 15, 1969, p. 1.

42. *The Economist para America Latina,* Vol. 3, No. 17 (August 20, 1969), p. 32.

43. *Ibid.*

44. *Ibid.*

45. *New York Times,* September 28, 1969, p. E5.

46. For details on the establishment of diplomatic relations and the signing of trade agreements with the USSR and the Eastern European Bloc see *Peruvian Times,* April 25, 1969, p. 1.

47. See Pearson Commission report of the Commission on International Development, October 1, 1969. See portions quoted, *New York Times,* October 2, 1969, p. 74.

48. *Peruvian Times,* April 18, 1969, p. 1.

49. *Peruvian Times,* January 10, 1969, p. 1.

50. The suspension of Peru's sugar quota could idle about 50,000 sugar workers. This unemployment, which would be concentrated on the north coast, could place additional internal burdens on the junta. Peru's sugar workers are unionized and are among the better paid workers in the country. For a detailed study of Peru's sugar industry and its labor elite see, *Vision,* Vol. 36, No. 7 (March 28, 1969), pp. 30–31.

51. Under the Fisherman's Act all captains are reimbursed by the U.S. government for fines resulting from fishing within the extraordinary limits (200 miles) set by numerous Latin American countries. Fines have varied from $5,000 to $20,000 and are based on ship tonnage.

52. *Washington Post,* May 25, 1969, p. Al.

53. *Marcha,* October 3, 1969, p. 18.

54. The President of Petroperu, General Marcos Fernandez Baca, stated that "the object of the Revolution is not the distribution of wealth for all Peruvians but an equitable distribution of the natural resources throughout the country." *Expreso,* July 10, 1970.

55. For a brief account of the enlarged role of the state in Peruvian economy and society, see President Velasco's Presidential message, *El Comercio* (Lima), July 29, 1970, pp. 4–5.

56. On the state's takeover of the commercialization of the fish-meal industry, see *Expreso,* July 2, 1970, p. 3.

57. *Peru: Estrategia del desarrollo nacional a largo plazo* (Lima: Instituto Nacional de Planificacion, November, 1968). See also "Lineamientos Basicos de Politica de Desarrollo a Mediano Plazo" (Lima: Instituto Nacional de Planificacion, April, 1970).

58. Interviews with informed officials in CENACOOP, the government agency for training peasants in co-op principles, revealed that attempts to encourage peasant control of co-ops resulted in the wholesale reduction of staff personnel. A documented account of the "new paternalism" is found through interview transcripts. See "Ciclo de Conferencias sobre Cooperativismo: Entrevista a Tres Trabajadores Contratados del Complejo Agro-Industrial de Cayalti" (Lima: *Centro Nacional de Capacitacion Cooperativa* [CENACOOP], March, 1970).

59. Referring to the expropriation of IPC, General Marcos Fernandez Baca referred to it as "an exceptional case." *Expreso,* July 10, 1970, p. 2.

60. *Ley de Industrias, Decreto Ley* No. 18350, Titulo VI.

61. Decreto Ley, Normativo de la Industria Minera, No. 18225.

62. See the tables and discussion in Pumaruna, "El Reformismo Burgues Peruano es pro-imperialista, Cuajone lo demuestra," *Vanguardia Revolucionaria,* No. 6, pp. 25–46.

63. Highly placed government officials admitted that the reason why the industries were not nationalized was to forestall a hostile U.S. reaction to the expropriation of U.S.-owned landholdings. Under the new industrial law (Article 7) the state reserves for itself basic industries which includes paper, pulp, and other industries owned by Grace and Company (See Article 4 [2]).

64. In discussion with members of the Planning Institute it appeared that they functioned as an idea-bank from which the junta could draw; on the other hand there was little or no indication that they had direct contact with mass pressure groups.

65. While the structure is predominantly technocratic it is not wholly so. CENACOOP officials stated that approximately 80 percent of the personnel of the co-ops are workers and employers, but only 60 percent of the delegates in the representative assembly and only 40 percent in the directionship of the enterprise are workers and employers. The majority of the directors in some co-ops are directly appointed by the government.

66. The enormous inequalities which still persist can be seen in the case of the cooperative of Laredo in Trujillo: the 240 employers average

5,829 *soles* per month while the 1,263 workers average 362 *soles* per month—the employers receive sixteen times the pay of a worker in this "cooperative." The difference between the highest-paid employer and the lowest-paid worker is sixty to one. See *Oiga* (Lima), August 7, No. 385, p. 12.

67. The level of tolerance of the military is relative: parties, pressure groups and publications which are mildly critical are permitted. On the other hand it appears that criticism which attacks the executive as such (rather than its policy) or even criticism which is a bit pointed (morality of officials) can be subject to government action. See *Oiga,* August 7, 1970, p. 11 and July 17, 1970.

68. Unemployment determined by the number of jobless members of the labor force seeking employment rose from 4 percent at the end of 1967 to 5.2 percent in mid-1969. Similarly, underemployment (determined by the number of persons employed less than 35 hours per week and desiring more work, plus all individuals earning less than a given subsistence salary) rose from 26 percent of the labor force in 1967 to 34 percent in mid-1969. *Report of the International Monetary Fund Staff to Members of the Executive Board of Peru,* January 8, 1970.

69. President Velasco has stated: "There are, thus, conditions of genuine confidence for all those who understand that money must also have a constructive social responsibility. There is confidence and government backing for investment that promotes the economic development of the country within a framework that respects the fair expectations of capital and the legitimate rights of the workers. There is confidence because in the country there is general political stability. . . . There is confidence because private investment has all the qualities that any modern entrepreneur could demand. From the beginning the Revolutionary Government has declared its backing and support for private investment including foreign (investment) that subjects itself to the laws of the country." "Mensaje a la Nacion del Presidente del Peru en el Primer Aniversario de la Revolucion" (Oct. 3, 1969), published in *La Politica del Gobierno Revolucionario* (Oficina Nacional de Informacion), No. 4, January, 1970, p. 61.

70. During the first full year, 1969, of military rule, the generals were singularly unsuccessful in obtaining private sector cooperation. In real terms the 1969 investments were barely equivalent to one-half those in the mid-1960s; the rate of growth per capital was −2 percent. IMF Staff Report, *op. cit.*

71. Discussing the new industrial law, President Velasco has pointed out: "The worker now does not need protection and to be on guard. There are not going to be stoppages and strikes—what for? Both, the capitalists and the workers will benefit. There will be harmony and they will act as if they will be [are] in a good family." *Expreso* (Lima), August 13, 1970.

72. See the special incentives in the industrial law for industries which locate outside of Lima—Callao. Titulo III Art. 9 (4), *Incentivos por Decentralizacion.*

73. General Artola, the Minister of Interior, succinctly described the authoritarian nature of the government when he stated: "Artola's finger appoints the mayors. Time has proven me right. The finger of Artola has given better results than the political elections that were failures." *Expreso,* August 9, 1970, p. 3.

74. See "Discurso del Ministro de Relaciones Exteriores del Peru, pronunciado en la XXIV Asamblea General de las Naciones Unidas," New York, September 19, 1969, (Lima: Oficina Nacional de Informacion), esp. pp. 14 passim.

75. The two legal measures which the government passed to control criticism and conflict are the Ley Organica de la Universidad Peruana (Decreto Ley No. 17437) which eliminates student participation in the governance of the University and the Estatuto de Libertad de Prensa y su Reglamento 1969–1970 (Decreto Ley No. 18075).

76. President Velasco attacked the previous government as a "false democracy" and went on to justify his government: "Our legitimacy does not come from votes, the votes of a system corrupt to its roots, because it never served to defend the genuine interests of the Peruvian people. Our legitimacy has its origin in the incontrovertible fact that we are transforming this country, just in order to defend and interpret the interests of this people that has been deceived with imprudence and for a price. This is the only legitimacy of a genuine revolution like ours."

77. One of the best-informed Peruvian political writers is Francisco Moncloa, whose series of articles on the Peruvian bureaucracy are well-informed. See his articles in *Expreso,* July 2, 5 and 17, 1970.

78. The conflict over the use of Article 45 of the agrarian reform law which allowed for the expropriation of farms which did not comply with labor regulations is a case in point. The Ministry of Labor through Ministerial Resolution No. 481–70–TR set up a commission to review each case when Article 45 was applied. While the agrarian reform agency was trying to expedite expropriation, under pressure from the peasants, the landowners had found an ally in the Ministry of Labor.

79. While many observers have commented on the inefficiency of the Peruvian bureaucracy few have studied carefully its political role in Peruvian society. The long delays and *tramites* of the bureaucracy are means by which the system postpones meeting popular demands, staggering them over a long period and only gradually providing a trickle of pay-offs. The state is the first *obstacle* to realizing popular demands and for that reason is a major institution defending the unequal distribution of goods and services. The bureaucracy dominated by the economic elites has to resist the pressures of the lower-

income groups who look to the state for services which legally they may be entitled to. If the bureaucracy were "efficient" and did respond to these pressures and demands for services it would come into conflict with the whole system; the current bureaucracy *which is largely an instrument of control* is being asked to transform itself into an instrument of development, a task it does not appear capable of currently undertaking.

80. The debate over the industrial law lasted over a month and a half and the result considerably modified the original proposal—as may the cumulative new decree-laws and regulations.

81. It is commonplace to observe for example that businessmen always complain about government policy, even of conservative regimes which pass generally favorable legislation. There is always the possibility of obtaining something more. The current military government in Peru is providing a stable political environment and economic incentives, yet businessmen are complaining about provisions that *may* infringe on some of their prerogatives in the future. It is obvious that a government which represents the interests of a class may come into conflict with that class over the particular policies in pursuit of those interests.

82. Alejandro Tabini, one of Peru's leading electrical manufacturers, complained of the lack of access to government that even "progressive" business not associated with the "oligarchy" had. Interviews with other members of the staff of the National Association of Industrialists confirmed Tabini's observation. Interviews, August 13, 1970.

83. The International Monetary Fund Report stated: "The (Peruvian) authorities also stressed that although the ownership of the agro-industrial complexes is to be given to cooperatives of farmers, these complexes will be run by government-appointed managers until the time when the farmers' cooperatives are organized and have acquired the needed managerial skills. The Peruvian representatives indicated that virtually all the agronomists and technicians of the refineries have remained on their jobs and the transfer of enterprises to the new managers was effected without any significant damage to production." *Report of the International Monetary Fund Staff to Members of the Executive Board of Peru.* January 8, 1970.

84. Minister of Industry and Commerce, Jorge Dellepiane Ocampo, in commenting on the opposition of the industrialists, shrewdly noted that in their manner of expressing themselves the industrialists appeared to be in disagreement with the government but if one judged by their specific points, the situation was quite distinct. *Expreso,* August 8, 1970, p. 3.

85. See the industrial law, Titulo VIII and Part IV, operative definitions "P."

86. Political and social stability was the most frequent response that the generals gave when asked what they could offer investors in ex-

change for their participation in the government's development program.

87. The full flavor of the "fundamentalist" approach of Peruvian businessmen can be seen in "Sociedad Nacional de Industrias Comunicado No. 1," *El Comercio,* August 4, 1970.

88. The chief of the department of Public Relations of the Ministry of Industry and Commerce stated that the business associations did not have juridical or legal status because they did not meet the requisites demanded by the industrial law—one man, one vote and the right of new members to join freely. *Expreso,* August 13, 1970, p. 2.

89. On the position of the APRA see *Oiga,* No. 384, July 24, 1970, pp. 14–15. The position of the Communist party (pro-Moscow) is found in *Unidad,* August 1, 1970—practically the whole issue is devoted to defending the government's industrial law.

90. *Un año de reforma agraria* (Lima: Ministerio de Agricultura, Direccion de Relaciones Publicas, June 24, 1970).

91. *Ibid.*

92. *Ibid.*

93. *Ibid.;* see also *Expreso,* August 8, 1970, p. 14.

94. For a brief but informative account, see Thomas F. Carroll, *Land Reform in Peru* (U.S. Agency for International Development, Spring Review Country Paper, June, 1970).

95. Interview with Benjamin Samanez, director, Agrarian Reform General Headquarters.

96. An example of worker opposition to technocratic control is described by a peasant trade unionist in Cayalti. See Edilberto Rivas, "Cayalti: de la hacienda capitalista a la cooperativa de los trabajadores," *Rikchay,* March, 1970, pp. 2–6.

97. One government official has stated that "existing community leaders are politicized, therefore they cannot be worked with; the best leaders are those without previous experience in leadership. In Tupac Amara the old political leaders were replaced by new leaders." Ingeniero Carrasco, director *de Organizaciones Campesinas del Ministerio de Agricultura.*

98. See Thomas Carroll, *op. cit.*

99. Interview with Alcides Roca, *asesor juridico, reforma agraria, Direccion General de la Reforma Agraria;* Luis Barrios, subdirector, *reforma agraria, zona* IV; Luis Valdivia, director, *reforma agraria, zona* IV; July–August 1970.

100. Interviews with Luis Valdivia and Luis Barrios. July–August, 1970.

101. *Ibid.*

102. *Cuadro de Afectacion con la Ley* 17716, June, 1970, *Oficina del Sub-Director de la Reforma Agraria, zona* IV.

103. *Cuadro de Afectacion en Valle de Canete, Oficina del Sub-Director de la Reforma Agraria, zona* IV.

104. Interview with Guillermo Figalo, president of the Agrarian Court, July, 1970. Many other high agrarian reform officials agreed that they could do a more adequate job with fewer but better trained officials—though the problem of the social origins and attitudes of agrarian reform officials was never handled adequately.

105. Carlos Bohls, general director, Agricultural Development, Ministry of Agriculture, estimated that 90 percent of the extension employees moved into agricultural development, August 6, 1970.

106. According to officials in Agrarian Reform General Headquarters in Lima, more conflicts occur between the officials directing the development side of the change than the redistributive side.

107. The "apolitical" technicians were in fact quite political: generally concerned with maintaining control over the decision-making process. Interview with Jaime Llosa, adviser to the director, *Centro Nacional de Capacitacion Cooperativa* (CENACOOP), August 5, 1970.

108. On August 6, 1970, the board of directors of the Center for Training and Research in Agrarian Reform (CENCIRA) was established after a prolonged struggle between different factions of the agro-bureaucracy. See *Expreso,* August 7, 1970, p. 4.

109. In the period just after land distribution the great majority of the reform beneficiaries become strong government supporters—and felt that the agrarian reform could be a success. *La Reforma Agraria en dos complejos agro-industriales, Cayalti y Tuman* (Universidad Catolica del Peru, Departamento de Ciencias Sociales, March, 1970), p. 95.

110. Much of the "statist" influence found in the industrial law was originally presented in a document published by the Institute of Planning earlier in the year. See *Lineamientos Basicos de Politica de Desarrollo a Mediano Plazo* (Lima: *Instituto de Planificicion,* April, 1970), p. 68 passim.

111. *Oiga,* August 14, 1970, p. 10.

112. Within the 10 percent of the profits to be distributed to the *trabajadores*—5 percent will be divided according to the pay scale of each employer. Hence the highest paid, managers and employers, will receive a higher proportion of the profit than will workers.

113. Cerro de Pasco Corporation has calculated that if no further increases of stock capital excepting capitalization of free shares given to the industrial community is made it could still take between eleven and fifty-three years for the community to arrive at 50 percent ownership. It is likely that U.S. firms will invest, in which case the industrial community will never achieve 50 percent. It is for this reason that U.S. firms have not been overly concerned with the new law.

114. President Velasco and other military leaders have argued that with the establishment of the profit-sharing, stock-holding industrial com-

munity, there will be no reason to strike or to have work stoppages; thus the basis is laid for the elimination of class organization.

115. "For this to be an authentic Revolution, we do not propose to merely modernize the old structures of our society but to replace them by others qualitatively different which will be the basis of a new and distinct socio-economic order in our country." President Velasco appeared to be very critical of the idea that he was modernizing society because he attacked the idea at least four times in the course of his speech. *El Comercio*, July 29, 1970, pp. 4–5.

116. See the first part of *Lineamientos Basicos de Politica de Desarrollo a Mediano Plazo, op. cit.*

117. Interview with General Jorge Fernandez Maldonado, July 15, 1970.

118. Interview with Comandante Hugo Lizarraga Menendez, July 17, 1970.

119. The government's accumulation of reserves rather than being an asset was the result of its inability to develop and invest in projects. *Expreso*, the pro-government daily, raised the problem in its editorial of July 16, 1970, p. 10.

120. Overall the economy grew at a rate of 6.1 percent during the first six months of 1970—largely due to increases in the export sector (fish-meal and sugar). New investment in the private sector continued low. *Expreso*, August 8, 1970, p. 14.

121. Minister of Housing Admiral Luis E. Vargas Caballero rejected the idea of an urban reform because it would undermine the private sector in the construction industry. *Expreso*, July 23, 1970, p. 3.

122. According to one planner "much of the success of social development depends on industrial development and the surplus generated to finance social development." This view assumes that once the "surplus" is generated it will automatically be placed at the disposal of the poor; the Mexican and Venezuelan experiences have shown however that industrial development can heighten inequalities—as appears to be the case in Peru's industrialization effort since 1950.

123. Both planners and industrialists seem to agree on this point though they draw quite divergent conclusions.

124. *Report of the International Monetary Fund Staff to Members of the Executive Board of Peru.* January 8, 1970. Peru's rate of growth in 1968–69 was −2 percent in per capita income terms. The resultant financial stability and the improvement in the balance of payments led the IMF to give a very positive assessment of the situation in Peru. *Expreso*, July 11, 1970, p. 2.

125. The position of the "progressive" entrepreneurs is best expressed by Samuel Drassinower. See *El Comercio*, August 5, 1970, p. 12. *La Prensa* August 5, 1970, p. 4. *Expreso*, August 5, 1970, p. 4.

126. Informed sources at the National Association of Industrialists felt that the uncertainty of the businessmen was as important if not more important than the actual policies adopted by the government.

127. The published advertisements of the National Association of Industrialists and the editorials of *La Prensa* and *El Comercio* give the full flavor of this position. See for example "Sociedad Nacional de Industrias Comunicado No. 1 and No. 2"; the editorial in *La Prensa*, August 2, 1970. See also the advertisement in *Expreso*, August 12, 1970, p. 2.

128. There are more immediate causes of the economic crisis. By 1968 the factors which had made for rapid economic growth during the decade—the fish–meal boom, heavy construction activity in the Callao-Lima area, and substantial private investment in manufacturing spurred by extremely generous tax incentives—had disappeared. Agriculture was stagnant. In the face of this crisis the government began to push for changes which it felt could bring about a new development spurt.

129. The pragmatic point of view was presented by Alejandro Tabini, a director of enterprises in the electrical industry. Interview, August 13, 1970.

130. *Ibid.*

131. In July, 1970, Haya de la Torre stated that "we asked for a dialogue and offer our support" to the military government. *Oiga*, No. 384, July 24, 1970, pp. 14–15. In his speech of July 29, 1970, Velasco explicitly rejected any collaboration with "the old political leaders responsible for selling out the country and people"—remarks aimed at APRA. See *El Comercio*, July 29, 1970, p. 4.

132. See especially *Unidad*, August 1, 1970. The General Confederation of Peruvian Workers (CGTP)—under communist leadership—also strongly supported the government and the industrial law though they have inserted clauses calling for full workers' control and maintenance of the trade unions—positions which are not part of the law. See *Expreso*, August 7, 1970; August 13, 1970, p. 2.

133. The emergence of a mass movement in the form of *Comites para Defender la Revolucion* (Committees to Defend the Revolution) was discouraged by the Government—and they withered away.

134. General Artola, the Minister of Interior, admitted that the people were reacting slowly to the series of changes. He attributed this to the fact that the people had become accustomed to demagogic promises. *Expreso*, August 9, 1970, p. 2.

135. On the first anniversary of the junta's seizure of power (October 3, 1969), President Velasco accused an unnamed group of industrialists and landowners of plotting against him through their "economic apparatus and the reactionary press." In his speech, he said that "oligarchs" were in collusion with foreign elements and were creating an investment crisis in the nation. For further discussion of Velasco's speech, see: *Marcha*, October 10, 1969, p. 19; *Washington Post*, October 5, 1969; and *The Economist* (for Latin America), Vol. 3, No. 21 (October 15, 1969), p. 31.

7

Total System Change: A Decade
of Revolutionary Government in Cuba

Internal Developments

The agrarian nature of the Cuban Revolution is undeniable. The problems of Cuba's single-crop economy which have their origins in the Spanish colonial period have consumed a great deal of the attention of the revolutionary leadership. At the same time that sugar was considered anathematic to long-run economic development, it was considered the short-run panacea for financing the revolution. The position of this agricultural crop in Cuba's economy and the significance attached to it by Cuba's leadership in 1969–70 may prove to be the most significant juncture in post-revolutionary history.

The year 1969–70 was referred to as the Year of Decisive Effort in the calendar of the Cuban Revolution. It was the year in which Cubans attempted to produce 10,000,000 tons of sugar; a target almost 45 percent higher than their previous record of 7,000,000 tons in 1952.[1] Although production totaled 8,500,000 tons (the largest in Cuban history) or some 1,500,000 tons short of plan,[2] the effort was indeed massive and illustrated the limits of mass mobilization within the confines of infrastructure (transportation) inadequacies. The nearly six-month mobilization of the entire Cuban work force was perceived as the basis for future development; hence, failure to achieve a production target of 10,000,000 tons which was set five years previously was, perhaps, not as important materially as it was symbolically. The experience with natural and human inadequacies may alter the character of Cuban management:

> There are objective difficulties, some of them have been pointed out. But we aren't here to discuss the objective difficulties. We must discuss the concrete problem. . . . We are going to begin, in the first place, by pointing out the responsibility which all of us, and I in particular, have for these problems. I am in no way trying to pin the blame on anyone not in the revolutionary leadership and myself. . . . I believe that we, the leaders of this Revolution, have cost the people too much in our process of learning. . . . We really believe the Revolution is faced by a challenge greater than any it has ever faced before, one of its most difficult tasks.[3]

The concrete problems as outlined by Castro included lack of administrative and technical personnel as well as actual production and transportation management:

> Our lack of cadres, of men with a high enough level of training and intelligence who are capable of carrying out the complex tasks of production [are great] . . . the problem of plant management . . . should [not] fall exclusively to the manager. It would really be worthwhile to begin introducing a number of new ideas. There should be a manager, naturally—for there must always be someone accountable—but we must begin to establish a collective body in the management of each plant. A collective body! It should be headed by one man, but it should also be made up of representatives of the advance workers' movement, the Young Communist League, the Party and the women's front. . . .[4]

It must be emphasized that what Castro made public after the harvest had been suspected by Cuban officials prior to the harvest;[5] namely, that human and other resource constraints would seriously hamper the 10,000,000-ton goal. The actual harvest operation was, in a sense, a test of Cuban management and technology—a test which confirmed many hypotheses but did not seriously endanger the reorganization of Cuban economy or society. The importance of the Year of Decisive Effort to Cuban agriculture, economics, ideology, politics, as well as administration is significant; therefore, this chapter will draw liberally from this most recent event to illustrate the extent of total system change during the decade since the revolution.

The development push was a revolution within the revolution. In development terms, the 1970 harvest was a decisive event. The Cuban economy up to then had been performing below the targets set forth by the leadership in the mid-1960s. Massive mobilization to produce 10,000,000 tons of sugar was perceived as the basis for future development.

The Cuban economy today stands at the crossroads. Up until the middle 1960s, the Cuban revolutionary process was largely concerned with redistributing wealth rather than focusing on the problems of production.[6] The first years of the revolution involved two agrarian reforms, 1959, and then later, 1962, which effectively broke the power of the foreign and Cuban entrepreneurs who owned and controlled most of the land and the transportation system.[7] Large farms were nationalized or distributed to peasants. Cooperatives and individual land holdings gave way to the establishment of state farms. In the urban areas rents were cut, houses were built, and educational and health programs were instituted on a massive scale. Illiteracy, for all practical purposes, was eliminated. The first five years of the Cuban Revolution largely involved the destruction of the old ruling class, and the redistribution of its goods and property. In the process of reordering society a number of costs were incurred. One major cost was the hostility of the U.S. government which responded by instituting an economic blockade. This seriously limited the ability of the Cubans to obtain spare parts. As a result, many of their industries and machinery were incapacitated despite the great ingenuity which the Cubans have shown in repairing and maintaining their machinery.[8]

The period from 1959 to 1964 and the whole period prior to the revolution created an ambience in which productivity was a secondary consideration. Top priority was given to breaking the power of the ruling class and to providing social benefits for the population. In a sense this was necessary in order to consolidate revolutionary power. The real social benefits that accrued to the working class and the peasantry during the redistributive phase provided the motivation and the enthusiasm which was to sustain the revolution during the development drive.[9] The specific measures were concrete manifestations of the popular program which the government was embracing and reinforced the allegiance of the lower class to the revolution and the revolutionary leadership. The ability of that leadership to call on its population to make the enormous efforts necessary for economic development was rooted in the fundamental changes which took place in the period from 1959 to 1964.

On the other hand certain negative features carried over into the developmental phase. One was the concern with the shortages of consumer goods found especially among urbanites. Prior to the revolution Cuban society experienced lopsided development.[10] Heavy emphasis was on consumer imports from the U.S. Though this was concentrated among a small sector of the population, especially an urban population, nevertheless the emphasis was on values of consumption as opposed to production. Cuba was not an industrial society and lacked a factory culture.[11] It was largely a market place for U.S. manufactured goods. In addition, because Cuba was a major tourist center as well as an agricultural exporting society, considerable emphasis was placed on the values of consumption at the expense of industrial activity. Prior to 1959, the Cuban population experienced deprivation within a consumer-oriented society. This was followed by a revolution which was largely involved in redistributing consumer items. Subsequently the Cuban leadership initiated a development program which demanded sacrifices from the population—a change that did not appeal to all segments of the urban population. In 1969 the most important factor about Cuba is not the benefits which the population is getting from the government or from society but the involvement of large numbers of people in economic activity which has very little immediate pay-off. The sense of working for the larger good over a long period of time is characteristic of Cuba in 1970. The conversion from consumptionism to productionism is a very important element in understanding much that goes on in Cuba today.

The long lines in the cities, the lack of consumer items, the deprivation that Cubans put up with in their day-to-day life are all part and parcel of the same society which can elicit extraordinary effort by average citizens to overcome serious economic bottlenecks.[12]

The Cuban economy has gone through a series of changes which have crystallized in the effort to maximize agricultural production. Today the Cuban economy is largely as it was ten years ago—agricultural. Yet there are very significant differences. Mechanized agricultural production based on nationalized property and small holdings is a major feature of the Cuban countryside. Most of the investments that are made in Cuba today are going into the agricultural sector and, within the agricultural sector, into the purchase of machinery. The developmental revolution is largely rooted in the countryside.[13] The most dynamic aspect of agriculture is located in the sugar-cane fields. The population in the countryside continues to receive a disproportionate share of the benefits; the government inputs into the economy continue to favor agriculture and rural workers. Most new construction and new welfare programs are located in rural areas, while, on the other hand, very little new housing is being constructed in the cities.

The symbols of socialist Cuba are largely agricultural implements or agricultural figures (the machete and the cane cutter). The whole society is mobilized to develop the agricultural sector, neglecting the urban population, industrial activity, and urban services, which show the signs of disinvestment. The urban population is being ruralized through large-scale mobilizations of voluntary labor.[14] Cuban education is more and more oriented toward agricultural production. New power and light facilities are concentrated in the countryside.

Contrary to the experience in Eastern Europe, the urban population is being squeezed for the peasantry. The peasant is relatively privileged, receiving subsidies and a higher proportion of government funds than many of his urban brothers. Children of peasants receive scholarships, attend live-in schools from the primary level through the secondary, and many go on to higher education. Unlike Eastern Europe and the Soviet Union, there is no "peasant problem" because in a very real sense the peasantry is being bought off. Their children are being educated and will become skilled agricultural workers or go into other agriculturally related activities or into nonagricultural work. Very few of them, if any, will go back to work on their parents' little plot of land.[15]

Cuba's development strategy is based on mechanized agriculture. Industrial development revolves around the production of machine products directly related to agricultural growth. On the input side, factories will produce farm machinery, while on the output side, industries will be built that process and transform agricultural products.

The proposed production of 10,000,000 tons of sugar was very important in solidifying Cuba's international financial standing. It was felt that if this goal had been achieved, it would have allowed Cuba to pay back its debts to the Eastern European countries and re-establish its credit with non-Communist countries on a much sounder basis. This was the short-run gamble of the revolutionary leadership to finance future development efforts through the use of the otherwise anathematic and certainly underdeveloped, one-crop, one-sector economy. Cuba's ability to obtain machinery and other goods on credit depends upon improvement of its international financial status. The production of the 10,000,000 tons would not have substantially benefited the consumer public but it would have provided the basis for further development. The impact of the failure to achieve this goal on Cuba's international financial standing is still uncertain at the present. To a degree, Cuba's financial standing will also be affected by the success of other development efforts of which the 1970 harvest was the first of several very intense efforts planned for subsequent years.[16]

Cuba's development policy has had a significant impact on the patterns of population migration. The Castro government initially promoted industrialization at the expense of agricultural development, a policy that has been popular throughout Latin America. When, in 1964, Cuba shifted toward placing high priority on agricultural production within the development plan, financial and physical resources were directed toward the countryside. As a result the "worldwide trend" of urban slumification characteristic of the Third World was reversed. Havana is the only capital city in Latin America which shows a declining proportion of the national population.

GREATER HAVANA'S PERCENTAGE OF THE
NATIONAL POPULATION
1958–1968 [17]

1958	1963	1964	1965	1966	1967	1968
20.8	22.2	22.1	21.9	21.7	21.4	21.1

Unlike the pattern found in the rest of Latin America, Havana is not surrounded by shack towns and makeshift dwellings put together by rural refugees fleeing the poverty of the countryside. Since 1963 there has been a movement in the opposite direction, from Havana to the countryside. For example, 28,203 individuals migrated from Havana province to Oriente in 1967 while 24,989 moved from Oriente to Havana.[18]

The total number of enrolled students reached a peak in 1964–65, dropped off, and has recently been on the increase. Apart from adult education, the tendency has been for the number of enrolled students to increase yearly. Primary students numbered 717,417 in 1959, 1,323,925 in 1964–65, and 1,460,754 in 1968–69.[19] Intermediary education accounted for 88,123 students in 1958–59, 214,941 students in 1964–65 and 254,111 students in 1968–69.[20] The sharpest decline registered was on the intermediary level, regarding enrollment of students in administration: from a peak year (1964–65) when 29,314 students were enrolled, it has declined to 1,630 students in 1968–69.[21]

Higher education in Cuba between 1959 and 1969 showed a very substantial increase in overall attendance, rising from 25,599 to 35,490 students.[22] More significant in terms of Cuba's economic and social development goals has been the change in the nature of higher education. The emphasis of Cuban higher education has been changing from a traditional legal-humanist orientation to one which is more directly relevant to Cuba's development needs. In 1959, 4,291 (out of 25,599) students were in the faculty of humanities; by 1969 this had declined to 1,196 (out of 35,490).[23] In comparative terms, during 1959 there were 1,617 students in the science schools, while in 1969 there were 3,152.[24] The technological faculty has expanded from 3,323 students in 1959 to 6,588 in 1969.[25] The greatest expansion has been in the areas of mechanical engineering (up from 232 students to 1,114) and chemical engineering (up from 412 to 1,093).[26]

The Cuban educational system is more and more geared toward economic development plans; the universities are increasingly producing scientific-technological cadres to overcome the historic problems of underdevelopment. The university is no longer a middle-class school for training lawyers and the underproductive "service employees" who had been largely at the service of tourists and foreign-owned firms.

To meet the needs of social development Cuban universities have increased the number of medical students from 3,947 in 1959 to 7,278 in 1969.[27] It has been reported that half of the 1969 graduating class in the medical school was made up of women, suggesting that sexual discriminatory practices common to both North and South American professional schools are being overcome.

The shift toward intensified agricultural development is clearly seen in the changes in enrollment in the School of Agricultural Sciences: in 1959 the school contained 1,202 students; during the "industrialization period" (1961) this dropped to 851; by 1968–69 this figure rose to 2,203.[28] Within agricultural studies, student enrollment in veterinary science has more than doubled.[29]

In addition to the transformation of the curriculum, the educational system has expanded to meet the needs of the workers and peasants for higher education. Worker-peasant preparatory schools have been established. In 1960, 68 students were enrolled, by 1964 there were 3,650, and by 1968–69 the number had climbed to 7,201.[30] Over 70 percent of the increase in enrollment in higher education between 1959 and 1968–69 can be accounted for by the enrollment in the worker-peasant preparatory schools.[31]

In the field of education the same pattern emerges. The School of Education recovered the level of enrollment of 1959 by 1965–66 and by 1968–69 the number of education students had increased by 20 percent.[32]

The same emphasis on training students for development needs can be seen in intermediary education: the number of students attending technical schools (industry, agriculture, fishing) has jumped from 6,259 in 1959 to 26,506 in 1968–69.[33]

During the initial five years of the revolution great efforts were made to redistribute land and income and to provide social services to the previously exploited strata of the population. Housing was one of the critical areas of social life with which the Cuban government was greatly preoccupied initially. Between 1945 and 1958 only 10,020 houses were built per year, producing a total of 143,170 houses,[34] a disproportionate number of which were built for propertied elites and white-collar employees. Assuming five individuals to a family, there were 23,583 new families a year, which means that the annual housing deficit amounted to about 13,500 per year, prior to the revolution.[35] During the first five years of the revolution, the government increased housing construction by 70 percent, an average of 17,089 houses being built from 1959 through 1963.[36] The housing deficit amounted to about 10,566 houses per year, a sharp reduction. Beginning in the mid-1960s, Cuba turned its primary efforts toward economic development. Having exhausted the possibilities for redistribution, the revolutionary government faced the problem of creating new sources of wealth. The result was a decline in the areas of social development, as can be seen in housing. The four years from 1964 to 1967 witnessed a decrease in the number of houses constructed: the average for 1964 to 1967 was 14,214 as compared to the earlier 17,089.[37] The housing deficit increased from 10,566 to 13,441 per year. The decreased construction of the later period, however, still exceeded gross output prior to the revolution and the houses were built for those in greatest need. Nevertheless, the conflict between demands for social expenditures and for investment in economic development may be one factor causing the increased tension which some observers have noted in Havana in recent years. Along with educational changes, the shift in priorities away from redistributive policies reflects the primacy of technological and economic development.

The revolutionary government has invested enormous sums of money in the construction of new health facilities and in training medical personnel. In 1958 there were only 33 urban general hospitals, 1 rural general hospital and 90 policlinics; in 1968 there were 77 urban general hospitals, 48 rural general hospitals and 260 policlinics.[38] Cuba has the lowest infant mortality rate in Latin America: 37.6 per thousand in 1966, compared to its closest competitor, Uruguay, with 42 per thousand.[39]

A recent publication, however, attempts to show that the enormous increase in medical facilities has led to a *decline in health standards*. The writer states, "The average rate (infant mortality rate) for 1959–66 is 37.2 per thousand, substantially above the pre-revolutionary rates (33)." [40] The writer cites United Nations figures to make his point. This comparison, however, does not take account of the fact that since much of pre-revolutionary Cuba's rural lower class lacked hospitals and could hardly afford or even locate doctors and medicine, they frequently buried their dead infants without the benefit of an official counter. It is precisely with the construction of hospitals and the visible presence of free medical facilities available to all the people that the lower class began to visit hospitals, report their illnesses and have their dead counted. In a sense, the pre-revolutionary figure is perhaps best taken as an indicator of the mortality rate of Cuban urban-bourgeois society. In underdeveloped countries when sudden and dramatic social changes occur after little public concern was previously evidenced, we should not be surprised to see a sharp *increase* in the number of illnesses, dental work, etc., reported. The statistical increase may merely mean that patients previously unattended are now being treated; lower rates may merely reflect pre-revolutionary neglect.

Nevertheless, while health standards of the masses have been greatly improved by the revolution in comparison with pre-revolutionary conditions, they have not substantially improved *during the revolution*. During the beginning of the drive for economic development between 1964 and 1968, the infant mortality rate rose from 37.8 to 40.7.[41]

Mobilization, military organization, and egalitarianism are major features of contemporary Cuban politics. Cuban society is one in which the leadership sets policy. Policy has been supported by the majority of the population.

Within that majority one can see a very substantial proportion of the population which is very enthusiastic and very committed to realizing the tasks set forth by the leadership. Parallel with the command structure of political life is mass participation in the tasks set forth. The masses participate in carrying out the specific duties which are outlined: they discuss implementation on the local level, not policy-making. Decisions are made at the top and carried out on the bottom. Discussion, where it exists, is largely over methods. The command-mass participation syndrome in Cuba is successful to the degree that the commands are obeyed voluntarily and with enthusiasm by the population. For the population few avenues exist for expressing disagreement over basic policies.

In terms of the political actors in Cuba one finds more and more the merger of the politician and the administrator. Politics in Cuba today is largely the administration of work, the allocation of manpower, and the organization of production. To a considerable degree the politician and the administrator are one. There is very little functional specialization: they administer farms, organize communities, participate in policy meetings, direct the distribution of welfare, organize production, direct security and vigilance, etc. They have a multitude of tasks, some of which are delegated to subordinates who are responsible to them.

The bureaucrat in Cuba is largely ambulatory. In the field, visiting projects, discussing with subordinates, workers, employees, peasants, the bureaucrat communicates with his home base by a two-way radio. He is constantly on the move attempting to locate problems and to solve them on the spot. Thus, while the politico-administrative chief maintains control over decision-making, the system is flexible and responsive to problems. Most bureaucratic activity focuses on specific problems encountered in specific areas. Attention is concentrated in an attempt to correct and rectify particular problems as they occur.

Most bureaucrats are generalists: officials quite often

change positions from one area of political-administrative life to another. Few stay in one position for long periods of time. Administrators can be found who have been in education, agriculture, industry, security, the military, etc. Very few are concerned with a career in one particular administrative area.

Another characteristic of the bureaucracy is that very few were prepared for their administrative careers. Many of the administrators are from lower-income or lower-status occupation groups. Many of them were previously industrial workers and, in some cases, agricultural workers. One can find many examples of administrators of large plants who once were skilled machine operators.

Foremost among the criteria in recruiting personnel for the Cuban bureaucracy is political reliability. Cubans allege that during the first years of the revolution hostile administrators attempted to sabotage many of their social and economic projects. The overwhelming majority of trained managerial personnel fled to the U.S. after the revolution. As a result, the bureaucracy has not been efficient in terms of the norms usually associated with bureaucratic organizations. The average educational level of a party member is a sixth-grade primary education. The politically reliable and technically efficient bureaucrat is the administrative ideal that Cuba is aiming to achieve. In recent years there has been an increasing flow of technically trained and politically reliable administrators. Nevertheless there is still a very acute shortage of managerial personnel capable of organizing production and rationally allocating labor in most Cuban enterprises. The current administrative inadequacies are transitory. The Cubans are training administrators who are politically attuned to the revolution. The difficult period is passing: the administrators who were politically reliable but lacking in technical and managerial skills are being replaced. The most acute shortages can be found on the middle and lower levels of the bureaucracy as the most competent officials usually go to the top quite rapidly.

In terms of overall administrative performance there are very serious problems in locating personnel capable of taking the initiative in making decisions. There has been a tendency to avoid making decisions which might turn out to be "mistakes." This lack of initiative has had its own ill effects on the Cuban development process.

One of the key areas where the Cuban development efforts have suffered greatly is that of information collection. Pre-revolutionary Cuba was not very well developed in the area of systematic collection and transmission of information to policy-makers. This problem was exacerbated by the emigration of managerial personnel. Especially with the emergence of a planned economy based on nationalized enterprises, information collection became crucial. During the last few years many faulty decisions were made because the information necessary to make rational decisions was lacking or was erroneous. During the 1970 harvest one of the key developments has been the establishment of a day-to-day information-collecting apparatus functioning down to the very smallest unit of production. Information is collected, transmitted to regional and then to national information bureaus and decisions affecting the particular unit are then transferred back to the local levels. How effective this new apparatus will be, remains to be seen.

It appears as if substantial progress has been made in creating channels for the upward flow of information. This is largely confined to administrative channels having to do with economic matters (performance, and production reports) and is not related to political and social matters. The Cubans have been very much involved in creating an efficient administrative apparatus which they consider critical to their economic efforts. Administrative weaknesses have been pointed to repeatedly as the source of many of the ills which currently afflict the Cuban economic effort. To the extent that this is so, the recent efforts in this direction both in education and organization should improve their situation, though it is too difficult to judge at this time.

In summary then, one can say that Cuba has gone through three revolutions. The first was the political revolution that overthrew Batista and ended in 1959 with his flight out of the country. The second revolution, the social revolution, between 1959 and 1964, largely demolished the old ruling elite and the social structure upon which it was based. The establishment of public ownership over the means of production, agrarian reform, and egalitarian norms characterized the second revolution. The redistribution of goods in general was the major feature of the social revolutionary phase. The third revolution beginning in 1964–65 initiated the drive for economic development. During this period a serious effort is being made to organize the population and to maximize the production of goods, services, and new productive facilities. In each revolution a conversion process occurs.

During the social revolution a diffuse kind of "oppositionist" political militant is converted into a cadre concerned with social problems and economic redistribution. Political rebels are converted into social revolutionaries. In Cuba this meant the conversion of guerrilla fighters into mass political organizers. This conversion was very successfully carried out in the process of consolidating the revolution. There were serious conflicts and defections along the way, first from the right-wing anti-communists who opposed the social revolution and later by those within the social revolution, the old Communists around Anibal Escalante, who attemped to replace the leadership and reorient the revolution around different political and social criteria. The process of conversion was successful, however, and Cuba's transformation from a political to a social revolution was carried out and the new cadre created.

The third revolution, the development revolution, required the conversion of social revolutionaries into technical and administrative cadre. This change has been much more difficult than the previous; rather than changing from one type of politics to another this required a totally new set

346 : CULTIVATING REVOLUTION

of qualifications: technical and administrative skills. The development revolution and the conversion of cadre were not as successful as the prior efforts. Many of the political leaders could not develop the proper skills to manage economic enterprises and as a result, serious errors have been made along the way.

The future Cuban development effort will depend more on creating new cadre than conversion of old cadre. In fact a new technical intelligentsia is developing which is taking over many of the managerial functions of economic enterprises. The growth of a new technical intelligentsia, however, raises new problems: whether the technical cadre, and those social revolutionaries who were successfully converted, can maintain their political identity and the revolutionary élan that propels the revolution. Can they maintain the values of the earlier revolutionary phase or will they be oriented toward a less egalitarian society, a society more geared toward social differences and a differential reward system as is found in the U.S.S.R.? The Cuban leadership is acutely aware of this problem. Thus the intense effort to inculcate the idea of collective and productive work in the technical personnel as they are being trained for their technical or their professional careers.

The whole Cuban population is heavily involved in the current effort at internal development. Despite external pressures, especially emanating from the U.S., the basic decisions regarding development strategy are products of Cuban policy-makers. The constraints imposed by the past pattern of development have also limited the options regarding choices in priorities. The overall thrust is accompanied by a heavy commitment toward the introduction of technological changes and rationalization of production. The command relations in the political sphere and the current pressures for work have generated some tension especially in the capital city.

The ability of the Cubans to succeed in their development drive without incurring popular opposition and without resorting to intense coercion will depend on how clearly the leadership recognizes the threshold of sacrifice and commitment among the labor force. This will require a broadening, not a narrowing, of the channels of discussion of policy. Regarding the short-term effort, workers and leaders are in agreement: the workers have accepted the development priorities and are voluntarily making an extraordinary effort to reach the production goals.

Cuba's development performance during the first years has been very uneven. Some sectors have done exceptionally well, while the overall performance of the economy has been less than satisfactory. Per capita national income declined from an index of 134 in 1964 (calculated from a base of 100 for 1962) to 121 in 1968.[42] Likewise the per capita social product for the same period stayed at the same level.[43] The inadequate performance of the economy can largely be attributed to the general stagnation experienced by Cuba's main product—sugar. On the other hand, certain products have done extremely well between 1964 and 1968: milk production jumped 33 percent, eggs increased almost sixfold, fish 58 percent, beef cattle by 33.6 percent and citrus products by 40.1 percent.[44] In addition, long-term investment in infrastructure which will have important consequences for future growth are apparent in the growth of dam building. The capacity of Cuban dams has leaped from 28.8 million to 862 million cubic meters.[45] Likewise industries linked to sugar production, like fertilizer, have increased almost three and one-half times.[46]

In terms of commercial patterns Cuba continues to trade mostly with the Communist countries: 74.7 percent of Cuba's exports went to and 80.3 percent of its imports came from the Communist countries in 1968.[47] Since 1964 there has been a trend toward increasing trade within the Communist bloc: in 1964, 40.8 percent of exports went to non-Communist countries; in 1967 this dropped to 18.8 percent.[48] In 1968 this increased to 25.3 percent and may signal a shift toward increasing trade with capitalist countries, especially with Spain. The same trend is in evidence with regard to imports: in 1964, 32.5 percent of total imports came from non-Communist countries compared to 19.7 percent in 1968.[49] Within the Communist bloc, trade with the U.S.S.R. is increasing: exports rose from 38 percent of total exports in 1964 to 44.3 in 1968; imports rose from 40.2 to 60.9 percent.[50] Meanwhile trade with China declined: China accounted for 11.4 percent of exports in 1964 but only 9.3 percent in 1968; imports went down from 10.7 percent in 1964 to 7 percent in 1968.[51]

Closer commercial relations with the U.S.S.R. and increasing emphasis on economic development and technical education suggest that Cuba will be mainly preoccupied in the next period with overcoming bottlenecks affecting critical areas of the economy. As a corollary this means less attention than before will be paid to revolutionary political developments elsewhere.

External Developments

Sometime between the defeat of Che Guevara's guerrilla movement in Bolivia and the mobilization of Cuban society to produce 10,000,000 tons of sugar, there was a shift in Cuba's policy away from supporting revolutionary movements in Latin America. Cuba's policy gradually began to shift from moral and material aid to revolutionary movements to largely propagandistic support. Beginning in 1968, and throughout 1969 and 1970, the major direction of Cuba's political efforts was in the area of internal economic development.

Five major factors appear to have converged and strongly influenced this shift in Cuban political priorities: (a) the death of Che Guevara, the main architect of continental revolutionary struggle and a major influence in shaping Cuba's efforts in support of the indigenous guerrilla movements; (b) the failures, defections, and fragmentation of the guerrilla groups leading to their diminished political significance, reduced size, and isolation from sources of political power; (c) persistent stagnation in the economy resulting in serious internal problems, a weak international trading position, and increased dependence on the U.S.S.R.; (d) emergence in Latin America of nationalist developmentalist regimes pursuing policies which conflict with U.S. policies and interests in a number of areas.

Guevara perceived the Cuban revolution as only the initial stage of the Latin American revolution.[52] In Guevara's view Cuba existed largely as a beachhead for Latin American revolution. He saw Cuba's survival as a revolutionary society to be intimately linked to the fate of the Latin American revolution; each victory in Latin America revitalized Cuban socialism; each defeat compounded Cuba's internal difficulties and extra-hemispheric dependency.

The Latin American revolution was viewed as an integral whole: national boundaries were largely artificial constructs that fragmented and weakened the revolutionary effort without in the least inhibiting U.S. imperialism from crossing national frontiers with its troops or agencies to prevent popular forces from advancing their goals. Guevara's internationalism was not rooted in romantic traditional Hispanic notions about common cultures (nor was it rooted in Bolivarian rhetoric); rather it was a logical and rational response to modern U.S. expansion, penetration, and domination of Latin American societies.

Guevara's mission to Latin America was the creation of international guerrilla movements capable of organizing revolutionary alternatives to the existing left-wing organizations which were largely "reformist" or passive. Between 1964 and 1967, while Guevara was organizing the new vanguard, he represented the internationalist conscience of the Cuban revolution: among the militants in Cuba and throughout Latin America, while Guevara lived and fought, there *was* no other choice but to support his action. Guevara's moral authority and the clear logic of his political perspective put Cuban advocates of national-economic development on the defensive. Guevara's advocacy of armed struggle as the only road to revolution was considerably strengthened by the aggressive interventionist policy that the U.S. chose in the cases of the Dominican Republic, Vietnam, and Laos.

Guevara and the Cubans were not discouraged by the fact that guerrillas had suffered serious losses, that counter-revolutionary forces were ascendent throughout Latin America, and that pro-Moscow Communist parties were renouncing all forms of revolutionary action (aided and abetted by the U.S.S.R.). It was thought that the forces of continental reaction were vulnerable and could be readily defeated; that the reformers would be won over by successful example; that the U.S., tied down in Vietnam, would not be able to commit forces; that the Latin ruling classes, their dependence on external forces exposed, would be discredited.

The death of Guevara and the defeat of the guerrilla force that he was leading in Bolivia was not only a great tragedy but it led to a serious reappraisal of the whole notion of guerrilla warfare as a uniform strategy of revolutionary struggle. The Guevarist analysis of Latin American politics contained more than a grain of truth—but the forms through which those truths were expressed were substantially different from those he envisioned.

The forces of continental reaction *were* vulnerable and capable of being challenged—if not totally defeated. In May, 1969, the Argentine working class went on a nation-wide general strike—taking over factories and in some industrial areas temporarily taking over sectors of cities. Argentina's May days were the most violent in recent history and severely shook Ongania's regime, although he managed to hold power.[53] In Brazil and Uruguay urban guerrillas have become increasingly active.[54] In Bolivia and Peru the generals responsible for assassinating guerrillas decreed a number of nationalist measures including the nationalization of U.S. oil companies, and managed to stay in power despite U.S. pressure.[55] Urban popular discontent first surfaced during the Rockefeller Mission's visit to Latin America: the massive popular demonstrations in Central America, Colombia, Ecuador and the cancellation of Rockefeller's visit by the Peruvian, Venezuelan, and Chilean governments were clear indications that a new cycle of popular mobilization was in the making.[56]

Guevara's analysis of the growth of nationalism and anti-imperialism was essentially correct; however, nationalism was expressed through mass demonstrations (not guerrilla units); nationalist measures were taken by military regimes (not popular governments). Guevara foresaw that mass conflicts would emerge; but these conflicts were experienced in urban confrontations involving urban workers —not peasants. The underlying basis for revolutionary political action, as Guevara perceived, was U.S. exploitation and the failure of the indigenous elites to carry out the democratic reforms of the Alliance for Progress; however Guevara was not able to diagnose the particular social forces that would express the discontent.

Up until Guevara's death, Cuban policy was strongly oriented toward international revolution and Guevara was the best symbol of internationalism.[57] With his death a significant change took place in terms of the meaning of the Guevara symbol: from being a symbol of internationalism he was transformed into a symbol of internal development. The austerity, work, dedication, and sacrifice of Guevara are projected to the Cuban people as ideals to which they should aspire.[58] The masses are told to dedicate themselves to development as Guevara dedicated himself to revolution. Politics and production are united. Thus, Guevara has become an important symbol in Cuba's current development effort.

Cuba, during the drive for 10,000,000 tons of sugar, in some ways resembled the period of War Communism in the Soviet Union. Much of the rhetoric and organizational forms were taken from a military vocabulary: brigades, columns, command posts, etc. Labor was requisitioned from urban centers and there was talk of militarizing the labor force.[59] Command relations and the techniques of military organization were harnessed to the needs of massive mobilization to overcome underdevelopment, the U.S. economic blockade, and overdependence on the Soviet bloc countries.

The omnipresent pictures of Guevara and the messages convey the same theme: the need to work, the need to sacrifice, the importance of social solidarity for economic development. Many values which were characteristic of Guevara have been transformed into social ideals for Cuban society. For example, Guevara's austerity has been a factor in rationalizing the shortage of consumer goods in Cuba. Personal sacrifice, another characteristic of Che Guevara, is translated into the idea of volunteer labor and in the formation of labor brigades. A movement of young people called "The Followers of Che Guevara and Camilo Cienfuegos" is engaged in efforts to carry out productive activity in the agricultural sector. Guevara's belief in social solidarity is translated into the collectivist ethic, the building of the new communist man who works for moral rather than material incentives. Guevara's commitment to work is now made an ideal for all the people. To be disciplined means to carry out assignments and tasks, to avoid absenteeism and tardiness at work, etc. Like Guevara all top officials engage in productive work (regardless of their rank) including the cutting of sugar cane.[60] This is not a symbolic gesture but actually involves spending weeks on end cutting cane alongside regular cane cutters.

The Guevara movement is one that reinforces the revolutionary leadership's attempt to mobilize as many human, financial, and physical resources in the shortest period for the greatest effort. The needs of Cuban development shape the use of the image and values of Guevara. In turn the values of Guevara influence the direction of Cuban development and inform that effort.[61]

In summary, Guevara, the revolutionary, has been posthumously converted by the Cuban leadership into the philosopher of development. The qualities of the heroic revolutionary are converted into the characteristics and qualities of the efficient and productive worker. The disciplined revolutionary is transformed into the disciplined worker. Revolutionary form is united with a total commitment to internal development.

Cuba has supported revolutionary movements in Latin America for almost a decade, providing moral and material support to indigenous revolutionary movements. Cuban volunteers have joined revolutionary movements and have died in battle.[62] Beginning in the early 1960s but especially after 1966, Cuban revolutionary thought was focused on the notion that revolution would occur only through rural guerrilla warfare and that the only correct policy was support for the guerrilla groups.[63] Cuban support continued despite repeated failures and defeats suffered by these movements. Throughout Latin America, Cuba gave as much support as it could afford to revolutionaries to counter the massive influx of U.S. goods and personnel—even at some risk to its own existence and at some cost to its own development. In Bolivia and Venezuela, material support, in not inconsiderable amounts, was sent to help the guerrillas and counteract the millions of dollars and huge military advisory missions that the U.S. was pouring into those countries.[64] Nevertheless, the U.S. through its greater resources was able to provide Latin elites with sufficient support to isolate or defeat rural guerrilla groups. In turn the guerrillas in Guatemala, Venezuela, and Colombia have split over issues of dubious importance.[65] The guerrillas, fragmented into competing groups, present the Cubans with the option of supporting one or another small isolated group or looking beyond the splinters toward factions in the ruling class which are amenable to bargaining over diplomatic and economic questions.

Contributing to the decline of the guerrilla groups was

the defection of Communist party members, especially in Venezuela and Guatemala.[66] After briefly participating in the guerrilla movement, the Communists defected, cutting the guerrillas off from most of the urban network, most of the finances and propaganda outlets. Military defeats, political fragmentation, and the defection of the Communists seriously weakened the guerrilla movement's ability to recruit new members and finance new operations. As a result of the decline in guerrilla effectiveness, the Cubans have turned from revolutionary internationalism toward internal development as a means of breaking out of isolation. The change is visible to anyone present in Cuba in 1969.

Each year Cuba celebrates a particular theme. In 1968 it was the Year of the Heroic Guerrilla. In 1969 it was the Year of Decisive Effort—referring to the production of 10,000,000 tons of sugar. In those two contrasting themes one gets some idea of what Cuba's priorities are today. Cuba is still interested in and supports the struggle of liberation movements in Latin America. But the overwhelming effort is being directed toward internal development and the practical problems of sugar production.

Cuba's international politics are pragmatic. The Cubans do not initiate or organize revolutionary activities in Latin America. They have maintained ties and fraternal relationships with ongoing revolutionary movements. They have supported those movements which have shown themselves capable of initiating serious struggles for power in Latin America. At the same time the Cubans do not commit themselves to movements that hardly exist or to tiny grouplets incapable of engaging in serious political warfare. In Latin America at this time there are no movements that have the capacity to mount a serious struggle for power. Where Communist parties have large popular followings, they are parties which are basically integrated into the legal political structures of their country.[67] The Cubans are not interested in subsidizing reformers whose intent is to ameliorate political and social situations, within a capitalist context.

Because the international situation is not very promising, because of their commitments to their own population, and because of their international financial obligations, the Cubans have turned toward building their economy. Currently the Cubans are not offering prescriptions for Latin American revolution. They have shown a considerable amount of flexibility in giving support to the "revolutionary measures" (as they characterize them) of the Peruvian military junta; they are conscious of important changes within the Catholic Church and in general show a willingness to consider new revolutionary developments as they occur.[68]

Concomitant with the ebbing of the revolutionary movements in Latin America, Cuba has experienced a period of extended economic stagnation. Despite high investment rates and moral exhortations the Cuban economy has continued to flounder. Administrative inefficiency, poor planning, and labor indiscipline coupled with leadership preoccupation with noneconomic problems produced an economy whose performance was less than adequate. In 1968 and thereafter the Cuban leadership "discovered" the seriousness of Cuba's internal and external economic situation. The cumulative effect of a series of poor years, resulting in excessive external debts, generated a dependence and vulnerability which could threaten Cuba's sovereignty if not its survival.

Lacking any basis for expecting a Latin American revolution to occur in the near future which might justify emphasizing international revolution at the expense of internal development, and perceiving that a continuation of the downward trend could lead to political disaster within Cuba, the leadership decided, in typical Fidelista fashion, to promote all-out mobilization for internal development. The original rationale for internal development was that current investment of energy and time in internal development would lead to even greater support for revolution . . . later.

In the meantime the Cubans in effect told the guerrilla groups that from 1968–69 they were on their own: Cuba was going to be strictly involved in struggling against internal underdevelopment—meaning the problems of work, organization, technical innovation and, above all, increasing production. In more ways than one Cuba was increasingly coming to adopt the strategy of building socialism in one country. Though internal problems weigh heavy in shaping this outlook they are not the only ones.

There is considerable warmth in Cuban-Soviet relations today in contrast to two years ago when bitter polemics were exchanged between Cuba, the Moscow-oriented Communist parties of Latin America, and the Soviet Union over strategy for revolution in Latin America.[69] These differences concerned the question of methods of struggle (armed revolution versus the policy of peaceful coexistence with its implicit acceptance of U.S. hegemony in the Western hemisphere) as well as policies for internal development. For the Cubans, revolution meant armed struggle; for the Soviet Union, Communist parties should be engaged in what is referred to as "progressive" politics, which largely consists of supporting middle-class movements or governments which are amenable to establishing commercial and diplomatic relations with the Communist Bloc.[70] The Soviet Union and its sister parties in Latin America have for a considerable time now eschewed any action which might jeopardize the legal status of the parties and diplomatic relations with the U.S.S.R. where they have been established. The Soviet Union continues to support Communist parties in Latin America; the Communist parties in Latin America continue to support the international policy of the Soviet Union, the line of peaceful coexistence.

The Soviet Union has, in recent years, increased its trade and assistance programs with right-wing and pro-U.S. military regimes.[71] Apparently commercial relations have completely replaced ideological concerns in the Kremlin. Up till 1968 the Cubans considered this policy opportunistic. The Cubans supported only those groups which were concerned with structural changes in Latin America. Cuba's support for movements calling for armed overthrow of regimes in Guatemala, Venezuela, and Colombia involved Cuba in serious conflicts with the U.S.S.R. and its "fraternal" parties. Beginning with Cuba's silence during the Mexican student revolt and culminating in the uncritical but cautious support of the Peruvian military junta, the Cubans have turned toward a policy of support of new bourgeois nationalist tendencies as they begin to challenge the authority of the U.S. in the hemisphere.[72] As a result, by 1969, political differences between Havana and Moscow had diminished.

The second difference between the U.S.S.R. and Cuba concerned strategy toward internal development and the construction of socialism. In his speech on the U.S.S.R's invasion of Czechoslovakia, Castro criticized the bourgeois style of life, the economic inequalities, and the emphasis on material incentives within the Soviet bloc which generated "liberalism." Castro counterposed the formation of the new communist man who is motivated by egalitarian and moral ideals.[73]

These differences between Cuba and the U.S.S.R. manifested themselves in two important international events. The Cubans did not attend the U.S.S.R.-sponsored conference of world Communist parties along with China and other dissident Communist countries.[74] Secondly, the Cubans refused to sign the test ban treaty despite the pressures and urgings of the Soviet Union. Since the middle of 1968 these differences have been played down. One important reason for the playing down of differences and the friendliness that the Cubans have shown toward the Soviet Union has been the fact that most of the important trade agreements came up for renewal in 1969–70. These agreements were vital for Cuban survival. Although the discussions surrounding the trade agreements lasted much longer than anticipated, giving support to the suspicion that a tacit understanding had been reached concerning certain rules that should be observed regarding political differences in the future, the agreements themselves proved satisfactory to the Cubans. The 1971 trade agreements were preceded by three months of negotiations which included the formation of a joint Soviet-Cuban commission to study ways to increase the efficiency of the Cuban national economy—a theme stressed by Castro following the inability to harvest ten million tons of sugar in 1969–70. These activities seem to indicate that the technical-managerial topics have replaced the need to iron out political differences, at least for the time being. The 1971 trade agreement itself represented an absolute increase of about $110 million in Soviet goods to Cuba over the previous (1970) agreement.

The second factor influencing the rapprochement in Cuban-Soviet relations is the fact that Cuba has turned toward internal construction rather than giving priority to international revolution. The Soviet Union may think that the Cubans are accepting their approach to international politics and internal development. Whatever the future direction of Cuban policy, in 1969–70 the Cubans turned toward internal development and this probably has favorably influenced the Soviet Union.

Another reason accounting for Cuban-Soviet rapprochement is China's relations with Cuba, which are "correct but cool." [75] The Cubans have not forgotten the ultimatum which they claim the Chinese issued in 1965. In effect the Chinese told the Cubans that either they supported the Chinese in their dispute with the U.S.S.R. or their action would be interpreted as hostile. As a result of this great-power arrogance and the abrupt reduction in the purchase of sugar and export of rice, relations deteriorated sharply. [76] The Cubans no longer are able to maintain a completely neutral position in the Sino-Soviet dispute and in that sense are more dependent within the Communist world on the Soviet bloc countries. The hostility, sectarianism, and great-power chauvinism of the Chinese have allowed the Russians to gain the friendship of the Cubans.

The fourth factor which may influence the growing rapprochement between the Cubans and the Soviet Union is probably due to Castro's support of the Soviet intervention in Czechoslovakia. The support was backhanded because of Castro's sharp critique of Soviet internal policy. Nevertheless Castro's pro-Soviet stand came at a difficult time for the Soviet Union and perhaps their gratitude is expressed by the greater support that they are giving Cuba today.

The rapprochement between Cuba and the Soviet Union may have several consequences. One possible result might be an increase in Soviet economic support this year and perhaps next for Cuba's development effort. At a minimum the Soviets will probably maintain the current level of trade and support for Cuba. Public polemics between the pro-Moscow parties in Latin America and Cuba are unlikely. Relations may not be one of warm embraces but they will probably be cordial. The Cubans will support specific measures taken by nonrevolutionary governments which they consider anti-imperialist while minimizing support for guerrilla groups. The Cubans will, however, continue to provide sanctuary and moral support for revolutionary movements, especially in those countries like Brazil where right-wing military dictatorships are in command.

On the whole, the rapprochement will have a moderate impact—moving Cuba closer to the U.S.S.R. and the pro-Soviet parties but it will not result in any drastic realignment within the Communist bloc. The Cubans will continue to maintain their independent position within the bloc, giving or withholding support, bargaining, and negotiating with the Soviet Union depending on the specific political question.

In 1969 Cuban policy became more sympathetic toward bourgeois nationalist groups, especially involving those that have state power. From the fall of Goulart and Brizola in Brazil to the rise of General Velasco in Peru in

1968, the Cubans maintained a fairly consistent policy which rejected all elites and regimes in Latin America, including so-called "progressives" (as the Soviets referred to them) like Frei and Belaunde.[77] Beginning late in 1968 and increasingly thereafter the Cuban press began to present favorable accounts of the Peruvian junta. In his speech on July 26, 1969, Fidel Castro made positive though cautious references to the "revolutionary measures" adopted by the Peruvian junta. Cuba's reappraisal of the revolutionary potentialities of elite groups, their possible contribution to the revolutionary process, is tied to Cuba's preoccupation with national development. Internal stagnation, the decline of the guerrillas and the nationalist posture of some elite groups account for Cuba's shift in policy. The convergence of external factors with specific internal needs has been instrumental in reshaping Cuban thinking.

From the point of view of Cuban policy-makers, the benefits of supporting the elites on short-range issues may outweigh the costs in terms of strategic developments. The elite "nationalists" offer concrete point of opposition to U.S. policy while the guerrillas are as remote as ever from power. President Velasco did nationalize the International Petroleum Company and the sugar plantations of Grace Company in defiance of the threats of the Hickenlooper Amendment. In contrast the Movement of the Revolutionary Left (MIR) and the other guerrilla groups have not been able to organize and initiate armed action for several years. The Cubans have not endorsed the Bolivian government's action nationalizing Gulf Oil because General Ovando—the current ruler—was implicated in the murder of Guevara. Nevertheless elite nationalists in Bolivia, Chile, and Venezuela have spoken of establishing relations with Cuba.[78] President Caldera of Venezuela has spoken of the "reintegration of this people (Cuba) into our organization (OAS)." [79] The break-up of the economic blockade of Cuba would facilitate internal economic development and ease some of the pressures. However, the price appears to be that Cuba cut off support to revolutionary movements in Latin America—a policy which will certainly have some initial negative effects on certain movements, especially in Venezuela.

Beginning in 1969 Cuba's relationship with the revolutionary Left in Latin America has been changing parallel with its new stance toward the new manifestations of elite nationalism. This shift in policy can be most clearly seen in Cuba's policy toward the Venezuelan guerrilla movement.[80]

Between 1962 and 1965 the guerrilla movement, the Armed Forces of National Liberation (FALN), contained both Communist and non-Communist groups. In 1965 the Communist party began a campaign to regain legality and to withdraw support from the FALN with the slogan calling for a "democratic peace." An intense debate and profound division occurred within the FALN between those who wanted to continue the guerrilla struggle and those who favored a return to legality. The old leadership of the Communist party supported the latter. In a speech on March 13, 1967, Castro spoke strongly in favor of those who wished to continue the guerrilla struggle and rejected the Communist assertion that they were the vanguard of the revolution. Castro provided a more "behavioral" yardstick for determining who constituted the revolutionary leaderships: "Their attitude toward the guerrilla struggle will define the Communist in Latin America." [81] Castro denounced the Communist leaders who abandoned the guerrillas and made their peace with the Venezuelan government, and gave his "support and solidarity" to FALN leader Douglas Bravo.

However, by April, 1969, the FALN was criticizing the Cubans for being distant, for not giving support to the revolutionary movements in Latin America, and for concentrating all attention on economic development.[82] In the same document, after analyzing Cuba's current priorities and policies the FALN concluded that the Cuban position was approaching the revisionist camp. The FALN still held out hopes that the Cuban leadership would reverse its position and that once again "the Cuban people take the road of Che and Bolivar." On January 15, 1970, Douglas Bravo, commander of the FALN, issued a communiqué accusing the Cuban leadership of abandoning the guerrilla movements.[83]

It is therefore not too surprising that Venezuela's conservative President Rafael Caldera became a leading advocate of recognizing Cuba—even though Venezuela had been in the past one of the most aggressively belligerent opponents of Cuba in the OAS.[84]

There are several other indications that Cuba has broken off or seriously curtailed support to the revolutionary Left in Latin America. During the massive, student-led demonstrations against the bureaucratic autocracy in Mexico, the Cuban press did not contain a single article either in support of the students or against the Mexican government. Mexico is the only country in the hemisphere which maintains diplomatic relations with Cuba and the Cubans apparently did not want to endanger ties. Throughout 1969 and early 1970 the Cuban press and government presented a completely favorable account of the Peruvian military government. No criticism was voiced of the $335-million-dollar investment contract signed with a U.S. consortium; no mention was made of the five-year sentence received by Ricardo Gadea, a leader of the Fidelista Movement of the Revolutionary Left (MIR); nor was there any reference to the junta's arrest of nine members of MIR for "subversion"; more important, the junta's crackdown on student power in the universities went unnoticed. In Bolivia, the guerrilla group, the National Liberation Army (ELN), apparently had to resort to bank robberies to finance its purchase of arms. As one journalist recently noted, concerning the lack of external support: "If urgent change is not produced in external solidarity toward the Bolivian guerrillas in 1970, one cannot be certain of the way in which the ELN could continue positively a task that is today heroic but that in a short period could be suicidal." [85] The discontinuance of positive support toward the guerrillas is matched by a complete absence of criticism toward the pro-Moscow Communist parties.

In the summer of 1969 declarations and statements by traditional leaders of Latin American Communist parties reflecting their legalistic reformist politics were printed in *Granma* (the official organ of the Cuban Communist party), without comment or criticism.[86]

The shift toward "building socialism in one island" has apparently two interrelated consequences: a tendency for the Cubans to reach out toward the new elite nationalists in Latin America while minimizing ties with the guerrillas, the latter being a condition for the former. Cuba still remains a sanctuary where indigenous revolutionaries can take refuge, as recently occurred with the Brazilian political prisoners exchanged for the U.S. ambassador.[87] The focus on consolidation of the Cuban economy is part of normalization of relations with as many existing Latin regimes as possible. In sum, international revolution is being subordinated to internal economic development.

While the Cubans may be changing their policy there are several factors limiting this change:

(1) Continued U.S. hostility—the economic blockade —and the opposition of pro-U.S. governments in most of Latin America. The most recent expressions of the intransigent opposition of the U.S. can best be seen in the Rockefeller report and in Nixon's policy speeches.

(2) The Vietnam War expresses the willingness of U.S. to invade and massively occupy a country to shape its internal politics. Thus Cuba cannot rule out the possibility of a similar occurrence in this hemisphere.

(3) Ideological bonds link Cuba's politics to those of revolutionaries in the Third World. Past and present ties have taken on a reality apart from the particular circumstances in which they arose.

While the priorities and dominant tone of Cuban politics may have shifted from internationalism to nationalism, from guerrilla struggle to agricultural work, the commitment to support revolutionary struggle elsewhere is still strong.[88] Cuba is far from accepting U.S. hegemony in the hemisphere, let alone seeking out a negotiated settlement on the basis of the existing established order in Latin America. Given the degree of U.S. penetration and the conservative nature of the political regimes in almost all Latin countries a general accord appears unlikely. Nevertheless the Cubans have opened the door to new currents in Latin America— the development of new nationalist formations from previously status quo oriented institutions—while continuing to support, as in the past, revolutionary groups in the countries still following U.S. leadership. Cubans have adopted a pragmatic attitude, supporting specific measures or positions adopted by the newly emerging forces without giving blanket support to any one group or government.

NOTES

1. Carmelo Mesa-Lago, *Availability and Reliability of Statistics in Socialist Cuba* (Pittsburgh: Latin American Studies, Occasional Papers No. 1, University of Pittsburgh, January, 1970). For more recent figures on sugar production, see Republica de Cuba, Junta Central de Planificacion, Direccion Central de Estadistica, *Compendio Estadistico de Cuba 1968* hereafter referred to as *Compendio*), p. 11.

2. For two different analysis and interpretations of the significance of the Cuban harvest, see: Les Evans, "How Can Strain on Cuba's Economy Be Relieved?" *Intercontinental Press*, Vol. 8, No. 28 (September 7, 1970), pp. 715–18; and coverage of Fidel Castro's July 26, 1970, speech by the *New York Times*, July 27, 1970.

3. Fidel Castro's July 26, 1970, speech, *Granma Weekly Review* (English translation of speech), August 2, 1970. See also his September 28, 1970, speech at the tenth anniversary celebration of the Committees for the Defense of the Revolution reported in *Granma Weekly Review* (English edition), October 4, 1970.

4. *Ibid.* See also Livro Maitan's analysis in "A Crucial Stage for the Cuban Revolution," *Intercontinental Press*, Vol. 8, No. 40 (November 30, 1970), pp. 104–46. For another account, see: "Cuban Econ-

omy Is Strained Because Sugar Falls Short of Goal," *New York Times*, December 11, 1970.

5. Interviews with Cuban officials, June–July, 1969.

6. On the early phase of the revolution, see Leo Huberman and Paul Sweezy, *Socialism in Cuba* (New York: Monthly Review Press, 1969); James O'Connor, *The Origins of Socialism in Cuba* (Ithaca, N.Y.: Cornell University Press, 1970); and Dudley Seers, ed., *Cuba, The Economic and Social Revolution* (Chapel Hill, N.C.: University of North Carolina Press, 1964). For additional information, see the statistics quoted by Castro in his July 26, 1970, speech cited above.

7. Edward Boorstein, *The Economic Transformation of Cuba* (New York: Monthly Review Press, 1968), and James O'Connor, *The Origins of Socialism in Cuba, op. cit.*

8. Boorstein, *ibid.,* Chapter 4.

9. Maurice Zeitlin, *Revolutionary Politics and the Cuban Working Class* (Princeton, N.J.: Princeton University Press, 1967), Chapter 11.

10. James O'Connor, *The Origins of Socialism in Cuba, op. cit.*

11. United Nations Social and Economic Council, Symposium on Latin American Industrialization, *El Desarrollo Industrial de Cuba,* ECLA/ conf. 23, 1. 63, March, 1966.

12. For a detailed account of political mobilization see Richard Fagen, *The Transformation of Political Culture in Cuba* (Stanford, California: Stanford University Press, 1969).

13. Martin Kenner and James Petras, eds., *Fidel Castro Speaks* (New York: Grove Press, 1969).

14. Fagen, *op. cit.,* esp. Ch. 3.

15. Twelve thousand *fincas* were sold to the state between 1967 and 1969. However, only 5,000 small farmers (less than 5 percent) are members of the Communist party. Interview with Pepe Ramirez, president of the National Association of Small Farmers (ANAP), July 15, 1969. Observations and interviews in Oriente province among peasants confirmed the assertion that children of small holders were abandoning the small farms as they graduated from high school and technical schools.

16. Fidel Castro's speech, "We are determined not to lose this battle," *Granma Weekly Review* (English translation), February 15, 1970, p. 5.

17. *Compendio,* p. 4.

18. *Ibid.,* p. 5. World Bank President Robert McNamara noted, "The cities of the developing countries are the centers which ought to serve as the basis of both industrial growth and social change. Instead . . . the cities are spawning a culture of poverty that threatens the economic health of entire nations." *Alliance for Progress Weekly Newsletter,* Vol. 7, No. 44 (November 3, 1969), p. 1.

19. *Ibid.*, pp. 32–33.
20. *Ibid.*
21. *Ibid.*
22. *Ibid.*, pp. 34–35.
23. *Ibid.*
24. *Ibid.*
25. *Ibid.*
26. *Ibid.*
27. *Ibid.*
28. *Ibid.*
29. *Ibid.*
30. *Ibid.*
31. *Ibid.*
32. *Ibid.*
33. *Ibid.*, pp. 32–33.
34. Carmelo Mesa-Lago, *op. cit.*, pp. 69–70.
35. Calculated from raw figures in *Compendio*, pp. 1–3.
36. *Ibid.*, p. 21.
37. *Ibid.*
38. *Ibid.*, p. 43.
39. *Ibid.*, p. 7.
40. Carmelo Mesa-Lago, *op. cit.*, p. 47.
41. *Compendio, op. cit.*, p. 6.
42. *Ibid.*, p. 8.
43. *Ibid.*
44. *Ibid.*, pp. 11–12.
45. *Ibid.*, p. 20.
46. *Ibid.*, p. 18.
47. *Ibid.*, p. 26.
48. *Ibid.*
49. *Ibid.*
50. *Ibid.*
51. *Ibid.*
52. See for example "Guerrilla Warfare: A Method," "Cuban Exceptionalism," and "Vietnam and World Struggle" in George Lavan, ed., *Che Guevara Speaks* (New York: Merit Publishers, 1967).
53. "Otro Mayo Argentino," *Cuadernos de Marcha* (Montevideo), No. 7, July, 1969. The entire issue is devoted to a discussion of the events of May, 1969.
54. A critique of the Brazilian Communist party from the position supporting armed struggle can be found in "Carta de Carlos Mari-

ghella al ejecutivo del Partido Comunista Brasileno solicitando su renuncia," *Pensamiento Critico* (Havana), No. 7, August, 1967, pp. 209–18. For further discussion on the Brazilian guerrillas see James Petras' articles, "A New Left in Brazil" and "A Look at Brazil's New Left," *Guardian*, December 20, 27, 1969.

55. On the military government in Peru see "Peru: Despues de un Ano," *Marcha*, October 24, 31, 1969, p. 11. Also Petras and Rimensnyder, "What's Happening in Peru," *Monthly Review*, February, 1970, pp. 15–28. On elite nationalism in Bolivia see Rene Zavaleta Mercado, "Ovando, el bonapartista," *Marcha*, January 30, 1970, pp. 16–17 and 20; "Bolivia: La Segunda Revolucion Nacional," *Cuadernos de Marcha*, No. 30, October, 1969 (the whole issue is devoted to the emergent nationalism of the Ovando regime); Augusto Cespedes, "Bolivia en guerra con la gulf," *Marcha*, November 21, 1969, p. 19; "Cerraremos los pozos pero Bolivia resistira agresion" (an interview with the Bolivian Minister of Mines and Petroleum, Marcelo Quiroga), *Marcha*, November 14, 1969, pp. 12–13 and 24; Rogelio Garcia Lupo, "Junto a los Nacionalistas Bolivianos," *Marcha*, October 31, 1969, pp. 2–3 (see also the interview of President Ovando on the same page in the same issue).

56. *New York Times*, May 25, 1969, p. 6; June 8, 1969, p. 4.

57. See for example Fidel Castro's "Eulogy for Che Guevara" in Kenner and Petras, eds., *op. cit.*, pp. 181–86.

58. A typical Cuban headline today reads: "The people of Cuba pay homage to Che and Camilo with nation-wide work drive," *Granma*, October 19, 1969, p. 1. During October, 1969, there was a nation-wide "guerrilla work drive." The following description appearing in the Cuban press best captures the new image of Guevara:

He was a pioneer of voluntary work. When a few dozen went, he would go to the canefields to cut cane or operate a harvesting combine, or be on the docks pushing a wheelbarrow or work in the mine—with complete faith in man, of confidence in the conscience of man. How he would have enjoyed seeing the people of Cuba with this willingness to work, with this readiness, with this attitude of going massively to wage their battle, their decisive battle for the economy, their decisive battle in work.

Granma Weekly Review (English translation), November 2, 1969, p. 1. The following quote from Guevara appearing in the Cuban press highlights the new emphasis: "Man begins to see himself portrayed through his works, and he understands his human breadth through the created object, through work that is carried out." *Granma*, August 1, 1969, p. 2.

59. "Our Revolutionary Armed Forces have mobilized for the 10 million ton sugar harvest as they would for war," *Granma*, November 16, 1969, pp. 1–3. During the author's visit to the Mayebeque region

in August, 1969, most government officials and party leaders stressed the need for "military organization" and referred to it as a model.

60. Among those whom the author found cutting sugar cane alongside ordinary cane cutters was the president of the national book publishing house and the president of the National Academy of Sciences. See photos of the Cuban leaders cutting cane in *Granma Weekly Review,* January 18, 1970, p. 12.

61. One of the negative side effects caused by the reaction to Guevara's death was the "accelerated depreciation of economic considerations in Cuba's development efforts." Interview with Carlos Rafael Rodriguez, August 15, 1969.

62. Brief biographical accounts of the Cubans who joined the Bolivian guerrilla movement can be found in *Granma* (Cuban edition), July 30, 1969, pp. 1–3. Also *Granma* (English edition), June 1, 1969, p. 12.

63. Fidel Castro, "Closing speech to the Tri-Continental Conference in Havana," *Granma* (special supplement on the Tri-Continental Conference, English edition; Havana), January 16, 1966. For an even more forthright presentation of the armed struggle thesis see Fidel Castro, "Our people have no other path to liberation than that of armed struggle," in Kenner and Petras, *op. cit.,* pp. 150–59.

64. On U.S. involvement in Venezuela see *U.S. Army Handbook on Venezuela.*

65. On the divisions within the Venezuelan guerrilla group see "Differences Among Venezuelan Guerrillas," *Intercontinental Press,* Vol. 8, No. 5 (February 9, 1970), p. 103. On Guatemala see Rudi Fion, "Report from Guatemala: Where the Guerrilla Groups Stand Today," *Intercontinental Press,* Vol. 7, 1969, p. 286.

66. For a critical analysis of the defection of the Venezuelan Communist party from the guerrilla movement see Ignacio Urdaneta, "Polemica en la revolucion," *Pensamiento Critico* (Havana), No. 7, August, 1967, pp. 117–58. See also Fidel Castro, "Their attitude toward the guerrilla struggle will define the communists in Latin America," Kener and Petras, *op. cit.,* pp. 128–49.

67. Latin America's largest legal Communist party is found in Chile. For a discussion, see James Petras, *Politics and Social Forces in Chilean Development* (Berkeley: University of California Press, 1969).

68. Fidel Castro, "This harvest begins today and it will not be stopped until we have ground the last bag of the 10 million," *Granma* (Cuban edition), July 15, 1969, p. 4.

69. The Soviet attacks on Cuba can be found in D. Bruce Jackson, *Castro, The Kremlin and Communism in Latin America,* Studies in International Affairs No. 9 (Baltimore: Johns Hopkins Press). Unfortunately, most of the author's discussion is speculative and ill-informed. For the Cuban side see Castro's "Their attitude toward

the guerrilla struggle will define the communists in Latin America" in Kenner and Petras, *op. cit.*, pp. 127–49. Inside Cuba a small pro-Soviet faction developed, but it was quickly eliminated. For a discussion of the "micro-faction" see Richard Fagan and Wayne Cornelius, eds., *Political Power in Latin America* (Englewood Cliffs: Prentice-Hall, 1970), pp. 341 passim. The clearest expression of Soviet-Cuban rapprochement can be found in *Granma*, July 27, 1969: The headlines read: "Soviet sailors cut cane as beautiful gesture of international solidarity." On page 8 of the same issue it was reported that 22 bilateral agreements were signed by Cuba and the U.S.S.R.

70. For a discussion of the position of the U.S.S.R. and the pro-Soviet parties see "Documents adopted by the International Conference of Communist and Workers' parties." *World Marxist Review*, Vol. 12, No. 7, esp. pp. 18–20. The Soviet Union signed commercial, cultural and financial agreements with the Colombian government the same day that the leadership of the Communist party was being arrested. For the full flavor of Fidel Castro's caustic remarks see "Their attitude toward the guerrilla struggle. . . ." in Kenner and Petras, *op. cit.*, pp. 146–48. For a sampling of the legalist approach see Luis Corvalan, "Alliance of Anti-Imperialist Forces in Latin America," *World Marxist Review*, Vol. 10, No. 7, pp. 44–51.

71. Soviet trade with Argentina rose from $27 million in 1967 to $30 million in 1968; with Brazil a new pact is being negotiated to cover approximately $100 million in term payments for the sale of machinery and heavy equipment. *Alliance for Progress Weekly Newsletter*, Vol. 8, No. 5 (February 2, 1970), p. 3.

72. On the Mexican events see the issues of *Granma* between July and November, 1968; on Peru see *Granma* between June, 1969 and February, 1970. Especially important to note is an article on Peruvian copper which appeared in *Granma Weekly Review* (English translation), December 2, 1969, p. 10, and which offers no critical appraisal of the Peruvian government's position.

73. Castro's speech on the Soviet invasion of Czechoslovakia appeared in *Granma* (English edition), August 30, 1968.

74. For a report on the international conference of 75 Communist and Workers parties which took place in Moscow from June 5 to 17, 1969, see *World Marxist Review*, Vol. 12, No. 7 (July, 1969), pp. 3–53. Cuba, Korea, China, Albania, and North Vietnam were not in attendance.

75. Interview with Oscar Pino Santos, former Cuban ambassador to China (1960–1967), July 20, 1969.

76. On January 2, 1966, the day prior to the opening of the Tri-Continental Solidarity Conference, Fidel Castro attacked the Chinese for cutting their rice shipments to Cuba from 285,000 tons in 1965 to 135,000 tons in 1966 and for cutting their imports of sugar from Cuba. *Deadline Data on World Affairs: Cuba*, May 20, 1966, p. 213.

370 : CULTIVATING REVOLUTION

77. Subsequent to a massacre of copper miners by the Chilean government, Fidel Castro said of Chilean President Frei: "He promised revolution without blood and he has given blood without revolution," *Ultima Hora* (Santiago, Chile), March 12, 1966, p. 14.

78. On February 20, 1970, it was announced that Chile had re-opened trade with Cuba (*New York Times,* February 21, 1970). And shortly after his inauguration in November, 1971, President Allende re-opened diplomatic relations with Cuba, thus fulfilling a campaign promise.

79. *Washington Post,* February 5, 1970, pp. 1 and 5.

80. On the development of the Venezuelan guerrilla movement, see James Petras, "Revolution and Guerrilla Movements in Latin America: Venezuela, Guatemala, Colombia and Peru" in Petras and Zeitlin, *Latin America: Reform or Revolution* (N.Y.: Fawcett Books, 1968). For a current discussion of the "slow growth" of the guerrillas and their changing perspective emphasizing the organization of the urban masses, see *Boletin Interno,* No. 1, *Partido de la Revolucion Venezolano* (FLN-FALN), Buro Politico del PRV (no date, but probably summer, 1969).

81. Kenner and Petras, *op. cit.,* p. 127 passim.

82. "Rectificacion Tactica o Estrategica," *Fuego* (Journal of the FLN-FALN), April, 1969, No. 1, Reproduced in *Rocinante* (Caracas), No. 13, August/September, 1969.

83. For the best single account of the splits within the Venezuelan Left and the differences among the guerrillas concerning Cuba see Ugo Ulive, "Division y unidad de la Izquierda," *Marcha,* February 20, 1970, pp. 20–21. "Differences Among Venezuelan Guerillas," *Intercontinental Press,* Vol. 8, No. 5, February 9, 1970, p. 103.

84. *Washington Post,* February 5, 1970, pp. 1–5. It is useful to compare President Caldera's views to Romulo Betancourt's attitude expressed in "Castro, Communism and the Attempt to Subvert Venezuela," Richard Fagan and Wayne Cornelius, eds., *op. cit.,* pp. 96–99. While Latin "moderates" perceive the change in Cuban policy, the Rockefeller Report contains little else except the usual clichés about "subversion" and Castroite terrorism.

85. Carlos Maria Gutierrez, "Informe sobre la guerrilla boliviana," *Marcha,* January 30, 1970, p. 20.

86. An example of changed attitude of the Cubans toward the pro-Moscow Communists can be seen in the fact that the Cuban press printed without comment an article from the Uruguayan Communist party newspaper *El Popular* criticizing the government for acting unconstitutionally by violating Uruguay's political traditions and acting contrary to public opinion. Hardly a revolutionary approach. *Granma* (Cuban edition), July 11, 1969, p. 7.

87. "Brazilian revolutionaries arrive in Cuba," *Granma,* October 5, 1969, p. 1.

88. On the priority of the politics of production in Cuba in 1970 the following quote clearly indicates the policy view of the Cuban leaders: "Because, in the first analysis, politics in its new context is no more than that: how to organize production and social life in general, insuring an ever more conscientious, and ever more enthusiastic and an ever more effective participation of the masses of the people in that production and in that social life." Speech by Armando Hart, organizational secretary and member of the Political Bureau of the Cuban Communist party. *Granma,* October 5, 1969, p. 4.

PART FOUR

THE UNITED STATES AND
SOCIO-POLITICAL CHANGE
IN LATIN AMERICA

U.S. policy has a great impact on the internal development policies of the countries of Latin America. The position taken by the U.S. with regard to change in the agricultural sector is the central concern of our discussion.

During the first years of the Kennedy administration a great deal of public discussion and debate centered on the need for sweeping changes in order that Latin American countries evolve into modern democratic societies. However, the means for bringing about these changes and the manner in which they might affect political allies and U.S. and Latin American propertied groups were not adequately discussed. As a result, a series of speeches evoking the need for sweeping changes was articulated; but in practice these pronouncements rarely affected the day-to-day operations of foreign aid administrators operating in the field. The disjuncture between public policy statements and the operating rules resulted in a great deal of cynicism and disenchantment among those forces in both North and South America who were awaiting a "new era" in hemispheric relations.

The purpose of this section is to analyze the nature of U.S. policy and the orientation of U.S. policy-makers toward change; to specify the points at which official rhetoric diverged from actual practice; and to determine some of the reasons why this divergence occurred.

8

U.S. Policy and Agrarian
Reform in Latin America:
The Alliance for Progress Decade

One of the most striking characteristics of Latin America is the uneven pattern of its social and economic development. This imbalance is evidenced by the overwhelming amount of economic-social-political power held by the few as against the extremely weak bargaining position of the many. Historically the power position of elites in Latin America is rooted in agrarian-based societies, more specifically in land ownership. Social movements and political analysts concerned with the gross inequalities in Latin America have of necessity focused on the issue of land reform. The proponents of the status quo, on the other hand, have sought to prevent or limit changes in land tenure by stressing factors affecting aggregate output. The issues of agrarian reform and agricultural development in Latin America transcend the South American continent.

The United States is the paramount political and economic power in the Western Hemisphere and has substantial agricultural interests in Latin America. Furthermore, U.S. policy-makers choose political allies and frequently provide aid which is decisive in determining the fate of a regime. The U.S. is a crucial determinant of Latin American agricultural development. A discussion of Latin American agricultural development must include an examination and analysis of United States policy and role. An analysis of the attitudes and policies of U.S. officials will provide us with a basis for evaluating the contribution that the U.S. has made in facilitating or hindering social change and the democratic restructuring of Latin American society. We will discuss the extent to which U.S. policy has followed a distributionist or productionist approach to agricultural development. Specifically we propose to examine the following propositions:

(1) that the redistributionist (structural reform) and productionist (incremental change) schools of thought exist among U.S. policy-makers, with the latter gaining ascendancy since the Kennedy administration;

(2) that this shift in approach has affected the type of programs and projects financed by the U.S., causing a drift away from projects of a distributionist type to more strictly productionist projects;

(3) that the productionist approach has been ineffective in terms of significantly raising agricultural production, increasing production of food, and reducing Latin America's dependence on food importation;

(4) that the original intent of the Alliance for Progress to restructure radically Latin American agriculture has been repudiated.

One strategy for dealing with uneven development is social mobilization, institutionalization of political power and implementation of legislation aimed at reforming present systems of income distribution so that benefits accrue more evenly.[1] This solution to societal maladies is within what many scholars label structural or comprehensive developmental changes. Another view of Latin American development sees the solution in "incremental" changes largely based on providing greater incentives to current investors. These two approaches[2]—structural reform versus incremental change—are diametrically opposed to each other in terms of rationale, strategy, and clientele even though on occasion similar tactics may be adopted. We will examine both approaches as they relate to U.S. policy and involvement in Latin American agricultural development.

U.S. agricultural policy toward Latin America, especially after 1961, has been an important constraint affecting the policy choices open to Latin American officials. By examining agricultural development and the U.S. role in these activities, we can evaluate the adequacy of competing approaches to development. By way of introduction, we will discuss the two contrasting approaches to development, those of structural and incremental change, and their respective strategies for agrarian development.

Two Approaches: Redistribution vs. Incremental Change

In the societies of Latin America, agrarian reform has been very widely considered an important component of any policy of structural change. Agrarian reform has, however, been given a wide variety of meanings. For some it entails the distribution of large land holdings among the landless and small farmers. For others it means better utilization of existing tenure patterns to increase the products available for consumption and export. Still another view sees agrarian reform as improving transportation, communication, and storage facilities to expedite the flow of farm products to marketing outlets.

Even among those who favor the redistributive approach, agrarian reform policy can vary; it can mean distribution of public or unused lands, division of private large estates, consolidation of small farms. The method of obtaining the land can be expropriation, taxation, confiscation, or a combination of these measures. Accompanying programs may or may not include technical modernization, increased educational facilities, diversification of products, and development of communications.[3]

In our use of the term, agrarian reform involves a re-distribution of political and social power in addition to fundamentally re-ordering the economic structure of the agricultural sector. Land ownership in Latin America involves social and political power in addition to the control of economic resources. To own land means to control the individuals who work the land. Social status and prestige are associated with ownership of land and the traditional style of life which accompanies it. Through traditional paternalistic social relations and physical coercion the landowner is able to control the political behavior of "his" peasants. The peasants are little more than pawns in the hands of the large landholders. Through their control over the peasantry the landowners influence the functioning of political institutions to perpetuate their privileged position. Possessing wealth, status, and votes (the captive voters of the rural areas), the landowners are able to influence legislatures, executives, bureaucracies, and judiciaries. Through their control over political institutions they influence taxation, government expenditures, and the use of the police and army.[4]

Because changes in land tenure can have multiple effects on the distribution of political, economic, and social power it is scarcely surprising that there is disagreement and conflict among scholars and politicians over the use of a comprehensive approach to agrarian reform. Some writers see Latin America's agricultural problems largely in terms of a more efficient use of the land and increasing technical capacity—in essence, agricultural development is merely a matter of technology. The ends of such a policy would be to increase production and to secure a larger share of the export market. Development and reform usually refer to building farm-to-market access roads, creating better marketing facilities, producing cheap fertilizers, importing farm machinery, rationalizing credit, diversifying output to provide a better balance between supply and demand in the country and, perhaps, broadening the export base. Since it is largely premised on the maintenance of existing land tenure patterns, the only type of land distribution consistent with this policy would be the development of previously uncultivated areas. The underlying assumption is that the overall growth of the agricultural sector will indirectly cause the income of small farmers and peasants to be raised, along with educational and health levels. This strategy of modernization from above (the gradualist approach) argues that development can best occur through increased production *without* land redistribution. Those unable to receive land in the countryside would migrate to the city as literate workers, thus supplying a labor market for industrial development.

Unfortunately, although intense exploitation of the peasantry and rural labor force has been commonplace throughout Latin America for the better part of four centuries, landowners have not utilized economic surplus to industrialize society. While in Europe, the Soviet Union, Japan, and even the U.S. coercion of the agricultural population to extract the economic surplus was a necessary accompaniment of rapid industrialization, this has not been the case in Latin America. Foreign investors and Latin elite have exported their earnings to the industrial capitalist world, invested in land, commerce, real estate, and have engaged in speculative activity. Historically the Latin American landowners have not fit Barrington Moore's description of the modernizers from above: they have exploited and coerced but they have hardly "developed."

Obviously, some elements or techniques of the two approaches are not mutually exclusive and could be integrated into a program for agricultural development. The fact that the "client" group emphasized is different in each case, however, presents an insurmountable obstacle to such a policy integration. Programs of land redistribution would not be successful without massive technical assistance to the new land title-holders, and the advocates of technical modernization do not totally ignore the living environment of the landless and marginal farmers. But, for the redistributionists, land reform is a necessary precondition to agricultural development. The emphasis here is on bettering the conditions of the *bulk* of the agrarian population. The productionists, on the other hand, stress nonhuman resources—the importance of technical innovation in development strategy. Most important are their contrasting views of the social forces which will implement the development program. A redistributionist strategy must be based upon popular mobilization, while the productionists work through existing channels and institutions. Modernization from above may bring greater technical efficiency and raise production. However, it will not alter, but it will probably enhance, the economic, political, and social resources of the few who own land at the expense of the many who work it.[5] Agrarian reform as an aspect of social change aims at altering inequality in the distribution of rights and income, thereby minimizing inequalities of access to the political system.

Agrarian Reform and Agricultural Development: U.S. Views, 1961–1968

The official U.S. view of agricultural development and agrarian reform in Latin America is a composite of three sources: the executive (presidential), legislative (congressional) and the operating or administrative (field staff). None of these three separate sources can individually claim exclusiveness in policy-making, although constitutionally the Chief Executive has total responsibility. In practice, legislative intent as well as administrative interpretation play major roles in shaping *and* implementing U.S. policies abroad. Even though conflict existed over the ideal nature of U.S. policy in regard to agricultural development/agrarian reform in Latin America, and more specifically over the operationalization of the policy in the field, a degree of consensus did develop early in the Kennedy administration which tended toward "gradualism" and "production." It is important to note that all three participating sets of U.S.

officials—members of the executive branch, congressmen, and U.S.A.I.D. field administrators—included both "structural reformers" and "advocates of gradual change." A historical examination of all three official sources illustrates the evolution of U.S. policy in this area.

The statements of U.S. officials since the inception of the Alliance for Progress in 1961 reveal a gradual shift in approach from redistributionist to productionist. The extent of the shift is clearly seen by contrasting the first Punta del Este Conference in August, 1961, with the second, held in April, 1967. In his message to the first conference, President Kennedy called for:

> Full recognition of the right of all people to share fully in our progress. For there is no place in democratic life for institutions which benefit the few while denying the needs of the many, even though the elimination of such institutions may require far reaching and difficult changes such as land reform and tax reform and a vastly increased emphasis on education and health and housing.[6]

The Charter which was subsequently drawn up encouraged:

> Programs of comprehensive agrarian reform leading to the effective transformation, where required, of unjust structures and systems of land tenure and use, with a view to replacing *latifundia* and dwarf holdings by an equitable system of land tenure so that with the help of timely and adequate credit, technical assistance, and facilities for the marketing and distribution of products, the land will become for the man who works it the basis of his economic stability, the foundation of his increasing welfare and the guarantee of his freedom and dignity.[7]

This section of the Charter explicitly stated that structural reforms, including "effective transformation . . . of land tenure" were necessary. The efficacy of technical assistance and infrastructure development to realize increases in rural standards of living would be contingent upon these reforms.

The 1967 Punta del Este Conference, while paying lip service to the need to guarantee the *campesino* full participation in the economic and social life of his country, makes no mention of the prior necessity of structural changes:

> In order to promote a rise in the standard of living of farmers and an improvement in the condition of Latin American rural people and their full participation in economic and social life, it is necessary to give greater dynamism to agriculture in Latin America.[8]

There goals were to be realized through:

> increasing food production in the Latin American countries in sufficient volume and quality to provide adequately for their population and to meet world needs for food to an ever-increasing extent, as well as toward improving agricultural productivity and toward diversification of crops, which will assure the best possible competitive conditions for such production.[9]

Thus, by 1967, executive emphasis had clearly shifted from the structural reform goal of redistribution of land to the productionist goal of increasing the output of foodstuffs and thus securing a larger share of the world agricultural market. Modernization from below was shelved in favor of infrastructure development—in a word, providing incentives and subsidies to improve the efficiency of current large landholders.[10] Limited expropriation of marginal and previously uncultivated land would provide a few new farmers with an opportunity to benefit directly in these changes.

While the contrast between 1962 and 1967 drastically highlights the change in U.S. policy, the shift took place slowly and can perhaps best be viewed over the entire five-year period. Events which marked this shift in policy occurred as early as 1962. From the beginning, congressional opinion was generally hostile to the redistributionist policy of the Kennedy administration. A report on agricultural development by the Subcommittee on Inter-American Economic Relations of the Joint Economic Committee stressed the need for "increased agricultural productivity, and still more increased agricultural productivity." [11] The subcommittee felt that land reform was a dangerous aspect of a program for the improvement of agriculture. Echoing the traditional landowners' elitist mistrust of the common man, the subcommittee spoke of the danger of the "illiterate or semi-literate cropper":

> It is frequently asserted, and even too frequently taken for granted, that an essential first step in increasing agricultural productivity and output of food and fiber for consumption and export in most of the South American countries lies in changing the landownership pattern.
>
> While the distribution of land to landless farmers may have justification on the grounds of equity and establishing the basis for free democracy, as land reform, the program ought not to rest exclusively on these grounds.
>
> The danger is that the illiterate, or semi-illiterate cropper on hearing of these plans will assume that he is soon to be freed from his traditional quasi-feudal role and have for his very own a plot in an Elysian field.[12]

As a result of their hearings and staff studies, the subcommittee called for an "official clarification" of the meaning and objectives of agrarian reform in the context of the Alliance for Progress. They were especially concerned with minimizing the role of the U.S. government as a participant, stating that a review of U.S. policy was not only in order but imperative. The subcommittee set forth its own guidelines:

The primary objective of agrarian reform measures should at all times be increased agricultural productivity . . .

Land reform is, thus, not exclusively a tenure problem but a problem of improved farming practices generally.[13]

The objective of land tenure changes is not to be punitively directed against large landholdings or absentee landowners as such: on the contrary, existing property rights under law are to be respected.

The programming and administration of agrarian reform is, and must remain, an internal matter for each of the several nations.[14]

Certainly the United States is not pressing for preconceived patterns of land tenure or agrarian reform; least of all can it undertake unilaterally to assure individual croppers of its support of ultimate landownership, no matter how seemingly meritorious cases may be.

As a first step in land reform and possible redistribution, the respective participating countries should look first to public lands and lands not presently under cultivation.[15]

The emphasis was on: (a) production; (b) improving farm practices generally; (c) protecting existing property rights (including absentee owners); (d) undermining attempts to reorient U.S. policy away from support of the big landowners ("internal matters"); and (e) focusing on public lands for distribution (apparently not an "internal matter"). It must further be noted that *nowhere* in the Alliance for Progress Charter is land redistribution set down as a sufficient condition for modernization. It is always linked to technical assistance, increased credit, better education, and improved roads and marketing facilities, all of which are seen as factors in bringing about increased productivity. The congressional warnings had a different intent. By keeping the focus on production and protection of property rights, Congress kept the pressure on the structural reformers. As a result, even in official definitions of the term "land reform," certain productionist themes are clear. For example, the Land Policy Statement, issued by the United States Agency for International Development (AID) on August 28, 1962, considered land reform to include only (1) natural resource surveys and inventories; (2) economic studies and research of land uses and tenure patterns in relation to productivity, efficiency, and social problems; (3) physical improvement of the land, e.g., fertilizers, reclamation projects; (4) land tenure adjustments through institutional changes in the adjustment of people to the land; (5) supervised agricultural credit; and (6) training and educational programs for officials and farmers.[16] The AID was limited to providing capital assistance in the form of loans and grants to help defray certain administrative costs involved in carrying on land reform programs: it could help finance the cost of supervised agricultural credit programs, land reclamation projects, and public facilities in areas where land reforms are being executed.[17] However, the Social Progress Trust Fund, instituted in the Eisenhower administration and incorporated within the Alliance machinery, was explicitly barred from allocating funds for the purchase of agricultural land.[18]

AID's interpretation of congressional intent regarding agricultural programs, congressional resistance to such use of funds, current AID emphasis on support for discrete projects rather than broad reform programs, and the pressure of U.S. and Latin American landowning elites made it likely that the prohibition against the use of U.S. funds to purchase land would exist in practice. Assistance for gradual change (for example, credit and technical assistance given to colonists who settled new lands) continued. Executive as well as administrative accommodation to conservative congressional pressure would seem to indicate that productionist values took precedence over those of the redistributionist at a very early stage. If this is the case, then the continuity in policy between the Kennedy and Johnson years seems to be greater than suspected—in the direction of a more conservative agricultural development policy. There is considerable evidence to substantiate such a position, quite apart from that presented above.

The legislation authorizing the Alliance gave priority to agrarian reform measures. Title VI of the Foreign Assistance Act of 1962 directed the President to

> assist in fostering measures of agrarian reform, including colonization and redistribution of land, with a view to insuring a wider and more equitable distribution of the ownership of land.[19]

The actual meaning of these general policy objectives was "clarified" by Lincoln Gordon (then a consultant to the President's Task Force on Latin America and later Ambassador to Brazil and Regional Assistant Secretary under President Johnson). The kind of agrarian reform policies which would be supported by the United States through the Inter-American Development Bank, according to Gordon, are clearly defined in accordance with the strategy of modernization from above:

> Senator Kuchel: . . . It was suggested that by reason of the veto which the U.S. has in the two-thirds loan situation that we would be interested in the internal affairs of those countries when we made loans perhaps to the extent of indicating our belief on land policy. Is that true?
> Lincoln Gordon: . . . I think it is a little more complex than that . . . The idea is to try to force the owners, if they don't want to pay the taxes (on the land), to sell the land and make it available for ownership by smaller farmers as a result. This also seems to us a very useful kind of redistribution. Our thought is that the Bank would in such cases make loans available for helping the small farmer to get properly settled on the land. They would be for agricultural credit, perhaps in certain cases it is inaccessible land, for building access roads, for assistance to cooperatives in developing marketing and storage facilities for food and other agricultural crops and things of that kind.[20]

The idea of taxing owners in order to make them productive and efficient certainly is an important component of the productionist approach. Gordon's notion that poor *campesinos* will be in a position to acquire those lands which will be put on the market surely overlooks the obvious; other large landowners, and even those not presently connected with the agrarian sector (industrialists) who want a "hedge against inflation," are in a far better financial position to purchase land made available by the process he mentions.

There are two themes in Gordon's statement. First, that land reform will be accomplished by taxing owners into selling unprofitable land. The result would seem to be that the land could only be purchased by those efficient farmers with excess capital—hardly the landless peasant class or those struggling in *minifundos*. Second, that the type of external assistance given should be oriented toward development of infrastructure. Gordon, having made clear what he means by "agrarian reform," goes on to suggest that U.S. aid will be used as a political lever: "We obviously can't say we are going to dictate the land reform legislation of another country, but we are going to provide help when the right kind of legislation is forthcoming and refrain from providing help where it doesn't [isn't]." [21]

The then (1962) Assistant Secretary of State for Inter-American Affairs, Edwin M. Martin, had a different set of priorities from those of land reform and other institutional changes:

> It is not possible to have a sound and constructive economic development program in a situation in which there is not a reasonable degree of political stability and political maturity. Unless you have a reasonable degree of political stability the normal course of business just won't be conducted. We've had a few examples quite recently of political instability and business just stopped. Unless it's a strong government which has the respect of the people, it will not be able to secure the sacrifices in money and personnel

that are required to do a job of political and economic and social development.[22]

Martin's emphasis on the need for stability, a "businessman's political climate," strong government, and "sacrifice" fits the traditional conservative political order in Latin America. One can hardly imagine any situation where significant distribution of land takes place without this leading to some social dislocation, at least temporary "instability," flight of capital, and perhaps changes in government. It is beyond doubt that a number of the institutional changes stressed in the Charter of Punta del Este would have had a profound unstabilizing effect on many existing governments.

Because of the Alliance for Progress, the rhetoric of agrarian reform became respectable. Most liberal and conservative governments made appropriate symbolic gestures in this direction by passing agrarian reform laws that were largely ineffective. The United States did not demand more than "gestures"—because U.S. policy-makers themselves were not convinced of the necessity of agrarian reform. Attempts to make extensive changes through existing political channels met with local resistance which was effective because the socio-economic groups involved held political power. Such changes, if carried out, would result in a change in the distribution of wealth. Social reform would seem to entail some degree of violence, or at any rate, instability. With his usual understatement, Galbraith made the obvious (but frequently obscured) point.

> If the government of the country is dominated or strongly influenced by the landholding groups—the one that is losing its prerogatives—no one should expect effective land legislation as an act of grace. . . .[23]

The policy statements cited above, which reflect a productionist approach, date from 1961 (Gordon's testimony) and 1962 (Martin's statement); both, of course, are well before the end of the Kennedy administration. A full-scale attack on the redistribution concept then appeared in the Clay Report of March 20, 1963. This report emphasized productivity, elite modernization, and the trickle-down approach to social improvement as the best strategy for the recipients of U.S. aid. Policies to be undertaken were largely derived from conservative economic theory which dictates goals and tactics such as monetary stability, balanced budgets, elimination of subsidies to government enterprises, and stimulation of private capital investment. The last item on the list was a reference to the desirability of measures for the better utilization of land to "increase income on the lower levels of society." The report's basic position was that:

> Latin America must be encouraged to see its essential choice between totalitarian, state controlled economies and societies on the one hand and an economically and politically freer system on the other, realizing that a society must begin to accumulate wealth before it can provide an improved standard of living for its members.[24]

The Clay Report clearly states the primacy of U.S. ideological and economic interests in the Cold War; development criteria which do not coincide with the interests of the propertied investor class are thereby relegated to the opposite camp. Not all State Department officials were in agreement with this rigid line (as was also the case with Kennedy's advisers), but the trend since 1963 was toward a much more conservative position. John Moors Cabot, a former Assistant Secretary of State for Inter-American Affairs, acknowledged the priorities and constraints imposed by U.S. corporate interests on U.S. policy: "Whereas our policy seeks to promote reform and social justice in Latin America, the need to protect our large economic stake injects a conservative note into our policies." [25]

The redefinition of U.S. policy to mesh with the demands of the productionists can be seen in two excerpts from speeches of Teodoro Moscoso, the first Alliance coordinator:

The people of the United States are not prepared to support a large scale effort which they think will result in the perpetuation of social and economic systems that are structured so as to benefit the few to the detriment of the many . . . We are insisting on reforms as a condition of our material support to Latin America. We would rather withhold our assistance than to participate in the maintenance of a status quo characterized by social injustice. . . .

Agrarian reform . . . (as a big chapter in the Charter of the Alliance) gave rise very quickly to the misconception that all that was wanted or needed was the splitting up of the large landed estates which were owned by a few wealthy men who also played a decisive role in controlling the political destiny of their countries. But it is not this simple . . . I prefer to speak rather in terms of modernizing agriculture. By that we do not necessarily mean taking land away, dividing it up and redistributing it, but orderly reorganization, including possible changes in land tenure, supervised credit and extension service, and farm-to-market roads. . . . This is the rational way in which the Alliance is tackling the problems of agriculture. It is the right way. . . .[26]

Subtle changes in the meaning of terms, shifts in emphasis and priorities, and acknowledgment of difficulties and complexities highlight the shift from policies directed toward redistribution of land (and redistribution, therefore, of economic, social, and political resources) to policies designed for the maximization of incentives to the existing elite. The rather strong productionist emphasis found in Moscoso's statement suggests that the usual image of the Kennedy team as strong advocates of social reform under the Alliance may perhaps have been inflated. Lincoln Gordon has noted that

Some observers associate the loss of glamor in the Alliance with the death of President Kennedy, but the historical record cannot sustain the interpretation. The failure of the Alliance to catch fire as a political watchword was already evident by mid-1962, and the atmosphere surrounding the São Paulo meeting of economic ministers in November, 1963, only a few days before the Kennedy assassination, was one of frank crisis, with many delegates audibly wondering whether the Alliance would survive another year.[27]

Whatever the initial assumptions were behind the rhetoric of the original Alliance for Progress, it now appears that both U.S. and Latin America signatories of that document were either unprepared for the political pressures at home or were simply engaging in verbal exercises in order to exorcise the specter of Castro's agrarian reform or perhaps both. Thus, from the early years, the modernization-from-above strategy predominated in the actions if not in the rhetoric of the Kennedy administration.

President Johnson's policy followed the same direction. On the third anniversary of the founding of the Alliance, he stated:

> Through land reform aimed at increased production, taking different forms in each country, we can provide those who till the soil with self respect and increased income, and each country with increased production to feed the hungry and to strengthen the economy.[28]

A number of points emerge both from what Johnson stated and from what he omitted. Production is the overriding goal. The pay-off for the *campesino* is "self-respect" and increased income, not land. The *campesino* will apparently continue tilling the soil for the *latifundista*. Thomas Mann, Johnson's Assistant Secretary of State for Inter-American Affairs, reiterated the productivity theme. While mentioning the abolition of the *minifundia,* Mann omitted the need to undertake the other half of the proposal in the Charter of Punta del Este—the abolition of *latifundia:*

> Archaic land tenure systems still exist which must be revised within the objective of increasing productivity. This means the elimination of plots too small to be viable as

well as placing into production lands underemployed or idle. It also means supervised credit, extension service, research and all the other items of successful farming.[29]

Mann's visions of increased productivity and efficiency suggest that U.S. policy was largely designed to pressure existing elites to adopt measures to achieve these goals.

A variation on the productionist theme is the "national markets" program proposed by W. W. Rostow, then chairman of the State Department Policy Planning Board and U.S. delegate to the Inter-American Committee of the Alliance for Progress (CIAP), the latter's principal coordinating body. Rostow's prescriptions for solving the problems of the countryside emphasized a reliable and fair price for the landowners, more technical assistance, credit at reasonable rates to help finance shifts to cash crops, and improved methods for supplying manufactured goods at reasonable prices.[30] On the national level, Rostow argued for a build-up of agricultural productivity, especially in the higher-grade protein foods; improved marketing of agricultural products in the cities to guarantee reasonable prices in urban markets; a shift of industry to the production of simple agricultural equipment and consumer goods for the mass market; and the introduction of improved marketing methods for cheap manufactured goods, especially into rural areas:

> Applied, for example, to the Alliance for Progress in Latin America, this strategy would give the whole enterprise a new cast, a new dynamism. It would not alter the need for improved methods of tax collection, for land reform in certain areas, for increased investment in education, housing, and health. But it would supply an operational objective in which private enterprise would have scope for real initiative and creativeness, a real basis for collaboration with governments, and a way of demonstrating to all the peoples its inherent virtues. What greater reality could the Alliance for Progress have than if it began to yield a drop in food costs to the urban consumer; a shift in rural population to new, higher quality and higher productivity

products; full utilization and rapid expansion in industrial plant; and an enlarged flow of fertilizers, farm equipment, and industrial products to the villages at reduced prices.[31]

Rostow's exhortation for better marketing conditions seems more suited to comforting the "true believers" of free enterprise than to dealing with the issues confronting the underemployed and unemployed landless *campesinos* of Latin America. The benefits of agricultural improvements within present-day society would increasingly become concentrated in the hands of those who already control important social and economic resources. Rostow's account furthermore fails to deal with the agro-commercial elites who monopolize the marketing of produce and credits. They would, of course, continue to flourish, given the free play of private enterprise that Rostow proposes. Capital-intensive farming, while it might increase productivity, would also increase rural unemployment, driving tens of thousands of *campesinos* from the farm to urban areas where industry cannot provide adequate employment. Rostow's proposals were based on the familiar but faulty assumption that an "invisible hand" arranges the social order to everyone's satisfaction—a proposition which hardly fits with the historical experience of those social classes adversely affected by the free play of free enterprise.

In 1967, Congress gave official approval to the modernization-from-above theme in a resolution which states in part:

> Whereas the achievement of this goal (self-sustaining growth) is in great part dependent upon an accelerated movement to integrate the economies of Latin American countries and a major effort to modernize the education and agricultural sectors, with special emphasis on science and technology. . . . Further, the Congress recommends that the United States provide an increase in assistance under the Alliance for Progress for programs of educational and agricultural modernization and improvement of health. The nature and amount of such assistance is to be depend-

ent on demonstrated need and adequate self-help within the recipient countries.[32]

Science, technology, and education were defined as the means for uplifting Latin America. Modernization no longer involved re-ordering the social structure. In the meantime, even the very existence of the problems was becoming less obvious to U.S. policy-makers—assistance was to be given on "demonstrated need." Furthermore, the aid for promoting the program of modernization from above was no longer to be so freely given—it was premised on "self-help." The conventional prescriptions of the 1950s were once again the vogue. Policy-makers no longer expressed the same urgency as in the years immediately after the Cuban agrarian revolution. Kennedy's revolutionary rhetoric of the early 1960s was increasingly displaced by greater emphasis on private enterprise and individual initiative, ideas supplied by those of his former advisers who continued to serve under President Johnson.

U.S. policy-makers now seemed increasingly to think of Latin American agrarian problems in terms of food production. Consequently they devised policies which were designed to increase production through improved technology, without much concern for the eventual distribution of either the food itself or the income derived from it.[33] In short, U.S. policy embraced technical modernization without structural reform.

In 1965, Simon Hanson pointed to the end of the era of reformist rhetoric when he noted:

The Latin Americans might still remember the social objectives envisaged in Kennedy's classic plea: "No society is free until its people have an equal opportunity to share the fruits of their own land." But the day of the dream was gone and the State Department hailing its departure from the land-distribution plan of land for the landless, put it flatly: "The main thing is to make available the range of services and supplies needed by farmers to increase their output." Achievement? [34]

The Triumph of Gradualism

From the very beginning, and except for a few "rhetorical" examples, the Alliance does not now appear to have been concerned with developing specific measures to implement a general redistributionist policy, but only with general denunciations of "unjust" systems of tenure. Even during the Kennedy years the emphasis of official rhetoric was not on expropriation of large landholdings, except in the case of the traditional *haciendas,* which were condemned because they were inefficient operations. Landless laborers on efficient plantations were not included in the redistributive plans of the Alliance. Intensity of land use as the basis for expropriation introduced a different concept of social justice. According to this notion, what was crucial was not peasant needs but the owners' efficiency. According to these criteria, the expropriation of large landholdings which were fully utilized was unjust. This would suggest that "land fulfills its social function when it is fully used," regardless of how it may be used and to whom the benefits derived may accrue.[35] The result of such a policy was to shift the emphasis from the elimination of social inequality stemming from unequal distribution of resources to the consideration of policy measures which would result in increased production. The ambivalence in the Kennedy administration on the redistribution-productionist issue was the basis for the subsequent easy transition to a completely productionist point of view.

Only President Kennedy himself, and then in a public speech, spoke of redistribution without co-reference to increased production and modernization of the rural sector. The most reasonable conclusion appears to be that U.S. policy-makers saw land redistribution only as one more or less equal variable that could affect production, to be considered together with credit programs, technical assistance, marketing facilities, transportation, and several others.

Redistribution was viewed as a tool to be used together with the others to produce greater production. It was not viewed as a critical social issue, but as an economic issue (and a rather minor one at that) and except perhaps for Kennedy, it was seldom considered as a primary social problem. Expropriation and redistribution only of unused and inefficiently used land was stressed from the beginning by the Alliance.

Additional evidence in support of the triumph of the productionists is found in the individual and collective attitudes of those U.S. officials who are responsible for implementing U.S. policy. A typical response by a senior U.S. AID official to the question of U.S. emphasis on agrarian reform is:

> everybody in the Agency (AID)—any economist—has argued himself out of it for a number of reasons. First, land reform means a decrease in production. Second, it means a disruption of marketing and credit and transportation. Third, it's just too costly. Fourth, and it's not said overtly, land reform is against the tide of history. History shows that the trend has been the consolidation of land . . . you can't resolve agricultural poverty. . . . Fifth, people are pessimistic about carrying the reform out. You just can't force vested interests to carry the load. . . .[36]

Another high-ranking official responded to a similar question—the U.S. response to Latin America's agrarian sector problems—revealing agreement on the value of production:

> The key is agricultural production. The mechanisms to do this are many. You can redistribute land and income, but the first fundamental thing to do is to increase production . . .[37]

In fact, the attitudes individually expressed in over forty in-depth interviews with the major U.S. AID officials connected with Latin American agricultural development programs[38] support the idea that productivity is the fundamental and highest priority item in U.S. response to Latin

American agricultural problems. In stressing productionist values, these officials revealed their hostility to structural reform.

The Impact of the Incremental Approach

The test of any public policy is its effectiveness in terms of fulfilling its objectives. The gradual-change or productionist approach to agricultural development in Latin America has had ample time to prove itself as an effective strategy in the development of viable agrarian sectors in Latin American nations. To measure the success of this approach we employed the same indicators as those proposed by the architects of this policy, namely the growth of: (1) per capita agricultural production, (2) per capita agricultural food production, and (3) agricultural imports. Tables I, II, and III summarize the results.

In terms of per capita agricultural production during the Alliance for Progress years, 1961–1968, the incremental approach has thus been a singular failure. By 1968, over half the Latin countries had failed even to maintain the 1961 level of per capita food production. Over one-third of the Latin countries had seen a decline of over 10 percent during this same period. Only one country achieved the 2.5 percent per capita growth rate which economists assumed to be an adequate minimum. Finally, the two most populous countries of South America, Argentina and Brazil, suffered a decline in per capita production between 1961 and 1968.

The performance of the Latin American countries in the area of food production was also dismal. The indices of per capita food production show that almost half of the countries regressed in the period between 1961 and 1968. Another third of the Latin countries showed little or no improvement. Only two countries, Nicaragua and Venezuela, achieved the minimum rates of growth projected in the Alliance for Progress. Stagnation and regression in the produc-

TABLE I

INDICES OF PER CAPITA AGRICULTURAL PRODUCTION,
BY COUNTRY, 1961–1968
(1957–59 = 100)

COUNTRY	1961	1962	1963
Mexico	100	106	104
Dominican Republic	94	93	90
Haiti	103	91	82
Costa Rica	105	101	97
El Salvador	115	111	120
Guatemala	108	120	121
Honduras	100	101	99
Nicaragua	113	128	135
Panama	95	91	91
Argentina	97	97	107
Bolivia	99	95	98
Brazil	104	101	103
Chile	95	90	96
Colombia	96	98	96
Ecuador	111	108	103
Paraguay	98	101	100
Peru	114	111	106
Uruguay	105	104	107
Venezuela	98	102	112
Latin America (19 countries)[1]	102	102	103

[1] Excludes Cuba, Guyana, Jamaica, and Trinidad and Tobago.
Source: *Indices of Agricultural Production for the Western Hemisphere* (excluding the U.S.), U.S. Department of Agriculture, May, 1969, p. 4.

tion of food may contribute to political insurgency and undermine attempts at industrial development.

In connection with declining production, between 1961 and 1966 Latin America as a whole has increased its imports of agricultural goods by 40 percent. Only two countries, Costa Rica and Venezuela, have lowered their dollar imports of agricultural goods through the substitution of

1964	1965	1966	1967	Prelim. 1968
109	114	111	108	111
86	77	78	73	69
79	79	73	70	67
88	88	96	98	106
119	101	102	108	97
115	128	113	117	112
104	107	97	103	103
164	145	148	142	138
98	109	105	103	105
103	93	98	103	95
97	93	93	87	88
91	115	100	104	98
92	95	94	94	96
97	93	90	92	93
103	106	107	111	102
95	95	88	97	88
109	104	103	97	93
114	109	99	86	94
110	113	114	117	114
98	105	100	103	99

local production. Because many of its agricultural products are geared to the export market, Latin America has failed to produce a diversified agricultural sector that can even keep up with the needs of its own population. These data give us some measure of the inadequate performance of the modernization-from-above strategy. The promises of efficiency and growth which were to result from the incrementalist approach have yet to be realized. If present trends are any indication of the future and if present policies are continued,

TABLE II

INDICES OF PER CAPITA FOOD PRODUCTION, BY COUNTRY, 1959–1968

(1957–59 = 100)

COUNTRY	1961	1962	1963
Mexico	101	106	105
Dominican Republic	92	93	87
Haiti	99	96	85
Costa Rica	98	100	92
El Salvador	97	104	103
Guatemala	100	105	110
Honduras	111	114	121
Nicaragua	94	91	89
Argentina	96	97	108
Bolivia	99	95	98
Brazil	105	108	109
Chile	95	90	97
Colombia	97	102	97
Ecuador	109	106	103
Paraguay	97	96	94
Peru	110	106	102
Uruguay	106	105	110
Venezuela	100	104	116
Latin America (18 countries)[1]	101	103	105

[1] Excludes Cuba, Guyana, Jamaica, Trinidad and Tobago, and Panama.
Source: *Indices of Agricultural Production for the Western Hemisphere* (excluding the U.S.), U.S. Department of Agriculture, March, 1969, p. 9.

social problems stemming from economic and political inequalities may be exacerbated rather than ameliorated. The increasing dependence on food imports and the increasing costs will limit the purchasing power of the lower classes and the capacity to import capital goods needed for industrial development.[39] Declining living standards and urban migration without industrial employment could provide a

1964	1965	1966	1967	Prelim. 1968
111	115	117	115	118
84	77	79	73	71
80	79	80	76	72
96	87	91	93	102
95	96	105	100	105
106	108	108	104	106
132	126	134	133	135
99	111	105	103	106
105	93	99	108	98
97	93	92	87	88
108	121	113	118	114
98	96	94	95	96
97	99	97	97	99
103	102	104	107	100
92	91	85	90	79
106	103	105	106	97
121	117	102	87	101
115	119	121	126	122
105	109	107	110	106

basis for explosive urban politics in the not too distant future. In brief, U.S. agricultural policy has failed to provide a viable alternative to the structural reforms advocated but not implemented during the early years of the Alliance.

Conclusion

It may well be that U.S. policy is concerned primarily with neither increasing production nor land reform, both of

TABLE III

AGRICULTURAL IMPORTS 1961–1966
(millions of U.S. Dollars)

COUNTRY	1961	1962	1963	1964	1965	1966
Argentina	85.0	76.6	59.8	97.3	112.7	110.5
Bolivia	17.8	25.8	27.6	26.9	26.4	24.0
Brazil	189.7	262.2	279.7	315.2	222.2	290.1[2]
Chile	97.2	129.4	176.6	172.2	146.0	166.2
Colombia	64.3	57.6	44.4	65.7	56.6	94.3[3]
Costa Rica	23.2	12.6	12.9	14.9	17.2	20.0
Dominican Republic	6.3	23.9	29.8	45.1	27.1	33.4
Ecuador	12.7	14.3	14.7	20.2	17.3	14.4
El Salvador	19.5	25.0	26.7	28.8	32.2	36.7
Guatemala	18.4	19.4	22.1	22.4	27.2	20.6
Haiti	5.4	6.9	7.6	6.8	8.9[1]	8.6
Honduras	8.5	9.4	11.4	12.5	13.4	17.4
Mexico	73.0	81.8	132.6	116.7	116.4	110.9
Nicaragua	7.6	10.7	10.2	14.3	17.1	19.3
Panama	18.2	18.8	18.6	21.6	20.9	22.0
Paraguay	5.9	6.3	6.2	6.8	6.8	6.7
Peru	76.1	83.6	88.3	96.9	121.4	134.1
Uruguay	28.6	25.6	24.4	29.1	20.4	44.5
Venezuela	186.6	172.7	174.5	176.1	179.4	148.1
Total	944.0	1,062.6	1,168.1	1,289.5	1,189.6	1,321.8

Total (excluding Cuba)
[1] ERS estimate.
[2] 1967 = 338.3.
[3] 1967 = 69.6.
Source: Data were kindly provided by William Gasser, chief, Western Hemisphere Branch, Foreign Regional Analysis Division of the United States Department of Agriculture, May 16, 1969.

which, as we have seen, have been at one time or another stated policy goals. It may be considered beside the point to evaluate the effectiveness of U.S. policy from either standpoint. U.S. policy-makers may have different criteria of success from those explicitly stated. U.S. agricultural policy may be considered a success from a political angle: it solidifies support among its traditional right-wing allies among the landholding elite. The productionist argument may be nothing more than code language for continuing support and cooperation with the traditional landed oligarchy. Historical and statistical data conclusively show that the landowners have not substantially improved agricultural production or the condition of the agricultural population. Theoretical discussion concerned with production may in fact be nothing more than ideological apologies for the political status quo. The landholding elite has usually favored close relationships with the U.S., consistently lines up with the U.S. internationally, and supports U.S. business and economic penetration of Latin American society. The quid pro quo is U.S. support of the traditional landowners, rationalized in the form of discourses on productionist values. In a word, for U.S. policy-makers economic considerations seem to be subordinate to political ones, i.e., the necessity of establishing counter-revolutionary alliances on a sound political basis.[40]

NOTES

1. Ernest Feder, "Land Reform in Latin America," *Social Order,* Vol. 11 (January, 1961), p. 2. It is interesting to note that in the two most recent articles on Latin America in the Establishment-oriented *Foreign Affairs* (the organ of the Council on Foreign Relations) no attempt was made to discuss Latin American agricultural development in a thorough, scholarly manner. Instead, both articles were little more than apologies for present U.S. Latin American development policy. See: George C. Lodge, "U.S. Aid to Latin America: Funding Radical Change," *Foreign Affairs,* Vol. 47, No. 4 (July, 1969), pp. 735–49; and Frances M. Foland, "Agrarian Reform in Latin America," *Foreign Affairs,* Vol. 48, No. 1 (October, 1969), pp. 97–112.

2. The following terms are interchangeably used for the structural reform school: comprehensive approach, redistributive approach, distributionist or distribution strategy, modernization from below, redistributionist policy. Synonyms for the incremental change school include: productionist, productionist approach, productivity theme, technical modernization, modernization from above, gradualist approach.

3. Victor Alba, *Alliance Without Allies* (N.Y.: Frederick A. Praeger, 1965), p. 194.

4. U.S. Congress, Joint Economic Committee, Subcommittee on Inter-American Economic Relationships, *Hearings on Economic Development in South America,* 87th Congress, 1st Session, 1962, p. 12.

5. Increased mechanization of agriculture eliminates the need for manual labor and, consequently, decreases jobs in the rural sector, resulting in the redundancy of the rural laborer. Given the very limited absorption ability of the industrialization process, the rural unemployed usually become the penny venders and slum dwellers who increasingly are found in and around all the major metropolitan areas of Latin America.

6. John F. Kennedy, "Alliance for Progress, A Program for the Peoples of the Americas," *Department of State Bulletin,* Vol. 45 (August 28, 1961), pp. 355–56.

7. "Charter of Punta del Este Establishing an Alliance for Progress Within the Framework of Operation Pan America," Title I, Section 6.

8. "Declaration of the Presidents of America" (Punta del Este: April 15, 1967), p. 15.

9. *Ibid.*

10. U.S. Congress, Senate, Foreign Affairs Committee, Subcommittee on American Republics Affairs, *Survey of the Alliance for Progress: Problems of Agriculture* (Testimony of William C. Thiesenhusen and Marion R. Brown), 90th Congress, 1st Session, 1967, p. 2.

11. U.S. Congress, Joint Economic Committee, Subcommittee on Inter-American Economic Relations, *A Report on Economic Policies and Programs in South America,* 87th Congress, 2nd Session, 1962, p. 21.

12. *Ibid.,* p. 22. The last sentence of this quotation reveals the cynical contempt which many U.S. officials have toward the expectations for improvement held by many Third World people. This statement and others like it will hardly impress the Latin American peasantry with the humanity and beneficence of U.S. policy-makers.

13. *Ibid.,* p. 23.

14. *Ibid.,* p. 24.

15. *Ibid.,* pp. 24–25.

16. V. Webster Johnson and Baldwin H. Kristjanson, "Programming for Land Reform in the Developing Agricultural Countries of Latin America," *Land Economics,* Vol. 39 (November, 1964), p. 357.

17. *Ibid.*

18. U.S. Congress, Joint Economic Committee, *A Report . . . , op. cit.,* Article I, Section 1.04 (a). The prohibition has been observed by U.S.A.I.D. as well.

19. U.S. Congress, Senate, Committee on Appropriations, *Hearings on*

Inter-American Social and Economic Cooperation Program and the Chilean Reconstruction and Rehabilitation Program, 87th Congress, 1st Session, 1961, p. 64.

20. *Ibid.*

21. *Ibid.*, p. 65.

22. Quotation from Edwin M. Martin, *U.S. News and World Report*, August 6, 1962.

23. J. Kenneth Galbraith, "Conditions for Economic Change in Underdeveloped Countries," *Journal of Farm Economics*, Vol. 33 (November, 1951), p. 695.

24. Committee to Strengthen the Security of the Free World, *The Scope and Distribution of United States Military and Economic Assistance Programs* (Washington, D.C.: 1963), p. 13.

25. *New York Times*, November 7, 1963, p. 19.

26. John C. Drier (ed.), *Alliance For Progress: Problems and Perspectives* (Baltimore: Johns Hopkins Press, 1962), pp. 94–95.

27. Lincoln Gordon, "Punta del Este Revisited," *Foreign Affairs*, Vol. 45, No. 4 (July, 1967), p. 635.

28. Kenneth L. Karst, "Latin American Land Reform: The Uses of Confiscation," *Michigan Law Review*, Vol. 63 (December, 1964), p. 327.

29. Simon Hanson, "The Alliance for Progress: The Third Year," *Inter-American Economic Affairs*, Vol. 18 (Spring, 1965), p. 107.

30. Walt W. Rostow, "Deeper Roots for the Alliance for Progress," *Americas*, Vol. 17 (April, 1965), p. 39.

31. Walt W. Rostow, *Americas, op. cit.,* p. 41.

32. U.S. Congress, House of Representatives, Committee on Foreign Affairs, *Support for A New Phase of The Alliance for Progress*, 90th Congress, 1st Session, 1967, p. 2.

33. U.S. Congress, Senate, Foreign Affairs Committee, Subcommittee on American Republics Affairs, *Survey of the Alliance for Progress: Problems of Agriculture, op. cit.,* p. 2.

34. Simon Hanson, *op. cit.,* p. 76.

35. Ernest Feder, "Land Reform Under the Alliance for Progress," *Journal of Farm Economics*, Vol. 47 (August, 1965), p. 658.

36. Interview with U.S. AID official, August, 1968.

37. Interview with U.S. AID official, September, 1968.

38. See Chapter 9.

39. Agricultural export sector earnings have increased to the benefit of those who produce Latin American export product specialties—bananas, sugar, coffee, etc.—and not domestically consumed foodstuffs. Such increases tend to benefit U.S. interests since a large portion of this sector is foreign owned.

40. Redistribution of land in and of itself may not lead to a revolutionary society, as Irish and Japanese experience can readily testify.

However, given the present political alignments in Latin America, it is hardly possible that land redistribution will take place without the occurrence of a violent revolution led by a revolutionary socialist movement. In those circumstances the agrarian revolution would form an integral part of a societal transformation condition that would seriously weaken the chances of a petit-bourgeois peasantry directing the post-revolutionary polity toward a traditionally conservative society.

9

Perceptions of Issues and Problems in Latin American Development by U.S. Officials: The Sixties

Introduction

A great variety of analysts and political figures have noted that United States aid programs and their vehicle for implementing assistance, the U.S. Agency for International Development or AID, have not contributed to the development of Latin America but have been self-serving. Former Peruvian President Fernando Belaunde once stated:

> AID is very feminine; it never says no, but it always says *maybe*. We told them what we wanted and they said *maybe*. What we need to do first (according to AID) is a preliminary study. That takes some time. Then I go back and present the preliminary study but AID says we now need a feasibility study. That takes time and by the time we finish the feasibility study, I am in a plane flying to Argentina.[1] *AID is a U.S. machine to export bureaucracy.*[2]

Harvey S. Perloff, former member of the Committee of Nine, Alliance for Progress, noted:

> One of the problems on the U.S. side (in assisting Latin American countries in development and reform) is that the AID program, as an integral instrument of U.S. policy, is

subject to the varied pressures and vagaries growing out of the complex U.S. policy interests in the hemisphere. AID is always susceptible to being used for advancing U.S. interests other than the development of its client countries.[3]

In terms of the strategic policy ends that are pursued, it has been noted that:

Over the last forty years, the survival of capitalism has rested on its ability to expand its control over resources and markets on a global scale. Expansion has been made possible by the increasing utilization of the state apparatus and a drastic increase in . . . "economic assistance." . . . The U.S. AID and its predecessors is by far the largest economic undertaking, utilizing some $130 billion since 1946. . . . (AID's programs) all promote and preserve "The Open Door" U.S. corporations now enjoy in trade and investment throughout the "Free World" . . . (Besides this major, indirect benefit from AID programs) several direct economic advantages are offered to U.S. business. . . .[4]

From different perspectives these critical assessments share the common belief that AID has not been employed as an instrument for encouraging the positive development of the countries in which it has operated. U.S. AID is almost always directed toward the interests of the United States, these interests largely coinciding with private corporate endeavors.

The foreign assistance legislation passed by Congress since World War II clearly indicates that this is in fact the proper interpretation of what constitutes U.S. interests abroad. Aid has too often been employed as an economic weapon or lever against a foreign government which seeks to exercise its sovereignty economically to the disadvantage of U.S. corporate interests.[5]

The activities of AID as an instrument of technical assistance or as a promoter of structural reform must be understood in terms of its priorities. These priorities include encouragement of development activities in recipient countries if and only if such activities do nothing to endanger the private, economic interests of the U.S. Nation-states which violate the international trade and investment policies of U.S. corporate interests may ultimately have to confront congressional displeasure and executive curtailment of aid.

In this context, it is important to discuss and analyze the issues and problems in Latin American development as perceived by officials of the United States Agency for International Development. We will concern ourselves with the AID interpretation of congressional and executive directives as they guide and illuminate program development and implementation during the decade of the sixties. We will consider the statements of values, program priorities, and general and specific goals and objectives made by those individuals closest to the operational aspects of foreign assistance.[6] The attitudes and perceptions of AID officials toward what constituted the major problems in Latin American development have relevance not only for our examination of the U.S. "contribution" to Latin American development in the preceding decade but are significant for what will occur in the 1970s.

To examine the AID perspective, we will discuss and analyze AID's perceptions of development, the role of agrarian reform in agricultural development, and strategy and techniques. Before proceeding, it is important to emphasize that it was AID which was assigned the technical and financial assistance responsibilities connected with the Alliance for Progress. It seems ironic that this agency, most of whose personnel had served with AID's predecessor agencies and, thus, were accustomed to serving U.S. interests abroad, was given the task of encouraging reform in Latin America. It was a case of the supporters of the status quo being given the opportunity to oversee "peaceful, revolutionary change." The following will examine how the AID bureaucracy handled the Kennedy call for structural reform as a requisite for U.S. financial aid and how AID contributed to what one observer called the "greatest failure for the Alliance for Progress." [7]

Perceptions of Development

AID officials held a variety of approaches and operational definitions of development.[8] Some strongly endorsed what they considered to be the current economic development fad: the Rostowian approach to economic growth. According to this viewpoint:

> Agricultural development is not a tough problem. Rostow's definition of agriculture is most useful. His view is most common on agricultural development. According to Rostow, development is the rapid extension to the wide population of command over resources, etc. You can measure development in terms of the expansion of production, the improvement of distribution, the increase in supplies available for consumption in marketing channels.[9]

Other officials were hostile to the Rostow approach:

> It's ridiculous to have a guy like Rostow in such a high position. His *Stages of Economic Growth* is a gross oversimplification of the development process.[10]

Most AID officials agreed that development, especially in the Latin American context, was a very complex process, involving many skills, resources, and a considerable amount of coordination—ingredients which, according to the same individuals, AID greatly lacked.

Among the AID personnel connected with Latin America, there appeared to be a split between those with tenure and those recently hired during the Kennedy/Johnson period. The old-timers resented the newcomers and articulated this resentment in the form of caustic remarks concerning lack of experience in AID missions and, of course, politics:

Kennedy let a lot of our people go. We used to have 6,000 agricultural people; then they cut us to 600. . . . We are losing a lot of our experienced people. I don't like the idea of some professor going out to manage a million dollar project when he doesn't have any experience. There is a definite shift in sending new people to Latin America. It's politics. You give the job to the people that help the party in power. The people in Washington are really inexperienced. They should choose people that have field experience.[11]

Likewise, the newcomers considered the agricultural technician as a representative of the past, an obstacle around which programs and administrators had to work. This conflict between old and new, the technician versus the economist, appears to have hampered any attempt to implement a consistent development policy within the agency headquarters:

> The mission director has great autonomy. His tenure is generally three years, really quite short. So he puts his emphasis on short-term projects. He usually wants to show a production increase in two or three years. So the system is biased against agrarian reform and other longer-range tasks.[12]

Although agreement on the meaning of development was lacking, there was consensus on the fact that it must be acceptable to prevailing elites:

> If a (Latin American) government leader says by pushing such a program that he is going to be overthrown, hell, do you think (the) State (Department) is going to push it?[13]

There was also a substantial amount of agreement regarding the key politico-economic factors in development:

> You must create jobs—in agriculture, banks, and services. In a capitalistic framework, you need attraction. Capital is international and impersonal. It moves when there is security, mobility, and profitability. Political stability is the key to the development process.[14]

AID's perception of development precluded wholesale, structural changes since such changes would be unacceptable to most Latin American political and economic elites and would therefore be unfeasible from AID's standpoint. AID officials tended to define development as a process to be implemented in partnership with landed and other political-economic elites, an arrangement which depended on stabilizing existing political and social relations. When a legitimate, government-sanctioned segment of the Chilean bureaucracy sought to initiate reforms from below (through peasant mobilization), AID officials were incapable of relating to the agency, and the Chilean agency, in turn, refused to follow AID's advice on reform:

> we had a small farm demonstration operation that was supposed to cost $90,000 but it cost us $40,000 in fact. INDAP was supposed to pick thirty farmers for the project; but they never found more than fifteen. This was supposed to be an "impact" project, but it had no impact. . . . INDAP, which we did most of our work with, was, frankly, leftist-oriented. They never wanted to carry through with AID projects.[15]

Perceptions of Agrarian Reform and Agricultural Development

AID perceptions of the role of agriculture and, to a lesser extent, agrarian reform reflect an uncertainty concerning the proper developmental "mix" in terms of sectoral priorities:

> In the 1940s and 1950s, industry was thought to be the key. Agriculture was seen as being something passive that you could drain resources from without need of replacement. In the 1960s, both the profession (economics) and the policy-makers (AID) see agriculture as playing the critical role. Now agriculture is seen as being on a par with the industrial sector.[16]

The program changes in individual countries illustrate the change from industrial to agricultural development. In Peru, for example:

> When the Alliance began, the strategy was more on the social welfare side. We had a big push in the Altiplano. Now the big pitch is productivity—a big increase in agricultural output on current farm land or increased land in production. There is little concern on raising the income of the farmer. . . . (This change occurred when) the macro-economists came into power. At the beginning of the period, Peru was not a food importer, it had the money to buy capital goods outside the country, it had foreign exchange reserves. By the end of the period, Peru had gone broke.
> There was also a shift in thinking among long-term agency personnel. The whole agency has changed. The changes in Peru antedated this. Now, the watchword is the "Green Revolution." [17]

The same was apparently true in the Dominican Republic:

> The first priority with the Dominican Republic is agriculture. . . . There has been a big impetus since 1965. The prime focus has been on productivity. . . .[18]

And for Ecuador:

> For three years (early 1960s), we were trying to set up a miniature USDA in Ecuador. Since then, the thinking has changed. We are now focusing on increased agricultural production, on developing new crops (rice).[19]

All country personnel interviewed responded similarly. Agriculture had increasingly captured AID's interest and attention. AID officials, following the lead of William S. Gaud, AID director, generally supported the notion that a Green Revolution was occurring and that this was the key to developmental success. Not all AID officials felt that agriculture and agricultural productivity had been given the priority it deserved. In fact, some indicated that in reality, agriculture was less of a priority sector now than prior to Kennedy/Johnson:

> Ever since the management people, the programmers, and planners came in, agriculture has been fifth or sixth in priority.[20]

On the whole, however, it was the consensus of most AID people that the Green Revolution strategy was the U.S. response to the ills of the underdeveloped countries:

> We have got to get these countries to be productive. We should concentrate on training and research. The emphasis should be on the technical assistance side.[21]

Also,

> I've long felt that agriculture is fundamental to developing economies. I was the first to believe so in the World Bank. You must improve agriculture in the first instance. The one thing most desperately needed is a substantial improvement in agriculture.[22]

Agrarian reform was not perceived as an integral aspect of agricultural development despite the supposedly reform nature of the Alliance for Progress:

> Agrarian reform was the cornerstone under Kennedy. But everybody in the agency—any economist—has argued himself out of it for a number of reasons. First, land reform means a decrease in production. Second, it means a disruption of marketing and credit and transportation. Third, it is just too costly. Fourth, and it's not said overtly (this is Lauchlin Currie's thesis in Colombia[23]), land reform is against the tide of history. The argument is that you should consolidate (the land) and as people move to the city, mechanize. They (Currie) say that you can't resolve agricultural poverty so it's cheaper to provide mass units of education and health. Fifth, people are pessimistic about carrying the reform out. You just can't force vested interests to carry the load. . . . (In fact,) AID programs in Colombia are diametrically opposed to land reform. They insist that certain lands not be expropriated. . . . We

(AID) are not pushing these countries (Latin American) on social progress. In fact, we are heavily against this in the Dominican Republic.[24]

AID programs in Latin America viewed agricultural development as a matter of production and as a means of maintaining the landed elite. Land reform was viewed as undesirable and, more importantly for AID programming, unfeasible.[25] The productionist stress is clearly seen in the following:

> At no point in time since the beginning of the Alliance has the U.S. approach to agricultural development been anything but productionist. One of the goals of the Alliance was agrarian reform. But the emphasis has been on increasing agricultural output. The main emphasis has been to increase the size of the economic pie; and then to worry about redistribution of income.[26]

AID officials were generally preoccupied with gross agricultural production figures, attacking agrarian reform as an obstacle to short-term growth. In addition, some officers indicated political reasons for the productionist approach:

> Of course, land reform is a risk because you're going to disrupt the marketing system, etc., and perhaps even suffer a drastic drop in production. But, the State Department does not want to take risks on reform.[27]

The rationale against reform was built on a blind faith in the operations of the market, the profit motive, and stability to ensure agricultural progress:

> Agrarian reform in Japan did not stem the tide. Just giving a guy the land is not going to help solve the problem. You must also do things like taking the lid off food prices in the cities to make farming profitable. This is what we've encouraged in Brazil. And in fact we are holding down inflation in Brazil because of agriculture.[28]

A fearful attitude toward social change reinforced this blind belief in the virtues of the existing free enterprise system:

little effort has gone into actual reform and most has gone into production increases. All of us, even with the best interests of the deprived at heart find it hard to overcome vested interests. They (the vested interests) are the big key to stability. (For example,) if the president supported a large-scale reform program in Guatemala, the government would be overthrown. In Guatemala (and elsewhere) it is an extremely delicate situation.[29]

Finally, in the countries which at least expressed a strong interest in reforming land tenure (Chile, for example), AID actually terminated some agricultural programs:

We really had only a few projects in agriculture. We just got a new mission director who had a new approach. We sent all of the agricultural technicians home. We pretty much got out of the agricultural area. We concentrated on higher priorities.[30]

AID's programs and priorities served to strengthen the status quo and to inhibit the redistribution of land (land tenure change). In this sense, AID officials reflected the prevailing thought and activities of the larger political and corporate interests which were also involved in Latin America.

AID Strategy and Techniques

The strategy and techniques employed by U.S. AID officials in the field supported those agricultural programs stressing productivity. The modernization-from-above approach required working closely if not entirely with landed elites. This was not a new strategy on the part of AID. In fact, contrary to the opinions of some AID officials,[31] working with Latin elites has been a cornerstone of U.S. technical assistance since the Good Neighbor Policy days:

We had to work with the oligarchy. To do demonstration work with limited funds, we had to work with the oligarchy. The main purpose of the *servicio* (a pre-Alliance institution) was to increase production. Since the big farmer had a lot of influence, you could have a bigger impact working through him. If you could get him to accept technological innovation, he'd pass it along to everyone below him.[32]

Although the rhetoric accompanying U.S. agricultural development assistance may have changed from pre-Alliance days to the Alliance period, the social orientation did not. Thus, AID officials revealed great similarities in describing present activities as compared with the past:

> We tie everything like agriculture to the middle and large-size farmers. We give aid to the farmers who have production capability and experience. The roadblock to development is not agriculture but a lack of industrialization and education.[33]

Some officials may not think that working through the elite is the most effective way to stimulate agricultural production, but they readily admit that this is AID's modus operandi:

> (I think) AID has consciously tried not to work exclusively with large farmers, but this is what has happened. AID has given large loans, given more credit to large landowners, many absentee ones. . . . AID does not go out and pick those farmers which were credit risks. In many cases, AID has over-capitalized farmers.[34]

Aid to small farmers or landless workers appears remote as far as AID officials are concerned.[35]

In terms of specific inputs and operations, the Alliance period did change AID operations at the highest levels:

> We got into capital development with Kennedy. All we had in the early days were technical assistance desks. Then State asked us for an overall economic picture of our countries and they wanted to know how much you needed to spend. I was terrified at economists like Hirschman coming in. Loans were made and they didn't move. The insti-

tutions in these countries didn't have the know-how to manage them.[36]

Large loans had a political purpose beyond stimulating economic development, according to some sources:

> The idea was to get leverage through loans. The idea was to tie a money transfer to a policy transfer.[37]

But there were some officials who opposed a large influx of money instead of skills:

> It's hard to put technical assistance on a loan basis. I think it's sad. Let's face it. Any minister of agriculture in Central America doesn't make more than $750.00 a month. O.K. Here we put in a loan and technical assistance, we insist on U.S. monitoring and technicians. Each guy you hire gets $25,000 a year. If you did that for the Latinos, you'd hear: "Are you selling out to the U.S.?" Many countries can't stand it (large amounts of money). A government (Latin American) man really isn't under our control. The guy says: "You give me a loan for technical assistance. I'm paying for the men hired. And you should tell me who I should have to hire?" Or, say, you bring in a top notch livestock man and the agriculture minister tells him to work on his and five friends of his farms. What do you do? [38]

Large loans were made available and were used by the landed elite for a number of purposes including, perhaps, agricultural development.

The consensus among AID officials as to the "necessity" of achieving agricultural development through elite modernization was matched by a uniformly patronizing view of potential lower-class clientele:

> You need supervision otherwise the farmer would probably spend the money on booze.[39]

AID attitudes toward Latin American development and the role of agrarian reform, and the strategy and techniques that were utilized were compatible with the wider interests of U.S. and Latin American propertied groups. By making available to elites considerable economic resources and, to a lesser extent, technical advice, U.S. aid contributed toward inhibiting basic social changes. The plight of the subsistence or below-subsistence farmer or the large number of landless agricultural workers was virtually ignored by AID. U.S. foreign aid bureaucrats assumed that what was good for the landlord would be good for the tenant. The result has been the maintenance of traditional patterns. As Perloff noted:

> Although both the U.S. AID Agency and the Inter-American Development Bank have given high priority to loans and technical assistance to Latin American farming, the results have been disappointing. The traditional crops are still the mainstays of agriculture in almost every one of the Latin American countries.[40]

The entrenched agricultural elites have little incentive to increase production as long as they can maintain their accustomed style of life—now subsidized by U.S. taxpayers. As one AID official observed:

> The Latin American landowner might spend his AID credit money on agriculture, but he puts his own funds into other areas. So there is not a net gain for agriculture.[41]

NOTES

1. This refers to his ouster from office and his exile first to Argentina and then the United States.

2. Interview with Fernando Belaunde Terry, President of Peru from 1963 to 1968, in Ithaca, New York, December 11, 1968. His emphasis.

3. Harvey S. Perloff, *Alliance for Progress: A Social Invention in the Making* (Baltimore: The Johns Hopkins Press, 1969), p. 194.

4. Hector Melo and Israel Yost, "Funding the Empire: U.S. Foreign Aid, Part 1," *Nacla Newsletter*, 4, No. 2 (April, 1970), pp. 1 and 2. Concerning AID, on June 7, 1970, the chief of U.S. Foreign Assistance Programs publicly admitted that AID funds were used to finance CIA activities in Laos. This immediately raises the question of how many other countries were similarly treated.

5. The classic example of this was the use of the Hickenlooper Amendment in reaction to the Ceylonese government's nationalization of U.S. oil companies in 1963. All aid was terminated to Ceylon in an attempt to "punish" the Bandaranaike regime.

6. Many of these individuals are no longer with the Agency. However, their statements still have validity for understanding what has happened and what will occur with regard to U.S. aid to Latin America since there is evidence to indicate that the Nixon administration will not substantially change the major use of U.S. aid or AID. At best, what will occur is reorganization of AID and aid following the guidelines of the Peterson Report which emphasized regionalism, multinational financial corporations, and multilateral institutions (see: Task Force on International Development, *U.S. Foreign Assistance in the 1970s: A New Approach* [Washington, D.C.: Government Printing Office, March 4, 1970]). As some scholars have indicated, it appears that the administration has moved toward "fixing a policy for the region" using both the Peterson and Rockefeller Reports as the blueprints (see: Melo and Yost, *op. cit.*, p. 3). This kind of reorganization plus a reduction in economic assistance to Latin America appears to be the agenda for the early seventies (Charles Meyer, Nixon's Assistant Secretary of State for Inter-American Affairs and formerly a Sears, Roebuck executive with international experience, was quoted in the October, 1969, issue of *Fortune* as saying, "Hard work, rather than soft loans" is the answer to the problems of Latin American countries; AID's 1970–71 appropriation—$2.3 billion—is the lowest foreign assistance expenditure since 1946; the reduction is here—the "hard work" is supposed to follow). However, as will be indicated in the following, this "comfortable" position of propping up regimes favorable to the U.S. through economic assistance was the position of the U.S. for the entire decade of the sixties.

7. "The failure of most Latin American governments to produce the promised reforms and the failure of the U.S. government (principally AID) and the international agencies to find more effective means of encouraging needed reforms or to identify themselves with reform objectives add up to the greatest failure for the Alliance to date. . . ." Perloff, *op. cit.*, p. 120. This "failure" to promote or identify with reforms was not a bureaucratic oversight, as this chapter will reveal.

8. In the unstructured interviewing of U.S. AID officials, we tried to approximate a disproportional stratified sample by focusing primarily on the separate subpopulation of U.S. AID officials who were engaged in Latin American agricultural development policy implementation. (For a discussion of the rationale underlying this approach, see: Hubert M. Blalock, *Social Statistics* [N.Y.: McGraw-Hill, 1960], p. 401.) The principal subunits sampled within AID included: (1) Office of Capital Development; (2) Office of Program and Policy Coordination; (3) Congressional Presentations Office; and (4) Rural Development Office. Included in the above were officials who had

field responsibilities in the following countries: Paraguay, Chile, Peru, Panama, Ecuador, Guatemala, Bolivia, and Dominican Republic. The levels of officials interviewed ranged from the lowest of the upper-management grades (General Schedule 9) to the higher upper-management grade (GS 17). The total number of interviews exceeded forty and were conducted in the months of July, August, and September of 1968. We wish to acknowledge and thank Michael Konnick for his assistance in conducting the interviews.

9. Interview No. 24, Latin American Bureau, U.S. AID, September 4, 1968.

10. Interview No. 3, Congressional Presentations Office, U.S. AID, August 19, 1968.

11. Interview No. 4, Rural Development, U.S. AID, August 20, 1968.

12. Interview No. 20, Office of Program and Policy Coordination, U.S. AID, August 30, 1968.

13. Interview No. 15, Sector and Market Analysis Division, Office of Program and Policy Coordination, U.S. AID, August 29, 1968. The last section of this chapter will discuss in greater detail working through indigenous elites.

14. Interview No. 5, Industrial Development Branch, Private Sector Development Office, August 20, 1968.

15. Interview No. 37, Latin American Bureau, U.S. AID, September 12, 1968. INDAP is the Institute of Agricultural Development. See Chapter 4 for a discussion of this agency's operations and impact vis-a-vis social reform in Chile.

16. Interview No. 20, *op. cit.*

17. Interview No. 27, Peruvian Development Affairs, U.S. AID, September 5, 1968.

18. Interview No. 7, Dominican Affairs, U.S. AID, August 21, 1968.

19. Interview No. 31, Ecuadorian Development Office, U.S. AID, September 9 and 10, 1968.

20. Interview No. 9, Agriculture and Rural Development Service, War on Hunger, U.S. AID, August 22, 1968. This reaction may have been related to the intense and earlier conflict between agricultural technicians and economists mentioned above. With the War on Hunger campaign and the accompanying stress on agricultural productivity, some of the agricultural technicians were "rehabilitated" to positions of some power within the agency. This individual probably was not and remembered that during an earlier time many of his colleagues had been dismissed from the missions. This reasoning was suggested in interview No. 16, Research and Institutional Grant Staff, U.S. AID, August 29, 1968.

21. Interview No. 34, Rural Development Division, Latin American Bureau, U.S. AID, September 11, 1968.

22. Interview No. 26, Capital Assistance, Office of Program and Policy Coordination, U.S. AID, September 4, 1968.

23. *See:* Lauchlin Currie, *Accelerating Development: The Necessity and the Means* (N.Y.: McGraw-Hill, 1966), especially pp. 66, 104, and 226–27.

24. Interview No. 14, Office of Policy and Program Coordination, U.S. AID, August 28, 1968.

25. The following section on strategy and techniques will underscore and elaborate on this point.

26. Interview No. 20, *op. cit.*

27. Interview No. 15, *op. cit.*

28. Interview No. 24, *op. cit.*

29. Interview No. 40, Office of Central American Affairs, U.S. AID, September 13, 1968.

30. Interview No. 31, *op. cit.*

31. One AID respondent claimed that the Kennedy era changed, radically, AID's approach to technical assistance:

> There was a shift when Kennedy came in. Under Kennedy, the idea was to improve the country without direct emphasis on the people. The idea was that if your country develops, the money will trickle down to the people. (Interview No. 4, *op. cit.*)

Other interviews contradict this interpretation not from the point that "pump priming" would not have a trickle-down effect but from the view that the Kennedy/Johnson administration changed AID's basic approach.

32. Interview No. 9, *op. cit.* This officer had had a long career in foreign assistance, dating from 1946. His faith in the large farmer as benevolent innovator, however, seems too unfounded in fact.

33. Interview No. 2, Rural Development, U.S. AID, August 19, 1968.

34. Interview No. 14, *op. cit.*

35. "There is talk of giving massive assistance to the little man (90 percent of agriculture is done by small men). But it's hard to administer." Interview No. 2, *op. cit.*

36. Interview No. 7, *op. cit.*

37. Interview No. 16, *op. cit.*

38. Interview No. 10, Rural Development Office, U.S. AID, August 22, 1968. His conclusion was that the U.S. would be better off offering technical assistance rather than large loans since "you can control the individual better."

39. Interview No. 2, *op. cit.*

40. Perloff, *op. cit.*, p. 70.

41. Interview No. 14, *op. cit.*

PART FIVE

PROSPECTS FOR RADICAL

CHANGE IN LATIN AMERICA

10

The Rise of Rural Radicalism

Introduction

Both Peru and Chile have experienced a gradual evolutionary pattern of socio-economic change. The frequent unconstitutional and violent political changes which have occurred in Peru were precisely efforts to maintain this pattern, having little impact on social and economic institutions. New institutions and social classes have emerged alongside older traditional colonial structures. While considerable change has occurred it has largely been grafted onto the ongoing social system. Both countries have experienced rapid urbanization, the growth of a substantial middle class, an expansion of public sector activities and employment, and the growth of a considerable manufacturing sector. In Chile and up till 1968 in Peru, a competitive electoral system based on a multi-party structure provided a variety of organized interest groups with opportunities to influence government policies, especially expenditures for development.

Alongside these changes, the *latifundio/minifundio* pattern continued to characterize the countryside; external economic interests continued to control the export sector; exports were largely composed of a few raw materials; control over financial and productive resources continued to be in the hands of a small domestic ruling class closely linked to foreign interests and members of the traditional agrofinancial oligarchy.

The social, economic, and political changes that have occurred have so far reinforced rather than undermined the power of the ruling class. Increased social mobility, the expansion of the educational system, and the growth of a large urban service sector provided the ruling elites with profitable new investment opportunities, and the skilled personnel to manage the new enterprises. Talented individuals recruited from the lower-middle class provided the political and organizational skills to control insurgent groups—a task which members of the traditional elite were either incapable of handling or which they found overtly distasteful.

In the post-World War II period, most Latin American ruling elites continued to follow the same gradualist path to development largely within the orbit of U.S. influence. Nevertheless, alternatives emerged largely through the efforts of new insurgent groups. In Bolivia, a large-scale revolt based on a coalition of workers, peasants, and the urban lower-middle class resulted in the expropriation of numerous landed estates and the tin mines. In Guatemala, the reformist Arbenz government sought to implement an agrarian reform and was violently overthrown by a CIA-financed military force. The successful Bolivian revolution of 1952 and the ill-fated attempt at reform in Guatemala in 1954 suggested that Latin America was headed for a period in which violent revolution and counter-revolution would be prominent features of political life. The political position of the U.S. as the great power in the area was revealed to be crucial to the outcome of the Guatemalan attempt at social change. The events of the 1950s seemed to suggest that revolution was inevitable and that it would occur soon. Influenced by past history, U.S. policy-makers continued to rely on their supporters among the traditional ruling class and the army to maintain and sustain U.S. economic interests and allegiance to U.S. policies in the international arena.

The Cuban revolution and its survival despite heavy U.S. pressure altered some of Washington's thinking regarding Latin America's future. Many of the tried and tested methods for undermining revolutionary regimes were put into practice and failed: economic blockades (cutting off trade, aid, etc.), subsidizing subversive activity (Bay of Pigs invasion), political and diplomatic pressures (breaking relations, expulsion from the OAS, etc.). Aided by the Soviet Union, Cuba survived stronger than ever, preparing for a period of economic and social development at home and support of social revolution abroad. With a social revolution firmly established ninety miles from the shores of the U.S., and with the growth of parallel social revolutionary movements and nationalist movements throughout the Latin American continent, the Kennedy administration proposed a series of social reforms to undercut the appeals of social revolutionaries—notably the declaration of the Alliance for Progress. The social reform goals of the Alliance for Progress were to be realized by the joint efforts of democratic reformers from both North and South America. Billed as the democratic revolutionary alternative to Communist revolution, the Alliance for Progress was ceremoniously inaugurated as a cooperative effort between concerned U.S. and Latin American officials.

Bargaining Systems and Socio-Political Change

While external factors have played an important role in constraining change, internal political systems have contributed mightily toward the same end. Both in Chile and Peru political institutions were heavily permeated by the outlook and values of elitist groups. The governing parties, the executive, the legislature, the courts, and the administrative system provided numerous opportunities for conservative politicians and propertied interest groups to influence agrarian reform legislation.

More important, perhaps, than even the institutional

arrangements, the procedures and rules of the game that dictated the manner in which the issue was acted upon severely limited the possibility of carrying out a massive transformation of the countryside. The debates and discussions, the studies and reports, negotiations and compromises all served to curtail the dynamic aspects of agrarian reform and to create instead a complicated set of regulations and procedures, exemptions and conditions that made the agrarian reform laws extremely difficult to deal with even for the most committed agrarian reform administrator.

The poly-class nature of the governing parties—including representatives of the economic elite as well as from the "marginal classes"—provided the conservative elites with a strong voice within the parties initiating change. Both in Chile and Peru, the dominant economic elites had representation within the Christian Democratic and Popular Action parties. The right wing of both parties served as the sounding board for landed interests and were able to limit the extent of expropriation, provide for exemptions, and build up pressure against drastic changes that were demanded by more militant sectors of the same party. The initial law in the first instance reflected a compromise with the representatives of propertied groups within the reform governing parties.

Legislative activity (especially in Chile) was a further extension of the same process. Debates and discussions led to delays, negotiations, and further delays. The period of congressional debate provided the antireform forces a platform to build up opposition through their disproportionate influence in the mass media. The oppositionists' buildup outside of legislatures—especially among investor and financial elites—created political anxiety and defensiveness among reform supporters within the government, making them more amenable to compromise. Congressional debate, as well as the intra-party bargaining, seemed to weaken the reform measure, strengthen the position of the elites, and thus weaken the potentialities for a redistribution of economic and political resources which could have contributed to the democratization of the two societies.

In the national legislatures, the largely middle-class representatives of former insurgent groups have been effectively socialized by the upper class. They accept the norms of civility and the civic virtues of reciprocity, negotiation, compromise, and moderation. Thus, the political institutions which purport to be instruments for representative democracy have, in fact, served as a democratic façade which serve to deflate mass movements through delays and symbolic activity while upholding exploitative social systems. Elite values permeate political and administrative structures, thus undermining attempts by agrarian reformers to utilize these institutions for an agrarian transformation.

The conglomeration of forces outside the formal governmental structure feed into this systematic bias against rapid change. The web of relations between semiautonomous agencies, landowner associations, the mass media, and U.S.-subsidized trade unions create strong pressure counteracting the attempts to implement the laws effectively. The inside opposition coalition of legislators, party leaders and administrators is reinforced by the external pressures generated by interest groups and social institutions. The bargaining political system is especially prone to being influenced by antireform groups and is singularly weak from the point of view of implementing a comprehensive agrarian reform.

The administrative problems which agrarian reform officials subsequently faced—principally a lack of finances and personnel and a fragmental organizational structure— were largely the consequences of the political decisions that were products of the bargaining process. The pressures of the landowners and their allies in government including especially those in the governing coalition were sufficient to limit the effectiveness of the agrarian reform legislation which was eventually passed. The fragmented authority and

430 : CULTIVATING REVOLUTION

lack of power of agencies formally responsible for implementing agrarian reform can be directly traced to the activities of governmental and nongovernmental coalitions. The limited expropriations and the failure of agrarian reform agencies to achieve the social goals that were originally set were, in fact, the result of the failure of the bargaining political system and its incapacity to reflect the needs and demands of excluded groups demanding entry into the polity.

Non-Bargaining Politics
and Socio-Political Change

If in fact the middle-class parliamentary system has shown itself incapable of dealing with twentieth-century problems in Latin America, what political alternatives can best serve to transform the agrarian sector?

We have noted three types of political action which have led to rapid and profound changes in the countryside. In Chile, because of the inadequacy of the Frei government's performance in the agrarian sector and under the prodding and encouragement of militant Christian Democratic and Marxist agrarian organizers, the peasantry in some areas began to take the initiative in bringing about change. To a degree, this can be described as limited, subsystem change through revolutionary means. Forcible, illegal land seizures organized by peasants who previously worked the land occurred with increasing frequency with the support and sympathy of most peasants in a particular region. These largely local land seizures frequently accomplished what the government's legislative and administrative activity had failed to do—redistribute land to those who worked it. Direct action, mass mobilization, and confrontation bypassed the bargaining processes that not infrequently had led to decisions favoring the landlord. While these land seizure actions were occasionally met by the government's dispatching of soldiers, it was also true that this sort of direct action pressured the government to accelerate expropriation proceedings. In that sense, peasant action strengthened the bargaining hand of the agrarian reform officials who favored a more dynamic approach.

In Peru, a military government which illegally and unconstitutionally seized political power at the expense of elected politicians and without the benefit of party machinery has initiated a far-reaching agrarian reform program, the likes of which have never been seen in Peru. At least up until 1970, the Peruvian military government has been able to expropriate most of the large commercial plantations without allowing the changes in the agrarian sector to affect the property interests of nonagricultural groups. Largely relying on its control over the means of violence, the military so far has refrained from any massive mobilization or organization of the potential beneficiaries of its program. In its concern with the redistribution of property, the military resembles the Cuban social revolutionaries; in its concern to carry out change without popular mobilization, the military resembles the strategists of modernization from above. In a sense, then, post-October, 1968 Peru represents partial change via a military-dominated system. It is too early to judge the success or failure of this hybrid approach which can be looked at as the agrarian reform-from-above approach.

In Cuba, a rural-based guerrilla-led movement succeeded in overthrowing a corrupt and conservative dictatorship and through a series of measures accompanied by massive popular mobilizations, to effectively transform the agricultural sector. As conservatives and U.S. policy-makers suspected, the spillover into urban areas was substantial, leading to a transformation not only of the countryside but of the urban centers as well. This was virtually social change via a totally revolutionary system.

As our case studies suggest, the legal, peaceful, or evolutionary approach to land tenure change has nowhere been as successful as the revolutionary approach. To solve the problem of maldistribution of land resources in Latin America and counteract the obstacles which the elite have set up to keep the masses out of the bargaining systems, revolutionary activity appears as a rational response which can contribute to democratic mass behavior.

The United States and Socio-Political Change in Latin America

Throughout the 1960s, U.S. policy-makers never seriously considered the revolutionary option, nor were they primarily concerned with the social aspects of the agrarian problem. The largely ineffectual measures ultimately projected by Latin Americans were, in part, a response to the public attitudes and behavior of U.S. officials. Neither U.S. policy-makers nor Latin governing elites seriously considered the Alliance for Progress.

U.S. policy toward the agrarian sector was largely oriented toward energizing and activating political allies among the landholding elite. U.S. officials held out financial rewards for those groups willing to cooperate with the U.S. in increasing the output of the agrarian sector. The close association and cooperation of U.S. and Latin elite segments was based on their mutual opposition to mass popular movements which threatened to change the social order. Official notions of social change in rural areas largely were couched in liberal democratic jargon; in fact, U.S. policy was geared to strengthen and consolidate the position of the elites while leading them toward more efficient modes of production. The formal declarations of policy on ceremonial occasions largely served to elicit support from the U.S. public and to mollify liberal opinion at home and abroad.

In Latin America, the gap between U.S. rhetoric and

behavior led Latin Americans to dismiss U.S. declarations of concern as mere propaganda—which is, in fact, what it has been. The consequence for the U.S. is a credibility gap of enormous proportion. Today, communication between the U.S. and Latin America is largely through the elites who govern; outside of official channels, the U.S. has little direct influence and therefore is heavily dependent on the elites to follow U.S. policy directives.

Through financial levers, the U.S. has become more intimately involved in the Latin American development effort than ever before. Latin American development decisions dependent on North American financing have resulted in the devolution of decision-making power into the hands of U.S. officials. The dependent financial status of Latin America has resulted in the penetration of Latin America's administrative structure and the shaping of development policies to accommodate U.S. interests. The notion that there is a coalition between U.S. and Latin elites—including public officials and private interests—is mistaken, since this implies a rough sort of equality between the members of the coalition. The significant change in the Western Hemisphere has been the obtrusive and persistent North Americanization of Latin America—incorporating the Latin American elites as agents who implement U.S. policy.

During the Kennedy period when public officials were articulating the ideology of democratic revolution, U.S. officials created the financial and administrative machinery that later served to promote a most undemocratic and elitist model of development. Whatever the original intentions of President Kennedy in calling for a redistribution of land, U.S. officials and legislators did not take the radical implications of his speeches seriously. Throughout the 1960s, U.S. administrators of aid programs showed a marked hostility toward agrarian reform programs and a decided preference for programs directed toward providing incentives to existing landowners. The liberal liturgy articulated on ceremonial occasions served to legitimate a conservative policy whose purpose was to solidify political support for global and regional U.S. interests.

Throughout the 1960s, U.S. policy-makers and Latin American governments—whether controlled by right-wing traditional elites or by modern middle-class parties—feared the dynamic social and political forces in their societies which were pushing for agrarian reform. Lacking control over the process of social change, the policy-elites feared the emergence of programs and projects of broad scope which would strengthen the political power of excluded groups and the ideological spokesmen of national-popular movements. Hence, U.S. policy-makers and their Latin counterparts appear to have been as ideologically hostile to agrarian reform as they were to the political developments which engendered it. Only in very limited situations—where social forces were largely immobilized—did the U.S. partially support some changes in land tenure, and then the results were largely a set of compromised, poorly financed programs with little impact on the countryside as a whole.

The modernization-from-above approach which was finally adopted was essentially a cause and an effect of the counter-revolutionary policies pursued by U.S. policy-makers—an attempt to dampen the process of social mobilization under way throughout the early sixties. It was one of a number of programs that grew out of and in turn nourished the status quo-oriented forces in Latin American society who were preoccupied with preserving the existing order.

The consequences of U.S. agricultural policy assume major importance because agriculture is the most numerous economic sector in Latin America; maintenance of illiteracy, poverty, nonparticipation and low productivity are some of the products of the modernization-from-above strategy.

The political problem that U.S. and Latin modernizing elites early recognized was that agrarian reform can affect the total structure of rural society with considerable spill-over into urban society. The possible linkage between radical agrarian reform and other societal-political forces and programs that could challenge the power of urban propertied classes was largely responsible for the U.S. decision to remain aligned with the traditional elites.

APPENDIX

APPENDIX

A Methodological Note on the Comparative Study of Bureaucracy

There are both advantageous and disadvantageous periods for field-researching public administrative agencies. Contacting key individuals, clearing research projects through official channels, and receiving official sanctions of all kinds are still the most time-tested and acceptable means of insuring the success of field research endeavors.[1] But at certain times and in certain situations, contacts and the most laudatory letters of recommendation cannot make public officials here or abroad receptive to the researcher's questions or requests for documents, statistical data, or access to personnel for the purposes of interviewing. Political factors which public agencies are subjected to and the time period within which the researcher is examining the public agency are critical determinants of the quantity and quality of data which will affect the end product of research. The political setting and timing can indirectly (even if subjectively) influence the amount and kind of information (or misinformation) about a particular agency's behavior (performance) and projected achievements. These two critical factors seriously affect administrators' willingness to make data and information available to outside researchers.[2]

We will examine four cases to illustrate the influence of the factors of timing and political environment on data collection. Three of these cases deal with foreign bureaucrats and public agencies, while the fourth is concerned with officials in the U.S. Agency for International Development (U.S. AID). On the basis of our discussion, we will outline an optimal period for data collection suggested by the experiences with all four public agencies.

By using four different research experiences, we intend

to relate data collection to the operational histories of the agencies examined. Each case study of an agency reveals differences regarding the availability of reports and documents (including critical materials) as well as access to agency personnel for either structured (survey) or unstructured (in-depth) interviews. Access to these sources of information can be related to the particular "crisis" or "noncrisis" period the agency may be in when field research is being conducted. Finally, we will discuss quantitative and qualitative indicators of optimal and unfavorable time periods and discuss how these factors affect field research (data collection) with regard to public agencies.

The Damodar Valley Corporation: The End of an Era[3]

The Damodar Valley Corporation (DVC) was a semiautonomous public corporation chartered by the Government of India in December, 1948, to specifically develop, on a unified water-shed basis, the water and other natural resources of the Damodar River.[4] This was an intergovernmental undertaking. The Government of India (central government) and the governments of West Bengal and Bihar (state governments) agreed initially to surrender certain powers to the newly established DVC for as long as required to develop valley resources. Not only were state government powers surrendered to a centrally established and controlled agency, but the states were also required, along with the central government, to financially underwrite the DVC's activities on a benefit-accruing basis.

When field research was conducted on the DVC, the agency was entering its 18th year of operation. Of post-independence agencies, the DVC best parallels the evolution of the Indian Union since its operations began during the first year of independence. Initial political support for this agency (Nehru, Roy, Sinha and lesser central and state Congress leaders) and initial enthusiasm with which it was received by other influential sectors of Indian society (especially elites of the press and Indian Civil Service), led to the conclusion that if any Indian agency were to "succeed," then the DVC would. However, with the initiation of research in 1966, it became apparent quickly that the DVC in 1966 was far different, by several measures, from the DVC of the early 1950s.[5]

In the Indian case, setting and timing affected perception of administrative performance, expected performance, and research reporting of administrative performance. A brief analysis of some critical points in the DVC's operational history will illustrate the point.

From 1949 to about 1956, the DVC administrators (by their own admission and by the studies done of this agency during this time period) could claim to have accomplished more in a shorter period than after the mid-1950s. When questioned as to why this was so, most administrators stated that the autonomous nature of the agency and the powers exercised by the chairman and board members bypassed decision-making delays by eliminating the need to secure consent from state and national governmental leaders. Since the corporation (construed here as the board, the chairman, and most department heads) shared a broad, all-India view of development (a view which is counter to the more limited state-level view), government of India officials did not feel slighted—an opposite position from that taken by state government officials. During the 1949–1956 period, perceptions of administrative performance tended to be positive and expected performance was much the same. Reporting of administrative performance was positive.

However, significant data were not made available for research.[6] In the middle 1950s, the powerful B. C. Roy (chief minister of West Bengal and leading Congress Party member) openly fought both the DVC and the government of India. He successfully stopped the DVC program of flood control by reducing the number of proposed dams from

eight to four. Furthermore, he began to agitate for the transfer of the DVC-built irrigation works from the DVC to the
government of West Bengal (this was consummated in
1959). Finally both governments (West Bengal and Bihar)
established their own state electricity boards in 1956 and
thus stimulated state competition in electricity rates, which
would translate into attempts to curtail and confine DVC's
power program. Hence the 1956–1966 period witnessed the
virtual abandonment of the unified valley development concept and the almost complete phase-out of the DVC as a
separate public agency.

By 1966, perceptions of DVC administrative performance, expectations of administrative performance, and the
reports on appraisals of the performance of the DVC made
by researchers became more negative. However, *research
opportunities increased.* Administrators who previously
might cover up agency blunders or withhold agency documents which would cast doubts concerning past or present
agency programs and/or personnel did just the opposite.
During 1966, one of the authors conducting field research
secured copies of documents previously unavailable and
also gained some highly critical observations from agency
officials who, in a sense, felt they had "nothing to lose."

Although "success" (defined as achievement of goals
and survival as an agency) is not the focus here, it is an
important factor affecting field research. The perceptions
which officials have of success or the potentialities for
achieving success appear to influence the extent to which
foreign researchers are permitted to examine an agency, its
officials, and its operations. Success or lack of success influences or determines the type and kind of written data
(documents, internal reports, etc.) agency officials will make
available to the researcher.

The DVC case illustrates how environmental factors
(in this case, adverse political pressures coupled with
threats to agency survival) and timing (1966 as versus
1955) affect availability of information and reports of per-

formance. The most propitious time period for studying the agency was the period when the agency's survival was threatened, a period of time when it was too soon to engage in postmortem examinations but too early to dismiss the DVC as a lost cause.

The National Office of Agrarian Reform: The End of an Administration[7]

The Peruvian National Office of Agrarian Reform (ONRA) was established in 1964 under Agrarian Reform Law Number 15037 of May 24, 1964. This agency, like its older sister agency, *Servicio de Investigacion y Promocion Agraria* (SIPA), had a semiautonomous status within the national bureaucracy of Peru. Both agencies (ONRA and SIPA) were accountable directly to the President without being directly controlled or supervised by the Ministry of Agriculture. ONRA was established to implement Peru's agrarian reform legislation.

Several important tasks were assigned to ONRA from the beginning. These included expropriation of land,[8] administration of land seizures,[9] and administration of land colonization projects. ONRA also had some responsibilities in the area of providing technical assistance and limited credit to small farmers—responsibilities which brought the agency into direct conflict with SIPA.[10]

Field research was conducted with ONRA in the summer of 1968—a little after the beginning of ONRA's fourth year of operation and just a few months before the military coup which overthrew the Belaunde government. Social reform of traditional institutions had not been effectively implemented during his term of office. Infrastructure projects and programs were stressed—and the problems of land tenure and social inequality remained unresolved. ONRA, which was supposed to be the instrument for implementing agrarian reform, early felt the President's restraint toward activity in that direction. ONRA's first director, a Christian Democrat, resigned within two years—a move that reflected a general exodus of reformist Christian Democrats from ONRA and the government. The new director, who was a member of Belaunde's party, indicated strong dissatisfaction with the lack of presidential support for the rather ineffectively reformist activities of the agency in 1968.

Unlike the Indian DVC, the Peruvian ONRA never had the extensive and initial political and financial support essential for at least a good start toward achieving organization objectives. ONRA was more of a "lip service" agency —a façade behind which Peruvian politicians could hide when other Peruvians asked what was being done with regard to the enormous social problem among rural dwellers. However, ONRA, in 1968, shared in common with the DVC, in 1966, the fact that both agencies were drastically limited in their ability to perform assigned tasks and both were on the verge of disestablishment.

As with the DVC, ONRA officials were very receptive to researchers. Permission was given to conduct intensive, in-depth interviews with all officials at the management level. Clearance and agency "blessing" was given for a stratified sampling of attitudes and perceptions of the entire ONRA universe (some 1016 individuals). Several classified reports were given to the research team and extensive personnel data were made available. In short, the same willingness to provide previously unavailable information including data which exposed agency failings as was observable in the DVC appeared during the field research effort in ONRA.[11] Although expectations regarding ONRA's administrative performance and expected performance in 1964–65 were much more optimistic than in 1968,[12] reporting of performance could have been similarly different.

The ONRA case illustrates the influence of unfavorable factors (lack of political and financial support) and timing (1968 as opposed to 1965) on an agency and the resultant favorable situation for the researcher: the data available measure both past and present administrative performance. ONRA was threatened with absorption in the old bureaucratic machinery which meant, in effect, that it was going out of business as a reform agency. ONRA's financial problems coincided with Belaunde's unwillingness to commit national resources to resolving Peru's social problems. As in the case of the DVC, timing favored our research. ONRA had not been abolished—it was too early to "dissect" a "dead" agency—but it was in the process of witnessing a severe financial cutback and personnel turnover disadvantageous to the goals of the agency. As a result, many functionaries in precarious positions did not feel obligated to defend the agency or government: they spoke freely and made available previously unavailable reports, including critical studies.

INDAP and CORA: Before the End [13]

The Institute of Agrarian Development (INDAP) and the Agrarian Reform Corporation (CORA) are complementary, semiautonomous public agencies responsible for the implementation of Chilean agrarian reform. As in the case of Peru, Chile placed the implementation of agrarian reform in the hands of public agencies separate from the national bureaucracy but responsible to the President.

Agrarian reform as a part of public discussion in Chile arose much earlier than in Peru. The right-of-center Alessandri government had enacted a weak law in 1962—the legal vehicle used by the Frei government to implement agrarian reform until the summer of 1967.

Both INDAP and CORA existed as semiautonomous public agencies before the Christian Democrat, Eduardo Frei, was elected President in 1964. When Frei took over the Presidency there was a large-scale personnel turnover.[14] Both CORA and INDAP began with new teams. The executive vice-presidents of INDAP and CORA, appointed by Frei, were rising figures within the Christian Democratic party (PDC). Both appointees were associated with the more reformist tendencies within the PDC. Personnel data reveal that some 75 percent of the CORA staff were from urban areas, and a majority had joined the corporation because of their commitment to social change. In 1964, INDAP and CORA were viewed as the agencies most involved in social reform.

Unlike the Peruvian agrarian reform effort, the program of social change through agrarian reform and the public agencies (INDAP and CORA) to implement it had been strongly supported by President Frei before and immediately after his election. From his numerous statements of support most observers felt that his government would give agrarian reform the highest priority. Most of the Chilean and U.S. press depicted Frei as a "democratic revolutionary" and the "last hope" for Chile.[15] Although subsequent events have indicated otherwise, initially it appears that Frei was favorably disposed toward change in the direction of improving the living conditions of the landless Chilean *campesino*. Hence, both INDAP and CORA had early presidential support for their programs of agrarian reform.

Prior to the enactment of the 1967 law, both INDAP and CORA operated under the 1962 law in implementing a threefold program of land expropriation (with the accompanying establishment of government *asentamientos*),[16] unionization of landless peasants (mobilization of peasants to generate demands for change), and establishment of credit facilities and technical assistance for the *minifundo* owners.[17] The clientele served by INDAP and CORA, therefore, included all rural dwellers except the powerful, large *fundo* owners. The 1967 law did not accelerate implementation of agrarian reform. Lacking political and financial support for expropriation and distribution of land to landless peasants, INDAP and CORA's operations proceeded at a snail's pace. However, the passing of the law, the

verbal support of President Frei, and the successful unionization of some 70,000 peasants gave the agrarian reform
agency heads some hope that more significant changes
would be forthcoming in the future.

Field research of both INDAP and CORA personnel
and operations took place in the summer of 1968. Unlike
the ONRA situation but like that of the DVC, previous administrative studies of the two agencies did exist.[18] Although critical of some aspects of administration, on the
whole, these previous studies were optimistic with regard to
the ability of the two agencies to achieve their organizational goals. Hence, performance up until 1968 was considered to be at least adequate, and expectations of performance in the future were not negative. Our field research was
conducted during a period when both agencies were having
their first doubts about their ability to achieve even partial
success in meeting their objectives. This was a critical factor
in data collection. Although financing was already a problem,[19] no massive personnel turnover had occurred (as was
the case of ONRA in Peru). The executive vice-presidents
of INDAP and CORA still felt that agrarian change was occurring. Our research commenced at a time when key officials still held some hope that agrarian reform in its broadest
sense might be accomplished,[20] officials who were important
"watchdogs" over access to agency reports and personnel.

Here again the time factor was critical for data collection. Clearance for any examination of operations or interviewing of personnel (both in-depth and survey methods)
for both agencies had to be forthcoming from the executive
vice-president of INDAP. During our interview with him he
expressed his hesitation about the examination of INDAP or
CORA "at this time." Conducting a survey similar to the
one proceeding in Peru was "out of the quesion" at that
time. Furthermore, a large portion of both personnel and
financial data was "classified." Only after considerable discussion did he permit in-depth interviewing of high-level
management personnel. Indirect means had to be employed

in gathering information on personnel and finances. Unlike the Peruvian or Indian cases, the Chilean case was researched at a politically sensitive time—a time when organizational leadership felt that any disclosure of its operations to any outside group would adversely affect its future operations (both agencies were under attack by conservative elements within Chile). However, unlike the previous two cases discussed, although INDAP and CORA were financially pressed, personnel quality was still high and both agencies were still able to function adequately. None of the originally assigned tasks had been dropped by either agency although emphasis on unionization was greater than on actual expropriation of land.

The INDAP-CORA case presents a situation in which research was being conducted at a time when the agency leaders felt they had a future with regard to agency functioning and administrative performance. The reason for the refusal to permit a survey study of either agency was the fear that revelations of their operations might be used against them by political opponents. Administrative leaders felt that they had "something to lose." Neither INDAP nor CORA was in the midst of an optimal period for analysis of their operations by anyone outside the two organizations. As a result, we had to reorient our research effort.

The Agency for International Development: Continuing Uncertainty and Crises[21]

The problems of AID predate President Kennedy's reorganization of AID's predecessor, the International Cooperation Administration (ICA), or even ICA's predecessor, the Foreign Operations Administration (FOA). Nonmilitary U.S. foreign aid has always lacked sizable domestic support. Characterized as a "temporary" measure, it has been subject to congressional opposition and straddled with such impossible tasks as "building democratic institutions" in aid-receiving countries. Compared to agencies such as NASA or the Department of Defense, AID has usually taken a back seat in appropriations and priorities.

Our research in AID activities, operations, and personnel focused on its relationship to social change and agrarian reform in Latin America. AID was responsible for implementing Alliance for Progress programs and projects, especially in the area of agrarian reform and/or development. Since the original Alliance Charter stressed reform, we were interested in examining the extent to which AID officials perceived either agrarian reform or agricultural development as the priority of the Alliance and U.S. involvement in Latin America.

Field research of AID took place during the summer months of 1968. During this period, several events occurred which affected agency behavior and data availability. The most important event was the announcement that U.S.A.I.D. for fiscal year 1968–69 would receive the lowest amount ever appropriated during the twenty-year history of U.S. aid efforts. This caused great concern on the part of AID officials since, as it was revealed, in some cases entire units within the agency were phased out, with the accompanying personnel departure.

AID was more secretive about its materials (more materials are considered "classified") than the other agencies studied. Nevertheless, a great deal of documentary material was gathered during the research effort. The factor which accounted for data availability was the "nothing to lose" attitude among agency personnel. Those officials who knew by middle and late summer that they would have to seek new positions were quite willing to discuss the agency's past and present failings as well as its potential for future "blunders." Even those officials who knew they would remain were very candid in their observations as well as critical of past, current, and what appeared to be future policy and its implementation with regard to Latin America. In short, the lack of political and financial support as well as the factor of time appear again, in the case of AID, to benefit the researcher.

U.S. AID was, by the fall of 1968, a demoralized agency whose director had publicly admitted the unfavorable political environment which surrounded the agency. In an address before the American Assembly at Columbia University, Mr. William S. Gaud stated:

> Today it is not the backward Indian peasant who blocks the road to food self-sufficiency—it is the indifferent American. . . . We ask for money to put out fires in Vietnam, in the Congo, in the Dominican Republic, and we get it. We ask for money to prevent fires, and we are accused of carrying on a give-away program. We have learned a lot about how to help underdeveloped countries move off dead center. We have learned less about how to help Americans visualize the grim future that faces them and their children so long as more than half the world ends each day hungry and hopeless.[22]

The attitude of the director appeared to be shared by his subordinates in the agency. This critical attitude toward past nonsupport from Congress as well as those who staff the White House certainly assisted our research efforts. U.S. AID is a prime example of a harassed agency whose program is ill-defined (due to inability to plan beyond one fiscal year) and underfinanced. The summer of 1968 was a particularly bad time for the agency and our researcher was able to capitalize on the willingness of agency officials to discuss past and present administrative performance with consideration about what the future might bring. In short, an environment of continuing uncertainty and crisis (in terms of agency survival and program continuation) that has characterized the agency for the past several years coupled with the factor of timing (1968 as opposed to an earlier, perhaps more hopeful period) combined to facilitate data collection and information gathering.

An Optimal Period for Field Research[23]

The four field research experiences related and analyzed above share certain similarities and differences. All deal with public sector agencies engaged in either natural resource development or social development or both. Three focus on foreign (non-U.S.) experiences while the fourth deals with the U.S. counterpart to foreign endeavors. In all four cases we found that timing and agency environment can either facilitate or hamper field research. Ranking the cases on the basis of optimal periods for research, the following order results: ONRA, DVC, U.S. AID, and INDAP-CORA. This ranking coincides with the order in which these agencies will either be merged (or disestablished) within their respective bureaucracies or suffer reorganization of an extreme nature (including substantial personnel turnover or termination).

Tables I and II illustrate the relationship between data collection, research timing, and political environment (including administrative factors). Both tables taken together suggest that threats to agency security that create great uncertainty among agency personnel increased research opportunities available to our research team.

Our experience suggests that time periods which coincide with unfavorable or adverse political conditions for agency survival tend to be the most advantageous ones, on the whole, for data collection on administrative behavior. Furthermore, these periods might be discovered by quantitative indicators. For example, an agency whose budget has been severely cut, has suffered a decline in political support (from executive, legislative, or bureaucratic groups or all three), has an unstable personnel cadre (large turnover in otherwise normal years—U.S. AID for example) would be in a prime period for analysis. Threats to organizational

TABLE I

POLITICAL AND ADMINISTRATIVE FACTORS AT TIME OF DATA COLLECTION

Agency	Status of Original Agency Objective(s)	Status of Leadership and Other Personnel	Political Support	Financial Support	Reorganization Activities (Internal)
DVC	Abandoned; single objective (power production) almost only function of agency	Changing; moderate but higher than normal turnover rate	Weak; under attack by state governments	Budget cuts but still financially viable	Reorganization discussions taking place; outcome in doubt; future uncertain
ONRA	Abandoned; only "lip-service" given to objectives	Changing; rapid turnover rate	Nonexistent; under attack	Budget cuts extreme; no longer financially viable	Rumors of absorption into Ministry of Agriculture; future very doubtful; large degree of uncertainty
INDAP-CORA	Still maintained; shift in emphasis (from expropriation to unionization)	Some leadership replacement; usual (normal) turnover rate	Some loss of support; under attack by rightists	Budget cuts but still financially viable	No activity
AID	Fiction of objectives maintained	Wholesale change; very rapid departure of personnel	Decreasing support from traditional supporters	Extreme budget cuts; many programs eliminated	Uncertainty; awaiting new administration

TABLE II

DATA MADE AVAILABLE AND RESEARCH TECHNIQUES APPROVED BY AGENCY

Agency	Personnel Interviewing		Statistical Information		Critical or Previously Suppressed Data of:	
	Structured	Unstructured	Personnel	Financial	Entire Agency	Certain Functions
DVC	Was not requested; felt approval could have been secured	Approved*	Approved	Approved	Approved	Approved
ONRA	Approved	Approved	Approved	Approved	Approved	Approved
INDAP-CORA	Denied †	Approved	Denied (received unofficially)	Denied	Denied	Denied (received from other sources)
AID	Was not requested; felt approval would not be given	Approved	Approved	Approved	Approved	Approved

* Denotes either official or unofficial approval (permission granted or information provided).
† Denotes official denial (permission not granted or information not provided).

survival tend to make officials want to "set the record straight."

Of course there are other variables which affect the availability or accessibility of data on public agencies—government-imposed security regulations, agency or personally imposed confidentiality, among others. However, awareness of these other variables does not negate the importance of timing and political setting.

Many reasons for agencies failing to achieve their objectives can be found *after* an agency has ceased to exist as a separate entity. The concept of optimal time periods for administrative analysis is useful in maximizing research opportunities, and in providing information on the interplay between political and administrative variables.

NOTES

1. For a more general discussion, see: Robert E. Ward, ed., *Studying Politics Abroad* (Boston: Little, Brown, 1964); and Klaus Knorr, "Social Science Research Problems and Remedies," *World Politics,* 19 (April, 1967), pp. 465–85. Other articles which consider related issues include: Hahn-Been Lee, "From Ecology to Time: A Time Orientation to the Study of Public Administration," *The International Review of Administrative Sciences,* 33, No. 2 (1967), pp. 103–13; and William Delany, "Some Field Notes on the Problem of Access in Organizational Research," *Administrative Science Quarterly,* 5 (June, 1960–March, 1961), pp. 448–57.

2. We advance the following evidence in support of the importance of these two variables. Our data suggest a relationship between the variables and the data concerning the agencies studied. We do not exclude the fact that other variables may be operating to affect data collection.

3. For a more complete treatment of this theme and this agency, see: Robert LaPorte, Jr., "Intergovernmental Change in India: Politics and Administration of the Damodar Valley Scheme," *Asian Survey,* 8, No. 9 (September, 1968), pp. 748–60.

4. The Damodar River flows through the present-day states of Bihar and West Bengal (its headwaters are in Bihar).

5. Most of the materials written earlier concerning the DVC were quite optimistic. See: Henry C. Hart, *New India's Rivers* (Calcutta: Orient Longmans, 1956). Critical materials were produced, how-

ever, but later. See: P. Prasad, *The Damodar Valley Scheme* (New Delhi: Indian Institute of Public Administration, 1963).

6. See DVC, *Proceedings of the Participating Government Conferences, 1945–1956,* 3 volumes, Calcutta: 1956, 1959, 1961. It is worth noting that no other works on the DVC (which the authors have examined) cite these important sources. Yet when the 1966 research was conducted, these materials were "released" to the researcher.

7. The data and field experience related below are pre-1968 coup but do not change the general direction this agency was heading nor concepts derived from the empirical data gathered.

8. Without going into detail, suffice it to say that "expropriation" has been very limited due to the loopholes in the law as well as the cumbersome, tedious, and time-consuming legal-adjudication process.

9. This refers to land in the *Sierra* seized by force by landless peasants; the government decided not to reclaim it by force but to oversee its use.

10. SIPA is no longer an autonomous agency; in the summer of 1968, it was being incorporated into the Ministry of Agriculture. Needless to say, those SIPA officials with long tenure were extremely unhappy.

11. At the same time, revealing the lack of support for mild reform by Peruvian politicians who have in the past championed, in public, agrarian reform. The extent of lack of support can be shown financially in that ONRA's 1967–68 budget was reduced quantitatively even though Peru had just devalued the *sol.* In fact, ONRA did not have enough money in the summer of 1968 to purchase gasoline for its vehicles.

12. Interview with Cesar Fuentes, former zonal chief (*Sierra*), ONRA, July, 1968.

13. The data and field research upon which the following is based were also gathered during the summer of 1968. One very noteworthy event since this research was conducted has been the resignation of Jacques Chonchol who was executive vice-president of INDAP and the acknowledged force behind agrarian change in Chile.

14. Chile is not unique, of Latin American countries, in the "patronage" nature of its national bureaucracy. For example, see: John C. Honey, *Toward Strategies for Public Administration Development in Latin America* (Syracuse, N.Y.: Syracuse University Press, 1968).

15. Leonard Gross, *The Last Best Hope: Eduardo Frei and Chilean Democracy* (N.Y.: Random House, 1967).

16. These are actually government-administered former *fundos* in which the government (through CORA officials) organizes and supervises the cooperative farmers until the farmers themselves decide whether to remain as members of an *asentamiento* or become independent landowners.

17. These are the subsistence-level agricultural producers whose small, inefficient plots produce barely enough for individual family consumption. INDAP's strategy was to increase these peasants' ability to produce by providing low-cost credit and free technical advice.

18. See: Plinio Sampaio, "Organizacion, Planificacion Y Coordinacion de las Instituciones del Sector Publico Agricola de Chile, A Nivel de Terreno" (Santiago: *Departamento de Administracion en Reforma Agraria,* ICIRA, December, 1966); and the annex to this work.

19. Inter-American Committee on the Alliance for Progress (CIAP), "Domestic Efforts and the Needs for External Financing for the Development of Chile," mimeographed (Washington, D.C.: Pan American Union, September 29, 1967).

20. In this case, mobilization of landless peasants so as to form a political base for generating demands for more land expropriation. Peasant unionization was the most significant change in the Chilean agrarian scene.

21. For data in support of the contentions revealed in the following section, the authors wish to acknowledge and thank Michael Konnick, research assistant, Institute of Public Administration, The Pennsylvania State University.

22. *New York Times,* Sunday, November 3, 1968, p. 12.

23. Although the optimal period may be hypothetical, the problem of agency uncooperativeness is very real. Just a few months prior to the field experience in Chile, another political scientist attempted to do a similar study of INDAP-CORA but did not even get beyond the discussion stage with Chilean bureaucrats and their foreign advisers. The outcome of this impasse was that the political scientist had to do an entirely different study of a different Chilean agency— a loss of several months, time, and energy. Another more costly example may be found in the case of the National Assessment of Education Project funded by the U.S. Office of Education. This is a multi-million dollar project which has taken four years in development. However, just recently the American Association of School Administrators announced their decision not to support these activities.

Index

About the Authors

JAMES F. PETRAS was born in Lynn, Massachusetts, in 1937. He received a B.A. from Boston University and a Ph.D. in political science from the University of California (Berkeley). As a Doherty Fellow, he studied Chilean politics during the critical years of the Frei administration. He is the author of *Politics and Social Forces in Chilean Development*. Together with Maurice Zeitlin, Petras compiled and edited *Latin America: Reform or Revolution*. His other works on Latin America include *Fidel Castro Speaks* and *Politics and Social Structure in Latin America*. Dr. Petras is the author of numerous articles and is Associate Professor of Political Science and Public Administration, The Pennsylvania State University.

ROBERT LAPORTE, JR., was born in 1940 in Detroit, Michigan, and received his B.A. and M.A. from Wayne State University. He has a Ph.D. from the Maxwell School at the University of Syracuse. Dr. LaPorte studied public enterprise organization and management in South Asia on a Ford Foundation fellowship and is at work on a study of the public sector's role in development in India, Pakistan, and Ceylon. He is Associate Professor of Political Science and Public Administration and Assistant Director of the Institute of Public Administration, The Pennsylvania State University. Professor LaPorte has written many articles for scholarly journals.